REELECTING
LINCOLN

REELECTING
LINCOLN

The Battle for the 1864 Presidency

JOHN C. WAUGH

CROWN PUBLISHERS, INC.

NEW YORK

Frontispiece: Abraham Lincoln in 1864. *(Library of Congress)*

Copyright © 1997 by John C. Waugh

Published by Crown Publishers, Inc., 201 East 50th Street, New York, New York 10022. Member of the Crown Publishing Group.

Random House, Inc. New York, Toronto, London, Sydney, Auckland
http://www.randomhouse.com/

CROWN and colophon are trademarks of Crown Publishers, Inc.

Printed in the United States of America

Design by Lenny Henderson

Library of Congress Cataloging-in-Publication Data
Waugh, John C.
Reelecting Lincoln : the battle for the 1864 presidency / John C. Waugh.—1st ed.
Includes bibliographical references.
1. Presidents—United States—Election—1864.   2. Lincoln, Abraham, 1809–1865.   3. United States—Politics and government—1861–1865.   I. Title.
E458.4.W38   1998
324.973'07—dc21   97–22759

ISBN 0-517-59766-7

10 9 8 7 6 5 4 3 2 1

First Edition

*For Dan and Eliza, who began as my children
and grew up to be my friends.*

Also by John C. Waugh

*The Class of 1846: From West Point to Appomattox—
Stonewall Jackson, George McClellan and Their Brothers*

Sam Bell Maxey and the Confederate Indians

CONTENTS

PREFACE

T HIS IS A BOOK ABOUT LINCOLN'S REELECTION CAMPAIGN IN
1864. But it is much more than that. The reader will find in
these pages more than just the story of an election: he or she
will find, as I found, that the campaign cannot be covered as an isolated
incident in a thirteen-month election cycle.

There are simply certain events, not necessarily political ones, that
can't be ignored or left out. The Gettysburg Address was not a part of
the campaign, but it is a towering incident in the time frame in which
the story told here occurred. So it is covered. The mid-election Confederate invasion and siege of Washington in July 1864 were not
overtly political—although they had political overtones and fallout.
They are also covered. You will find here not only the story of an election, but of a year, a very important year, in the Civil War and in American history, and of the major actors in it.

This book is not a historical treatise, a monograph, or an analysis; it
is a story not without analysis but written as a reporter—which is what
I am—might have covered it as it was happening 130 years ago. It is a
big story writ large, about arguably the most critical election campaign
in our history.

I was drawn to the story, as I am drawn to every story in history, by
its drama. Set yourself down anywhere in the past—anywhere at all—
and something fascinating and dramatic is happening. Somebody is
doing something interesting, and probably doing it to somebody else.
And in few human activities is somebody doing something to somebody else more emphatically than in an election campaign.

I was trained as a reporter; for years I covered national politics as
they were playing out in the twentieth century. When I finally realized

how much I loved the nineteenth century, I began to report politics and events as they were being played out then. The only difference I find between covering an event in this century and covering an event in any other century is that all my sources are dead. But that is no disadvantage. My sources all left vivid tracks of one kind or another. They always do.

So what I hope I have given the reader in the pages that follow is a dramatic reliving of this important election year in 1864, the first democratic election ever successfully held during a civil war anywhere, at any time, an election in which the issue was what kind of nation this was going to be—unified, however painfully, without slavery or permanently split with or without it. It was an election campaign in which the issue was truly our young nation's future. What our nation is today can be tracked directly to the outcome of that election campaign in the middle of the Civil War.

Because it is told as a narrative story by a reporter, and not as a treatise by a historian, although I view myself as both—"historical reporter" describes me precisely—it is full of the sights and sounds and smells of a political campaign, the characters, the color, the plot, and the drama of the times. And the wonderful thing is that it is true. It really happened. Nothing is made up. I have held strictly to the facts as clearly as I could know them.

My hope for it is that the reader, when finished, can say it was fun to read, and that the historian can say yes and it's true, it really happened that way.

REELECTING
LINCOLN

PROLOGUE

A WALK TO THE TELEGRAPH OFFICE

A UTUMN HAD COME TO WASHINGTON, AND THE NATION WAS about to enter the third winter of what Abraham Lincoln called "this great trouble."[1]

Nearly three years of civil war had left their stamp on the capital city of the North. A correspondent of the *London Daily Telegraph* would describe Washington in the final month of this year, 1863, as a "great, scrambling, slack-baked embryo of a city basking in the December sun like an alligator on the mud-bank of a bayou. . . ."[2]

But now it was October, and the city was just shaking off the dog days of summer, a summer the president's young secretary, John Hay, had thought as dismal as a defaced tombstone, "as dull . . . as an obsolete almanac."[3] As winter approached, Washington was, as it had been throughout the war, a bustling, busy, and corrupt city of camps, corrals, and soldiers—a fair number of whom were everlastingly drunk, or worse, wounded and dying.[4]

Within sight of the White House, painted women fluttered "their shame upon the streets." Gambling dens demeaned the principal avenues, and bribery and corruption were everywhere.[5]

The newcomer to Washington this autumn would scarcely believe there was a "great trouble" shadowing the nation. New houses were going up in every part of the city; bursting prosperity was apparent in every direction. It was the social season, and the theaters were thronged. "Hilarity and self-satisfaction are everywhere manifested," wrote Charles Mason, an Iowa judge just returned to the city after half a year absent. "From all that is visible one would not be led to conclude that the existence of the Nation was at stake."[6]

On this mid-October evening, Lincoln was crossing the shaded grounds between the White House and the War Department building. The president's tall, ungainly form could be seen as many as three or four times a day on this crossing. Nearly every evening before retiring he made this pilgrimage, for the telegraph office in the War Department was his ear on the war and his window on the world. He was on his way there again this evening, for elections had been held in several key states that day, and he needed to know the results.[7]

It is not likely that as he walked he paid much heed to the tall trees and thick shrubbery on either hand. As the war had dragged on, he had become progressively more inward-turning and meditative. The immediate external world had become a thing of diminishing interest to him over these three hard years. Except in conversation, he tended to pay it little notice. He was not unmindful of what was stirring about him as he worked in his office or walked through the White House grounds, but such particulars were secondary to him now, much in the background. His mind was ever busy in reflection, as it very likely was this autumn evening. There was much to reflect about. The war, the country's future, his own political career, seemed at a critical turning point.[8]

Looking out on the Union, Lincoln saw signs that at long last the skies were brightening, that the time might be coming, as his friend Noah Brooks, the correspondent of the *Sacramento Daily Union,* had written in March, "when peace shall end this troubled night."[9]

Ahead was a presidential election year. Looking at the prospects, it was perhaps not unreasonable for Lincoln, who tended to be cautious about such things, to believe that if he ran again he might be reelected.

Union victories in early July—at Gettysburg in the East and Vicksburg in the West—had turned the war around. Port Hudson on the Mississippi had been stripped from the rebel grip. For the first time since the war began, the great river was now Confederate-free and open to navigation for its entire length—from Minneapolis to New Orleans. The Cumberland Gap had been cleared, liberating east Tennessee. If the Union army could beat the Confederates back from the gates of Chattanooga—the issue was at that moment in doubt—then all of Tennessee would be Union ground. Fort Smith and Little Rock in the Trans-Mississippi West were now in Federal hands; Confederate military power in Arkansas had been broken, giving the Union army a firm foothold in that distant theater of the war. The mouth of the Rio Grande was now Federal territory, closing off yet one more rebel lifeline to the outside world. The Union naval blockade of the Confederacy, ratcheted up over the three years, was now so tight that rebeldom was virtually cut off from normal commerce. It was slowly strangling, confined within strictured limits, not likely now to expand, but doomed to shrink further still. There no longer seemed a danger of another full-scale invasion of the North. The rebellion at last seemed to be reeling. The hard blows were wearing it down. Lincoln believed that the rebel power was at last beginning to disintegrate, "that they will break to pieces if we only stand firm now."[10]

The rift in the leaden clouds had let in a broad beam of sunlight, and given fresh courage and larger faith to the country. There was a change of feeling in the air. Public sentiment was more confident. To a degree, the North had even become hardened to the killing and casualties and chaos of the conflict. There was prosperity not only in the capital city, but throughout the free states. Business was humming everywhere. Money was plentiful.

Lincoln could look back this evening in 1863, nearly three years into his administration, on a record of achievement.

Human freedom had made big, hard-won strides. Lincoln had emancipated the slaves in all conquered territory of the South. Congress had abolished slavery in the capital; prohibited it in the territories; declared all Negro soldiers in the Union army, and their families, free; and repealed the fugitive slave laws and all other laws that recognized or sanctioned slavery. Slavery now existed for the most part only behind rebel lines, in territory over which the Confederacy still held military sway. The only small exception was in the border states of the North. All that could be done short of a constitutional amendment outlawing slavery forever throughout the land had been done.[11] And such an amendment would surely be introduced when the Congress reconvened in December.

In foreign affairs, Lincoln had managed to maintain peace with Britain and to keep her neutral in the conflict. He had also won and held the goodwill of most of the rest of the world. Much of this had been his doing personally, the harvest of his own outgoing generosity, friendliness, and kindness to foreign leaders and foreigners generally.

Domestically there had been striking legislative breakthroughs, which, without the overarching shadow of war, would have glowed even brighter. The Homestead Act, opening the West to widespread settlement, had been passed in 1862. A College Land Grant Act was now law. A transcontinental railroad—the Union Pacific—had at last been chartered, to run from Nebraska to California. A Department of Agriculture had been established, a National Academy of Science founded. All of these achievements signaled a new era of advancement and prosperity for the country.

The nation was flexing and growing. West Virginia had become a state, Nevada was ready to become one. Washington Territory had been organized. A new territory embracing the Montana country was not far from reality. And beyond territory lay statehood. The nation was expanding, pulsating, pushing its frontiers ever westward.

Lincoln had also learned perhaps more than he ever wanted to know about how to run a war. Weaponry new to warfare had emerged, from observation balloons to breech-loading rifles to ironclad warships. Lincoln himself marveled at "this extraordinary war" with its "extraordinary developments . . . such as have not been seen in former wars."[12] The nation had a new national banking system, and Secretary of the Treasury Salmon P. Chase had found innovative new ways to pay for war on a scale such as the world had never seen.[13]

It was no longer the same country it had been when Lincoln was elected president nearly three years before. It was no longer what it was in 1860, when he had been nominated and had told Donn Piatt, the Ohio newspaperman and Republican politician, that "I must run the machine as I find it."[14] The machine he had found then no longer resembled the one he was running now.

None of this meant, however, that the clouds had fully lifted. The rebellion still lived stubbornly on; it still had sting. The Confederacy had partially rebounded from the back-to-back summertime disasters at Gettysburg and Vicksburg. The rebels had since halted one Union drive on Charleston in South Carolina and thwarted another at Sabine Pass in Texas. They had routed the Union army at Chickamauga in Tennessee and driven it back on Chattanooga.

And now, even as Lincoln walked from the Executive Mansion to the telegraph office, General Robert E. Lee's Confederate Army of Northern Virginia had pushed across the Rapidan and driven the Union Army of the Potomac under Maj. Gen. George Meade back toward Washington. Lee had moved by the Federal right flank, attempting— unsuccessfully so far—to slip behind Meade. It had been a worry for Lincoln these past few days. Three times he had anxiously wired Meade: "How is it now?" "What news this morning?"[15]

Even at that moment the two armies faced one another along Bull Run within a morning's carriage ride from Washington, skirmishing, probing, testing, each apprehensive to know the other's strength and

intentions. Lee was clearly trying to take advantage of a Federal reduc-
tion in forces on his front. Union troops had been pulled from Meade's
army and sent west to relieve Chattanooga. Other soldiers had been
temporarily furloughed to go home and vote in the important state
elections.

There were other worrisome matters pressing on the president this
evening as well. He had resorted to the draft in the spring, and yet
another call for volunteers to keep his armies at full strength would
soon be necessary. The draft had not been popular. Neither would the
new call for volunteers. And despite these things, he still couldn't get
the Army of the Potomac to move against the Confederates with its full
might and power. He would like to bring Maj. Gen. U. S. Grant, the
hero of Vicksburg, a proven fighter, east. But he didn't think that would
do, not just yet anyway.[16] He had decided to send Grant instead to
Chattanooga, to give him command over all Federal operations from the
Mississippi east to the Alleghenies. Chattanooga was at this moment the
more pressing demand.

So clouds still moved on the horizon. But things had to be kept in
perspective. It was a brighter day now than any Lincoln had yet seen in
the nearly three winters of war. There had been enough good news this
past summer and fall to cause him, only a few days before, to set aside
the last Thursday of November as a day of national thanksgiving.

In August, Lincoln had written a letter to his friend James C. Conkling in Illinois, to be read at a giant mass meeting of Republicans in
Springfield in September. Lincoln's two young secretaries, John Nicolay
and John Hay, had thought it a fine "stump-speech."[17] Hay had called
it "a great utterance of a great man. The whole Cabinet could not have
tinkered up a letter which could have compared with it. He can snake
a sophism out of its hole, better than all the trained logicians of all
schools."[18] Lincoln himself thought it "a rather good letter."[19]

The letter said what he might have been thinking this evening as he
walked from the White House to the telegraph office: "The signs look
better. The Father of Waters again goes unvexed to the sea. . . . And
while those who have cleared the great river may well be proud, even
that is not all. It is hard to say that anything has been more bravely, and
well done, than at Antietam, Murfreesboro, Gettysburg, and on many
fields of lesser note. Nor must Uncle Sam's Web-feet be forgotten. At all
the watery margins they have been present. Not only on the deep sea,
the broad bay, and the rapid river, but also up the narrow muddy
bayou, and wherever the ground was a little damp, they have been, and

made their tracks. Thanks to all. For the great republic—for the principle it lives by, and keeps alive—for man's vast future—thanks to all."

He had added that "peace does not appear so distant as it did. I hope
it will come soon, and come to stay; and so come as to be worth the
keeping in all future time. It will then have been proved that, among
free men, there can be no successful appeal from the ballot to the bullet; and that they who take such appeal are sure to lose their case, and
pay the cost."[20]

The ballot was very much on Lincoln's mind this mid-October
evening. He was anxious about the returns in the important state elections held that day in Pennsylvania and Ohio. For they would be the
keys to that even larger political event a little more than a year away:
the next presidential election.

The national canvass in 1864 would be a dangerous passage at a
dangerous time. Lincoln had temporarily reconstituted his Republican
party to rally political enemies as well as friends to the Union cause. He
had renamed it the National Union Party, and he believed that if it
failed to win the presidency, these three winters of death, deprivation,
and sorrow would have been in vain. At stake was a reunited, reknit
nation, what he had been working for so hard for all those three
calamitous years. If his party lost, that goal was also surely lost. He
believed that the coming canvass, the first wartime presidential election
in this or any democratic nation's history, would be no less than a contest between a Union and a dis-Union candidate, and that permanent
disunion would surely follow a Democratic victory.[21]

Some believed that simply to conduct a successful presidential canvass in the midst of the war would be a triumph, perhaps even a miracle, no matter who won. But nobody had seriously considered not
holding one, certainly not Lincoln, the man who had the most to lose.

Even now, thirteen months from that canvass, the country was
already humming with speculation—with "the buzzing of presidential
intriguing," as Count Adam Gurowski, the Washington diarist, put it.
Gurowski, an acid-tongued Polish exile, called politicians "gnats and
musquitoes . . . the race of hell." And he wrote that they were "at work
like moles, to counteract each other and to undermine the respective
presidential candidates."[22]

A good deal of the buzzing of the gnats and mosquitos was over
whether Lincoln would run again, and could he win if he did? Both
questions were in the air. Both were at issue. Both awaited answers.

Various members of the race of hell had been out over the summer and early fall, testing the air. Lincoln's political friend from Ohio, former governor William Dennison, had told John Hay not ten days before that he had conversed much with leading men in different parts of the country and found a widespread and constantly growing feeling in favor of Lincoln's reelection. He said that feeling was evident throughout the West, and spreading. He had even found it in that rankest of Democratic strongholds, New York.[23]

Schuyler Colfax, the Republican congressman from Indiana, so generally genial and friendly that people called him "Smiler,"[24] had also been out testing the sentiment in the country. Wherever he had been that summer, Colfax had found evidence of a very powerful popular feeling in the president's favor. He was about to tell Lincoln he thought it would continue, "unless you do something to check it in your message [the upcoming presidential message to Congress in December] or public utterances or acts this winter."[25]

To the question "Will Lincoln run again?" Lincoln was saying nothing. His friend Noah Brooks, one of the small army of newspaper correspondents in Washington who called themselves "Bohemians," thought he knew. He had written in a dispatch to his paper in Sacramento less than ten days before that "there is no longer any need of concealing or ignoring the fact that Lincoln is a candidate for renomination." Brooks said he had it on the highest authority that the president did not seek the nomination, but greatly desired it, that he considered his reelection less risky in these iffy times than "swapping horses in the middle of the stream."[26]

Brooks, who stared out at Washington and the world through pince-nez glasses on a cord and smoked good cigars, was pretty close to Lincoln. He might, therefore, be pretty close to the truth.[27]

But whether Brooks was right or not, so much now depended on circumstance. Nothing was certain. Anything could happen. And nobody on this mid-October evening a year before the election knew that better than Lincoln himself. The matter was very much on his mind as he ended his walk from the White House and stepped inside the War Department telegraph office.

1

THAT SUBJECT OF
THE PRESIDENCY

———

THE TELEGRAPH OFFICE WAS ON THE SECOND FLOOR OF THE WAR
Department building at the corner of Pennsylvania Avenue and
Seventeenth Street. Even on the most miserable of days, when
the wind whistled through Washington's dirt streets, filling the city with
driving dust and obscuring the avenue from end to end, the dim outline
of the distant war could still be seen from the telegraph office, and its
echoes heard.[1]

It had often been an unhappy echo that reached Lincoln there. The
poet-editor James Russell Lowell wrote of the "insidious treachery . . .
of the telegraph, sending hourly its electric thrill of panic along the
remotest nerves of the community."[2]

Two of the most powerful men in the North were often there in the
telegraph office, waiting, listening for, dreading that electric thrill. Secretary of War Edwin Stanton rarely left. He looked upon the telegraph
service as his "right arm." It was so much his right arm that the office
it occupied adjoined his own, separated only by a door, nearly always
left ajar. Lincoln spent more of his waking hours there than at any
other place except the White House. He called this room his "office."

The president had spent endless hours of suspense, exultation, and
sorrow there. He had written the first draft of the Emancipation Proclamation in the telegraph office on pieces of foolscap between disastrous
messages from the Peninsula in the bleak summer of 1862. That summer had been particularly forlorn. Maj. Gen. George B. McClellan's big
Army of the Potomac had been driven back to the banks of the James
River after seven days of punishing attacks from Robert E. Lee's
smaller Confederate army. It had been a summer of smashed hopes, res-
onating for weeks over the telegraph wires.

Sometimes Lincoln came alone to the telegraph office, without escort. More often, as fears for his life deepened with the war, he was attended by a small guard of soldiers. Sometimes he stayed the night— on those nights when his armies were fighting and bleeding on some battlefield and the issue was in doubt. But routinely, on quieter nights, he returned to the White House, attended often after dark by the head of the telegraph office, Maj. Thomas T. Eckert.

Lincoln was in good hands with Major Eckert, who had a penchant for breaking soft iron fireplace pokers over his arm, and presumably could do the same with heads. The first time Eckert broke pokers for Lincoln's entertainment, the president turned to John Potts, chief clerk of the War Department, and said, "Mr. Potts, you will have to buy a better quality of iron in the future if you expect your pokers to stand the test of this young man's arm."

Lincoln stepped into his "office" on this evening in October 1863 and hung his shawl over the top of the door opening into Stanton's room, as was his custom. He was instantly among friends. The cipher operators were his boys. Few men were in closer contact with the president day in and day out than they, except his cabinet officers and his private secretaries.

The room housing the telegraph office was a peculiar setting for such a function and for such men. It was more suggestive of an athenaeum than a throbbing wartime information clearinghouse. It had been the War Department library before the war. About half of its space was given to bookcases set back in alcoves between five tall windows looking out on Washington. On those shelves were stacked volumes dating as far back as 1800. The alcove doors were generally kept locked to keep the collection intact, but the cipher operators had access for reading and study in their leisure moments between messages.

Without question the most useful volume in the collection was a copy of *Roget's Thesaurus,* fast becoming dog-eared, with which the puzzled operators attempted to deal with Assistant Secretary of War Charles A. Dana's esoteric vocabulary. Dana laced his messages with such obscurities as "truculent" and "hibernating," words these young cipher operators had never heard before and had no idea what they meant. They looked to the thesaurus to enlighten them.

Lincoln could have told them what those words meant, for he had had firsthand experience in these weary three years of civil war with truculent generals and hibernating armies. Often on troubled evenings he bent over the shoulders of these young operators, peering anxiously at incoming messages even as they were being deciphered.

This evening, as on all evenings, Lincoln strode first to the little drawer in the cipher desk where incoming dispatches were filed as they were received. He read each from the top down until he reached those he had already seen his last time there.

He then said, "Well, boys, I am down to raisins."

One day one of the operators asked him what he meant by that, and Lincoln had told them a story: A little girl had celebrated her birthday by eating freely of many wonderful things, topped by raisins for dessert. During the night she was taken violently ill, and when the doctor arrived she was busy casting up her accounts. The genial doctor, investigating the contents of the upchucking, noticed the small black objects that had just appeared, and assured the anxious parents that the danger was past, the dessert was coming up, the child was "down to raisins."

Lincoln found a measure of peace and serenity in this telegraphic retreat that he found nowhere else—despite its urgent messages of chaos and upheaval. It was in fact his Bethany, his harbor in the storm, even though the news clattering in over the wires was so often of war and killing. Besides virtually living there when a battle was being fought or when votes were being counted, he often dropped in when nothing was happening, just to escape the swarms of office-hunters and favor-seekers thronging the White House hallways. This library-cum-telegraph office had often been the site of important conferences with the president and members of his cabinet, generals, congressmen, and other insiders. Most of them knew that if they couldn't find Lincoln in his White House office, they could probably find him here, settled in at Eckert's desk after he was down to raisins.[3]

The midterm state elections in October the year before had given Lincoln one of his longest nights in the telegraph office. Those elections in 1862 had been a disaster for him and his party. Five of the key states he had carried in 1860—New York, Pennsylvania, Ohio, Indiana, and Illinois, heavy hitters all—only two years later had sent Democratic majorities to Congress. The Republicans had held onto a bare eighteen-vote edge in the House of Representatives only because of large, steadfast Republican majorities in New England and the border states. A solid swath of Northern states from the Mississippi to the Atlantic that had gone for Lincoln in 1860 had defected to the Democrats in the midterm elections of 1862. The same outcome in 1860 would have beaten Lincoln 127 electoral votes to 86. He would not now have been president.

The most important race in 1862 had been in New York, the biggest state in the Union, where a Democrat for governor, Horatio Seymour, had beaten a Republican, James S. Wadsworth, by nearly eleven thousand votes. The New York Democrats had also elected a majority delegation to the U.S. House of Representatives. The Democrats had won only two of the six governorships up for grabs, Seymour in New York and Joel Parker in New Jersey. But the strong anti-administration tide had coursed relentlessly through congressional races nearly everywhere.

William W. Orme, an Illinois Republican, said, "The democracy have carried everything, and I think the country is ruined. The result of these elections will palsy the arm of the President." *The New York Times* called the election a "vote of want of confidence" in the president.[4]

The reasons for that midterm Republican disaster nationwide in 1862 had been clear enough. The Union army had failed to win the war. From First Bull Run to Antietam, the Army of the Potomac had been humiliated at worst, frustrated at best. So much money and so many lives had been spent, with so little to show for it. This lack of success on the battlefield had undercut the popular confidence in the young Lincoln administration throughout the North.

Another reason for the Democratic victory in 1862 had been Lincoln's preliminary Emancipation Proclamation, announced in the fall following the battle of Antietam, only a few weeks before the election. Emancipation had not sold well with many in the North. Indeed, George William Curtis, the popular New York editor-orator, wrote of "the mad desperation of the reaction" to the proclamation nationwide.[5]

Many northerners thought it had turned the war into a fight to free the slaves instead of to reunite the Union, and they couldn't buy into that. A year later the *New York Herald* was still complaining editorially about "the destructive measures and controlling malign influences of the abolition Marplots at Washington," whom many believed had hold of Lincoln and had caused him to pen the detested document.[6]

The Democratic catchphrase of the campaign in 1862—"the Constitution as it is and the Union as it was," with slavery unimpaired—

sounded reasonable to many Northern ears. Emancipation did not. Lincoln, who tended to put a light face on anything he could in that sad time, paraphrased that slogan: "the Union as it was, barring the already broken eggs."[7]

That had not been particularly humorous to candidates such as H. S. Bundy, running on the Union Party ticket for Congress in Ohio's Eleventh District. Just before the election, Bundy predicted that the proclamation "will defeat me and every other Union candidate for Congress along the border."[8]

Nor were the unwon war and the Emancipation Proclamation the only two things working against Lincoln in the elections in 1862. There had also been some trampling on individual rights by the Executive in the act of waging war against enemies external and internal: arbitrary arrests, imprisonments, and violations of habeas corpus. The Democrats had looked on these as a shameless, cynical, dangerous misuse of administrative power, and had pushed the issue hard in the state canvasses. They had pictured Lincoln as a tyrant, and his administration as a dictatorship.

All of those things together had defeated Lincoln's party at the ballot box in the autumn of 1862. And the defeat had suggested that the president's policies were in serious trouble throughout the country, and that he was on politically unsteady ground. His reelection two years hence looked out of the question. The new year, 1863, had opened on widespread pessimism and gloom in the North, not helped by another bloody Union army disaster at Fredericksburg in mid-December, just before the old year ended.

The popular writer-lawyer Richard Henry Dana put what it had all come down to by March 1863 in a letter to Charles Francis Adams, Lincoln's ambassador to Britain. "As to the politics of Washington, the most striking thing is the absence of personal loyalty to the President," Dana had written. "It does not exist. He has no admirers, no enthusiastic supporters, none to bet on his head. If a Republican convention were to be held to-morrow, he would not get the vote of a State."[9]

But since then the clouds had started to lift. There had been Gettysburg and Vicksburg. And at the ballot box earlier in the year there had also been better news. New Hampshire, in an election in the spring, had given the Republicans a victory. But even that was a victory laced with lingering bad portents. The ongoing bitter hostility of the Democrats to the prosecution of the war was sharply evident in the results. New Hampshire senator Daniel Clark wrote Lincoln that spring that "scarcely a Democrat supported the Administration. Almost every one who had heretofore avowed himself for the Union and the country turned in for peace and party. Yet we have beaten them. They have retired from the field. The two houses in convention will choose a Republican governor. . . ."[10]

Two other springtime elections, in Rhode Island and Connecticut, also went to the Republicans, signaling a hopeful backlash against the peace-at-any-price Democrats, and a move back toward the Union Party side. More recently, elections in California and Maine had gone the same way. This augured well. Lincoln's political fortunes, like the war, might be turning around.

Now, in the autumn of 1863, Lincoln was waiting in the telegraph office again for election news—this time from two "October states," Ohio and Pennsylvania. They would tell the story. How they went would tell Lincoln if there was now a realistic hope for his own nomination and reelection in 1864.

At about ten o'clock in the evening he wired Columbus, Ohio: "Where is John Brough?"[11]

Brough was the candidate for governor of Ohio on the Union Party ticket. And he was in the telegraph office in Columbus when Lincoln's wire arrived. So Lincoln inquired, "Brough, about what is your majority now?"

Brough wired back, "Over 30,000."

Lincoln asked him to remain at the telegraph office through the night, and a little past midnight he wired him again: "Brough, what is your majority this time?"

Brough replied, "Over 50,000."

At about five o'clock in the morning Brough's next answer came back: "Over 100,000." Lincoln wired him, "Glory to God in the highest. Ohio has saved the Nation."[12]

Ohio had been crucial. The governor's race in that state had been the most clear-cut contest yet between the war and peace parties in the country, between conservative, pro-Union war Democrats and Republicans on the one hand and the peace Democrats—called "copperheads"—on the other.

In Ohio the Democratic party had nominated the man known as "the king of the copperheads," Clement Vallandigham, to run against Brough. No line could have been cleaner drawn. Vallandigham was a former congressman, a tireless critic of the Lincoln war policy, an emotional searcher for peace at any price. His seditious public tirades against the administration had landed him in arrest under a military edict against such talk earlier in the year, fueling to white heat the charges of arbitrary arrests. Lincoln would not have sanctioned the arrest had his approval been sought beforehand, but it hadn't been. And now he had to support the general who had done it.

Rather than sending Vallandigham to prison, however, Lincoln, in an act not without humor, sent him instead to the Confederacy, which really didn't want him either. By the summer of 1863, Vallandigham, now a martyr to the antiwar, pro-peace cause, was nominated for governor in Ohio by the Democratic party, and was running in absentia from Canada against John Brough.

Vallandigham's platform was peace now, at any price, slavery and all. Brough's cause was the Union Party's cause: to fight the rebellion to its end and reunite the shattered Union, without slavery. The choice between him and Vallandigham was wholly undiluted, up and down, black and white. The New York Herald, guiltless of sympathy for either alternative such races represented, wrote that it all boiled down to "whether the copperheads or the niggerheads are more obnoxious to the great conservative body of the people."[13]

The great conservative body of the people of Ohio appeared to be finding the copperheads more obnoxious. The race had drawn the largest vote ever in the state, and it was translating into a landslide that was not only sweeping Brough into office, but an emphatically pro-Union state legislature with him. The New York Herald, reporting the result two days later, called it a chastisement that the copperheads could not possibly misunderstand.[14]

Between reports from Brough, Lincoln also anxiously reached out through the cipher for early returns from Pennsylvania. There the issue wasn't so clear-cut. But it was just as important as a harbinger of the larger struggle in 1864.

In Pennsylvania the strong pro-Union Republican governor, Andrew Curtin, was running against a state supreme court judge, Democrat George W. Woodward, who had a strong antiwar reputation. The New York Daily Tribune thought Woodward "the Vallandigham of Pennsylvania," but a far craftier politician with "an excellent talent for silence."[15] Judge Woodward was not as extreme as the Tribune had painted him. Although tilted toward peace, he was hardly a Vallandigham. He was popular in Pennsylvania, strongly supported by the mass of his party.

But Curtin was also popular. His unstinting and practical support of the war had been a sturdy prop for Lincoln from the beginning. He was genial and witty and had a way with a speech. His genuine care and concern for the well-being of the Pennsylvania troops in the field had won him a reputation as the "Soldier's Friend," and made him a hard man to beat. Everybody knew it would be a close race.[16]

By early morning, Lincoln was liking all he heard clacking in over the wires from both states. By five o'clock, when Brough reported his 100,000-vote landslide, the president knew Curtin had won, too. The margin was far narrower in Pennsylvania than in Ohio, but the trend showed Curtin riding toward a 15,000-vote win. Lincoln's war policy was being impressively sustained in the two big states where it counted the most. He was being vindicated. He and his party were bouncing back from the dark October of 1862.

When Secretary of the Navy Gideon Welles dropped in at the White House the next morning to congratulate Lincoln, it was a far happier president than he had found there the day before. Lincoln confessed to Welles that he had been more anxious about the outcome of that election than he had been for his own in 1860.[17]

If Lincoln had watched and worried, he had also pulled levers and played politics. He had authorized a fifteen-day leave for all government clerks from Ohio and Pennsylvania to go home and vote. He arranged for the railroads to give them passes and saw that they were assessed a fraction of their pay for the support of the party. Commanders in the field were authorized to furlough troops home to vote in Pennsylvania, since they couldn't vote yet in the field. There were so many soldiers absent from the armies, the Democrats charged, that Lincoln had put Meade's army in jeopardy between the Rapidan and the Potomac. On election day, workers in the Philadelphia arsenal were driven to the polls en masse—"like cattle to the slaughter," somebody suggested.[18]

Big-name Republican politicians had converged on the contested states. The Republican governors of Illinois and Indiana had stumped for the ticket in Ohio. Secretary of the Treasury Chase, for the first time since the war began, also went home to Ohio to stump and vote for Brough and deliver "previously deliberated addresses" from railroad platforms. His audiences had called him "Old Greenbacks," and he had called the victory "the battle day of the republic." He said that the people of the great states, asked whether they would sustain their armies in the field, their credit at home, and their honor abroad, had "decided them for the country . . . decided them for all time." Chase was particularly pleased with the size of the victory in Ohio, telling an audience in Columbus on October 15 that a 10,000-vote majority for Brough would not have sufficed, but the grand old 100,000 had done the job.[19]

The *Chicago Tribune* had called these 1863 elections "the hot canvass."[20] And Zachariah Chandler, the radical, pro-Union, rebel-hating senator from Michigan, wanted Lincoln to keep the heat on. Chandler wrote that Lincoln must, in his upcoming message to Congress in December, "stand firm" against the timid Republican conservatives. "Conservatives and traitors," Chandler wrote Lincoln with his accustomed lack of delicacy, "are buried together." For God's sake, he urged the president, "don't exhume their remains in Your Message. They will smell worse than Lazarus did after he had been buried three days."[21]

Lincoln wrote back, "I am very glad the elections this autumn have gone favorably, and that I have not, by native depravity, or under evil influences, done anything bad enough to prevent the good result. I hope to 'stand firm' enough not to go backward, and yet not go forward fast enough to wreck the country's cause."[22] That probably didn't satisfy Chandler, but it would have to do.

As Lincoln had once told Maine's radical Republican senator, Lot M. Morrill, "I don't know but that God has created some one man great enough to comprehend the whole of this stupendous crisis and transaction from end to end, and endowed him with sufficient wisdom to manage and direct it. I confess that I do not fully understand and foresee it all. But I am placed here where I am obliged, to the best of my poor ability, to deal with it. And that being the case, I can only go just as fast as I can see how to go."[23]

Did he really want to deal with it for another four years? Illinois congressman Elihu Washburne had written him only the day before the October elections, demanding to know. "Notwithstanding the troubles that surround us," Washburne wrote, "the time has come when we must confront the question of our next presidential candidate. I think you ought to let some of your confidential friends know your wishes." On October 26, Lincoln wrote Washburne only a qualified commitment: "A second term would be a great honor and a great labor, which together, perhaps I would not decline, if tendered."[24]

Lincoln's reporter friend, Noah Brooks, believed the president liked to look on himself not as the people's ruler, but as their attorney. He told Brooks privately that "if the people think that I have managed their case for them well enough to trust me to carry up to the next term, I am sure that I shall be glad to take it."[25]

From the beginning Lincoln had had a love-hate relationship with the presidency. Even as he was leaving Springfield to come to Washington to take the job in February 1861, he told his law partner, William H. Herndon, that "I am sick of office-holding already, and I shudder when I think of the tasks that are still ahead." Later, in New York, en route to Washington, he had said, "I think when the clouds look as dark as they do now, one term might satisfy any man."[26]

Early in the year ahead he would tell representatives from the Philadelphia Union League visiting the White House that he would shrink from nothing that might be required to save the country. "I shall not shrink," he told them, "from another man's nomination for the Presidency with any greater hesitation than I would from my own. If it shall be made to appear in any way that the elements upon which the salvation of the country is to depend can be better combined by dismissing me, the country can have no difficulty in getting rid of me." But he also would not shrink from being used further if that appeared to be the best way to save the country.[27]

Second terms were rather out of style just then. No president had been reelected since Andrew Jackson in 1832. Running again had become the thing not to do. To run again, Lincoln would have to buck thirty years of tradition. And there was plenty of doubt in plenty of minds in late 1863 whether he should even try it.

There was, however, no doubt about it in the minds of Lincoln's two young personal secretaries, John Nicolay and John Hay.

Neither Nicolay nor Hay was yet thirty years old, and Count Gurowski, in his diary, called them the White House's "political little ones."[28] They called Lincoln "the Ancient," "the Tycoon," and "the Premier."[29] They were young enough to have unqualified opinions about nearly everything, and after seeing Lincoln up close now for three years, they had an unqualified opinion about him: they were swollen with admiration. At those times when their idolization was bursting all bounds, they called him "the American."[30]

Hay had written Nicolay in August that "I am growing more and more firmly convinced that the good of the country absolutely demands that he should be kept where he is till this thing is over. There is no man in the country, so wise, so gentle and so firm. I believe the hand of God placed him where he is. . . . I believe the people know what they want and unless politics have gained in power & lost in principle they will have it."[31]

In September, Hay had written in his diary, "I do not know whether the nation is worthy of him for another term. I know the people want him. There is no mistaking that fact. But politicians are strong yet & he is not their 'kind of a cat.' I hope God won't see fit to scourge us for our sins by any one of the two or three most prominent candidates on the ground." No matter what happened, Hay believed "next winter will be the most exciting and laborious of all our lives. It will be worth any other ten."[32]

What was going to make it so exciting and laborious and worth any other ten was the fact that Lincoln's own party was so schism-rent. Its moderate, conservative wing, which Lincoln led, was for pushing the war to final victory, followed by a lenient, liberal reknitting of the shattered nation. But the party had another wing, a powerful, vindictive, and unhappy radical contingent. These Republican radicals agreed with the president about pushing the war to final victory. But they were not at all inclined to be either lenient or liberal. They wanted to control the reconstruction of the South, and they wanted no part of being lenient about it. They were abolitionists for the most part, who deplored the kindhearted president's approach. They wanted vengeance, a stern and relentless punishment of the rebellious South and its slaveholding leaders, and a reknitting of the Union in their image.

By this autumn in 1863, the Republican radicals had a decision to make. James Gordon Bennett at the *New York Herald* put it this way: "It is no joke that President Lincoln is a candidate for another term of four years in the White House. We think the time has arrived when the radical wing of the republican party must decide whether they are to take 'Honest Old Abe' for another trial or run a scrub ticket against him."[33]

The only thing that gave Lincoln hope in the face of this opposition within his own party was the even deeper split in the Democratic party. Most Democrats bitterly opposed the Emancipation Proclamation that had gone into effect in January. They considered it abolitionist, unconstitutional, and unnecessary to winning the war. They deplored the high-handed tactics of the Lincoln administration in prosecuting the war, the roughshod manhandling of habeas corpus, and other offenses. The Democratic party was called "the united democracy" by its members (because, as the ever-sardonic *New York Herald* explained, "it was hardly ever before so fragmentary and disunited").[34]

Like the Republicans, the Democrats had two warring wings. One of these, the war Democrats, agreed with Lincoln about the need to first crush the rebellion. That done, they would then shape a peace that restored the Union as it had been. But the party's other wing, the peace Democrats—called copperheads—wanted an immediate end to the war and peace at any price, even if it meant letting the South go its own way and leaving the nation forever divided.

The Democrats' problem had been relentlessly compounded by whole-sale defections to the new National Union Party, that temporary fusion of Union-minded Democrats and Republicans under a single banner. Like many things national, this fusion started as a local movement. It was the brainchild of the politically ever-present Blair family of Maryland and Missouri.

There had been a Blair at the highest levels of American politics since the days of Andrew Jackson. The patriarch of this politically powerful, pro-Union family, Francis P. Blair Sr., had been one of Jackson's closest friends and advisers—a member of his "kitchen cabinet." He enjoyed access on the presidential level still, for Lincoln liked the old man and listened to him. Lincoln also had two of Blair's sons to listen to. One of them, Montgomery, was in his cabinet, his postmaster general. The other, Francis Junior—called Frank—was a major general in the Union army, and also a congressman from Missouri. It was, in fact, Frank who first changed a local Republican party into a Union Party and set the whole movement in motion.

As civil war approached, Missouri was on the border both geographically and emotionally. Pro-Southern sentiment was in the minority in Missouri. However, the state had a governor and a legislature that were pro-Confederate and ready to take it out of the Union the minute the break came. What emphatically wasn't pro-Confederate in the state was Frank Blair. And he wasn't going to put up with any such apostasy as a Confederate Missouri. Unshakably pro-Union, as all of his family was, Blair by January 1861 was preparing to keep Missouri from seceding, by force if necessary—and it would probably be necessary.

Blair was convinced that a civil war was surely coming. He was also convinced that the word "Republican" was an uncomfortable umbrella for pro-Union war Democrats to gather under. So he began recruiting all Union sympathizers, Democrats and Republicans together, into Union Clubs, uncaring and unmindful of what party they belonged to.

Mixing Democrats and Republicans and conditional Unionists (for the Union up to a point) and unconditional Unionists (for the Union, no matter what) in Missouri, was like mixing cats and dogs. It took somebody as resolute and unbending as a Blair to make such an unnatural fit stick. Many Republicans balked when he began shuffling them into pro-Union fighting units alongside Democrats. "I don't believe in breaking up the Republican party just to please these tender-footed Unionists," one unconditional Republican partisan objected. "I believe in sticking to the party."

"Let us have a COUNTRY first," Blair said, "and then we can talk about parties." In two meetings in January 1861 in St. Louis he fused the antisecessionist, antislavery movement into one entity, and formed the first Union Party in the country.[35]

By the elections of 1862, the idea had spread. There were similar informal, often uneasy, pro-Union coalitions in every state. In some cases they were about as unpopular as they had been at first in Missouri. The Ohio Republican senator John Sherman not only didn't like these unnatural alliances, he blamed them in large part for the disaster that year at the polls.

"The Republican organization was voluntarily abandoned by the President and his leading followers," Sherman complained to his brother, Union Maj. Gen. William T. Sherman, shortly after the 1862 elections, "and a no-party Union was formed to run against an old, well-drilled party organization. This was simply ridiculous. . . . If they [the Republicans] have the wisdom to throw overboard the old debris that joined them in the Union movement, they will succeed. If not they are doomed."[36]

Lincoln, however, was convinced they were doomed if they didn't unite with the old debris. In 1862 these uneasy, unnatural political coalitions that supported his war policy had been only unstructured, local, and informal. After the 1862 elections Lincoln resolved to formalize them, and the Republican party temporarily became the National Union Party. This further infuriated Republican radicals such as John Sherman, but it was moving toward a unified center position, where Lincoln believed the votes were. His idea was to harness as many factions as possible to pull together in support of winning the war. This broad fusing of pro-Union Democrats and Republicans into an alliance under a single umbrella seemed to have paid off in the autumn elections of 1863. It must be made to do so again in 1864.[37]

When all sixteen state elections had been held, by early November, all—not just Ohio and Pennsylvania—had come in with thumping

Union majorities. As the *New York Herald* put it, the outcome was "like the handle of a jug—all on one side."[38]

By the end of October, the buzzing over what it all meant for 1864 had reached such a pitch that even Lincoln was tired to death of it. "I wish they would stop thrusting that subject of the Presidency into my face," he snapped at John Hay. "I don't want to hear anything about it."[39]

The subject, however, seemed to be there to stay, not likely to be out of his face for another twelve months.

2

LITTLE MAC

———❧———

T HAT SUBJECT OF THE PRESIDENCY WAS ALSO IN GEORGE Brinton McClellan's face. It had been there already for a year now. With twelve months yet to the election, it was still there, a gnat in endless, gyrating orbit.

Ohio's Democratic congressman, Samuel S. Cox, who occasionally dined with the enemy, explained it all to John Hay over dinner. Cox was a Democrat with a difference. He was deeply religious, a scholar who read broadly, wrote prolifically, had a prodigious memory, and was an independent thinker. He had such an affinity for describing setting suns that friends and enemies alike called him "Sunset."

"The whole horizon full of golden, impenetrating lustre . . . ," he had described one sunset, "a long polished belt of azure, worthy of a Sicilian sky."[1]

Cox also had a fondness for the lustrous hue of his own voice, and never let an opportunity pass without a word or a crack or a joke. Noah Brooks of the *Sacramento Daily Union,* who was so ready to describe every notable public figure who came within the range of his pince-nez, classified Cox as "caliber, light; range, limited"—despite his broad reading and prolific writing.[2]

Cox thought he had the range on who his party was going to run for president against Hay's boss in 1864.

Who? Hay asked over dinner.

"General McClellan," Cox answered. "We will run McClellan. He is our best ticket. . . ."[3]

If that was so, rarely would a fired employee ever have such a spectacular and public opportunity to get back at the boss who sacked him.

Lincoln had dismissed McClellan as commander of the Army of the Potomac more than a year before.

McClellan had been the first Union general of the war to win victories. In May to July 1861, his Ohio, Indiana, and West Virginia troops had won three little skirmishes in the mountains of western Virginia—at Philippi, Rich Mountain, and Corricks Ford. The North had embraced these small victories, the only ones so far, as signs of hope, hailing this hero of the West as the "Little Napoleon," for both his compact physique and his battle-winning ways.

Following the Union defeat at Bull Run in late July, Lincoln had called McClellan to Washington from over the mountains and put him in command of the army in the East. McClellan had picked up that beaten and demoralized army, renamed it the Army of the Potomac, reorganized it, rebuilt it, drilled it, and made it, by the winter of 1861–1862, into the finest fighting force ever seen on the American continent. But then he had maddeningly refused to take it into battle until he believed it was thoroughly and overwhelmingly prepared, which he never seemed to think it was. The uncharitable called him "the Unready."[4]

Pressed into doing something, McClellan finally met the Confederates on the Peninsula in 1862. But instead of attacking in force, he himself was instead savagely attacked by the Confederate Army of Northern Virginia under Lee, and driven back in July, weary and on the run, to the sanctuary of Harrison's Landing on the James River.

When another Union army, under Maj. Gen. John Pope, was also routed by Lee in front of Washington in August, Lincoln in desperation turned again to George McClellan, that gifted organizer, in hopes that he could knit the shattered Union forces back together, restore morale, and find a way to beat the Confederates at last.

Buoyed by two successive victories over two Union armies, Lee invaded Maryland in September. But he then divided his army in front of McClellan and overreached himself. McClellan cornered Lee's scattered army across Antietam Creek, with its back to the Potomac, on September 17. Never had the Confederate army been in such danger of destruction. But McClellan—with an army twice the size of Lee's, and after holding back until he felt he was ready—struck him only piecemeal, division by division. Not only did he fail to deliver the knockout blow, but he let Lee slip quietly away a day later, under the cover of night, across the Potomac, and then failed to pursue until it was too late. So, in November, Lincoln fired him.

But, by doing so, the president also made him into his likely Democratic opponent in 1864, for McClellan in military exile became the darling of the most powerful and influential Democrats in the North.

Like many famous generals before him, McClellan was a politician despite himself. His years at West Point had trained him to be an engineer and a soldier, not a politician. And he thought like a soldier, not a politician.

He had a basic nonpolitician's view of the presidency. It was his conviction that no man should seek that high office, at least not publicly, but that no true man ought to refuse it, either, if it was spontaneously offered him and he was satisfied that he could do the country good by accepting it. It all came down to a question of duty.[5]

In the year since his sacking, he had both lived by that belief and violated it. All through the year McClellan had expected to be reassigned to another command in the Union army. He was still the senior general on the army's active list, though he was only thirty-six years old. But he had been put on the shelf. Secretary of War Stanton had ordered him to Trenton, New Jersey, the day he was relieved, and had never communicated with him again.

McClellan almost immediately moved from Trenton to nearby New York City, and began writing a report vindicating his fifteen months as commander of the Army of the Potomac. Governor Horatio Seymour had enlisted him to help organize a militia call-up in New York State, but otherwise McClellan had waited. As he waited, his old army endured more disasters, first under Ambrose Burnside at Fredericksburg, and then under Joe Hooker at Chancellorsville. And with each disaster there was pressure on Lincoln to call McClellan back once more to save the Union. The Union victory at Gettysburg had eased the pressure, but done nothing to blunt the boom that had been building in the Democratic party to make "Little Mac" its standard-bearer in 1864.

McClellan had laid low publicly, trying, as he told Charles C. Fulton, editor of the *Baltimore American,* "to remain as quiet as possible."[6] He worked on his report and avoided writing letters for publication.

But the mere act of moving to New York City, into the Fifth Avenue Hotel, after he was shelved, had injected him into politics. The city was a steaming Democratic hotbed, the largest party stronghold in the North. Cheering partisan crowds greeted him at the door of the hotel and followed him all over town. The New York newspapers carried a daily schedule of his movements. He could not go to the theater, the opera, a dinner party, or a grand ball without notice. Nor could he avoid being seen with the leading Democrats in New York. They had made him their special project. Governor Seymour conferred with him. August Belmont, the rich and powerful financier and chairman of the Democratic National Committee, befriended him. John Van Buren, son of the former Democratic president, now the New York state party chairman, flattered him. Dean Richmond, a leading party strategist, whispered in his ear. Such major corporate and financial powers and party supporters as Samuel L. M. Barlow, William Aspinwall, John Jacob Astor, and William B. Duncan became his closest New York friends. They presented him with a handsome, fully furnished, four-story brick house on West Thirty-first Street in one of Manhattan's most upscale neighborhoods. Barlow had headed the effort and contributed much of the $20,000 it had cost.[7]

The editors of the two most powerful Democratic newspapers in the country, Manton Marble of the *New York World* and William C. Prime of the *Journal of Commerce,* became McClellan's friends and advisers. By throwing in with such Democratic luminaries, the general was allying himself with Lincoln's most powerful enemies. These were all men who entertained grave reservations about the war McClellan had fought for fifteen months as general of the Union army, and who opposed the Lincoln administration root and branch.

Manton Marble had but one political aim for his *World,* where daily he lashed out viciously against Lincoln's war. Marble intended his paper "to do all it possibly can to unite every Democrat in solid column to break down the present administration, for that is the condition *sine qua non,* of all any intelligent patriot can hope for of Union or Peace or Liberty."[8] The patriot Marble wanted to lead the Democrats to victory was McClellan.

The general's cozying up to the Democratic powers of New York City through the past year had alarmed many of his friends. For many of them, these Democratic leaders were a suspect crowd. McClellan's brother's brother-in-law, Edward H. Eldredge, thought them "as near secessionists as they dare to be." He called them "seeming friends who may prove his worst enemies." Many of McClellan's former soldiers from the Army of the Potomac believed as Eldredge did. They saw these Democrats befriending their former beloved commander as copperheads—whether it was true or not—peace-at-any-price politicians whom one of them likened to poisonous reptiles.[9]

But McClellan was ideologically comfortable with these men. He basically believed as they did, and had for a long time. They were friends, with whom he had been corresponding regularly for a year or more. Their cause was his cause. Like them, he believed the war could never be won or the nation successfully reunited under Lincoln's Republican policies. That didn't mean McClellan was a copperhead himself, or that they were. McClellan differed sharply from the peace wing of the party, for he believed, with Lincoln, that the war must be vigorously pushed with reunion as its aim. Reunion, however, was his sole condition for peace. Emancipation was to him a mistake and should never have been entered into the equation. Like nearly every Democrat still loyal to the party, he wanted "the Constitution as it is, the Union as it was."[10]

McClellan's politics had long been suspect by the Republicans. Stories had been circulating from the beginning of his meteoric military career that he was seeing a presidency in his future, and using his military position to get him there. He denied that notion then, and he was denying it now.

But the taste was in his mouth. He was an ambitious man, and the presidency was ambition's ultimate prize. It was within his reach. In McClellan's mind, it was unfortunate that he must go through politicians to seize it. He had come to detest and distrust politicians in his dealings with the Lincoln administration. He considered them inferior beings, beneath contempt.[11]

That he might be viewed as one of them was not the image he sought. His image of himself was more messianic and detached. He viewed himself as a man ordained to save the Union. Shorn of his military power, the only power left him was political. It would have to do. But the strategy he chose was that of the reluctant lover.[12]

There had been open overtures to him to plunge into partisan politics in the year since his sacking. Sunset Cox had written him in May 1863 from Ohio, urging him to permit his name to be put before the Ohio Democratic State Convention as a candidate for governor. McClellan had been an Ohio resident before the war. "You can be nominated with a perfect furor," Cox wrote him, "and an election would be a foregone conclusion." Cox feared that if McClellan didn't accept the nomination, Vallandigham surely would, and that would bring disaster for the party in Ohio. McClellan declined, and Cox was right about Vallandigham and the disaster.[13]

Much of this pressure to flush McClellan out into open partisan warfare was his own doing. It had all begun when he wrote a letter to Abraham Lincoln from Harrison's Landing on the Peninsula in the summer of 1862. In it McClellan stepped over the line of military science into political science, offering advice to the president not just on war, but on policy. The president had ignored it, but the Democratic politicians hadn't, because it expressed their sentiments exactly.

The Union must be preserved, McClellan advised Lincoln in his Harrison's Landing letter, whatever the cost in treasure, time, and blood. It should never be a war upon the Southern people or the Southern way of life, however, but only upon their armies and the political organizations that ran those armies. Slavery must not be touched: "Neither confiscation of property, political executions of persons, territorial organization of states or forcible abolition of slavery should be contemplated for a moment." In short, the letter said, there should be the constitution as it is and the Union as it was.[14]

This letter signaled the beginning of what Lincoln's young secretaries, Nicolay and Hay, would come to consider McClellan's "distinctively political career." They believed he had always been more or less in sympathy with the Democratic party and consequently in an attitude of dormant opposition to the administration. As early as late 1861 he had been approached by Democrats to declare himself openly on their side. He had been tempted then, but had declined, being a general serving a Republican administration. The Harrison's Landing letter in July 1862, however, had telegraphed his political sentiments. By late 1862, after he had been relieved of command and gone to New York to socialize and be seen with powerful Democratic leaders, his sentiments, if not his aspirations, were entirely out in the open.[15]

But he was still lying as low politically as he could. He was not committing himself publicly, not getting involved directly by word or deed. But neither was he discouraging presidential speculation. If it was his credo not to reach openly for that high office unless it was spontaneously offered, he was not against its being offered, and was seen as working quietly to see that it was. He managed to walk that tightrope—not surfacing publicly, but massaging his candidacy privately—all through 1863, until the day before the October elections in Pennsylvania.

On October 12, only a scant thirteen hours before the opening of the polls, McClellan fired off from New Jersey an endorsement of Judge

Woodward, the Democratic candidate for governor in Pennsylvania. An article in the *Philadelphia Press* a few days before the election had suggested that McClellan favored Curtin, the Republican candidate. It was a logical assumption, since McClellan and Curtin were longtime personal friends.

Not so, McClellan protested, in his wired endorsement. The telegram said, "I desire to state clearly and distinctly that, having some few days ago had a full conversation with Judge Woodward, I find that our views agree, and I regard his election as Governor of Penna called for by the interests of the nation."

The views on which they agreed, McClellan said, were that both of them favored the prosecution of the war until the military power of the rebellion was crushed. Both agreed that there must be no violation of private rights and property, including that most disputed of all properties, slaves. Both agreed that the sole object of the war should be to restore the unity of the nation—in effect, to preserve the constitution as it is and the country as it was. In his eleventh-hour telegram, McClellan said, "Believing that our opinions entirely agree upon these points & that he feels, as I do, that the maintenance of our national unity is of vital necessity, I would, were it in my power, give to Judge Woodward my voice & my vote."[16]

McClellan had stepped for the first time across the line and into the glare of the open political arena.

The endorsement offended Curtin, who felt his friendship betrayed, and it didn't help Woodward—he still lost. And it further alarmed many of McClellan's already alarmed friends.

One of them wrote Barlow, "Why should *he* step from a dignified & secure position into the depths of partizan mud? He has hazarded everything by this 'change of base' & I think & fear, lost all. The Oracle is unveiled, & a partizan is presented—that's all he has done."[17]

The pro-Republican *New York Times* loved it. The *Times* said, "Gen. McClellan, who was so slow in the military field, is rather faster in the political. We have at last a dash from him—a regular slap-dash." He sped, as he never sped before, to the rescue, the *Times* wrote, "just as the sun was descending beyond the Schuylkill—thirteen hours and three quarters, by the best watches" before the polls opened on election day. The *Times* suggested that McClellan was showing admirable versatility: his case was as hopeless in politics as it was in war.[18] In short, he had not succeeded as a general—usually a requirement for any soldier running for president. But that didn't seem to matter, for the failed general was just as readily running on failure as if it had been success, blaming the failure on the administration he was running against.

Democratic insiders such as Sunset Cox read the Woodward letter and nodded knowingly. They all knew that the endorsement had been pushed on McClellan by Pennsylvania's Democratic party leaders as the price of their support for his covert presidential candidacy.

Cox had explained it all to John Hay over dinner. "He lost some prestige by his Woodward letter," Cox conceded. "But it was necessary. He never could have gotten the nomination without it."[19]

The *New York Daily Tribune*, no more pro-McClellan than the *Times,* thought the Woodward letter just bad strategy. "McClellan is the true and rightful Pro-Slavery candidate for President," the *Tribune* editorialized, "'which nobody can deny.' But being such, it is all wrong to have him backed about and used up in this way. . . . He is to-day as strong a candidate as you can pick from that side, and has been the strongest. But he will be used up before next July if all manner of seedy, dyspeptic, passé, played-out politicians are allowed to use his name freely to advance their own selfish ends. A few more such back-sets as his Woodward letter . . . will finish him."[20]

A month after his last-minute Woodward endorsement, McClellan decided he ought to write Abraham Lincoln another letter. He began it with a review of his military record—well known to both men, although each put a slightly different spin on it. Then he said, "I have been now for more than a year unemployed, and it is evident that my services are no longer desired by your Excellency." Under these circumstances, McClellan wrote, "I feel that I can be of no present use to my country by retaining my Commission, and I am unwilling longer to receive pay while performing no service. It is now my duty to consult my private interests and those of my family—which I have entirely ignored and sacrificed during my continuance in service." He said, a bit wistfully, that he would have preferred to retire from the service knowing he still retained Lincoln's approbation. "As it is," he wrote, "I thank you for the confidence and kind feeling you once entertained for me, and which I am unconscious of having justly forfeited."[21]

The fact of the matter was, McClellan had been offered the presidency of the New Jersey Railroad and Transportation Company, by his wealthy Democratic friend John Jacob Astor. It would pay him $5,000 a year, nearly replacing his $6,000-a-year salary from the government. In the end the new job didn't work out, and neither his letter to Lincoln

nor his letter of resignation to the War Department got mailed. Nor
had he yet had the Democratic presidential nomination spontaneously
conferred upon him, nor was he yet openly seeking it, despite the
Woodward letter. But his candidacy, by the end of 1863, seemed written in the stars. He was clearly the Democratic front-runner.

The general had long since moved his family out of the gift house on
Thirty-first Street in Manhattan to a home he had purchased in
the peaceful Orange Mountain region of New Jersey. There he had
found some serenity in the rising storm, out of the public spotlight—
something of a political Harrison's Landing. On his thirty-seventh
birthday, in December 1863, McClellan spent most of the day in
Newark at the christening of his friend Col. Edward H. Wright's baby
boy. McClellan was the baby's godfather, and the christening had gone
well. As McClellan wrote his mother three days later: "The baby did
not cry & I did not drop him!! You see I am becoming quite skilful."

His mother, the gracious and genteel Elizabeth McClellan of Philadelphia, had written her son that "the Democrats say, the *War Democrats,*
that George B. McClellan, is to be the next President. . . ."

"I feel very indifferent about the White House," McClellan answered
his mother, "—for very many reasons I do not wish it—I shall do nothing to get it & trust that Providence will decide the matter as is best for
the country."[22]

It was December now, and he was still trying to be true to his political credo—not seeking that high office, but waiting for something
spontaneous to happen so he could not refuse it, either.

3

BUSY LAYING PIPE

T HE LATE-AUTUMN WEATHER HAD TURNED POLAR IN THE EARLY days of November 1863, with bitterly cold winds that cut to the marrow and raised whirling clouds of dust over Washington. A few flakes of snow had already fallen, foreshadowing the coming descent into winter.[1]

On November 7, Meade's army had pushed to the Rappahannock and, after severe fighting at Kelly's Ford and at Rappahannock Station, had muscled Lee back across the Rapidan. It was not the major Federal offensive the president longed for, and it was cautiously done, but it had returned the two armies to roughly where they had been before Lee's election-time offensive.

In late October, Union artillery had opened fire on Fort Sumter in Charleston harbor in South Carolina. Now, on November 12, after a pause, the guns were thundering again, and both sides wondered how much more shelling that embattled and shot-scarred fortress could stand before it crumbled or collapsed.

It was slightly warmer in Washington on the twelfth. It had been dry and dusty all day, and as Lincoln dressed for Kate Chase's wedding that evening, Sumter was one of his worries. Chattanooga was still under siege in the West by Gen. Braxton Bragg's Confederate Army of Tennessee. And as Lincoln climbed into his carriage for the mile-long ride to the home of his treasury secretary, Chattanooga was a worry as well.[2] He made a weary figure with too much to do and too much on his mind.

Salmon Chase, the secretary of the treasury, was dressed for his oldest daughter's wedding in a coat of rich black cloth, white French silk grenadine vest, and black cashmere pantaloons special-ordered from his tailor. His greeting of the president was not entirely comfortable, for there was an awkward strain in their relationship, caused by something new even in this not-too-high-minded political time, or anytime: Chase was running for president against his boss. He wouldn't admit it, but he and Lincoln and everybody else in the wedding parlor knew it. "Chase is straining every nerve, and will present a very formidable front," a friend had written Senator Lyman Trumbull that very day from Alton, Illinois.[3]

"There is nothing fixed on either side," the New York Herald had said only a few days earlier, "except what the Rev. Henry Ward Beecher would call 'the great central facts'—that President Lincoln is prepared to serve another term, and that Mr. Secretary Chase expects to supersede him."[4]

But perhaps it wasn't too surprising, considering the makeup of Lincoln's cabinet. The president had put virtually all of his chief rivals for the presidency in 1860 into his cabinet: William Seward as secretary of state, Edward Bates as attorney general, Chase as secretary of the treasury, Simon Cameron—since replaced by Edwin M. Stanton—as secretary of war. With Gideon Welles as secretary of the navy, Montgomery Blair as postmaster general, and John P. Usher as secretary of the interior, the cabinet was about as ill-assorted and heterogeneous a body of men, one observer thought, as were ever called together as ministers and advisers to a great government. John Bigelow, a Republican politician, said it "had the appearance of being selected from a grab-bag."[5] Count Gurowski described it as "a violent mixing . . . of inimical and repulsive forces."[6] A bunch of "poor sticks," said the ever-irreverent James Gordon Bennett of the New York Herald.[7]

Chase was the cabinet's odd man out, the one who had never let go of his ambition to become president of the United States—a particularly "crooked piece of timber," as Bennett described him.[8] That ambition, amounting to longing, smoldered sleepless in Chase's breast, like a glowing ember in an undying fire.

Chase was six feet two inches tall—a giant for his time, nearly as tall as Lincoln himself—broad-shouldered, austere, and proudly erect. He was clean-shaven, and his unusually large head was slightly bald. Noah Brooks found him easy and gentlemanly in his manners, but with a painful way of holding his head straight, which led one to fancy that his shirt collar was crowding his ears.[9]

Lincoln, who admired him for his ability if not for his ambition, said of him, "Chase is about one and a half times bigger than any other man that I ever knew."[10]

Brooks suggested that "if he should be the next president of these United States the executive chair would be filled with more dignity than it has known since the days of Washington." Brooks found him inaccessible, dignified beyond all account, and aristocratic. Part of this aloof persona may have had something to do with the fact that he was also painfully nearsighted, often appearing frosty and remote even to his nearest friends, until on closer approach he recognized them.[11]

Chase was a man of Jovelike serenity, and in his nearly fifty-six years of life he had not yet learned the art of subordination.[12] A Union general who had come to know him believed it was difficult for him to follow the lead of any man.[13] It was suggested that each morning as he surveyed himself in the glass, he said, "Good morning, Mr. President."[14]

If Chase indeed greeted himself in this way, it was not a greeting in jest, for nobody had yet found any humor in him. Sobersided lawyer that he was, it was as though he considered laughter inadmissible in the courtroom of life. He therefore didn't laugh at Lincoln's jokes, and on those rare occasions when he tried to engineer one himself, it was never built right and always collapsed of its own weight. The wag who had said, "It required a surgical operation to get a joke into his head," could well have said it of the secretary of the treasury.[15]

Chase always spoke carefully, and with provisos—a very literal-minded man. He was not a gifted orator. His delivery was heavy and imposing, he lacked platform grace, and his deep voice came with a slight lisp. But if rich rhetoric was missing, thorough preparation and powerful argument were not. As a lawyer and politician, he was an awesome and convincing advocate.[16]

Because he was solitary by nature, his learning was rooted almost entirely in books, which he loved and accumulated. Some two thousand volumes lined the shelves of the study of his house at Sixth and E streets, among them twenty or thirty dictionaries. He was not known for misspelling words, and he could also have told the cipher operators in the telegraph office what *truculent* and *hibernation* meant. His tastes tended to history, politics, and law, but very little to poetry and never to fiction. He could read fluently in French and German.[17]

But he was not, with all of his learning, a student of the passing parade. He seemed little versed in the ins and outs of human nature.

His nearsightedness, even his friends admitted, extended to his understanding of people, whose motives seemed to him as indistinct and blurred as faces across a room.[18] There was a saying: "Mr. Chase is nearsighted and does not see men."[19]

Nor was unsheathed frivolity permitted under his roof. Chase abominated waltzes, barely tolerated quadrilles, and was not known for stepping either one. He never went to the races or the theater, and his exercise was limited to the two indoor and one outdoor games he loved—chess, backgammon, and croquet—at which he hated to be beaten.[20]

His closest friend in Washington was Charles Sumner, the U.S. senator from Massachusetts, his equal in humorless austerity, righteousness, and ideology. They dined together often and, when one of them was out of town, corresponded with regularity. Chase was also fond of the young Ohio general James A. Garfield, whom he treated rather like the son he never had. Garfield lived with the Chases for a time in the fall of 1862, and the two men played chess in the evenings and discussed the conduct of the war together over the bishops and kings.[21]

Chase had been unlucky in love and marriage. He had buried three wives, all of whom had died young, and was not without his longings. To Mrs. Carlotta Eastman, a widow for whom he felt a particular, although reserved, attraction, he would write, "I think of you constantly; and, if any feeling is left in me, with the sincerest affection. We have been friends a long time, and I hope shall be better friends, instead of worse. How I wish you were here in our house—in this little library room—that we could talk, instead of this writing by myself, while you are—where?" And he would take letters from her to bed with him on a Saturday night, to read and "to inspire my dreams."[22]

Chase had never been without dreams. And uppermost in those dreams had been the ascent to the ultimate summit of prestige, power, and public service. He had been a U.S. senator, a governor of his state, and now secretary of the treasury. But the dreams had always reached higher than all of these lofty posts. And there was only one thing higher.

As to his ability, Noah Brooks observed, "it is only a trifle below [his] dignity, or the Secretary is greatly deceived."[23] Even his enemies admitted his competence, and his integrity was beyond question—as unbending as his body and his mind. In a job where he could have made himself a fortune on the side, he had never done anything to line his own pockets. He boasted, "I am not a rich man, and I am glad to be able to say that I have become poorer instead of richer from public employments."[24]

Perhaps it was a measure of his ambition for the ultimate prize that Chase was never entirely comfortable as secretary of the treasury. As he wrote the New York editor Horace Greeley, early in 1863: "I have neither love nor hate for the position I occupy, and have two regrets connected with it: one, that I ever took it; the other, that, having resigned it [following a cabinet crisis in December 1862], I yielded to the counsels of those who said I must resume it."[25]

But over and over again, day out and day in, this dogged, ambitious, stiff-backed man did resume it. He rose daily in summer at six and in winter no later than seven. Work began instantly, in his library dictating letters or receiving visitors until the breakfast hour at eight-thirty. After breakfast—by nine-thirty, sometimes earlier—this operation-already-in-progress, with no room in it for procrastination, was transferred directly to his office at the Treasury building, a mile away. It was an office to match a cabinet minister's dignity, with its broad, tesselated floor, its long, low-hanging chandelier, and its four towering windows facing the street and rising nearly to the ceiling, with bookcases equally tall on one side wall and a fireplace on the other. At each window, heavy drapes framed the Washington that Chase could only indistinctly see.

Chase went to this office six days a week, but never, if he could help it, on Sunday—not even to write a letter or lick a stamp. It was also a rule with Chase, just as doggedly kept as the Sabbath, never to transact business with ladies. There was only one exception to this, and that was his beautiful daughter Kate, who, on this glittering evening in November 1863, was about to marry one of the richest men in America.

Chase liked visitors to his own table, but cared little to sit at the tables of others. When life required that he get from one place to the next, passage was generally taken at a rapid gait that tolerated no stops.[26]

It was the way Chase would have liked to have proceeded to the presidency. But that was a passage encumbered with troublesome stops. The worst interference on the way had been this man Lincoln, whom he considered his woeful inferior. The president's young secretaries, Nicolay and Hay, believed that Chase's opinion of Lincoln varied "between the limits of active hostility and benevolent contempt."[27]

He held so poor an opinion of Lincoln's intellect and character in comparison with his own, Nicolay and Hay said, "that he could not believe the people so blind as deliberately to prefer the President to himself. . . . He could not bring himself to feel that the universal demonstrations in favor of the reelection of Mr. Lincoln were genuine. He regarded himself all the while as the serious candidate, and the opposition to him as knavish and insincere."[28]

He believed the president was a political accident, that a terrible mistake had been made at Chicago in 1860 when Lincoln and not Chase had been nominated by the Republican party. He believed it was his duty to see the mistake rectified in 1864.[29]

Chase's widespread correspondence was laced with digs at the way Lincoln ran the government. "There is in fact no administration, properly speaking," he wrote one correspondent. There were departments and there was a president. But the president left nearly everything to the heads of the departments, who acted with absolute independence from one another, amounting almost to anarchy. "Had there been here an administration in the true sense of the word—" Chase wrote, "a President conferring with his Cabinet and taking their united judgments, and with their aid enforcing activity, economy, and energy, in all departments of public service—we could have spoken boldly and defied the world."[30]

The cabinet met now and then, Chase conceded, but it was catch-as-catch-can, on whatever subject happened to come up. There was no grave consultation, particularly with Chase, on the important subject of the salvation of the country. "We have as little to do with it as if we were heads of factories supplying shoes or clothing," he wrote. There were no regular and systematic reports of what was done, even to the president, certainly none to the cabinet. It was painful, he wrote, "to hear complaints of remissness, delays, discords, dangers, and feel that there must be ground for such complaints, and know at the same time that one has no power to remedy the evils complained of. . . ." It was to Chase like seeing a house on fire, feeling sick at heart to watch it burn, but being unable to do anything to stop it.[31]

Chase had been wanting to be president for at least a decade. He had been wanting it since 1856, since the Republican party was born and he had joined it. He had been a leading candidate in 1856 and again in 1860 and been denied both times. "He never forgave Lincoln for the crime of having been preferred for President over him," said one Republican.[32] And ever since, he had been "laying pipe" to win the nomination in 1864.[33]

It was not an obvious thing, although everybody knew it. It seeped out in Chase's far-flung correspondence. And it generally took the form of a nagging understated dig at Lincoln, followed by the opinion that a different nominee was needed in 1864, followed by a denial that he considered himself that person, followed by a statement that he was nonetheless available.

"If I were controlled by merely personal sentiments," he was to write his new son-in-law, Rhode Island senator William Sprague, "I should prefer the reelection of Mr. Lincoln to that of any other man. But I doubt the expediency of reelecting anybody, and I think a man of different qualities from those the President has will be needed for the next four years. I am not anxious to be regarded as that man; and I am quite willing to leave that question to the decision of those who agree in thinking that some such man should be chosen."[34]

If "no, no" was written in the text of such letters, "yes, yes" was written between the lines. And meanwhile, the pipe was being laid.

It was commonly believed that Chase had mobilized his huge army of treasury agents and officeholders into a political machine. In effect, he had at his disposal more than 10,000 political mercenaries in his patronage domain. John Nicolay called them "the treasury rats." Noah Brooks called them "the Chase impracticables."[35] But it offended Chase that it was thought he made appointments with politics in mind. "I should despise myself if I felt capable of appointing or removing a man for the sake of the Presidency," he said.[36]

Chase's reputation for personal integrity lent a ring of truth to what he said. Washington observers such as Navy Secretary Gideon Welles, however, were being told of an active, zealous, and formidable movement operating around the country to seize the Union Party nomination for Chase.[37] Reports were filtering back that treasury officials were "remorselessly decapitating every subordinate believed or suspected of being in the least tainted with Lincolnism."[38]

It did not seem to occur to Chase that his maverick candidacy showed any disloyalty to Lincoln. In his mind, the field was clear and open, and the job should by all rights be his anyhow; he had been born for it.

This self-assurance amounting to self-ordination, which most politicians found as myopic as his eyesight, continued to amaze some and amuse others. Senator Ben Wade of Ohio, who was nicknamed "Bluff Ben" for good reason, said bluntly, "Chase is a good man, but his theology is unsound. He thinks there is a fourth person in the Trinity."[39]

Chase's hunger for the office was palpable. The presidency is "glaring out of both eyes," one politician said of him.[40] Everybody saw it. Richard Henry Dana had seen it as early as March. "Chase looks and acts as if he meant to be the next President," Dana had said then.[41] "I'm afraid Mr. Chase's head is turned by his eagerness in pursuit of the presidency," Attorney General Edward Bates observed in October.[42]

Chase was trying not to let it show. He "tries to have it thought that he is indifferent and scarcely cognizant of what is doing in his behalf," Welles told his diary, "but no one of his partisans is so well posted as Chase himself."[43]

None of this escaped Lincoln. He could see the presidency glaring out of Chase's eyes as well as anybody. "I suppose he will, like the blue-bottle fly, lay his eggs in every rotten spot he can find," Lincoln told Hay.[44] But Lincoln also could sympathize with such presidential cravings. "No man knows what *that gnawing* is till he has had it," he said.[45] He told Hay that he was entirely indifferent to the success or failure of Chase's egg-laying as long as he did his duty as head of the treasury department. Chase was a good secretary, and Lincoln had determined to shut his eyes to it all and keep him where he was. If he becomes president, then all right, Lincoln told Hay, "I hope we may never have a worse man."[46]

In the privacy of their bedroom, Mary Lincoln tried to change her husband's lax attitude toward Chase and his candidacy.

"Father," she would say to him, "I do wish that you would inquire a little into the motives of Chase."

Lincoln, lying carelessly on the sofa reading a newspaper, answered, "Mother, you are too suspicious. I give you credit for sagacity, but you are disposed to magnify trifles. Chase is a patriot, and one of my best friends."

"Yes, one of your best friends because it is his interest to be so. He is anything for Chase. If he thought he could make anything by it, he would betray you to-morrow."

Lincoln protested, "I fear that you are prejudiced against the man, mother. I know that you do him injustice."

"Mr. Lincoln," Mary insisted, "you are either blind or will not see. I am not the only one that has warned you against him."

"True, I receive letters daily from all parts of the country, telling me not to trust Chase; but then these letters are written by the political enemies of the Secretary, and it would be unjust and foolish to pay any attention to them."

"Very well," Mary warned, "you will find out some day, if you live long enough, that I have read the man correctly. I only hope that your eyes may not be opened to the truth when it is too late."[47]

Lincoln worried about Chase more than he let on. It was getting to him that fall. Late one evening about the time of Kate's wedding, the Pennsylvania politician-editor Alexander McClure was visiting in the White House. For an hour Lincoln talked worriedly about Chase. At every turn McClure reassured him that Chase could not be the Republican candidate, whoever might be, and that he regarded Lincoln's renomination as reasonably certain.

When McClure rose to go—it was about midnight—Lincoln followed him toward the door. Swinging one long leg over the corner of the cabinet table nearest his desk, Lincoln started out again on a new aspect of the Chase problem that had just occurred to him. When he got through that, McClure again said good night and started for the door. Lincoln followed him to the other end of the cabinet table, where he again swung a leg over one corner and started afresh. It was now nearly one in the morning. McClure said good night for the third time and got as far as the door. But just as he was about to open it, Lincoln called to him and, with a merry twinkle in his eye, said, "By the way, McClure, how would it do if I were to decline Chase?"

"Why, Mr. Lincoln," said McClure, "how could that be done?"

"Well, I don't know exactly how it might be done, but that reminds me of a story of two Democratic candidates for Senator in Egypt, Illinois, in its early political times."

And there, at one in the morning, Lincoln told the sleepy Alexander McClure the story of two candidates running for the same office in Little Egypt, a Democratic stronghold in southern Illinois:

Day after day they were meeting in debate and growing more and more exasperated with one another. Their discussions soon disintegrated into disgraceful wrangles. Ashamed of themselves, they finally agreed that either could say anything he pleased about the other, and that it shouldn't be taken personally. From that time on the campaign progressed, paved with mutual insults but lacking further outbursts of temper.

On election night, the two candidates met to receive the returns together, and the contest was uncomfortably close. A distant precinct, which one of them had confidently expected to win by a big margin, was reported instead to have gone heavily against him and lost him the election. He was profoundly surprised. The other candidate, however, said he shouldn't be so astonished, as he had taken the liberty of declining him in that district the evening before the election. He reminded his disappointed opponent that since they had agreed that either was free to say anything about the other without offense, he had gone to that district and taken the liberty of announcing that his opponent had retired from the race.

"I think," Lincoln told McClure with a hearty laugh, "I had better decline Chase."[48]

McClure didn't think Lincoln was joking. He probably did intend to "decline" Chase. But McClure knew that Lincoln for now would just play a waiting game. He knew from past experience that when the president didn't know exactly what to do, he was the safest man in the world to trust to do nothing. He would simply wait until he could by some lucky circumstance remove Chase as a competitor, or by some manipulation of politics make him a hopeless one.[49]

Another astute Republican politician, Congressman George Ashmun of Massachusetts, agreed. He had also been to visit Lincoln in the White House recently, and he was convinced that there would eventually be a showdown with Chase. Ashmun believed Lincoln would wait for an opening in which Chase was clearly in the wrong. "He thinks that Mr. C. will sufficiently soon force the question," Ashmun wrote a friend. "In the mean time, I think, he is wise in waiting till the pear is ripe. . . ."[50]

But the pear was not yet ripe and it was November 12, and Lincoln was going to Kate Chase's wedding.

Kate Chase was no ordinary bride. She was devastation in a woman's body, a host unto herself, an army of dazzling enchantment that regularly laid waste to all of social Washington. To describe her as "very attractive, agreeable, and sprightly," as the British newspaper correspondent William Howard Russell did, was the equivalent of calling the Taj Mahal a pretty good-looking building.[51]

Kate was an enchantress. Her figure was statuesque, tall and slender, wavy and willowy. Her skin was marble white, pale and soft, the color of moonlight. Her hair was a rich chestnut, with tones of red-gold, copper, and mahogany, pulled severely back and wound into a Grecian knot at her neck. Her eyes were large, languid, and proud, flecked with green, dark and inquiring. Her lashes were long and black, her eyebrows arched and crescent. Her voice was low, melodious, and magical.

It was not so much the parts that made her such a provocative package, it was the whole. She was not a classic beauty. Her nose tended to tilt upward and perhaps would not have passed muster with a severe connoisseur of faultless grace. But it was always audaciously tipped, and it fit the rest of her face perfectly. Her beautiful head rested upon perhaps the most perfectly swanlike neck in the country, and she moved through space with elegance and majesty to match. She glided into rooms and let herself down upon chairs "with the graceful lightness of a bird that, folding its wings, perches upon the branch of a tree."[52] She was imperial and captivating and held majestic sway over men's imaginations.

But as conspicuously stunning and elegant as were her beauty, her form, and her movements, even more devastating were her character and her mind. She possessed a man's vigor and a woman's delicacy. She was keen and clever rather than profound, with a quick intelligence. She read much and forgot little.

And she had the gift of politics. While still in her teens she was one of the most astute politicians in Ohio. And now in 1863, at age twenty-three, she was one of the most astute politicians in Washington.

But the most devastating thing of all about Kate Chase was neither her beauty nor her mind, but her mindset. She was, perhaps more than any other woman ever born, her father's daughter. Her father called her "Katie," and respected and trusted her political acumen above all others. And for him she had an absolute and overmastering love, a dedication that gave new meaning to the fourth commandment. His ambition was her ambition, never sleeping. This made her into what some thought a rather nervous and nail-biting beauty.

She and her father were physically perhaps the handsomest father-daughter pairing in the country. Without question they were politically the most potent. Kate longed for the White House even more acutely than her father did. For there she would be *de jure* what she already was *de facto*—the social divinity of Washington. She would be the official hostess in a Chase White House, and a power behind the president—for her father had not remarried, and she would see that he never did. The Chases were not wealthy, but Senator Sprague, her husband-to-be, had money beyond measure, and money was the necessary ingredient for such powerful presidential ambition.[53]

It was for what Kate Chase was and what she hoped to be that Mary Lincoln hated her so. But Mrs. Lincoln could scarcely brook anything in petticoats who ever came near Mr. Lincoln, particularly one so smart, stunning, and ambitious. Elizabeth Keckley, Mrs. Lincoln's seamstress and friend, who overheard perhaps more than she should in the bedrooms of the White House, told of a dialogue between Mr. and Mrs. Lincoln, so often repeated before receptions that it amounted to ritual:

"Well, mother," Lincoln asked, pulling on his gloves, "who must I talk with tonight—shall it be Mrs. D.?"

"That deceitful woman!" exclaimed Mrs. Lincoln. "No, you shall not listen to her flattery."

"Well, then, what do you say to Miss C.? She is too young and handsome to practice deceit."

Mrs. Lincoln exploded at mention of Kate's name. "Young and handsome, you call her! You should not judge beauty for me. No, she is in league with Mrs. D., and you shall not talk with her."

"Well, mother," Lincoln implored, buttoning his glove with a mock expression of gravity, "I must talk with someone. Is there anyone that you do not object to?"

"I don't know as it is necessary that you should talk to anybody in particular. You know well enough, Mr. Lincoln, that I do not approve of your flirtations with silly women, just as if you were a beardless boy, fresh from school."

"But, mother, I insist that I must talk with somebody. I can't stand around like a simpleton, and say nothing. If you will not tell me who I may talk with, please tell me who I may *not* talk with."

"There is Mrs. D. and Miss C. in particular. I detest them both. Mrs. B. also will come around you, but you need not listen to her flattery. These are the ones in particular."

"Very well, mother," replied Lincoln with a merry twinkle in his eye, "now that we have settled the question to your satisfaction, we will go down-stairs." And with stately dignity he offered her his arm and led the way.[54]

Kate Chase and William Sprague, the wealthy young senator, former governor of Rhode Island, and sometime general, were something of an unnatural fit. She was restless, relentless, vivacious, electric, domineering, and headstrong. Made rich by an inherited textile empire, he was a bit indolent, dull, and diffident, drained of life and animation except for rare bursts of audacity, too often kindled by alcohol. He was fueled by drink, she by soaring ambition. She was turned on by society and politics, and he wasn't. They carried on an uneven courtship, but in the spring of 1863 they became engaged, and were now, in the late fall, about to marry in the most spectacular social event of the war.[55]

Cynics said it was all for the sake of his money; he was reputed to be worth $25 million, more than enough to fuel a presidential campaign for the father of the bride. Not many seriously believed this was a marriage of love. But Sprague's love was real. "Let me here, my dear Sir," he wrote his father-in-law-to-be after the engagement was announced, "thank you from the bottom of my heart for the treasure you have reared and given to me."[56] Chase liked the young man, but then both men were strikingly nearsighted.

Whatever the cynics thought, Kate Chase was marrying William Sprague. And the evening before her wedding, alone in her room, life had seemed so real to her—"My heart so warm and keen with sympathy, hope so confident, ambition high, and holy things so sacred." She spent the night, she later wrote, "in one long prayer, that in my new relation, I might fill each office to completeness, that to my waiting husband, I might be the messenger of every joy, and holding him above all, the dearest and the best, I might become his companion, friend, and advocate—that he might be, in a word—a husband satisfied. All there is of love and beauty, nobleness and gentleness, were woven in this fair dream, and I believed *no* future brighter than that our united lives spread before us. . . ."[57]

The next evening at her father's house at Sixth and E streets, Washington was at her feet. Carriages jammed the roads leading to the house. Inside, the president and the cream of the political, military, and diplomatic worlds waited. At eight-thirty the bride and groom entered the wedding parlor. Kate was sheathed in a white velvet wedding gown with a long following train. Crowning her regal head was a glittering diamond tiara. The groom wore black with a vest of white silk.[58]

The ceremony was read by the Reverend William Newton Clarke, the Episcopal bishop of Rhode Island. The stirring notes of the "Kate Chase Wedding March," composed for the occasion and played by the U.S. Marine Corps Band, floated out on the night to the crowd gathered on the street. Secretary Chase saluted his daughter with a kiss, and two parlors, hung in the national colors, were thrown open to the huge concourse of reception guests. The bride, whom Henry Adams likened to Jephthah's daughter, sacrificed to her father's ambition, greeted them with a languid smile on her beautiful lips.[59]

The tables, the *Washington Chronicle* reported the next day in an account reprinted in *The New York Times,* were spread with "edibles and viands . . . of the choicest description imaginable." The Marine Corps Band "discoursed most eloquent music," and "twinkling feet" stepped a light quadrille. Grace and loveliness were at every hand. Among the belles was the daughter of the Brazilian minister, whose dazzling beauty was the cynosure of all eyes. On the dance floor the main attraction was the elegant footwork of Maj. Gen. Irvin McDowell's young and beautiful daughter.[60]

It was said that the gifts for the bride and groom were valued at $100,000, breaking all records for recent American weddings. Lincoln himself had given one of the simplest and least pretentious of gifts, a small fan. The economics of this colossal event were probably nagging at the back of the treasury secretary's mind as he watched the eating, drinking, and dancing. The wedding had cost $4,000. He still owed over $1,400 for his daughter's trousseau, and his bank account was overdrawn by more than a hundred dollars. But no matter, Kate was marrying into millions.[61]

The wedding report of "Agate," the correspondent of the *Cincinnati Daily Gazette*, ended in a rhyming tribute:

> *Deck, O flowers, this bride so rare;*
>   *Come with beauty, blush and scent;*
> *Roses twine her silken hair—*
>   *Queen of all the continent.*
> *The bravest weds the one most fair,*
>   *And love is lilied with content.*
> *Idly pass, O autumn hours,*
>   *For your fairest task is done;*
> *Music floats from field and bowers,*
>   *Deep purpled in the setting sun.*
> *Sweet benedictions, heavenly powers,*
>   *Pour on these two hearts linked in one.*[62]

For the two Chases, father and daughter, it had been the biggest social night of their lives. The next big one—far bigger even than this, if all went well—would be the one in the White House in early 1865, celebrating his inauguration as president of the United States and her coronation as the first lady of the land.

4

THE MEN WHO
FACED ZIONWARDS

THEY WERE ON THE MOVE AT GETTYSBURG, THE LIVING AND THE dead.

After the battle, bodies were buried in shallow graves in the scattered fields where they had fallen in those three desperate, bloody days in July. For weeks now, burial parties had been at work systematically disinterring the Union dead and carrying them to a seventeen-acre site on Cemetery Hill, on the outskirts of the town. By the middle of November, only a third of the bodies had been dug up and reburied, and the work was still under way.

The living had begun streaming into the little Pennsylvania town as early as the Monday after Kate Chase's wedding. It was as difficult to get into Gettysburg as it was to get out. There was but a single thread of railroad line snaking into the town from Hanover Junction, twenty-six miles away—a rickety little branchline with meager rolling stock under poor management.[1]

But they were coming, and the little town of 2,700 inhabitants, with its inadequate lodgings, was groaning under the massing burden. They were coming from all the seventeen loyal states whose soldiers had fallen there, to dedicate and consecrate the seventeen acres of Gettysburg's ground to the honored dead.

It had been the idea of Pennsylvania's governor, Andrew Curtin, with the cooperation of the other sixteen governors, to set aside a cemetery as a permanent consecrated site, and in the late summer the reburial had begun. The dedication ceremony had been scheduled for October 23. But Edward Everett of Massachusetts, who was to deliver the oration, needed more time. This was no ordinary speech, even for the man widely regarded as the greatest living American orator. So the ceremony had been postponed at his request to November 19.

In early November, David Wills, the thirty-two-year-old Gettysburg lawyer and civic leader acting as Curtin's special agent on the project, wrote Lincoln, inviting him formally to set apart the grounds to their sacred use by "a few appropriate remarks."[2]

The date, convenient to Everett, could hardly have been less so for Lincoln. He was reluctant to leave Washington. It was a busy time, a bad time. Tad, his ten-year-old son, was coming down with something and was in bed sick. Lincoln was not feeling well himself. Mary was urging him not to go. But this dedication was important. It was an opportunity to address the people on the meaning of the war. He must go.[3]

It was a six-hour train ride from Washington to Gettysburg, through Baltimore and Hanover Junction. The president and his party left on special cars at about noon on November 18, the day before the ceremony, and arrived that night, a frazzled and hungry band. When the train pulled into the Gettysburg station at about dusk, the president could see the stacked coffins still awaiting burial. Also waiting, to greet him, were Everett, Wills, and Ward Hill Lamon, Lincoln's old friend from Illinois and now marshal of the District of Columbia. Lincoln greeted them with his weary smile, and they escorted him to Wills's home, the largest house on the town square, where dinner and almost two dozen other distinguished guests waited. During the evening, serenaders, "bewildering the night with music," gathered before the Wills house and sang for the president, "We Are Coming, Father Abraham, Three Hundred Thousand Strong." After dinner Lincoln retired to his room on the second floor overlooking the square, and there he passed the night.[4]

At sunrise the next morning, the day of the dedication, a cavalry call drifted in over the town square from Cemetery Hill. A cannon bellowed, its salute thundering across the now quiet battlefield, "a stern and mighty requiem for the brave."[5] It was a raw November day. In the early part of the morning, successive showers of cold rain fell, but then the skies began to brighten, and Lincoln rode out in a carriage to visit the battle sites. It was still desolate ground. The decayed carcasses of dead horses lay on the field where they had fallen. Trees and buildings, ripped and battered in the battle, still showed their scars. Patches and shreds of clothing, old hats, soleless boots, toeless shoes, moldy bayonet sheaths, rotten knapsacks, and rusty cartridge boxes—the useless and decaying debris of battle—were still strewn everywhere. Most of the more romantic remnants of the fight—the shells, shot, bullets, broken bayonets, and sabers—had long since been gathered up and carried away. At the cemetery itself, bodies in neat coffins, laid side by side, arranged by regiment where possible, still awaited burial. It had been slow, hard work—only sixty or so bodies a day, weather permitting.[6]

Lincoln reemerged from the Wills house at about ten in the morning, when the procession to the cemetery was scheduled to begin, and mounted a brown horse. The ride to the burial ground was to be on horseback, for carriages were impractical in the crush of the 10,000 to 20,000 people gathering there. The president was dressed in black, with flaring white gauntlets on his big hands. Around his high silk hat he wore a black crepe band in memory of his own dead son, Willie. The procession formed itself "in an orphanly sort of way" on Carlisle Street, about fifty yards north of the square.[7] At its head, the U.S. Marine Corps Band, which only a week before had played "The Kate Chase Wedding March" in Salmon Chase's parlor in Washington, now waited to play the dead march on the battlefield. After a delay of nearly an hour, minute guns barked and the procession began moving slowly away toward Cemetery Hill. It was a ragged march, everybody seeming to get there as best they could. As the president arrived on the burial ground, the guns thundered a salute.

The dignitaries mounted the platform, which faced north, toward the Union. Lincoln took his place at the center of the dais in a rude, high-backed, wooden rocking chair. The reporter from the *Cincinnati Daily Commercial* noted his "thoughtful, kindly, care-worn face, impassive in repose, the eyes cast down, the lids thin and firmly set, the cheeks sunken." How weary he looked, the reporter thought, and in anything but good health.[8]

Everett arrived half an hour late. When they were all present and seated, Lincoln in his rocker between Seward and Everett, the reporter speculated that perhaps upon no other American platform, ever, had there been such a conjunction of all that is distinguished by official position, statesmanship, learning, and eloquence.[9] The reporter for the *Washington Chronicle* marveled that "the occasion has had no parallel in modern times."[10]

The Birgfield Band of Philadelphia struck up a solemn dirge, and the Reverend Thomas H. Stockton, chaplain of the U.S. House of Representatives, rose. Stockton was a celebrated ecclesiastical orator in his own right, with a fame as wide as Everett's. He was tall and gaunt, his face thin and worn, his great eyes staring, it seemed, as if bent on the future. "Addressing the Throne of Grace," he delivered an invocation that ran four times as long as what the president intended to say. John Hay noted that it was "a prayer which thought it was an oration."[11]

The Marine Corps Band played, then Everett rose, gripping a cambric handkerchief, which somehow seemed part of his elocution. The great orator wore a tightly buttoned, close-fitting frock coat. His hair was soft, "sunny, silken, clinging," and as white as the snows of the seventy winters of his life. His every word, faithfully memorized, began to pour out in a stream of powerful eloquence that rolled steadily on for two hours. As the oration climbed to its emotional climaxes, Everett's arms rose majestically above him, the fingers quivering and fluttering like the pinions of an eagle, raining down on the audience the emotions with which they seemed to vibrate.[12]

It was, said one witness, an oration wreathed in splendid metaphors, classical allusions, eloquent diction, lofty statements, and clear and logical reasoning—including a lucid and concise recounting of the battle itself.[13] For the space of two hours, agreed Nicolay and Hay, "he held his listeners spellbound by the rare power of his art."[14]

A dirge followed the oration, then Lincoln rose, deliberate, hesitating, awkward, "like a telescope drawing out." He walked to the edge of the platform and bowed to the assemblage in his homely manner. He put on his reading glasses and took a page of foolscap from his coat pocket, quietly unfolded it, and began to speak. His voice was high, to the point of shrill, a tenor with a Kentucky twang. But it had the merit of carrying power. He spoke his 272 words slowly, the most ungainly of men uttering the most graceful of words. In 135 seconds it was over, and a choir from the Gettysburg churches sang a dirge.[15]

Ward Lamon would later report that Lincoln turned to him when it was over and said, "Lamon, that speech won't *scour*! It is a flat failure and the people are disappointed."[16] Whether he said that or not, it was difficult to know what the people did think. It had all happened so fast.

Everett himself, a connoisseur of speechmaking, had never thought much of Lincoln's oratory. In 1861, when Lincoln was the president-elect on his way to Washington and making desultory speeches at stops along the route, Everett had listened in disgust and told his diary: "These speeches thus far have been of the most ordinary kind, destitute of everything, not merely of felicity and grace, but of common pertinence. He is evidently a person of very inferior cast of character, wholly unequal to the crisis."[17]

But on this day at Gettysburg, Lincoln had made a believer of the connoisseur. The day after the dedication ceremonies, Everett wrote Lincoln a letter and said, "I should be glad, if I could flatter myself that I came as near to the central idea of the occasion, in two hours, as you did in two minutes." Lincoln was gratified by this praise from so true a source. He wrote back, "I am pleased to know that, in your judgment, the little I did say was not entirely a failure."[18]

In the calm perspective of hindsight, others would read in the words what Everett had heard. Homer Bates, one of Lincoln's cipher operators, had said of the president's Thanksgiving proclamation what he probably also believed about the few appropriate remarks at Gettysburg: "No ruler of millions, since King David the Psalmist, has clothed great thoughts in sublimer language." A British observer was to say of the address, "It may be doubted whether any king in Europe would have expressed himself more royally than the peasant's son."[19]

Count Gurowski's line on the speech was as expected. "Lincoln spoke," scoffed the count, "with one eye to a future platform and to reelection."[20]

Whether it had been a stump speech or an utterance of unutterable majesty, the peasant's son left Gettysburg in his railroad car to return to Washington in the early evening of the nineteenth. He arrived at the White House after midnight, now as sick as his son Tad.

Tad had scarlet fever. Lincoln had the varioloid, a mild form of smallpox. He thought of the petitioners thronging the White House hallways, smiled through his misery, and joked, "Now I have something I can give to all of them."[21]

The White House wasn't put under quarantine, but it was turned into a minor smallpox hospital. And the malady hung on longer than expected, nearly three weeks, with fever and severe headaches, and some unproductive days in and out of bed. He was up and down, carrying a light workload, attended by his family physician, Robert King Stone.

The varioloid was inconvenient and irritating—but no more so than the Missouri radicals, who had also come to plague him earlier in the fall.

He now understood why the mule prospered in Missouri. More than any other single state, it showcased the ongoing antagonisms, schisms, and divisions within his own party. Lincoln knew that as the 1864 election year drew near, he had to do something about the Missouri radicals or risk seeing his reelection hopes crushed.

The trouble in Missouri had been going on for a long time. By the fall of 1862, Lincoln's party in the state was split into two warring factions, both with names suited more to characters in a minstrel show than to politics: Charcoals and Claybanks. The Charcoals were the radicals; they wanted one thing very urgently: immediate emancipation of slaves everywhere, and particularly in Missouri. The Claybanks were the conservatives, those who favored emancipation, but wanted it gradually. There was a third group who didn't want emancipation in any form, and who were known as Chocolates, but they had never amounted to much in the party. If they were Chocolates, they lived in St. Louis and were probably Democrats.

This party split in that one stubborn border state mirrored the radical-conservative split within his party everywhere. But it was more intense, bitter, and unforgiving in Missouri than anywhere else.

The radicals were in the majority in Missouri, but the state government was in conservative hands. The governor, Hamilton Gamble, was a conservative and, more important, so was Frank Blair, who had control of western patronage. Blair was mainly interested in keeping trade open on the Mississippi, which would permit continued conservative control of the state. But trade on the river had been proscribed by an order of Secretary of the Treasury Salmon Chase. This, among other things, had made Chase the principal natural ally of the radicals in Missouri, and an enemy of the Blairs. But the Blairs had never liked Chase anyhow, and they liked him even less now that he was not so covertly running against Lincoln for president.

Chafing under their lack of political control and hungering to deal a death blow to the hated Blairs, the Missouri radicals desperately wanted three things: First, they wanted to be rid of the Union general in command of the Missouri Department, John Schofield, who in their eyes favored the conservatives; instead they wanted a good, solid radical general such as Benjamin F. Butler appointed in his stead. Second, they wanted the state militia abolished and replaced by Federal troops, for much the same reason—it was in the wrong political hands. Third, they wanted the right to vote denied to all persons who had engaged in the rebellion, again for somewhat the same reason—that such votes worked against radical interests.

Hopelessly at odds and unable to agree among themselves on a policy or on persons to execute a policy, these two wings of the party had been hitting on Lincoln with their rival points of view for nearly a year, giving him little rest. Lincoln had tried to keep out of the quarrel. But in May 1863 when he replaced a general whom the radicals liked with Schofield, whom they didn't, the radicals immediately demanded that the appointment be suspended. Lincoln found himself in the middle of the struggle whether he wanted to be or not.

Doubtless wondering why there had to be a war everywhere he turned, Lincoln wired back: "It is very painful to me that you in Missouri cannot or will not settle your factional quarrel among yourselves. I have been tormented with it beyond endurance for months by both sides. Neither side pays the least respect to my appeals to your reason. I am now compelled to take hold of the case."[22]

Lincoln knew that the situation was political dynamite. He knew, as Nicolay and Hay did, that "a certain unreasoning radicalism which pervaded the whole North might, and probably would, range itself behind this unreasonable radicalism of these Missourians, and that the whole acting together might prevent his nomination or reelection."[23]

By late September the radicals had had about all of conservative control they could stand, and a delegation of seventy of them entrained for Washington to lobby the president personally—to see if he "would ride in their wagon or not."[24]

As they approached, Lincoln was perhaps reminded of the story he later told a visitor from New York. The problems in Missouri, he told his visitor, "remind me of a field I once had when I was farming in Sangamon County. It was a very good field—very good land in it; but in one corner there were some stumps, so tough and long-rooted that they couldn't be grubbed up with the hatchet and axe; so wet that they couldn't be burned out. Well, what could I do? I could only plough round them." He figured that was what he would have to do now with these Missouri radicals, too—"plough round them."[25]

When the delegation arrived in Washington, it went first to see Chase, who was quietly sympathetic with any up-and-running anti-Lincoln political movement. The next day the delegation went to see the president, who was anything but sympathetic.

Leading the Missourians into Lincoln's office was Charles D. Drake of St. Louis, the state's leading radical. Drake, like many in this topsy-turvy political time, had once stood 180 degrees from where he stood this September. He had started out a Democrat friendly to slavery. He was now one of the most relentless antislavery radicals in Missouri. He had switched when the first cannon shots of the war fell on Fort Sumter in 1861 because he believed that slavery had been the cause of it all.[26]

Drake dramatically read the three demands and the bill of particulars, and for three hours the delegation hammered Lincoln with its arguments. Lincoln, never one for a hasty answer to anything, told them he would study their demands, consider them carefully, and answer them at his earliest convenience. He didn't tell the delegation he intended to plow round them. Four days later the Missourians sent four supplementary demands to the White House.

On October 5, Lincoln answered, denying most of what they had asked. He refused to remove Schofield, and refused to abolish the militia. He agreed to their demand to deny the franchise in Missouri to anybody who had been allied with the Confederate cause. That was easy enough to do. For all the trouble the Missouri radicals had gone to, Frank Blair still had control of patronage in Missouri. Basically, Lincoln had told them he wasn't going to ride in their wagon.

It was this reluctance to ride in their wagon that angered radicals in Lincoln's own party everywhere. They had all rushed to the support of the Missouri claims, and were just as outraged with the result.

Plowing around radical outrage nationally was a far bigger problem for Lincoln than simply plowing around it in Missouri. To a man, radicals everywhere were upset with him. They thought him too slow, hesitant, and weak, not decisive and active enough against slavery, and lacking proper energy. He was too friendly with the hated Blairs and that "arch criminal" he insisted on keeping in his cabinet, William Seward. The president was a patronage disaster, forever naming the wrong kind of people—"dishonest men" who disagreed with them—to high position, then being too much influenced and controlled by them. The radicals thought him wrong on reconstruction—far too lenient toward the South. For some he was a worse disaster even than that: a coarse joker, an imbecile guilty of "damnable blunders." He lacked backbone, encouraged corruption, squandered millions, and was a flat failure as a military commander-in-chief. The best any of them could say of him was that he was "too angelic for this devilish rebellion," for none of them, even his bitterest critics, could say he wasn't kindhearted and well-meaning. Too kindhearted and well-meaning—that was the trouble.[27]

One particularly vocal radical newspaper, *Wilkes' Spirit of the Times* in New York, called Lincoln's government "this albino administration, and its diluted spawn of pink eyed patriots—this limp result of the feeble embrace of half-furnished conservatives and limited emancipators."[28]

It was a common thing to hear Republican radicals abuse the president and his cabinet. Brooks compared these critics to bumblebees in a bottle who fancied that the entire world resounded with their buzzing.[29]

Much of the political world did buzz with them. It was not just radical members of Congress who were critical of the president and impatient with his policies; nearly everybody else in Washington was too. Many Republicans deplored the weaknesses and incompetence of his administration. Nearly all were dissatisfied with his cautious way of doing things, and thought he should reconstitute his cabinet. Nearly all, not just the radicals, thought the administration was corruptly and inefficiently managed, an inept, ineffective, and disorganized bureaucracy run by a well-meaning but incompetent president lacking in political sagacity.[30]

But it was not just over style that the radicals differed so with Lincoln. It was over doctrine—what they called his "rose water policy"[31]—and that made their opposition to him far more deep-rooted, bitter, and unbending. They were not satisfied with simply putting down the rebellion and restoring the Union without slavery. That was what Lincoln sought. They wanted that, too, but far more. They wanted subjugation of the South and vindictive punishment of the rebels, the overthrow of their state governments, and confiscation forever of their lands and their homes. The radicals would colonize the South with new populations from the North and West. Gideon Welles called their program an "atrocious scheme of plunder and robbery."[32]

The radical view held that the Southern states had seceded. They had established a government and waged war. They had sown what they were about to reap. The North would win this war, and when it did, the Southern Confederacy would become conquered territory, its lands, its people, and its political future all at the mercy of the victor.[33] Their point of view was "let there be justice even though the heavens crumble."[34] Thaddeus Stevens, the blunt-talking radical leader in the House, was willing that the South "be laid waste, and made a desert," then "repeopled by a band of freemen."[35] Senator Zachariah Chandler of Michigan, one of the fiercest, most unforgiving and unbending of the radicals, put it this way: "A rebel has sacrificed all his rights. He has no right to life, liberty, property, or the pursuit of happiness. Everything you give him, even life itself, is a boon which he has forfeited."[36] These radicals wanted a remorseless war on the South followed by a vengeful reconstruction of the Union.

Lincoln, on the other hand, steeped in a sympathy and understanding bred of years of contacts with southerners—indeed, he had been born a southerner himself—was, in the radical view, far too compassionate and generous-hearted toward the enemy. He denied the validity of secession altogether, arguing that the Union was perpetual, that wrongheaded men had simply seized the governments of the Southern states and were using them for wrongheaded ends. The states were temporarily out of their "proper practical relations" to the national government. The task, as he saw it, was to restore them to their proper practical relations—but with slavery purged.[37]

As Welles put it, Lincoln had no desire to take bloody vengeance on southerners, "no desire to kill them, to exile them, to subjugate them, to confiscate their property, or deprive them of their legal and constitutional rights for mistaken views or even for their criminal conduct."[38]

Lincoln said, "Are we ever again to be united and fellow countrymen? If so, there is, by my theory, much to forgive. Those who are in this new movement seem to think there is nothing to forget. I am for conciliation: they seem to be governed by resentments. They believe we can be made one people by force and vengeance: I think we are not likely to bring about unity by hatred and persecution."[39]

Behind the radical strategy was a not-so-hidden political agenda. They were abolitionists, and many of them had welcomed the war. It had stripped away Southern Democratic representation in Congress, put their party in the majority for the first time, and given them their longed-for opportunity to destroy slavery forever and to drive slaveholders into oblivion. The war for them was an opportunity to tip the balance of political power in the country forever away from the Democrats to the Republicans. Their idea was to change radically the political and economic landscape of the country. They foresaw a Union no longer subject to the will, whims, and designs of the Southern slaveholders, who had for so long been the base of Democratic strength in the antebellum Union. They envisioned a reconstituted South that was a fiefdom for their own wing of the Republican party. They therefore opposed any plan, even if it might shorten the war, that would readmit the South before their fundamental reforms had transfigured it into what they wished it to be.[40]

The radicals opposed anything that delayed the emancipation of slaves everywhere. Lincoln wished slavery ended, too, but he had put off issuing his proclamation for even limited emancipation until he believed that the country was ready for it and that it would help win the war. The radicals' animosity was driven by their impatience with his slowness to act on that issue and his failure to prosecute the war with more vigor.

Through 1861 and 1862 they had hounded him until he acted. Radical spokesmen made almost daily pilgrimages to the White House to demand an emancipation policy. One day Lincoln was telling a visitor how they came singly, in pairs, and all together to argue a forthright and immediate assault on slavery. As he spoke he stepped to the window, and sure enough, three of them at that very moment were hurrying up the White House walk to hector him again—Massachusetts senators Charles Sumner and Henry Wilson, and Pennsylvania congressman Thaddeus Stevens.

It reminded Lincoln of the story of the Sunday-school lad who had been chosen to read aloud the account of the three Hebrews in the fiery furnace—Shadrach, Meschach, and Abednego—but who found their names unpronounceable. In terrorized anticipation of the semantic disaster that lay just ahead, the lad read on until his eye lit again on the fearsome three names. In his pain and anguish he cried out, "Look! Look there! Here comes them same three damn fellers again!"[41]

One of the damn fellers who came often to lobby Lincoln was the radical Ohio senator, Ben Wade. One day Wade, who had a very short fuse, lost his temper and accused Lincoln of numerous military blunders caused by keeping inept and unfaithful men—such as George McClellan—in command of the army.

"You are on the road to Hell with this government," Wade shouted, "and you are not a mile off this minute."

That amused Lincoln. "A mile from Hell, Senator?" he asked. "That is just about the distance from here to the Capitol, is it not?"[42]

It wasn't so much that Lincoln wasn't coming around to what the radicals wanted, it was that he was coming around with such maddening slowness. And few of them were able to forgive him for it. One exception was Congressman Owen Lovejoy of Illinois, an old friend of Lincoln's, a radical who had more sympathy for the president than most. Lovejoy was a man of considerable brains and a good deal of body, with a big, bushy head and a tremendous, cannonlike voice.[43] He was as impatient as any other radical, but somewhat more resigned.

The year before, in a speech at the Cooper Union in New York, he had pictured Lincoln on the slow road to righteousness. "The President," Lovejoy had explained, "is like a man driving a horse in the thills of a buggy, and leading another behind him by the halter-strap.

The one in the shafts is a most superb animal—broad between the eyes, ears small, short around the throat, stifle full and hard, short coupled, and can clear ditch and hedge, high spirited and fast." This was the radical steed of Lovejoy's allegory, champing to pull driver and buggy along the road to freedom. But trotting behind the rig was the conservative nag in the halter-strap, holding up everything. And Lincoln was far too solicitous of the nag, reining in the radical steed to keep it from going too fast for the rest of the apparatus. But then, Lovejoy concluded in his frustration, "if he does not drive as fast as I would, he is on the right road, and it is only a question of time."[44]

The radicals believed their sole hope for a quick end to the war and the subjugation of the South was to get rid of this slow driver. Lincoln knew that his biggest challenge in the coming campaign would be to keep his contentious party—steed, nag, buggy, and all—moving forward together and himself still in the driver's seat. After all, the two wings were not that far apart. The radicals wanted a war to abolish slavery and remake the South. The conservatives mainly wanted to reestablish the divided Union. There had to be compromise and conciliation in there somewhere. Lincoln knew he must somehow hold to a policy in the coming months that would not lose him the political support of either side.

For most conservatives in his party, the radicals were anathema. Frank Blair viewed them as simple partisan plunderers.[45] John Hay called them Jacobins.[46] But Lincoln could not bring himself to dislike them, despite their antipathy to him. Musing one day with Hay about the ones from Missouri, he said, "They are nearer to me than the other side, in thought and sentiment, though bitterly hostile personally. They are utterly lawless—the unhandiest devils in the world to deal with—but after all their faces are set Zionwards."[47]

5

THE DRUMROLL
OF RECONSTRUCTION

N<small>O TWO RADICALS HAD THEIR FACES MORE FIRMLY SET ZION-</small>
wards, or were more unhandy to deal with, than Charles Sumner in the Senate and Thaddeus Stevens in the House.

Sumner was chairman of the Senate committee on foreign affairs. He
reminded the German-born politician-general, Carl Schurz, of some
Englishmen of distinction he had seen. Sumner was tall, nearly as tall as
Lincoln, and well built, with a handsome, strong face—a good-looking
man with a smile of peculiar charm.[1]

An English traveler described him as "that great sturdy English-
looking figure, with the broad massive forehead, over which the rich
mass of nut-brown hair, streaked here and there with a line of grey,
hangs loosely, with the deep blue eyes, and the strangely winning smile,
half bright, half full of sadness. He is a man whom you would notice
amongst other men, and whom, not knowing him, you would turn
round to look at as he passed by you. . . . A child would ask him the
time in the streets, and a woman, I think, would come to him unbidden
for protection."[2]

Indeed, mothers often named their children after Sumner, and he
always urged them never to do that. No child should be named after a
living man, he believed, since the jury was still out; there was as yet no
telling how dismally that man might fail or grow faint or turn aside to
false gods.[3]

Lincoln, who was wont to take his feet off his desk whenever Sumner came to visit, viewed him as "just my idea of a bishop."[4] The senator dressed his stalwart frame and commanding figure in clothes to
justify Lincoln's description: a brown coat and light waistcoat, lavender-
colored or checked trousers, and shoes with English gaiters. He sat in

the Senate with unbending dignity, explaining one day to the reporter Noah Brooks that since habit was everything, he never allowed himself, even in the privacy of his own chamber, to fall into a position he would not assume in his seat in the Senate. Senator James W. Nesmith of Oregon once speculated, "I wonder how Sumner would look in his nightshirt?" No one seemed to know.[5]

This English-looking giant was unforgiving and magisterial in thought and action, as unbending as his body, committed to what he viewed as the cause of the ages: the immediate emancipation of slaves and the destruction of slavery everywhere.

Sumner viewed slavery as "an intolerable, Heaven-defying iniquity." Alas, he said, "there have been crimes in human history; but I know of none blacker than this. There have been acts of baseness; but I know of none more utterly vile."[6]

He didn't hesitate to say so, which had gotten him nearly caned to death at his desk on the Senate floor in 1856 by a Southern congressman outraged by his latest speech. For when Sumner spoke, he delivered screeds, crushing, insulting, name-calling philippics, that tended not just to offend, but to inflame. It was said that he practiced these thunderbolts before a mirror in his chambers, then went to the Senate floor to deliver them abrasively in what John Hay called "that high-priced style of his."[7]

Sumner's speeches were studded, nearly top-heavy, with quotations from the classics, poetry, and history, and they were delivered as cannonballs, in a voice sonorous, deep, and mellow, "like the roar of a lion, or the bay of a St. Bernard."[8] His friend, the poet Henry Wadsworth Longfellow, described him as standing like a gunner on the Senate floor, gesticulating as if he were ramming down cartridges.[9]

Gideon Welles believed that Sumner's knowledge of men, like that of his good friend, Salmon Chase, was imperfect, nearsighted, and unreliable.[10]

The poet Julia Ward Howe asked Sumner one day if he had yet seen the actor Edwin Booth. "Why, n-no, madam—I, long since, ceased to take any interest in *individuals*." To which Howe, who was always ready with pertinent verse, lyric, or observation, said, "You have made great *progress*, Sir. God has not yet gone so far—at least according to the last accounts."[11] Sumner's fellow senator from Massachusetts, Henry Wilson, said of him, "Sumner thought any thing that did not originate in his own brain or the Almighty's, was not worthy of consideration."[12]

Sumner liked Lincoln personally and was a frequent visitor to the White House, not just on emancipation business, but socially, for he was a favorite of Mary Lincoln's. But Lincoln frustrated Sumner nearly beyond endurance. "He is hard to move," Sumner complained in a letter to his English friend, John Bright.[13]

Sumner desperately wanted to move Lincoln around to his way of thinking about things, and would do it if it killed him. For Sumner was the kind of man who would not take no for an answer, and who believed he "must do my whole duty, without looking to consequences."[14] And there were sometimes consequences, dire ones. James Gordon Bennett of the *New York Herald* called Sumner "the John Brown of politics," who "runs ahead of the radicals, strikes the first blow for them, and is always hung up for his pains."[15]

Another firebrand who cared little for consequences was that quintessential radical in the House, Thaddeus Stevens.

People called him "Old Thad," and he was a gambling man. The faro table drew Stevens like a magnet. In the evenings after his mulatto housekeeper, Lydia Hamilton Smith, had served him his supper, he would go down Pennsylvania Avenue to Hall and Pemberton's Faro Bank, one of the four poshest of Washington's more than one hundred gambling establishments.

They called these gambling halls that hummed in Washington's darkest recesses "hells." They ran along Pennsylvania Avenue and up the streets that intersected it, recognizable by the heavy gilt house numbers and the heavily curtained windows that emitted a dim glow of gaslight and suggested intrigue inside. Within lay another world, brightly lit, strangely hushed, and magnificently furnished, offering not only a way to lose money, but free food and wines of the highest quality. The carpets in the best of the hells were so rich and yielding that the tramp of a thousand feet could scarcely raise an echo. Ceilings and walls were lavishly frescoed and adorned by the choicest works of art. The curtains at the windows were of sumptuous material that deadened all sound from without and within. Splendid chandeliers with scores of gas jets shining through cut-glass globes shed a brilliant glare throughout the rooms.

Within the rooms themselves stood the irresistible green tables where, as Donn Piatt said, "men wagered their money and lost their souls." Like sirens, the fatal green tables called and some of the greatest men in the country came—governors, senators, congressmen, executive officers, high ranking officers of the army and navy, and Thaddeus Stevens. Stevens was not a big-scale bettor, he never wagered a lot or lost much. The playing seemed not to lose him his turbulent soul, but to soothe it.[16]

Stevens was the gray eminence of the House of Representatives, the friend of all slaves, the scourge of all slaveholders and copperheads, and a thorn in the side of Abraham Lincoln. He was well built, nearly six feet tall, with brooding, overhanging brows, and a foot clubbed from birth. His complexion was a uniform and melancholy sallow, his underlip defiant and protruding. Over a head shorn bald by an attack of "brain fever" earlier in life, he wore an ill-fitting reddish brown wig that never pretended to be anything but what it was. His cavernous eyes were dull and blue-gray, and in times of scorn seemed to shoot minié balls that could rive, blast, poison, and consume.[17]

Stevens was the oldest man in the House, chairman of the all-powerful Ways and Means Committee, and generally judged the ablest parliamentary politician of the day.[18] Someone had once said that whoever cracked Thaddeus Stevens's skull would let out the brains of the Republican party.[19]

He had been born in Vermont only ten years after the Revolutionary War ended. His clubfoot made him a sickly, outcast youth with a sympathy for the suffering and downtrodden that he never lost. At home in Pennsylvania he had a reputation as perhaps the most accomplished all-around lawyer in the state and an avowed foe of special privilege of any kind. He was a lifelong bachelor, but it was generally believed that the attractive mulatto, Lydia Smith, was more to him than just his housekeeper.

When Stevens rose to speak on the floor of the House, he rose by degrees and, once on his feet, stood like a column of iron, thundering his anathemas as though each weighed a ton.[20] "He cannot be said to debate," one observer remarked. "With him it is but assault."[21]

As another observer said, he could "make the fur fly." To please, penetrate, and persuade was not his forte. He often hobbled into the House from a night at the faro tables and hour after hour "frightened and coaxed, and bullied and controlled the members . . . along the path of humanity."[22]

He had several nicknames—the Great Commoner for one, and Old Sarcastic for another. His sarcasm was venomous; it bit and withered and defamed. In an earlier time, when he was a representative in the Pennsylvania Assembly, a fellow legislator spoke sharply against one of his measures. Nailing his critic with his cavernous eye, Stevens addressed the chair: "Mr. Speaker, it will not be expected of me to notice the thing which has crawled into this House and adheres to one of the seats by its own slime."[23] And on the floor of the House at a later time he said, "I yield to the gentleman for a few feeble remarks."[24]

His own remarks, never feeble, were delivered in a hollow voice devoid of music, but often laced with sardonic humor, which, said Schurz, "he made play upon men and things like lurid freaks of lightning."[25] "He is never tender, winning, or conciliatory," Noah Brooks noted through his pince-nez, "but always argumentative, harsh, ironical, grim, and resolute," full of gall and denunciation.[26] He upheld a principle with unsmiling intolerance. Beneath the sardonic cynicism, however, and not readily seen, ran a rich vein of human kindness and sympathy, evident in many good works in Pennsylvania for friends, fugitive slaves, widows, orphans, and others in need.[27]

But for the rebellious South and its leaders he had not a shred of compassion. They were traitors, and with them there was to be no compromise. They were to be crushed with force and then subjugated as a foreign nation. "Let no Slave State flatter itself," he said, "that it can dissolve the Union now and then reconstruct it upon better terms."[28] He held that the Constitution was not in force for those states that had consented to its overthrow, and he was impatient with anything he thought might be lenient. "Let the cursed rebels lie on the bed they have made," he said.[29] He was, as his fellow Pennsylvanian, Alexander McClure, described him, "the master-spirit of every aggressive movement in Congress to overthrow the rebellion and slavery."[30]

The South returned his venom in kind. One Southern writer called him "this demon . . . this malicious, pitiless, pauseless enemy . . . this misanthrope . . . this viperous, heartless, adulterous beast . . . this living sepulchre of all hideous things . . . this lonely, friendless, and unfriendly man." That same writer was to speak of Stevens's clubfoot as "hell's seal of deformity . . . fixed in his mother's womb."[31]

What these merciless radical opponents of slavery and rebellion who faced Zionwards feared most of all—what Charles Sumner and Thaddeus Stevens and every other radical feared—was that Abraham Lincoln, by his gentle, kindly, lenient, and forgiving nature, would not scourge the South, but would let slip away the fruit of victory wrested from it by war. Because they feared this, Lincoln's chances for renomination and reelection in 1864 were in peril.

The knotty question of reconstruction had begun to rise in the North in earnest that summer of 1863, after Gettysburg and Vicksburg. It had been recognized as an important question in Congress long before that—since the start of the war. But not until the fortunes of war began to tilt toward the North with those two victories in the summer was it forced into the public consciousness as a major political issue. By the fall of 1863 it was as much on Lincoln's mind as the question of the election itself.

Union control of the Mississippi and Grant's defeat of the Confederates at the gates of Chattanooga in late November had cleared the way to move ahead without rebel interference in at least three freed states, Louisiana, Arkansas, and Tennessee. And as the radicals in Congress watched fretfully, Lincoln reached immediately for the controls. Indeed, even before that, without consulting them, he had begun the process.

Lincoln knew that the Congress would have to approve final readmission of any seceded state's congressional delegation back into its ranks. The Constitution was clear on that. But he was as loath to leave the process that led to that point to the vindictive radicals in Congress as they were to leave it to his tender heart.

Undergirding radical concern, at the bottom of it all, was the question of whether emancipation must be a condition for readmission of a seceded state into the Union. Although the radicals disagreed widely on details and method, they absolutely agreed on that requirement; it must be in every new state constitution, and it must be there in concrete. The question through the summer and fall of 1863 was, how committed was Lincoln to that one essential point? As the opening of Congress in December drew near, attention was riveted on the position he would take in his annual message. Visits up the walk to the White House by "them same three fellers," and many others with them, increased.[32]

Co-partner to the concern over Negro freedom was that question of who was going to control the process, who would call the shots. Fixed in the radical mind was the belief that the Congress was the actual motor of government, that they controlled the engine, and that the president was but their tool. In their view, that was the true nature of things. Sumner believed the president was constitutionally subordinate to Congress on this issue, that he was assuming powers that belonged not to him, but to them.[33] Sumner's fellow senator from Massachusetts, Henry Wilson, said he would rather give a policy to the president than to take one from him. Lyman Trumbull, the scholarly U.S. senator from Illinois, said of the president that he could only execute the laws Congress passed, that "he is just as much subject to our control as if we appointed him, except that we cannot remove him and substitute another in his place"—no matter how desperately they wished they could. And Stevens said, "We [Congress] possess all the power now claimed to be under the Constitution, even the tremendous power of dictatorship."[34]

In Lincoln the radicals were finding a devil as unhandy to deal with as they were themselves. And they feared his face was not as sufficiently set Zionwards as theirs. Every day Lincoln was making dramatic invasions into their legislative territory, pushing the envelope of executive power to unprecedented limits, limits not even dared by that all-time presidential power pusher, Andrew Jackson. Lincoln was constantly increasing the size of the army and navy beyond the limits set by statute, suspending habeas corpus, and declaring martial law. And now he was meddling in reconstruction.

The struggle for control was clearly on. At stake was which point of view would prevail in how the South was to be reconstituted—in short, the future shape and nature of the Union itself.

By the summer of 1863, Charles Sumner was so worried about the issue and its stakes that he did what he always did when provoked— ran out ahead of the radicals to strike the first blow, only to get hung up for his pains. In a long article, "Our Domestic Relations," which ran in the *Atlantic Monthly* in July 1863, he made the radical case for killing forever any compromise with slavery and for congressional control of reconstruction.

He quoted Edmund Burke: "When men . . . break up the original compact or agreement which gives its corporate form and capacity to a State, they are no longer a people; they have no longer a corporate existence." The rebel states, Sumner argued, had done that by seceding. They had senselessly "sacrificed that corporate existence which makes them living, component members of our Union of States." They had abdicated their places in the Union, and thereby had fallen under the exclusive jurisdiction of the Congress. They were now simply territories again. "The whole broad Rebel region," Sumner argued, "is *tabula rasa,* or a clean slate, where Congress, under the Constitution of the United States may write the laws." And it was clearly Congress and only Congress, he argued, that was empowered to do this. The president, he believed, clearly needed to step aside.[35]

Postmaster General Montgomery Blair, who watched radicals as a mongoose watches a snake, read Sumner's ukase in the *Atlantic*

Monthly, and his temperature shot up. This particular Blair, a brother to Frank, was tall, straight, spare, and erect, with a face, one observer said, "in which fanaticism was tempered by enthusiasm." He was a lover of good books and works of art. Soft-spoken, with a pale voice, he was deeply religious, a lay reader in church.[36] Noah Brooks described him as "awkward, shy, homely, and repellent," the best scholar and probably the meanest man in the cabinet.[37] When Assistant Secretary of War Charles Dana described him as capable, sharp, and keen, but "perhaps a little cranky, and not friendly with everybody," he was being kind.[38]

The radicals believed him and all his kin to be "a family of Maryland serpents." Despite his mild and scholarly ways, Montgomery was also a West Pointer, and battle was in his blood. He is once reputed to have said, "When the Blairs go in for a fight, they go in for a funeral."[39]

It was a funeral Montgomery Blair had in mind when he went to Rockville, Maryland, in early October to address a Union Party meeting. The intended corpse was Sumner's congressional-supremacy thesis. Just when it appeared peace was nearly won, the rebellion destroyed, and slavery suppressed, Blair began, "we are menaced by the ambition of the ultra-Abolitionists, which is equally despotic in its tendencies, and which, if successful, could not fail to be alike fatal to Republican institutions."

The aim of these radicals, Blair said, was to dominate the country, to assume for the Congress absolute power over the states recovered to the Union without allowing them any representation in that body whatever. He flailed Sumner's theory that the states had committed suicide. He argued that the states shouldn't be held responsible for the treason of the disloyal who took them over and caused them to secede. They still existed as states, he argued; they must only be restored to loyal hands and set up in business under new management—what Lincoln, in effect, was trying to do. You can't say, Blair contended, that just because a state government has fallen into the wrong hands, it is therefore no longer a state, but only a territory to be dictatorially controlled by Congress.

Having thus blasted the radical program, he then praised the president's. Lincoln's approach was simple, he said: to "dishabilitate" the rebels and their usurpation and "rehabilitate" the loyal men and their republican governments. This was the president's way of saving the Union, by putting the powers of government, as soon as a state was redeemed, into the hands of loyal men and permitting it, under them, to resume its normal place in the councils of the nation, with all its rights restored. That was what the president was attempting to do in Louisiana, Arkansas, and Tennessee. And that, Blair said, was a "safe and healing policy." The radical program would carry the states back into colonial bondage. It would be the annihilation of a third of the states of the Union, on the pretext of the destruction of slavery.[40]

Blair's speech landed in the radical camp like a bomb with a lit fuse. It was reprinted in papers around the country and put out as a pamphlet, and everybody assumed it was launched with Lincoln's approval. The fact was, Lincoln had yet to speak publicly on the issue himself. Nobody was certain what his program was in detail. They only knew he had one, and was pushing it. All attention in early December therefore turned to the Thirty-eighth Congress, convening in the Capitol. It was there, and over the message he was preparing for it between bouts of the varioloid, that the battle would now be joined.

Washington was unclouded but cold on December 7 as the members of the new Congress began filing into their respective chambers to find their seats.

The view from the Capitol dome toward the city—over the "magnificent distances," as a Senate page had once described it—was captivating. Pennsylvania Avenue was a long ribbon linking the Hill to Georgetown in the distance. Old-timers could remember antebellum times, before the streetcar line was laid, when the avenue was an undulating, rutted, dirt surface, and when carriages making their way had tossed and heaved upon its bosom like ships at sea.

Now the streetcar line ran down its center, a sign of the times. An even more striking sign of the times was the fact that the Washington Horse Railroad Company recently had, to conciliate public opinion, put in big letters on the sides of the cars, called "c'yar boxes," this staggering concession: "Colored Persons May Ride In This Car." Until then Negroes could only ride the city's street horsecars standing on the exposed front platforms in the rain, snow, heat, and cold. Integration of the insides of the cars had been a signal victory in the war of emancipation.[41]

The view down the Mall began with the botanical gardens, an oasis, one observer said, that "seemed to have been plucked out of the heart of a tropical land and planted in our midst." It was a favorite with the members of Congress, who were fond of showing it to their visiting constituents. Beyond the gardens towered the turrets of the Smithsonian Institution, a showcase of architectural grace and beauty. Beyond that, in the center of the Mall, loomed the unfinished marble stub of the Washington Monument. Farther along still, Georgetown was visible, and the spars of the tall ships at anchor in the river beside it. On the high banks of the Potomac above the town and the river rose the graceful spires of Georgetown College.

To the northwest of the Capitol lay the social center of Washington, the section of the city where the dignitaries lived. Far on the eastern outskirts lay the Congressional Cemetery, where dignity was only remembered—with its 150 cenotaphs, one in memory of each congressman who had died in office since the beginning of the republic.[42]

The Capitol itself sparkled on the opening day of the new Congress in early December. Over the summer its interior had been renovated, refitted, and "cleansed of the dirt of the Thirty-seventh Congress." It was now ready, Noah Brooks wrote, for the dirt and wickedness of the Thirty-eighth. The hallways had been thoroughly purified, the lobbies and corridors whitened, and much of the unfinished painting of the frescoes in the Senate wing completed. The Capitol's heating and ventilating apparatus was clanging and hissing in good operating order.[43]

Even the Capitol building's crown was now in place. The Statue of Freedom, which had for so long lain on the ground nearby, waiting for her pedestal atop the dome to be readied, had been hoisted only five days before. She was a figure worthy of her place, nineteen feet six inches high, weighing seven and a half tons, and costing $23,796. Thaddeus Stevens noted with satisfaction that she stood "with her face toward the loyal States, and her back turned to the Rebellion." She had been lifted to her pedestal three hundred feet above the ground on the lantern of the dome at noon on December 2. The field battery of thirty-five cannon on the Capitol grounds had thundered a salute, echoed by the guns in the defenses ringing the city.[44]

The opening day of Congress on Monday, December 7, was a quiet one in the seats of war, only three small skirmishes that day—in Tennessee and Mississippi. In Richmond, only ninety miles to the south, the fourth session of the Confederate congress was also convening.

In Washington, the House galleries were packed by noon, glinting with the flashes of color the women wore. The floor was jammed with overflow all around the outside of the bar. Inside the bar, the members clustered about on the richly carpeted floor in knots and informal caucuses. The unclouded December sun filtered warmly through the stained glass of the skylights in the chamber roof. On the Senate side, the members filed sedately in, stiff and stuffy in their black broadcloth frocks and silk hats. At noon the gavel fell and the Thirty-eighth Congress was pounded to order.[45]

In the House, "Smiler" Colfax, dressed in black, which gave him a funereal aspect, was ready to rise to the occasion. Colfax was a teetotaler, but also an inveterate cigar smoker. A stogie was everlastingly sticking out through his ever-present smile. He was also a lightning-fast talker. It was said by the House stenographers, who ought to know, that he could put more words into an hour than any man in Congress. His smile didn't endear him to everyone. Maj. Gen. Frank Blair, about to assume his other job as a congressman from Missouri, considered him a little intriguer—implausible, aspiring beyond his capacity, and untrustworthy. After a decade in Congress representing a district in Indiana, Colfax aspired to be speaker of the House. His chances were good because he was generally viewed as one of its best parliamentarians. But, even more important for his prospects, he was the favored candidate of that other great parliamentarian, Thaddeus Stevens.[46]

Schuyler Colfax had to be grouped with the radicals. He had never forgiven Lincoln for leaving him out of the cabinet, and he had publicly announced he would not support the president for reelection in 1864. That didn't mean he didn't like Lincoln. They were still personal friends, often going to Ford's opera house together "to regale ourselves of an evening, for we felt the strain on mind and body was often intolerable." There they found "real relaxation" watching "those southern girls with their well rounded forms, lustrous hair and sparkling voices. We thought it a veritable treat to see them dance and hear their song."[47]

Smiler Colfax was elected speaker on December 7 by a vote of 101 to 81. The runner-up was Sunset Cox, with 42 votes. One of the first acts of the new Congress under its new speaker was a vote to strike a medal of thanks to U. S. Grant for the newly won victories at Missionary Ridge and Chattanooga. No fur was expected to fly until the president sent up his message the following day or the next.

Nicolay and Hay brought the message to the Capitol the morning of the ninth. Here it was at last, in black and white: Lincoln's plan for reconstructing the South, together with a Proclamation of Amnesty and Reconstruction. The members listened intently as the clerks in both houses began reading it aloud.

Lincoln's plan would grant full pardons, with all property rights, except slaves, restored to all who had participated in the rebellion— upon taking, subscribing to, and keeping an oath to faithfully support, protect, and defend the Constitution and the Union. The Emancipation Proclamation would hold throughout the South; all slaves would be freed.

There were some classes of rebels who would not be allowed to take the oath: any who were civil or diplomatic officers or agents of the Confederate government; all who had left judicial posts in the Union to aid the rebellion; all Confederate military or naval officers above the rank of colonel in the army or lieutenant in the navy; all who had left seats in the U.S. Congress to aid the rebellion; all who had resigned commissions in the army or navy to fight for the Confederacy; and any who had engaged in any way in treating black Union soldiers or whites in charge of them otherwise than as prisoners of war.

When eligible voters in any of the rebellious states equal to ten percent of the vote cast in the 1860 presidential election should take the oath and not violate it, and reestablish a republican state government, that state would be recognized as a loyal government and welcomed back into the Union, subject to congressional approval.[48]

That was it, Lincoln's plan, plain and simple, as Montgomery Blair had said. It came at the end of the message, attended by the Proclamation of Amnesty and Reconstruction. Nicolay and Hay had stayed to listen and, with great anxiety, to watch the reaction. What they saw was gratifying. Whatever may be the results or the verdict of history, Hay thought, the immediate effect of the paper was "something wonderful." Sumner was beaming, Chandler seemed delighted. The other radicals appeared equally pleased.[49] They had heard the one thing they had wanted to hear: slaves would be freed throughout the South, slavery would not be restored—Lincoln had vowed in his message never to go back on the Emancipation Proclamation, no matter what. In its most important particular, therefore, Lincoln's plan was consistent with the radical position.

In Lincoln's mind, few particulars of the plan were set in concrete. He was keeping an open mind. In a letter a week later he wrote: "I have not put forth the plan in that proclamation, as a Procrustean bed, to which exact conformity is to be indispensable; and in Louisiana particularly, I wish that labor already done, which varies from that plan in no important particular, may not be thrown away." Otherwise there were only two things he considered inviolable. He spelled them out in another letter: "The restoration of the Rebel States to the Union must rest upon the principle of civil and political equality of both races; and it must be sealed by general amnesty."[50]

He had gotten across his basic idea, a plan that was not vindictive and that worked toward the earliest possible restoration of peace and a reknit nation free of slavery. *The New York Times* praised the president's message for its "intrinsic excellence." But it added, "Of course Faction will bark at it."[51]

Indeed, Faction began barking soon enough. At first there was no outcry of opposition. Most Republicans, including the radicals, seemed to support the plan. Requiring oaths of only ten percent of the electorate seemed a little small to Sumner's liking. But Lincoln was leaving the admission of any reconstructed state to the Congress, he had stressed that the program was provisional and flexible, and he had included a ringing affirmation of his Emancipation Proclamation. Sumner could live with that. There might be differences over the details of admitting states, but he believed "these will drop out of sight, and nothing remain but the great principle of the irrevocability of the proclamation."[52]

But observant men had seen a spark of wrath on some radical faces as they listened to the message and the amnesty proclamation.[53] And soon a slow burn was setting in. The radicals began having serious second thoughts. The House appointed a committee to frame legislation to implement Lincoln's plan. But the more closely they looked at the way Lincoln was proceeding in Louisiana, the more alarmed they became. For one thing, the president seemed willing to reconstruct Louisiana under its antebellum constitution, with only the pro-slavery clauses stricken. That would continue to rest political power in the hands of the hated planters after only ten percent of them had taken a simple oath of future loyalty. Indeed, a labor system was being set up that continued to tie the freedmen to the plantations. There was even a possibility slavery might continue, since New Orleans and the surrounding parishes had been excepted from the Emancipation Proclamation. Such a program would negate all the gains of the war. As soon as the slaveholders repented and took the oath, they could resume control of their state governments and return to seats of power in Washington. This would never do.[54]

The radical abolitionist orator, Wendell Phillips, breathing fire, charged that Lincoln's plan "leaves the large landed proprietors of the South still to domineer over its politics, and make the negro's freedom a mere sham."[55]

The select committee in the House that had been appointed to hammer out legislation to implement Lincoln's plan abruptly shifted gears and began work on a different plan altogether. The basic problem remained: they must somehow wrest control of reconstruction from Lincoln's hands. While they awaited the alternate plan, the radicals dug in, determined meanwhile to reject any slate elected to the House or Senate by the new governments. As the Congress set its feet, and its committee worked to shape an alternative, Lincoln continued to push ahead according to his plan in Louisiana, Tennessee, Arkansas, and Florida.

The old year was about done and the new one about to begin, and Tad Lincoln was throwing a fit. It was the day before Christmas, Jack the Turkey's neck was stretched on the block, and the executioner's ax was about to fall. Tad had tearfully exacted a momentary stay, and was now racing for the office of the one man in the nation empowered to pardon the condemned, his father the president.

Tad was a merry, warm-blooded, kindly little boy, perfectly lawless, and full of odd fancies and inventions. Hay called him the "'chartered libertine' of the Executive Mansion." He was named Thomas after Lincoln's father. But he had been born with an unusually large head for his little body. For that reason Lincoln had playfully called him a little tadpole, and he had been Tad ever since. He ran continually in and out of cabinet meetings, interrupting the gravest labors and discussions of war and policy. He would often perch on his indulgent father's knee, sometimes even on his shoulder, while the weightiest conferences were in progress. He was Lincoln's youngest, left alone in the White House after Willie died. He had an impediment that made his speech almost unintelligible, and he evoked Lincoln's tenderest feelings. The son, like the father, was bighearted, often circulating among the crowds of petitioners thronging the White House corridors, ever the hot champion of the distressed, the disinherited, and the discontented.[56]

Some months before Christmas, one of Lincoln's friends had sent a live turkey to the White House to be killed and eaten on Christmas Day. Tad had won the confidence of the turkey, whom he named Jack, and whom he fed and petted until it followed him, slavelike, around the White House grounds. Now Christmas had come and Jack's life was in mortal danger, and Lincoln was at the moment in an important conference with one of his cabinet officers. Tad burst into the room like a shell shot from a cannon, crying out in rage and indignation that Jack must not be killed; it would be wicked.

"But," reasoned the president, "Jack was sent here to be killed, and eaten for this very Christmas."

"I can't help it!" Tad sobbed. "He's a good turkey, and I don't want him killed!"

Pausing in the midst of the pressing business of state, Lincoln took a card and wrote out a formal reprieve for Jack. Tad fled with it joyfully to the executioner and Jack's life was spared.[57] This wasn't the first time Tad had won an executive pardon for something named Jack. A doll with the same name had also been presidentially reprieved in the earlier days of the administration.

It is probable this holiday season, as on other Christmases, that Lincoln had already visited Joseph Schot's Toy Shop with Tad in mind. Lincoln was a frequent visitor to the shop, kept by an old crippled soldier who had fought in Napoleon's army and who now carved wooden soldiers for the children of Washington. [58]

The day after Christmas, Lincoln had also been able to give another gift, to a friend, Usher F. Linder, in Chicago. Linder's son, a Confederate soldier, had been captured. Lincoln had talked with the boy, then sent him to Stanton with a written order. He had then telegraphed Linder: "Your son Dan. has just left me, with my order to the Sec. of War, to administer to him the oath of allegiance, discharge him & send him to you."[59]

Lincoln was being Lincoln this holiday season, lenient and tenderhearted as usual.

Count Gurowski, who was seldom lenient or tenderhearted, but sometimes sympathetic, wrote in his diary on Christmas day: "More and more orphans and desolated homes, more hearths under cold ashes, and more broken hearts." A week later, on the last day of the year, Gurowski was feeling no better about things. "So ends this 1863," he told his diary. "Oh! dying year!" And on New Year's Day he spoke directly to the year just born: "Your mission is great, O 1864! and I hope you will fulfill it."[60]

For Lincoln, the election year had come, and with it another year of trying to manage a divided nation in war and a divided party in politics. He could only agree with all the count had written.

6

THE COMMON MAN

<hr/>

THE OLD YEAR LEFT ON A SEVERE NORTHEASTERLY RAINSTORM. New Year's Day, Friday, opened clear and sunny, but Greenland-cold. Water pipes were freezing, Noah Brooks noted, "as tight as the money market."[1]

And it was going to get colder still. The thermometer would drop to seven degrees by the weekend. The next day, Saturday, the wind would be blowing malignant off the Potomac, bringing the first snowstorm of the year by the beginning of the week. The entire East was Siberian. On New Year's Day the Susquehanna froze rock-hard. The railroad ferry-boat, with three hundred passengers aboard, shuddered to a stop in the middle of the river, and remained locked tight in its icy grip for the next sixteen hours.[2]

The Washington social season had blown in with the cold, and would last until Lent. This was the way it was every year. Through the bleak autumn the town was "sunk," as John Nicolay put it, "in its original Rip Van Winkle somnolence."[3] But with the new year came the gay season, a time of parties, receptions, and levees.

Before this New Year's Day ended, there would be receptions and levees at all of the traditional places. At Navy Secretary Gideon Welles's home, later in the day, there would be the accustomed gathering, with its "very large infusion of fogy."[4]

Welles struck people that way. His long white beard and a stupendous snowy wig, parted in the middle, gave him an apostolic mein, and caused people to call him "Father Welles." He wore such an air of ponderous deliberation that many thought him slightly fossilized, and wondered if he had ever clearly realized that the country was in an urgent civil war. But he was kindhearted, affable, and accessible. Aside from his looks, however, there was nothing decorative about him. As Charles Dana said, "There was no noise on the street when he went along." Receptions at his house tended to be like him—sedate.[5]

It would be a disappointing evening this New Year's Day at the Chase mansion. Kate Chase Sprague seemed to some the only real reason to go there, and she was on her honeymoon.

But there would still be the much-anticipated levee at Secretary of State Seward's house. Seward was a slight little man, not nearly as long, one English visitor believed, as his diplomatic dispatches. The *New York Herald* estimated that within the first two years of the administration, Seward had written "a mass of diplomatic correspondence which no living man will read through in ten years." Among the secretary's more notable physical characteristics was a prominent nose, which, when he sat in a room smoking his ever-present cigar, was said to rival the marble busts, engravings, flowers, and paintings as the most salient object there. Mary Lincoln didn't like him any better than she liked the Chases. She called him "that abolition sneak." But he threw good parties and he was good company. And if he chose to step outside to answer a call for a serenade, he would do so in a slow, artificial, metallic tone, throwing out his sentences, as one observer said, "like clanging oracles into the night."[6]

The best, most popular levee in town that day, however, was the one at the White House itself, an annual event with monumental social meaning. One had to see and be seen there, if nowhere else.

The diplomatic corps and the army, navy, and marine officers came first that morning, beginning at eleven o'clock. Seward led in "his pet lambs of the diplomacy," gorgeously arrayed in their stars, garters, and medals of honor. Among all that show, Brooks thought Seward looked like a molting barnyard fowl amid peacocks. The secretaries of war and the navy came escorting their generals and admirals. A few of the generals, led by the general-in-chief, Henry Halleck, wore their epaulets and feathers, but most came attired in battle dress.[7]

"There they parade in splendid array, the *starred* ones! misnamed generals," Count Gurowski snarled into his diary. "Marses who very well know how not to do it. Halleck, the mighty do-nothing Commander; Meade, the disorganizer of victory, and the man of manoeuvres, they and their adjuncts. All of them bats, not eagles."[8]

At noon the White House doors were thrown open to all, and a living tide poured through. For two hours the stream of humanity, rich and poor, great and humble, famous and obscure, surged past the president and his lady, past the pool of cabinet officers, where it eddied for a moment before sweeping on into the cavernous East Room. It was a maelstrom of living flesh decked in all styles of dress—a melee of uniforms, frock coats, and gay gowns. The scene was brilliant, the toilettes magnificent, the uniforms and gowns glittering, and the music fine. The women were, as always, stimulating. There were the lithe beauties among them, whom John Hay called the "young exquisites," some of whom he doubtless thought "prettier than is necessary." And there were among them those less lithe, less pretty, and far older, whom he called the "maiden antiques."[9]

Noah Brooks observed that, as always, "the crushing and jamming of bonnets and things were fearful." One woman became separated from her family. Her shriek, heard above the crush, convinced her young son that his mother was being slain, and he began wailing piteously.[10] Four blacks, reticent at first, but whom Secretary Chase thought "of genteel exterior and with the manners of gentlemen," passed through the line and shook hands with the president. This had never happened before at a White House levee, a sign of the changing times.[11]

Mary Lincoln stood on the banks of the raging human river next to Lincoln, greeting the throng as it passed. She was vividly dressed this first day of the new year in a gown of purple silk trimmed in black velvet and lace and ending in an enormous train. At her throat was a pearl pin and in her hair a white plume. Her outfit was, as Lincoln might have said, a pretty fair "trotting harness."[12] She was in fact radiant, looking anything but "the Hell-cat" Nicolay and Hay believed her to be.[13]

Lincoln at a levee had been compared to "a man sawing wood at so much per cord," or at a pump handle vigorously drawing water.[14] He shook hands seemingly unconscious of what he was doing, murmuring some monotonous greeting into the river as it flowed by, his eye dim, his thoughts far withdrawn. Then he would sight some familiar face in the passing tide. His eye would brighten and his lanky frame grow attentive. He would greet this familiar with a hearty grasp of the hand and a ringing word, and send him with a cheery laugh along to Mary. Whatever speech a passing guest thought to deliver to the president had to be compressed into the smallest possible space, or it would never get finished. The crowd, John Hay thought, was particularly adept at jostling perorations out of shape.[15]

One peroration at least didn't get jostled out of shape this day. Lincoln had just taken Congressman Isaac Arnold's hand in his own great, rugged, furrowed one—a cast-iron grip, anybody who had ever felt it agreed, that was the next best thing to a vise. Arnold congratulated Lincoln on the battlefield victories of the past summer and fall, then said, "I hope, Mr. President, that on next New Year's Day I may have the pleasure of congratulating you on three events which now seem very probable."

"What are they?" Lincoln asked.

"*First,* That the war may be ended by the complete triumph of the Union forces. *Second,* That slavery may be abolished and prohibited throughout the Union by an amendment of the Constitution. [Such an amendment had just been introduced in the new Congress.] *Third,* That Abraham Lincoln may have been re-elected President."

Lincoln smiled, and said, "I think, I think, my friend, I would be willing to accept the first two by way of compromise."[16]

Lincoln was looking better on this New Year's Day than Noah Brooks had seen him in a long time. The varioloid must have agreed with him. His complexion was clearer, his eyes less lackluster, his hue of health better. He was standing up manfully against the crush in his loose-fitting white kid gloves, bearing up to the day's work at the pump handle like a martyr.[17]

To describe the quaint man at the pump handle from head to toe, one had to start six feet four inches off the ground. The whole structure, hugely elongated, was topped by what the London *Times* reporter William Howard Russell described as a "thatch of wild republican hair."[18] The hair was coarse and black, and only beginning to streak with gray. It seemed generally to have a mind of its own. At best it lay floating where the president's fingers had put it or the winds had left it, piled up and tossed about at random, uncombed and uncombable, standing out in every direction at once, an unraked stubble field. Lincoln himself called it "a bird's nest," with "a way of getting up as far as possible in the world."[19]

A high, narrow forehead spanned the distance between the presidential hair and the eyebrows, which cropped like jutting rock from the brow of a hill. The eyes beneath this ledge were gray and penetrating, sunken and deep-set, often shadowed by a sad, preoccupied, faraway look. But they also seemed lit by an inner tenderness that suggested a kindness that would always forgive. They were eyes, one man said, of "pathetic sadness," from which "his soul looked forth—clear, calm, and honest, yet piercing and searching; not to be deceived, yet practicing no guile."[20]

Lincoln's left eye rode slightly higher than his right, and his head tended to tilt—almost imperceptibly—to the right.[21] His nose was large and long, which, like his ears, made it appear to some as if it must have been transplanted by mistake from a head twice the size.[22] It was a nose that stood out from the face, William Howard Russell thought, "with an inquiring, anxious air, as though it were sniffing for some good thing in the wind."[23]

The ears likewise stood out, appearing to some to run at nearly right angles from the sides of his head. The cheekbones were high, sharp, and prominent, the cheeks themselves leathery and saffron-hued. Lincoln was lantern-jawed, and his chin was long, strong, and bearded. A lone mole lodged on his right cheek a little above the corner of his mouth, and deep lines of thought and care plowed furrows around it.

All of these elements, taken together, produced a face which Nathaniel Hawthorne described as a "very remarkable physiognomy"—a "sallow, queer, sagacious visage."[24] Another described it as "furrowed, wrinkled, and indented, as though it had been scarred by vitriol."[25] Lincoln's law partner, Billy Herndon, who had stared at that face for years in Springfield, Illinois, described it as long, narrow, sallow and cadaverous, shriveled, wrinkled, and dry—and generally woestruck.[26] David R. Locke, who, as the humorist Petroleum V. Nasby, had a gift for making Lincoln laugh, said of it, "I never saw a more thoughtful face, I never saw a more dignified face, I never saw so sad a face."[27]

Lincoln's expression was remarkably pensive and tender in repose, as if a reservoir of tears lay just under the surface, as if a deep melancholy resided in his soul. It was so sad a face that the young painter Francis B. Carpenter, who would be at the White House constantly through six months of 1864, painting the signing of the Emancipation Proclamation, knew days when he could scarcely look into it without crying himself.[28] Yet it was a face that was capable of great mobility and mirth. At such times the eyes lit up and the countenance showed every shade of laughter and emotion. At such times, David Locke said, it was like a gleam of sunlight upon a cloud; it illuminated, but did not dissipate the sadness.[29]

This remarkable face was set in a head that was long, tall, and narrow, like the body beneath it. It accommodated a stovepipe hat seven and an eighth inches across, measured on the hatter's block.

The body beneath was as striking as the head above. It was thin, wiry, sinewy, raw, and heavy-boned, narrow through the chest and across the shoulders, which were slightly stooped. Lincoln was what

Herndon described as consumptively built. There were only 180 pounds distributed over the six-foot-four-inch frame. Yet it was a very powerful 180 pounds. The whole organization of it, the structure and functions, worked slowly. The blood had a long run from his heart to his extremities, and his nerve impulses had to travel long distances before his muscles heard from them. The entire apparatus, Herndon thought, worked creakingly, as if it needed oiling. When Lincoln walked, it was with caution and firmness and with an even tread, the inner sides of his feet parallel. He planted the whole foot down flat at once, not landing on his heel. He likewise lifted his foot all at once, not rising from the toe. Hence there was no spring to his step. He walked in an undulatory, up-and-down motion, "catching and pocketing time."[30]

The body, in motion or in repose, was odd, angular, and weather-beaten. A mock biography issued for the 1864 campaign said "his anatomy is composed mostly of bones, and when walking he resembles the offspring of a happy marriage between a derrick and a windmill."[31] The editor Donn Piatt compared him to "a huge skeleton in clothes." "Bent and slab-sided and ungainly," suggested another—a lank man in an Ichabod body.[32]

There was "no elegance about him, no elegance in him," said a woman visitor, who found him one day as he usually was, plainly clad in an ill-fitting suit of black. But the fit was no fault of the tailor, she decided, since such a figure could not be fitted. When he sat, in a folded-up sort of a way in a deep armchair, she believed one would almost have thought him deformed. Another visitor, seeing him seated at his desk with his feet planted on the top of it, his hands clasped on his head, thought he looked "exactly like a huge katydid or grass-hopper."[33]

It was hard not to conclude that Lincoln was homely. Many believed he was irredeemably so—about the homeliest man they had ever seen.[34] Lincoln himself believed it was so. During their celebrated debates in Illinois in 1858, when Stephen A. Douglas accused him of being two-faced, Lincoln said, "If I had another face, do you think I'd wear this one?"[35]

He was not created to adorn fashionable society, concluded one politician, who supported him anyhow.[36] Besides, there were extenuating circumstances: it was not Lincoln's fault, but nature's, that he looked so.[37]

Even Hawthorne, who found him homely, found him by no means repulsive or disagreeable.[38] A young Union cavalryman, seeing him for

the first time, believed him "not half so ugly as he is generally represented."[39] An old man "who knowed" him, said, "There's no denyin'
he was long and lean, and he didn't always stand straight, and he wasn't
pertikeler about his clothes. . . ." But "he wa'n't homely."[40]

One day Thaddeus Stevens brought a grieving mother from his district in Pennsylvania to plead with Lincoln for the life of her son, who
had been sentenced to death or long imprisonment for a crime with
extenuating circumstances. After a full hearing of the matter, Lincoln
turned to Stevens.

"Mr. Stevens," he asked, "do you think this is a case which will warrant my interference?"

"With my knowledge of the facts and the parties," Stevens replied,
"I should have no hesitation in granting a pardon."

"Then, I will pardon him," Lincoln said. And he signed the paper.

The mother, with a feeling too deep to utter speech, walked in silence
down the stairs with Stevens. Suddenly, partway down, she turned to
him and exclaimed, "I knew it was a copperhead lie!"

"What do you refer to, madam?" asked Stevens.

"Why, they told me he was an ugly looking man," she said. "He is
the handsomest man I ever saw in my life."[41]

An English visitor to Washington in this new year said of his physiognomy, "It is not beautiful—Mrs. Lincoln herself could not make it
so; but at any rate you will see a winning smile in his eye . . . and note
the instinctive kindliness of his every thought and word, and say if you
have ever known a warmer-hearted, nobler spirit."[42] His friend Noah
Brooks spoke of "his homely, heart-lighted features, his single-hearted
directness and manly kindliness."[43] David Locke said of him that "he
was as tender-hearted as a girl."[44]

It was this tenderheartedness that struck nearly everybody who met
him. Joseph Holt, the war Democrat who was the nation's judge advocate general, told the artist Francis Carpenter one day that the president
was "without exception the most tender-hearted man I ever knew."[45]

Herndon saw "this long, tall, bony, homely, wiry, sad, gloomy man"
as "a very sensitive, diffident, unobtrusive, natural-made gentleman."
Within the gangly body was a mind that was "strong and deep, sincere
and honest, patient and enduring, with a good heart filled with the love
of mercy and with a conscience that loved justice." Herndon believed
Lincoln "read less and thought more than any man in his sphere in
America," perhaps in the world, that "his reason ruled despotically all

other faculties and qualities of his mind," and that his heart was ruled jointly by his great reason and his conscience.[46]

Not all were as sympathetically inclined to the way Lincoln's mind worked as Billy Herndon was. The radical New England preacher Henry Ward Beecher said of it, "His mind works in the right *directions,* but seldom works clearly & cleanly. His bread is of unbolted flour, & much straw, too, mixes in the bran, & sometimes gravel stones. Yet, on the whole the loaf will sustain life, tho' it makes eating a difficulty, rather than a pleasure."[47]

Lincoln was known to be strange, incalculable, undomestic, and unparlorable. Socially he was magnificently inappropriate and disconcerting.[48] But nobody ever visited him without coming out with an unforgettable memory of him. The former slave and abolitionist orator Frederick Douglass visited him for the first time in the summer of 1863. "When I entered," Douglass said, "he was seated in a low chair, surrounded by a multitude of books and papers, his feet and legs were extended in front of his chair. On my approach he slowly drew his feet in from the different parts of the room into which they had strayed, and he began to rise, and continued to rise until he looked down upon me, and extended his hand and gave me a welcome. I began, with some hesitation, to tell him who I was and what I had been doing, but he soon stopped me, saying in a sharp, cordial voice:

'You need not tell me who you are, Mr. Douglass, I know who you are.'"

Douglass said, "He was the first great man that I talked with in the United States freely, who in no single instance reminded me of the difference between himself and myself, of the difference of color. . . ."[49]

The politician-general Carl Schurz said of Lincoln that he lacked higher education and his manners were not up to European conceptions of the dignity of a chief magistrate. But he was a man of profound feeling, correct and firm principles, and incorruptible honesty, possessing common sense to a remarkable degree and a strength born of conviction. His failings, Schurz said, "are those of a good man."[50]

Lincoln spoke in parables. Stories flowed from him in a natural stream, rarely the same one twice. A sentry in the Army of the Potomac overheard him telling stories one night and concluded that he had "a powerful memory and mighty poor forgettery."[51] The Washington writer-reporter Benjamin Perley Poore compared his stories to "the successive charges in a magazine gun," the next cartridge always ready "and always pertinently adapted to some passing event." When not telling his own stories, he was often reading somebody else's—aloud. He was inclined to read the works of David Locke, alias Petroleum V. Nasby, or other humorists to visitors, no matter who they might be or what their business was. Locke believed that the president seriously offended many of the great men of the Republican party by reading Petroleum V. Nasby to them.[52]

The Executive Mansion where the people were thronging on this clear but cold first day of the election year in 1864, was Lincoln's house, office, bedroom, parlor, and kitchen. It stood back from Pennsylvania Avenue and was approached by an ordinary semicircular drive. On quiet days there was often nobody in sight, no guard, outside or in, not even a house dog on watch.[53]

Within, however, in the room Lincoln used for his office, the watch on the war never ended. It was a long, high room with a window that looked south, across the grass to the Potomac beyond. On a clear day the president could see prominent objects in Alexandria, six miles downriver. It was a war room, with walls thickly hung with maps, which brought the battlefields to Lincoln. The maps depicted the contested ground of the war with pencil lines tracing the paths of the armies. A separate loose lithographic map, usually leaning against the leg of a desk or a table, showed at a glance the slave populations of the Southern states in graduated shades of gray and black. Lincoln consulted it often.

The table where he worked backed against the window in the farthest end of the room. To the left of it ran a long table before a fireplace grate, at which the cabinet met. The carpet underfoot was trodden thin, its dyes long since faded. The chairs at the long table were of the formal cabinet class, stately but only semicomfortable. There were bookcases crammed with books. And there was but one photograph among the nest of maps on the wall. It hung above the marble mantel and was a likeness of the pro-Union English parliamentarian John Bright. On Lincoln's table were more books, among them invariably the volume or two of humor to lighten the dark nights of trouble and sorrow— Orpheus C. Kerr, Artemus Ward, John Phoenix, or Petroleum Nasby— with which he solaced himself and with which he offended the earnest men in the Republican party.[54]

Lincoln rose early each day—his sleep was light and capricious—and was generally at his desk by eight in the morning. His breakfast was like his sleep, light and capricious—an egg, perhaps, and a cup of coffee. He

began receiving visitors at ten. But long before that, the anxious crowds
had the doors under siege. There were not just petitioners seeking office
or favors, but visitors of importance as well, on urgent official business—
senators, congressmen, generals, and cabinet officers—elbowing through
the crowd. "Congress," John Nicolay complained, "sends up a hungrier
swarm of gadflies every morning to bedevil the President, and to generally retard and derange business."[55]

Lincoln compared himself to a man who was so busy renting out
rooms at one end of the house that he couldn't stop to put out the fire
that was burning at the other end.[56] On some days he ordered the doors
flung open to all who were waiting, and they swarmed into the room
all together, where he took them one at a time, and called it "the Beggars' Opera."[57]

Some came only to shake his hand and wish him Godspeed. Others
came asking help for themselves or a loved one in the army; these usually pressed forward, careless in their pain about who overheard their
prayer. Still others lingered reluctantly in the rear of the room or along
its edges, leaning against the wall, waiting, hoping to be the last and to
be able to discuss things in a private tête-à-tête. Lincoln often made sad
havoc of their plans with a loud, hearty, "Well, friend, what can I do
for you?" compelling them to speak, retire, or wait for a more convenient season.

They came for as many reasons as there were needs. But Lincoln
seemed particularly to enjoy inventors, often men of originality and
eccentricity and more a source of amusement than annoyance. He liked
to tell in particular, with much merriment, of the inventor from deep in
the backwoods who advised him one day that "a gun ought not to
rekyle; if it rekyled at all, it ought to rekyle a little forrid."

On cabinet days—Tuesdays and Fridays—the interviews closed at
noon. The presidential lunch was rarely more than a biscuit and a glass
of milk, or a plate of fruit in season. The afternoon wore away in much
the same manner as the mornings—until late in the day, when the president often drove out with Mary for an hour's airing in a barouche. At
six he dined, eating sparingly of one or two courses, drinking little or
no wine, and never using tobacco. In the evenings he was generally
back in his office, although occasionally he remained in the drawing
room after dinner to entertain visitors or listen to music, his ear tuned
to simple ballads.

He was not often left alone evenings, even in his office, but frequently passed it with a few friends in frank and free conversation

about the course of war or politics; or in telling stories—being once more the lawyer of the Illinois Eighth Circuit, which he had traveled so often in quieter times. On some evenings he read aloud into the night from Shakespeare—*Hamlet, Macbeth,* and the histories—often with a single secretary for an audience.[58]

In the hot summer months the first family moved out to the Soldiers' Home, four miles from Washington on the Maryland side, where Lincoln passed the sweltering evenings. The presidential cottage sat on a wooded hill reached by a winding path and shaded by a spreading panoply of green branches. There the evening air was soft and cool and permeated by the woody odor of oak and willow. It gave escape from the heat, if not from war and politics.[59]

Lincoln rode into Washington from the Soldiers' Home in the mornings and out in the evenings, generally attended by an escort of twenty-five or thirty cavalry. The poet Walt Whitman, "a gentleman of the pavement," saw him nearly every day as he passed Vermont Avenue near L Street at about eight-thirty in the morning. Some days Lincoln rode horseback on an easygoing gray, at a slow trot toward Lafayette Square, with his cavalry escort following two-by-two. On some days he came riding in a barouche. In his plain black suit and high black hat, the president looked about as ordinary in attire as the commonest man. Whitman plainly saw his dark brown face, with the deep-cut lines, the expression of latent sadness. As Lincoln passed, the two men, who were never to meet, looked into each other's eyes and exchanged cordial bows.[60]

The cavalry escort wasn't Lincoln's idea, but Secretary of War Stanton's. The men in it often wondered why they were there at all. When they told Lincoln they thought they were of little use and were needed at the front, he said, "You boys remind me of a farmer friend of mine in Illinois, who said he could never understand why the Lord put the curl in a pig's tail. It never seemed to him to be either useful or ornamental, but he reckoned that the Almighty knew what he was doing when he put it there. . . . I don't think I need guards, but Mr. Stanton . . . thinks I do, and as it is in his Department, if you go to the front he will insist upon others coming from the front to take your place." Then, with a twinkle in his eye, Lincoln added, "and boys, I reckon it is pleasanter and safer here than there."[61]

An English visitor watching this entourage approach one day was hard-pressed to call the escort cavalry. Whitman said they rode with sabers drawn and held upright over their shoulders, making no great show in uniform or horses. The Englishman said, "I cannot call them cavalry, nor mounted rifles, nor *gendarmes,* nor anything else. The animals on which they rode had four legs, and an odd tail or two, and more or less the shape and manner of a horse, and I suppose they were intended for horses; but such a lot of bow-legged, cow-quartered, dead-alive quadrupeds I never saw. Of the riders themselves I can say less. They were dressed in the uniform of the Invalid Corps, light-blue, veritable shoddy, mud-bespattered, and threadbare as an Irishman's coat; such an ill-conditioned set of ruffians as Falstaff never would have led through Coventry."[62]

The escort, as the Englishman could see, was worthy of its charge, for this was a very democratic cortege. The barouche was "a very dirty, tumble-down machine, with an enormous hood, looking like a bathing-machine with the awning out." Lincoln, exiting this apparatus, completed the tableau to perfection: "a long, lank, lath-like, darkly-clad figure that seemed to unfold itself like the Genie of old before the gaze of the astonished fisherman, as if it were never coming to an end. But we watched patiently and at last the end came—and such an end. Such a pair of terminations were planted on the pavement as could belong to no biped but a Western Yankee or a Dodo."[63]

But that was Lincoln, who never pretended to be anything but what he was. And what he was was a common man who spoke the vocabulary of the common people. He had had a dream only the week before the New Year's levee at the White House. He was in a party of plain people in his dream, and as it became known who he was, they began to comment on his appearance. One of them said, "He is a very common-looking man." The president replied in his dream, "Common looking people are the best in the world: that is the reason the Lord makes so many of them."[64]

The editor Horace Greeley, who was wont to criticize the president politically, saw this commonness as well. Greeley would one day write, "There never yet was a man so lowly as to feel humbled in the presence of Abraham Lincoln; there was no honest man who feared or dreaded to meet him. . . ."[65] Lincoln was never quite comfortable with being called "Mr. President." One day he told an intimate friend, who called him that, "Now call me Lincoln, and I'll promise not to tell of the breach of etiquette—if you won't—and I shall have a resting-spell from 'Mister President.'"[66]

Carl Schurz said of Lincoln that "he personifies the people," that he was "the living embodiment of the popular will," who "felt instinctively the convictions and determination of the people because these went through the same course of development in him as in the masses; and what he said and did was the popular opinion expressed in the popular speech and fulfilled in the popular manner."[67] Others also saw in Lincoln what Schurz saw. The Massachusetts Republican congressman George S. Boutwell said of him that he possessed "the almost divine faculty of interpreting the will of the people without any expression by them."[68] He seemed possessed of an inner political tuning fork, set to the rhythms of the common man.

This, some suspected, was going to make him hard to beat in 1864. One day, one of Lincoln's common men, visiting Washington with his family, accidentally encountered the president on the portico before the White House. "The Lord is with you, Mr. President," the man said. Then, after hesitating a moment, he added, "And the people too, sir; and the people too!"[69]

Perhaps he was right. Many politicians didn't believe it—or didn't want to believe it. But the election year was here, and the country was about to find out if this common man so busy at the pump handle on this New Year's Day was reelectable. Time would soon tell.

7

STORKS BY
THE FROG POND

———

THE COUNTRY WAS STILL AN ICEBOX, AND NEW YORK CITY WAS IN her winter dress. She always looked fairest then, when snow was in the streets. And it was in the streets this January. All was bustle and excitement. Sleighs shushed in trafficky profusion along the white-clad avenues. Ladies with fur muffs chattered and giggled on their way to the frozen skating ponds of Fifth Avenue and Central Park.[1]

On January 12, in the early evening, the members of the Democratic National Committee began making their way through the bustle of the city and over the ice and snow to the Fifth Avenue mansion of financier August Belmont. It was the first time they had met since the summer of 1860. The hard early-January weather had kept a handful of western committeemen away. Otherwise they were all there.

Meeting them as they arrived at his door was Belmont himself, the national chairman, pale, sleek-headed, dapper, and smooth. He moved with the self-assurance of wealth and position, but with a permanent limp, the legacy of a duel fought over a lady's honor more than twenty years before.

Belmont was fifty now, an immigrant to America, an Austrian Jew born in the Rhenish Palatinate village of Alzey in 1813. He had been trained to the banking business in the famed Rothschild international investment house in Frankfurt. In 1837 he had migrated to the United States, established his own firm, and become Rothschild's agent in America. For a time in the 1840s he had been the U.S. counsel general to Austria, and in the 1850s ambassador to the Netherlands. Now, on this January evening in 1864, he was a banker of international celebrity and the leader of the Democratic party.

In 1849 Belmont had married Caroline Slidell Perry, the fourth daughter of Commodore Matthew C. Perry. Belmont called his bride the "beautiful & well-bred Caroline," and they were wed in November in New York's Protestant Episcopal Church of the Ascension.

The couple bought a splendid country house on upper Manhattan Island, in which, over the years, they had hosted some of the most famous visiting actresses and prima donnas in the world. Belmont was fond of masquerades and private theatricals, in which he often played the leading characters himself. He also owned a farm on Long Island where he ran his string of racehorses. And in the late 1850s he had acquired the mansion at the corner of Fifth Avenue at Eighteenth Street, where he and Caroline had continued to entertain with elegance and style. Belmont was a member of the exclusive Union Club, "the mother of clubs" in New York City. He was spectacularly connected, economically, socially, and politically.

He had been a Democrat since his naturalization in 1844. And in 1852 he had offered his political services to Caroline's uncle, Louisiana congressman John Slidell. He therefore started in politics at the top, cutting his teeth in James Buchanan's first run for the Democratic nomination for president in 1852. Buchanan lost, but by then Belmont was hooked on politics. Switching to the cause of the successful nominee, Franklin Pierce, he campaigned hard throughout the canvass.

Even when abroad in the years that followed, Belmont kept in touch with politics at home. As the presidential election of 1860 approached, and his friend, Illinois senator Stephen A. Douglas became the Democratic nominee, Belmont threw himself into that campaign. After the nominating convention in Baltimore, Douglas, as a reward, made Belmont the party's national chairman. When the war came and Douglas died, Belmont became, by default, the party leader and spokesman.

He was as pragmatic in politics as in finance, more interested in the practical perils of disunion than in the moral and humanitarian objections to slavery. He wished to save the Union from firebrands North and South. And when it suddenly fell to him to lead the party out of the election disaster and the postsecession chaos, he had acted as Douglas would have acted. He led a loyal opposition to Lincoln's side, contributing importantly to the war effort through his contacts abroad and in Northern financial circles.

But like every other Democrat, and many Republicans, Belmont now wanted a president other than Abraham Lincoln. By the evening of January 12, as his fellow national committeemen were arriving at his Fifth

Avenue mansion, he had become a strong McClellan man. Indeed, he had been working quietly for McClellan's nomination since 1862.[2]

Belmont opened the meeting and told his colleagues that the Democratic congressional delegation in Washington, at his request, had wired a preference for the time and place of the party's nominating convention. They had picked Cincinnati in May. Several committeemen, including Belmont, objected. Too early, they argued. If anything was working for the party it was time, the more of it the better—time to let further defeats on the battlefield, heavier taxes, and Lincoln's conscription policies take their toll on the Republican incumbent. So the committeemen fixed on July 4 for the convention instead of May, a late date for a convention, but full of pregnant patriotic meaning. They also overruled the congressmen on place, choosing Chicago over Cincinnati, as a tribute to Douglas.

Several present, Belmont among them, wanted the national committee to do more that evening than just set a time and place for the convention. They wanted to venture into policy making as well. They moved that the committee articulate for the country what it regarded as the party's authentic position on key issues. But that was too bold a step for most of them. It was usurping the national convention's function. The motion was voted down.[3]

August Belmont was a pacifier by inclination, ever interested in healing splits and papering over differences. He belonged to the right party, for at no time in its history had the Democratic party been this deeply split and at odds with itself. At no time had its differences needed so urgently to be papered over.

When the war came, many war-minded Democrats began bailing out, moving over to the new Union Party and into an unnatural alliance with the Republicans. It was a hard and radical step for many of these longtime Democrats. But even harder for them was the smack of treason that was attaching itself to their own party. Several Democratic stalwarts had defected: Daniel Dickinson of New York, David Tod and John Brough of Ohio, Ben Butler of Massachusetts, John Logan of Illinois, Andrew Johnson of Tennessee, and even Secretary of War Edwin Stanton. But they were difficult to number and pinpoint. It had been a revolt of the elite. The Democratic masses had largely held firm for the party. And even some of those who had jumped to the Union cause in 1861 and 1862 had become disillusioned. They had understood when they went over to the new party that Republican policies were to be dropped for a simple program of supporting the war. Slavery was not to be an issue. All differences were to be submerged solely in the common cause—winning the war and putting down the rebellion.

It hadn't worked out that way. The policies of the new party had turned out to be Republican party policies after all. And after the Emancipation Proclamation, many of the war Democrats had returned disillusioned to their old party, feeling that Lincoln had yielded to the Sumners and the Stevenses and their radical cohorts.

What was left, when the party's entire Southern contingent was shorn away by secession and many war Democrats had jumped to the Union Party, were two warring wings: the war Democrats who remained, such as August Belmont, who were faithful to both party and the war cause; and peace Democrats who were faithful to the party, but not the cause. The war wing supported a total prosecution of the war and the immediate reestablishment of the Union. In that, they were with Lincoln and the Republicans. The peace Democrats wanted peace and were willing, if necessary, to let the cotton states form a new nation—to let them go in peace, as Horace Greeley had once put it in a weak moment.[4]

This basic split was making it harder and harder to hold the party together long enough on a single united course to make a successful run at the presidency. They were as often as not fighting among themselves, spitting venom at one another instead of at the Republicans.

James Gordon Bennett, the sardonic editor of the *New York Herald*, put it this way: "They have a peace leg and a war leg, but, like a stork by a frog pond, they are as yet undecided which to rest upon."[5]

The seat of strength of the war Democrats was New York City, where Belmont lived. The seat of the peace Democrats was the Midwest and along the border, in Ohio in particular, where Clement Vallandigham, the prince of the copperheads, lived. The term "copperhead" had been coined in 1861 as an epithet, evoking the image of serpents of conspiracy in the northern Eden—"like copperheads and rattlesnakes in winter, cold in their stiff and silent coils," the "blind and venomous enemies of our government found in our midst," as the *Cincinnati Daily Commercial* had described them.[6]

Bennett called them the "peace patriots" and said, "Of all the small, insignificant, contemptible cliques that have ever disgraced the politics of this country the peace clique is the worst. It is equally despised by honest Union men and honest rebels." A reader of *The New York Times* wrote: "A copperhead is one who has all the instincts of a *traitor* without the pluck to be a *rebel*."[7]

By the fall and winter of 1862 the epithet was in general circulation in the North, and even the copperheads used it. Their slogan was "the Constitution as it is, the Union as it was, and the Negroes where they are." That precisely summarized their position. Their idea of reform was to overthrow the tyrant in the White House, end the war at once, and call a convention to restore the old Union on a compromise footing.[8]

Besides Vallandigham, the peace Democrats had George H. Pendleton, also of Ohio, who had assumed Vallandigham's mantle in Congress; Daniel Vorhees of Indiana; and Representatives Alexander Long, another Ohioan, and Benjamin Harris of Maryland.

These four peace leaders had recently been joined in the House by Fernando Wood, the former mayor of New York City. Wood was thin and elegant, with dyed hair and mustache. One critic said of him that "he has a perpetual smile on his face, which, cold and hollow, is well described by the word *smirk*. . . . There is an insincerity about him, which you feel whenever he speaks to you."[9] Wood not only tolerated secession, but was into it himself. As mayor of New York City as the war approached, he had suggested that it secede as well and become a free city. That had amused Lincoln, who said it would be like the front door setting up housekeeping on its own account.[10]

If Lincoln thought the radicals in his own party were unhandy devils to deal with, he could sympathize with the war Democrats trying to cope with their peace wing. The *Chicago Tribune* called the peace Democrats "doughface fanatics," and said, "They might as well . . . undertake to recall the Egyptian mummies to life as to save slavery. It is past doctoring. . . ."[11] The *New York Daily Tribune* found them to be an oxymoron. "A 'Peace Democrat,' when our country is fighting for existence," it had written just this January, "is rather a novelty. Usually, a Democrat, when he sees war made on the Stars and Stripes, 'goes in' for the old flag, without much inquiry as to whys or wherefores. To be 'ag'in the Cholera and in favor of the next War' used to be a test of Democracy."[12]

George McClellan, a firm war Democrat, considered peace Democrats fools who would destroy the Union for their own political purposes—the worst kind of viper in his book of virtues, no better than the blackguard politicians in the administration who had kept him from winning the war.

But they needed each other, these two wings of the party. It wouldn't be easy staggering along together. As Sunset Cox said, "We carry weights."[13] But pulling together was the only way the party could wrench power and the presidency from the Republicans. They agreed that Lincoln and the Republicans must go, but they couldn't agree on how to make it happen. They still had a few things working for them, however. Despite the defections and the differences, they were yet a potentially cohesive unit. Many of them, as one of them said, would vote the party ticket "if Gabriel's drum was sounding."[14]

The two wings of the party also still had much in common. Both abhorred the way the war had been broadened into an abolition crusade. Both believed that while waging a war to free the slave, the administration was also laying waste to civil liberties in the North. Both agreed that every action of the cursed government was a usurpation of power, a violation of civil liberty, a subversion of the Constitution. Both saw the Republican radicals promoting partisan ends by subduing Democrats and uplifting Negroes—all in the interest of remaking society and politics as they wished them to be. This must not be allowed. Belmont himself had said that Democrats were willing to fight for the Union, but not to fight a war of Southern extermination such as the Republican radicals had in mind. And in the Democratic view, the Republican radicals, not Lincoln, were calling the shots in Washington.

Lincoln's conscription act had outraged all Democrats. They saw it as contrary to the American experience and destructive of liberty, another step by an autocratic government unconstitutionally to control individuals and their behavior. The proper object of the war, they believed, was not to crush and conquer the South nor to destroy its social system, but to subdue its armies—while leaving Southern rights and property intact and Northern liberties uncompromised. They opposed the war's being perverted to any purpose of party aggrandizement, revolution, or other end than its original objective: to preserve the Constitution and the government—the simple and naked issue of restoring the Union. Freeing the slaves was thought by both wings of this beleaguered party to be unnecessary to that end.

A strong racist strain ran through the rhetoric of both wings of the party. They both talked of Lincoln and his "nigger-crazed counselors" and their plans to let "hordes" of slaves overrun the North, take land, compete with white workers, and, worst of all, marry white women. The drive to enlist Negro troops in the army was but the beginning. The Republicans had "nigger on the brain."[15]

The black former slave Frederick Douglass believed this racism that ran through Democratic party rhetoric showed them up for what they were. The party "has had but one vital and animating principle for thirty years," Douglass said, "and that has been the same old horrible and hell-born principle of negro Slavery. . . . Though it has lost in numbers, it retains all the elements of its former power and malevolence."[16]

Despite their similarities, their differences persisted. Many peace Democrats remained intransigent, many war Democrats impatient. It was still unclear, as the national committeemen met in Belmont's mansion in New York on January 12, whether they could work together when the crunch came. Despite their differences, the Democrats had a proven resiliency that made Republicans nervous. The abolitionist orator Wendell Phillips compared the party to a raft that no storm, however violent, was able to sink.[17] Besides, the war itself was a loose cannon. Anything could happen. No party was safe, and everybody knew it.

Though they still had sting, and the war itself made everything uncertain, it was not a good time to be a Democrat. The party was caught between those two monster isms of the times—the Scylla of abolitionism in the North and the Charybdis of secessionism in the South. And it had a problem it had never had before: How could it oppose Lincoln and the Republicans without seeming also to oppose the war, and therefore appear treasonous? In short, how could it avoid being lumped with the rebellion?

Many Democrats, such as August Belmont, were finding to their dismay that they couldn't. As one of Senator Ben Wade's friends said darkly, it was obvious "that there was a party in the North that did not enter cordially into the work of crushing the rebellion."[18]

The genial secretary of state, William Seward, could have told them, as he told John Hay one day, that such an image was death to a party. "One fundamental principle of politics," Seward told Hay, "is to be always on the side of your country in a war. It kills any party to oppose a war." Lincoln himself told Hay the story of an Illinois politician who was asked at the beginning of the Mexican War if he were not opposed to it, and he had said, "No. I opposed one war. That was enough for me. I am now perpetually in favor of war, pestilence and famine."[19]

Hay himself called the Democrats, including his friend Sunset Cox, "foul birds . . . croaking treason."[20] And everywhere epithets such as "copperheads," "secesh," "semisecesh," "disloyalists," and "assistant

Rebels" were being tossed about to describe all Democrats.[21] It was not unusual to hear somebody say of a Democrat that he was "entirely loyal—as much as any 'Democrat' can be."[22] If there was anybody ever damned with faint praise, that was it.

Unfortunately, Democratic prospects were tightly tied to how the war was going. If it was going badly, if the Union armies were taking a beating in the field, and the North was discouraged, their prospects brightened. When things were going well on the battlefield, their skies darkened. Even more so than the Republican radicals who opposed Lincoln on entirely different grounds, if they were to succeed, they needed the war to go sour. Nothing helped them so much as a defeat for Union arms.

This was not a new problem for an opposition party in time of war. But never was it so acute as in this one. To have one wing of the party that was against the war and seeking to appease the South at any price was an acute embarrassment for that wing of the party that wanted somehow to oppose only how the war was being waged and for what reasons. The peace Democrats made the whole party a sitting duck for the "traitor" label. Neither wing of this divided party dominated entirely. Since Douglas was dead, no one person now stood above all others in the party as its acknowledged leader and national symbol— not August Belmont, not anybody. But every Democrat, peace-minded or war-minded, knew the party had to work together if it hoped to win in November. Together they had a good chance; divided they had none.

Belmont and his fellow war Democrats thought they had the ideal solution to the party's problem in George McClellan. McClellan seemed the one man who could legitimize the Democratic opposition to the administration without having its loyalty questioned. He could challenge the Lincoln administration on its execution of policy without casting doubt on the party's patriotism. A year before, following the 1862 midterm elections, it had seemed that Horatio Seymour's nomination was a foregone conclusion. But he had mishandled the New York draft riots in July 1863 and his viability had worn thin.

Now the man of the hour was McClellan. The trick was how to get him nominated. Many peace Democrats thought him no better than Lincoln and the radicals. When he was commanding the Union army early in the war, he had suppressed civil liberties in Maryland in the interest of military security. They had never forgiven him for that. They said that they would support his nomination only on a peace platform and on no other. The party was in a fix, between the rock and the hard place.

McClellan, meanwhile, was on his peaceful mountaintop in New Jersey, trying to stay out of the fight, or above it at least, until spontaneously called. He was being counseled by his backers to take the peace wing's sensitivities into account. Try to be civil to them, he was urged, and keep an open mind to any honorable opportunity for peace and union.[23]

For his part, McClellan believed he was being put upon unreasonably. When a friend wrote him late in the old year with words of praise and encouragement, he wrote back on New Year's Day: "In these days when I sometimes hear that one old friend is angry with me because I said something, another because I said nothing, a third because I would not do something that was impossible to do, a fourth because I did something that I could not avoid doing, it is most gratifying to hear that I still have some . . . friends left. . . ."[24]

McClellan's report on the Army of the Potomac while under his command had just come out. It was long, a thousand printed pages, longer twice over, the unsympathetic *New York Times* noted, than Caesar's *Commentaries*. "Wellington, though seven years in the Peninsula, never wrote a paper that would fill twenty of these pages," the *Times* said. All of Grant's reports, one atop the other, could be read in sixty minutes, McClellan's hardly begun in that time. "If it is less than a Report," the *Times* complained, "it is also more than a Report. It is less than a Report, because numerous dispatches of the time are omitted from this collection. It is also more than a strictly military Report, because its basis is an elaborate, historical, and argumentative recital. . . . Its purpose seems to be less to record a series of military transactions than to vindicate his conduct and arraign the Administration."[25]

But the report was important to McClellan. It was to serve as an unofficial opening shot in his presidential campaign.

The presidential campaign was indeed opening for the Democrats already. The national committeemen had met at August Belmont's house. McClellan's report was out—to mixed reviews. A propaganda arm, the Society for the Diffusion of Political Knowledge, had been organized to pump out anti-Lincoln pamphlets and was already cranking up.

A consortium of New York war Democrats headed by Belmont and S. L. M. Barlow had bought their own newspaper in September 1862, an independent religious sheet called the *New York World*. They had changed it, making it over into the party's leading national voice, coming out daily, pounding the Republicans unmercifully.

Its young editor, Manton Marble, was not yet thirty years old and about to be married. But he was an experienced journalist beyond his years. And he had a clear presentiment of the peril that lay ahead for his party. "For myself," he would write a friend early in this election year, "I say that I believe any man who runs for the Presidency on an open Peace Platform, McClellan, Seymour or any one else is doomed to an utter rout at the polls. There ends all hope of Union & of the old form & spirit of govt."[26]

Yet that was precisely where this tortured party seemed headed in this new year. The prospects seemed as cold as the weather. But there was laughter on the skating ponds, and spring lay ahead and summer just beyond that. Anything could happen between now and then, and probably would.

8

CRAZY JANE
AND BEAST BUTLER

———•◆•———

O N THE DAY THE DEMOCRATS MET AT AUGUST BELMONT'S
mansion in New York, Washington was ice-locked. The roads
were clogged with snow, and the Potomac was frozen from the
Capitol to Alexandria. Teams of horses were crossing on the rock-hard
river. Noah Brooks believed it frozen solid enough to bear the weight
of the entire Confederate army.[1]

In the city the sidewalks were slippery and sleighs were in heavy
demand, renting for as high as fifteen dollars an hour.[2]

The seasonal round of winter maladies had blown in with the cold.
Washington was what one English visitor described as "an over-grown
watering-place" where "everybody is a bird of passage," mere lodgers.[3]
It also tended to be, as Brooks reported, "the very paradise and manu-
factory of coughs, colds, and influenza," where not just one handkerchief was needed, but a minimum of four a day—half a dozen for the
worst nose cases.[4]

A smallpox scare had come in with the cold and the coughs. The hospitals throughout the city were reporting twenty to thirty deaths a day.
It was an epidemic, serious enough to cause Lincoln to wire his son
Robert, who had planned to bring friends home from Harvard on a
winter break, that he might want to reconsider. "There is a good deal
of small-pox here," the president warned. "Your friends must judge for
themselves whether they ought to come or not."[5]

Lincoln was thinking, however, more about his party's coming nominating convention in Baltimore in June and the election in November
than about the lesser threat of smallpox. Two of his sometime political
confidants, Leonard Swett of Illinois and Thurlow Weed of New York,
had recently visited him at the White House.

"Do you know that the people begin to talk about your renomination?" Swett ventured.

Lincoln turned in his chair and, after a moment's pause, said, "Swett, do you know that same bee has been buzzing in my bonnet for several days?"[6]

It was more than a buzzing in Lincoln's bonnet. On back-to-back days in early January, he met to discuss the presidential campaign—with Gideon Welles, old man Blair, and former Ohio governor William Dennison on January 10, and with Dennison again and Montgomery Blair the following day.[7]

Lincoln wasn't a politician to sit and wait for things to happen. He was not a man, his law partner, Billy Herndon, said, who "gathered his robes about him, waiting for the people to call. . . . He was always calculating, and always planning ahead. His ambition was a little engine that knew no rest."[8]

Early in January, Welles was telling his diary that he thought a pretty strong current was setting in Lincoln's favor as the Union Party candidate. Welles, for one, believed it a good thing, best for the country, to reelect the president, and wrote that "if I mistake not this is the public opinion."[9]

There was indeed no lack of continuing interest in the president by the public. As Welles was about to enter a cabinet meeting in mid-February, an attractive lady from Dubuque pressed him to tell the president she wished to see him. Welles told Lincoln, who invited her in. She said she had come all the way from Baltimore just to have a look at him.

"Well, in a matter of looking at one another," Lincoln said, "I have altogether the advantage."[10]

James Russell Lowell had been looking at Lincoln as well, and weighing his political assets. Writing in the *North American Review* in January, Lowell analyzed the nearly three years of Lincoln's presidency and pronounced them good for the country.

He cited the steady progress of those jarring years, and said it was "mainly due to the good sense, the good humor, the sagacity, the large-mindedness, and the unselfish honesty of the unknown man whom a blind fortune, as it seemed, had lifted from the crowd to the most dangerous and difficult eminence of modern times. . . ."

Lowell wrote that "if we wish to appreciate him, we have only to conceive the inevitable chaos in which we should now be weltering, had a weak man or an unwise one been chosen in his stead"—a Democrat, for instance. "Perhaps none of our Presidents since Washington," Lowell said, "has stood so firm in the confidence of the people as he does after three years of stormy administration."

It seemed to Lowell that, despite the country's impatience, Lincoln "has always waited, as a wise man should, till the right moment brought up all his reserves." He seemed to know, as wise men do, not only when he was ready, but when he was not ready, and was "firm against all persuasion and reproach till he is." The president was not one "to run straight at all hazards," but rather proceeded about things with a "cautious but sure-footed understanding." He first assured himself, with his setting pole, where the main current was, and kept to that. "He is still in wild water," Lowell concluded, "but we have faith that his skill and sureness of eye will bring him out right at last."[11]

Lowell's panegyric was the strongest gun that had yet boomed for the president. And it caused a stir in the country and a rash of sullen grumbling among the radicals.

There was nothing certain about this election. As John Nicolay had confided in the year just ended, in one of his regular letters to his fiancée in Illinois, "So much depends upon the success or failure of our arms that it seems idle to speculate at all about the results." That was still the case. The new year had come in with doubt, darkness, and uncertainty, despite the battlefield victories of the past summer and fall. The war had taken its toll, and no certain end to it was yet in sight. But Nicolay also believed that nothing could prevent Lincoln's renomination and reelection but a series of disastrous setbacks on the battlefield.[12]

Congressman Owen Lovejoy was one of those radicals whose sternness was tempered with affection. He and Lincoln were both from Illinois and had been friends for years. Lovejoy liked the president personally, while chafing, as every other radical did, under his plodding policies. Among other things, Lovejoy appreciated Lincoln's sense of the ridiculous. The Illinois congressman had once gone to Secretary of War Stanton with a presidential order, which Stanton read and refused to carry out.

"But we have the President's order, sir," Lovejoy protested.

"Did Lincoln give you an order of that kind?" Stanton demanded.

"He did, sir."

"Then he is a d——d fool."

Lovejoy was aghast. "Do you mean to say the President is a d——d fool?" he asked.

"Yes, sir," said the secretary, "if he gave you such an order as that."

The scandalized Lovejoy took this conversation back to Lincoln. Lincoln listened, then asked, "Did Stanton say I was a d——d fool?"

"He did, sir, and repeated it."

After a moment's consideration, the president looked up and said goodnaturedly, "If Stanton said I was a d——d fool, then I must be one, for he is nearly always right, and generally says what he means."[13]

It sounded like Stanton, all right. Lincoln had an understanding with his irascible secretary of war that if he sent over an order that could not be consistently granted, Stanton was to refuse it, which he sometimes did, often with an embellishment such as this one. When another petitioner at another time likewise returned to Lincoln empty-handed to complain of Stanton's intransigence, Lincoln had explained, "I [haven't] much influence with this administration, but [expect] to have more with the next."[14]

Lovejoy hadn't been feeling well in this new year. Indeed, he had been desperately ill. But even in his illness he sensed something about Lincoln's prospects. "It is of no use talking, or getting up conventions against him," Lovejoy told the young painter Francis Carpenter. "He is going to be the candidate of the Baltimore Convention, and is sure to be reelected. 'It was foreordained from the foundation of the world'. . . . He is too strong with the masses."[15] And Lovejoy was content with that. "If he is not the best conceivable President," he wrote the abolitionist William Lloyd Garrison in February, "he is the best possible."[16]

There were others who were seeing the same thing, even though they were hedging their bets. "No man at this moment has so sure a hold of the national heart," *Harper's Weekly* editorialized early in the new year. "If the Presidential election took place next week, Mr. Lincoln would undoubtedly be returned by a greater majority than any President since Washington. And unless he is deserted by his great sagacity, or some huge military disaster befalls the country, or some serious blunder is committed by the Union men in Congress, his election is as sure as the triumph of the nation over the rebellion."[17] At about the same time the *Chicago Tribune*, out in the country's heartland, was editorializing: "God meant him for President, or the nation is deceived."[18]

Even that most adamant of the slavery-slayers, William Lloyd Garrison, seemed to be agreeing with both God and his friend Owen Lovejoy on the subject. Garrison himself would admit that for every word he had ever spoken in Lincoln's favor, he had spoken ten against him. But by early this election year he was speaking that one in ten *for* him.

Garrison told a meeting of the Massachusetts Anti-Slavery Society in January that, "taking all things into consideration—especially in view of the fact that he has not only decreed the liberation of every slave in Rebeldom forever, but stands repeatedly committed, as no other man does, before heaven and earth, to maintain it so long as he is in office—in my judgment the reelection of Abraham Lincoln to the Presidency of the United States would be the safest and wisest course. . . ."[19]

Out in the country, Lincoln partisans were moving to set this sentiment in concrete. Wielding patronage either as stilettos or bludgeons—whatever it took—they were quietly lining up delegates and endorsements. The first sign of this came in New Hampshire. There, Lincoln agents moved in on the state Union Party convention at Concord in January and rammed through a resolution calling for his renomination. The New Hampshire endorsement was a wake-up call for Pennsylvania. There the Union Party's contingent in the state legislature heard of it and also hurried to endorse the president's nomination and reelection. Watching from Washington, John Hay said, "They saw their thunder stolen from their own arsenals. They fear their own endorsement will be *passee* before long and are now casting about to get some arrangement for putting him in nomination at once."[20]

Endorsements from legislatures and party conventions had either come in or were in the works as well in Connecticut, New Jersey, Maryland, Minnesota, Kansas, Missouri, California, Indiana, Illinois, and New York. There seemed to be a bandwagon moving early in this election year. And the sentiment was strongest in the small towns in the nation's heartland. Small pro-Union newspapers everywhere were saying good things about Lincoln and calling for his reelection.[21]

The same could not be said for some of the powerful partisan newspapers in the big cities, however—or for most politicians in Washington. They were not seeing the same thing others were seeing—or were not wanting to see it. These early preconvention endorsements were not pleasing them.

They were particularly not pleasing George Wilkes, editor of the radical mouthpiece *Spirit of the Times*. Wilkes was convinced of Lincoln's inferiority and unworthiness. "Manifestly," he had recently written, ". . . this excellent man, though honest as the sun, and perhaps the best story teller in the world, is not the statesman to pluck this groveling country from the mire. . . ." Wilkes called the rush of endorsements an attempt "to steal . . . the *nomination,* and to *cheat* the usual convention of the people." He accused the president of being "thoroughly cognizant of the whole movement, and . . . plunged to his arm-pits in the succulent patronage which he is doling out in its support."[22]

James Gordon Bennett at the *New York Herald* was no less insulting. "What has President Lincoln done to entitle him to a re-election?" Bennett protested in late January. "We contend that he has done nothing to earn this high distinction, but that, on the contrary, in the conduct of the war, his deplorable mismanagement of our most important armies, with the disastrous and alarming consequences, have furnished evidence sufficient to convince the country that he is not the pilot to carry us through the perils of this war into the broad and secure anchorage of a re-established Union." This was followed by a plug for General Ulysses S. Grant for president.[23]

The truth of the matter was, nobody knew for sure what the country was thinking. And much of whatever thinking there was, particularly by anti-Lincoln politicians in Washington, was wishful.

No one was more wishful than Thaddeus Stevens. On the House floor in January he had said, "If the question could be submitted to the loyal people of these United States whom they would select for their next President, a majority of them would vote for General [Benjamin F.] Butler."[24]

George Ashmun of Massachusetts was one politician who was not thinking wishfully. He was certain where all this opposition was leading: nowhere. He wrote in early February, "There are weak men enough, too many, in & out of Congress, ready to embark in the most preposterous enterprise; but the sum of the whole is that the good sense of the country will demand the re-election of Mr. Lincoln so emphatically as, by the by, to render all opposition not only futile, but injurious to those who may have risked their fortunes in it."[25]

Into the cold January weather drifted a figure as warm and mesmerizing as summer sunshine, a phenomenon as unlikely as a Stevens endorsement of Abraham Lincoln.

Anna Elizabeth Dickinson had only just turned twenty-two. But she was the phenomenon of the nation's oratorical circuit. On January 16 she was to address a public meeting in the hall of the House of Representatives. Lincoln had received her in the White House earlier in the day, and planned to attend her lecture in the Capitol later that evening.

If there was ever a comet from nowhere, bursting without warning on the public ken, dazzling it with brilliant light, it was Anna Dickinson. Until age eighteen, she had been an obscure Quaker girl from

Philadelphia, working in the United States mint. Her unsuspected talent for oratory had erupted unheralded one evening in early 1860 at a meeting of the Association of Progressive Friends in Philadelphia. A man had made a case for female inferiority that had lit Anna's fuse. She had leaped to her feet, the oratory had poured eloquently out, and a star was born.

In the following months her part-time speaking career away from the mint rocketed spectacularly. She became locally celebrated, holding Quaker and antislavery meetings around Philadelphia in thrall with her blunt and volcanic oratory. People began flocking to see and hear her. William Lloyd Garrison caught this teenaged prodigy for the first time at a speech to the annual meeting of the Pennsylvania Anti-Slavery Society in October 1861, and was as dazzled as everybody else by her "remarkable oratorical fluency."[26]

Under his wing she quickly became the sensation of the national antislavery speech circuit, second only to Wendell Phillips, drawing crowds like a magnet. Her flying mane of hair, her rapid-fire delivery, her withering sarcasm, her beauty, and the sheer novelty of a girl among the good old boys of abolitionism, set audiences gasping, then cheering.

Following the battle of Ball's Bluff, a small Union disaster south of Washington in October 1861, Anna had boldly embraced military criticism for the first time, raking poor George McClellan unmercifully, charging him not simply with ignorance and incompetence, but with treason. She had not let up on him since. Her outburst against the general lost her her job at the mint and catapulted her full-time into oratory. She was only nineteen then, afire with passion for emancipation and the abolition cause.

One reporter called her "this most charming of female Demosthenes."[27] Many admirers, looking for a comparison easier to pronounce and relate to, began calling her the new Joan of Arc, a Maid of Orleans for these troubled times.

It was but a matter of time before she was a hot item on the Republican campaign circuit and a potent tool for the radicals. She made her stump debut in the fall campaigns of 1863 in New Hampshire, speaking for James A. Gilmore, the Republican abolitionist running for governor. She delivered more than twenty speeches on his behalf, mostly in small towns, attracting the largest crowds of any speaker. From New Hampshire she had gone by popular demand to Connecticut, "sent from on high," one editor suggested, "to save the state."[28]

Connecticut's was perhaps the most clear-cut race in the country—a very radical Republican against a very copperhead Democrat, as black and white as the contest in Ohio. The Republicans sent in a phalanx of speakers, blanketing the state. But none had Anna's impact. She traveled and fulminated for a fortnight to overflow crowds, finishing with the campaign's windup address in the state capital. When the Republican incumbent, William A. Buckingham, beat the copperhead Democratic ex-governor, Thomas H. Seymour, Anna got most of the credit.

She was likened not only to Joan of Arc, but to Portia, Pythia, Evangeline, Juliet, and Cassandra. She had become a prophetess. The Democrats, understandably less enchanted, called her that "spiritual medium," that "political witch," that "parrot," that "crowing hen."[29]

But suddenly she was a national political force. And here she was in Washington on January 16, in the big election year, a girl of twenty-two, invited by both houses of Congress, and booked to speak in the hall of the House of Representatives. It was unprecedented.

Anna was open-faced, sunny, and bright. Her nose was Grecian, her chin set. Her eyes were large and gray and flashing, her hair was short and black and wavy, curling slightly and tossing about her head as she spoke. She was of medium height and slender, but with a full, graceful figure. Early in her meteoric career, she had kept that figure clothed in simple Quaker gray with its white surplice. But as her fame grew she began dressing in "a style halfway between that of Quakerism and the world." By 1864 she had become a fashion plate known on occasion to wear diamonds and lace. Newspaper reporters debated among themselves whether she was "beautiful" or merely "handsome" and "prepossessing."[30]

Her voice was a strong contralto "of remarkable power and sweetness," one reporter wrote, which she tended to use as a lash.[31] The most devastating weapon in her oratorical arsenal was her sarcastic scorn, which she heaped with searing effect on any foe of the principles she supported. She hooted and jeered her villains, the Southern slaveholders and their Northern sympathizers, the Democrats. Even Lincoln was a stock character in her oratory, pictured as a hero when his behavior was satisfactory, as a villain when it wasn't. When he dragged his feet on emancipation, she called him "an Ass . . . for the Slave Power to ride."[32]

Her tongue-lashings, distinctly enunciated, had a penetrating effect. She had no trouble making herself heard in the remotest corners of the nation's largest lecture halls. She was not an original thinker, but depended on the more gifted abolitionists and radicals for the powder in the pyrotechnics she hurled from her platforms. And by this January in 1864 she had become a powerful weapon in their arsenal.[33]

The cold weather had let up in the week before her scheduled oration in Washington. The thermometer was still falling below freezing overnight, but the days had been milder. The temperature would drop below freezing again this night, but it wouldn't keep the crowd from the lecture hall.[34] This was an event not to be missed. Never before had a woman been invited to speak in the halls of Congress—much less a mere girl. Tickets had gone on sale two days before, and had been quickly snapped up.[35]

On the evening of the oration, she entered the hall at seven-thirty, escorted by Speaker Schuyler Colfax and Vice President Hannibal Hamlin. More than 2,500 persons thronged the floor and galleries of the hall, among them congressmen, senators, cabinet members, Supreme Court justices, reporters, diplomats, and generals. The hall was brightly accented with the gay attire of ladies in their velvets, flowers, and brilliant hues. Anna herself, her wavy black hair in short curls, wore a black silk gown with red velvet furbelows and a long train—nothing of the Quaker in it, but wholly of the world.[36]

A temporary platform had been erected in front of the clerk's desk for her, Hamlin, and Colfax. Hamlin introduced her, comparing her to the Maid of Orleans, and she began pacing the platform—to quiet the stage fright she always felt but never let show—and launched into her oration, titled "Words for the Hour."[37]

To and fro she paced. Her words for the hour thundered and volleyed. Her graphic descriptions and word pictures of the battle of Missionary Ridge and kindred scenes were vivid, bringing down the house "with thunders of applause." Noah Brooks, somewhat leery of the whole thing, described her speech as a series of random sketches loosely strung together into "a pleasant bit of mosaic, with here and there a patch of very common earthenware dovetailed between the sparkles of wit and hearty good sense." Brooks thought, "She will flash out her brief and splendid career and then subside into the destiny of all women and be heard of no more."[38]

But on this evening she was being heard clearly. And just as she was venomously raking Lincoln's liberal reconstruction policy, the president and Mary arrived. Lincoln took a seat directly in front of the platform and began to listen with bowed head as she soared into her scathing peroration. His sudden entrance had somewhat discombobulated the young orator. Having roundly smitten his policy, she suddenly, in a spectacular turnaround, endorsed his reelection, ending with mention of the work that "was left for his second term of office."

That wasn't exactly what she had planned to say—or what her radical mentors had in mind—but then she always spoke extemporaneously and was given to immoderate statements. It was right in character, and it was just the correct climactic touch. The audience, at first stunned by this abrupt turnabout in drift, broke out in "volleys of cheers." Lincoln's careworn face seemed to droop further still— whether caused by her endorsement or the idea of another four years of this, nobody could tell.[39]

The next day the *Washington Chronicle* applauded her "graceful allusion" to a second term and said her lecture ended on a peroration "whose beauty it were a shame to mar by synopsis."[40] Anna went on the road from Washington to other platforms, where she stepped up the venom of her attacks on the president's policy, unencumbered from then on by an accompanying endorsement.

It had been an evening to remember. One of Anna's friends wrote her, "You have conquered Washington—you have taken the capital. . . . I only wish you could take Richmond as easily. . . ." Not everybody was enchanted, however. A London correspondent called her a "crazy Jane in a red jacket," and wondered how Congress could have let her into its halls with such an exhibition. One Democratic congressman called her speech a partisan "political rhapsody," and introduced a formal resolution of condemnation.[41]

If Anna Dickinson couldn't easily get to Richmond, Lincoln had another visitor, a few days later, who figured he could, and was making plans to do so—not just to Richmond, but politically far beyond. If anything, this visitor was more striking than the girl orator—not in looks, certainly, but in moxie. And he now commanded the Union army's Department of Virginia and North Carolina headquartered in Fortress Monroe, at the very gates of Richmond.

No two men could have been less alike or more the same than this visitor, Maj. Gen. Benjamin F. Butler, and his White House host. Butler was radical, Lincoln was conservative; Butler was unforgiving, Lincoln merciful; Butler was rashness personified, Lincoln patience incarnate;

Butler was inflammatory, Lincoln conciliatory. Lincoln was humble and Butler was anything but. They were both outstanding politicians, however, and they both needed each other. They were the North's political odd couple.[42]

Butler came often to the White House—ignoring the military chain of command—to talk things over with Lincoln when he wanted something or had something to suggest. He was there again on January 20 for another long afternoon interview with the president. Butler was going to be a player in this election year, and Lincoln always took time and care to deal with players.

Butler had been a slight, sickly youth and young man, a ninety-seven-pound weakling, when he graduated from Waterville College in Maine at age twenty. But that had been twenty-five years ago, and he now had his full ration of bodily avoirdupois to go with his thick, bald, bullet-shaped head. But Butler's most startling physical characteristic was his eyes. They were wildly, blatantly crossed, a textbook case of strabismus. One observer who had had the misfortune to be hailed before him when he was the military governor of New Orleans two years earlier testified that those two eyes also were at cross purposes, vastly different in function and expression. "From one seemed to look out benignity," that victim remembered, "and from the other, malignity."[43]

Under Butler's bullet dome, behind those crossed eyes, resided one of the most shrewdly calculating intelligences in the country. A judge who knew him from his lawyering days told John Hay that Butler was "the smartest damned rascal that ever lived."[44]

He had been thought a rascal since childhood, known in his neighborhood in Deerfield, Massachusetts, where he grew up, as "the dirtiest, sauciest, lyingest child on the road."[45] By the time he had reached manhood and was practicing law in Lowell, he was being called much worse—an "infamous arch demagogue" and "political scoundrel."[46] Part of this animosity owed to the fact that he was also devastatingly effective. He was a tough man to beat in a courtroom, adept at getting evidence in and keeping it out.

Butler prided himself on being a man who always paid his debts—meaning he always got even. "He learns everything and forgets nothing," an admirer said of him when he was the military governor of New Orleans. He had shown himself gifted beyond measure at lawyering, politicking, and making money. It had been heard frequently among Union men that they wished Butler was president, for though he would make millions for himself during the first three months, he would finish the war in three months more.[47]

Butler's wife, Sarah, who loved him dearly, and was at least as shrewd as he was, but of a much more romantic nature, said of him affectionately that he was a man who liked the tempest and evoked the thunder and the flashing lightning.[48]

It was in his choice of a wife that Butler had been at his shrewdest. Sarah Hildreth Butler was the daughter of a Massachusetts physician. Her passion for drama and Shakespeare had made an actress of her, before she met and married Ben Butler. She was beautiful, articulate, popular with soldiers and politicians alike, a tremendous political asset for her socially grating husband. And Butler, no fool, saw this talent and attempted always to use it. Wanting to win some influence with General U. S. Grant, Butler urged her, "If you do all that your knowledge of the world, tact, and genius will enable you to do, then you will do a thousand times more in captivating the woman [Mrs. Grant] than I could possibly do with the husband."[49]

Butler deeply loved and trustingly confided in this partner of broad, lucid intelligence. He viewed her as "an adviser, faithful and true, clearheaded, conscientious and conservative, whose conclusions could always be trusted. . . . All that she agreed to was right and for the best; and if there is anything in my administration of affairs that may be questioned, it is that in which I followed the bent of my own opinions."[50]

Butler was born on November 5, 1818, a date celebrated in England for Guy Fawkes, a noted demolitionist who had conspired to blow up Parliament with gunpowder in 1605. Butler's father was a notorious privateer who died in the West Indies of yellow fever when Ben was only four months old.

The privateer's son was frail in body, but vigorous in belligerence. He was also a relentless reader, with a gift for total retention. He soon had the four Gospels memorized, every word.

This was appropriate, since his mother's most ardent hope was for her talented son to become a Calvinist Baptist clergyman. Failing to get into West Point, his own ardent hope, he tried it her way. But at Waterville College his interests had soon drifted off into such secular sidetracks as chemistry, particularly alchemy. And after college he took up law instead of religion.

Law turned out to be Butler's natural calling. By the beginning of the Civil War he was arguably New England's most skillful and successful attorney. He had also made a large place for himself in politics. A war Democrat, he had used his political clout and know-how to make himself a brigadier general from the outset, one of the very first of the political generals, and easily one of the worst. Virtually every engagement or battle that he had anything to do with had failed dismally. When John Hay suggested to the president that he thought Butler was the only man in the army to whom power would be dangerous, Lincoln said, "Yes, he is like Jim Jett's brother. Jim used to say that his brother was the damnedest scoundrel that ever lived, but in the infinite mercy of Providence he was also the damnedest fool."[51]

Butler was, however, spectacular at innovative administration and military politics, which made up for any drawbacks on the battlefield. To Butler went credit for instituting the practice of holding runaway slaves as contraband of war, a precedent that in late 1861 inspired the Confiscation Act, and made Butler the darling of the radical Republicans. Many of them, early in 1864, clearly favored Ben Butler over Abraham Lincoln—even over Salmon Chase—as the next president.

Butler's most memorable tour of duty, the one that had made his reputation North and South, had been his stint as the military governor of New Orleans following its capture in the spring of 1862. He had ruled the city with a fist of iron. When one Southern gallant burned the American flag in the streets of New Orleans, Butler had him hung. When the ladies of New Orleans spat on Union soldiers, insulted them on the streets, and doused Admiral David Farragut with a chamber pot of "not very clean water,"[52] Butler issued an order that they were all to be treated henceforth as prostitutes. The hanging put a damper on desecration of the flag, and the "woman order" stopped the insults and the unauthorized dumping of chamber pots.

The South, outraged when he hung the flag burner, was incensed by his woman order. It offended Southern gallantry to its core and inflamed the Southern heart as did nothing else in the entire war. From that day on, Butler became known and detested throughout the Confederacy as "Beast" Butler, public enemy number one. Jefferson Davis put a price on his head. If captured, Davis ordered, he was to be treated as a felon, "an outlaw and common enemy of mankind," and hung on the spot.[53] This was gratitude for you, for only two years before, at the Democratic National Convention in 1860, Butler, then a Democrat, had voted fifty-seven times for Davis as the party's nominee for president.

Those who didn't call Butler "Beast" called him "Spoons," for it was alleged he stole silver spoons and other valuables from the mansions of wealthy southerners in New Orleans. But whatever he was called, he had been an effective administrator. He had enforced order, maintained quiet, cleaned the city, wiped out the dreaded yellow fever, and ruled with a harsh but equitable hand. A villain in the South, he was a hero in the North. Because of this, and given his ambition and his political savvy, he was a force to be reckoned with in the coming election year.[54]

Lincoln knew Spoons was a man worth keeping an eye on—for more reasons than one. Whenever he came to town he was welcome to stop in.

9

THE PUDDING
DON'T RISE

———※———

EBRUARY IN WASHINGTON WAS SENDING OUT SIGNALS OF A GOOD
year. Lent had come, but the partying—John Nicolay called it the
"gayiety"—which generally tailed off with the beginning of the
holy season, still roared gaily on.[1]

Even the weather was kind. The terrible winter seemed to be loos-
ening its grip at last. It had been mild for nearly two weeks, the frost
was out of the ground, and the roads were drying. Washington was
expecting an early spring and an early beginning of armies moving
southward en masse—and perhaps an end to the war at last. It had
grown a little colder again by the tenth of the month, and on that day
the wind was high and the dust was kicking up. But it was still bright
and beautiful.[2]

At about eight-thirty that evening, the fire broke out. To everybody's
horror in the White House, the stables were on fire. Lincoln raced out
of the Executive Mansion, leaped over the boxwood hedge that
enclosed them, and demanded to know if the horses had been removed.
When he learned they hadn't, he flung open the stable door. The whole
interior was aflame. Any attempt to rescue the horses was futile. Lincoln appeared ready to enter anyhow, but was caught and restrained.
All six horses perished. Lincoln's coachman, who had been fired that
day, was arrested the next on charges of arson. Tad was inconsolable.
He had nearly lost Jack. Now his two ponies were dead, perished in the
fire. Suddenly, for the Lincolns, it was looking like anything but a good
year.[3]

Three days later, Saturday the thirteenth, was a beautiful springlike
day, bright and warm, and Attorney General Edward Bates was
tempted out for the first time after a two-week confinement with a deep

cold. He saw some friends, conversed for a while in passing with Maj. Gen. Dan Sickles, then called on the president.

Edward Bates had been around for nearly as long as weather itself. Joseph Medill, the often unsympathetic editor of the *Chicago Tribune,* described him as "a fossil of the Silurian era—red sandstone at least— who should never have been quarried out of the rocks in which he was embedded." Bates was a man with an old-fashioned interior and exterior, the oldest member of the cabinet at seventy-two. He had been a foremost politician from Missouri for what seemed eons. The hair on his head was still dark and ruddy, though his beard was now shrubby and pure white. Lincoln affectionately explained that was "because Bates uses his chin more than his head." He was slight of build, with a gentle but rugged face, a vigorous nose, heavy brows, and pensive and questioning eyes. He was said to be a literal logician, wholly lacking in imagination, who believed solely in God, the law, and the Constitution. He kept a daily diary, noteworthy for its disregard for correct spelling. He was deeply immersed in classic lore, he wrote with a rather crabbed pen, and they all called him "Granny Bates."[4]

Bates hardly disagreed with this description. He spoke of himself as a "garrulous old man," and nobody seemed willing to disagree.[5] He was still a Whig at heart, now belonging to no party and glad of it. "When the Whig party committed suicide, in 1856, and thereby left the nation without a *bodyguard,*" he explained, "I died with it."[6]

He was still alive enough to be a force. "I know very little of what is going on in politics and electioneering . . ." he admitted. "Nobody approaches me, to make interest, nor thinks it worth while (or perhaps safe) to tell me what he is aiming at. . . . But in my own quiet way—by letters to friends, and by the inculcation of principles, in my opinions and other public documents—I give Mr. Lincoln the best support I can; and I believe that, in some quarters, it is not without effect."[7]

On this springlike day in February the garrulous old man stopped in at the White House to see about giving Mr. Lincoln some of the best support he could, early in this election year. For half an hour they talked, mostly about the presidential canvass and the radicals. Both were on everybody's mind just then.

Lincoln was "fully apprehensive of the schemes of the Radical leaders," Bates told his diary that evening. "When I suggested some of their plots, he said they were almost *fiendish*. He is also fully aware that they would strike him at once, if they durst; but they fear that the blow would be ineffectual, and so, they would fall under his power, as *beaten enemies;* and for that reason only the hypocrits try to occupy equivocal ground—so that, when they fail, as *enemies,* they may still pretend to be *friends.*"

The president told Bates that the extremists—Bates called them the Chase men—had called several caucuses in the hope of finding it safe to take open ground against his nomination. Bates tried to impress on the president that the radicals needed him quite as much as he needed them—that they were cunning and unscrupulous, and that when they found they dared not openly oppose him, they would instead try to commit him to as many of their extreme measures as possible, so as to drive off his other friends. This would go on, Bates predicted, until the president was weakened down to their level and it became safe for them to cast him off. Bates believed Lincoln saw that plainly.

"I remarked to him," Bates told his diary, "that if he stood out manfully against the unprincipled designs of the Radicals, I thought it would be easy to bring all the old Whigs to his support." Lincoln thought that was probably true, not only of the old Whigs but of the better sort of Democrats as well. Bates thought the president seemed very hopeful that the designs of the radicals would fail and that in the end his friends would be able to counteract them.

"My chief fear," Bates confided to his diary, "is that the President's easy good nature will enable them to commit him to too many of their extreme measures, so that a wall of separation between them will be too thin to stop the fire of their bad principles, and save the constitution and laws, from the universal conflagration, which their measures plainly portend."[8]

Bates was no radical. But Salmon Chase was. And by this Saturday in mid-February the treasury secretary's undercover campaign to replace Lincoln as the Union Party nominee was at full throttle. Lincoln had not yet been able to "decline" him. What the *New York Herald* called "the war in the Cabinet" was still raging.[9]

The *Herald* called Chase "the Moses of the radicals,"[10] and Lincoln was putting up with his ill-concealed candidacy in part because sacking him would only further enrage those men with their hearts set Zionwards. He didn't need them any more upset with him than they already were.

Chase's radical credentials were in good order, because of his lifelong abolitionism. In his young lawyering days in Ohio he was known derisively in neighboring Kentucky as the "attorney-general for runaway negroes."[11]

His abolitonism was somewhat tempered, however. "I never was an abolitionist of that school which taught that there could never be a human duty superior to that of the instant and unconditional abolition of slavery," he had recently written a friend. "But, for more than half my life, I have been an abolitionist of that other school which believed slaveholding wrong, and that all responsible for the wrong should do what was possible for them, in their respective spheres, for its redress."[12]

That seems to have been good enough for the radical abolitionists of the other school. Chase was abolitionist enough. He had never liked it when Lincoln, that man whose abolitionism was suspect at best, had taken over emancipation. Chase thought that issue, as well as the presidency and—if Senator Wade was to be believed—the fourth spot in the Trinity, was rightfully his alone.[13]

A formal Chase organization was now up and running, and had been since December. On December 9, the day the president introduced his reconstruction and amnesty plan in the Congress, a group met calling themselves the "Organization to Make S P Chase President." The meeting had been called by three or four congressmen, two of whom were from Ohio, and four other men, of whom two—one a paymaster for the army, the other a newspaper correspondent—were also from Ohio. This nucleus was listed as the "Advisory Committee." But other, far more potent, names were on the list of the organization's backers, whether they knew and approved of it or not: Maj. Gen. Robert C. Schenck, Massachusetts senator Henry Wilson, Tennessee's military governor Andrew Johnson, Vice President Hannibal Hamlin, former Ohio governor William Dennison, and Indiana governor Oliver P. Morton.[14]

Central, state, and local committees had been appointed at that first meeting that night, and soon the organization had expanded into a larger national executive committee, with Kansas senator Samuel C. Pomeroy at its head. Pomeroy was a large man with a bold, high forehead and a bushy beard. Noah Brooks described him as "an unctuous and sleek man, with a rosy countenance and a suave manner."[15] He also had something of the mind of a Judas. His antipathy for Lincoln was related to patronage. He had been getting the smaller piece of the Kansas patronage pie, while the other Kansas senator, James H. Lane, whom he detested, had been getting the bigger slice. Pomeroy resented that.

Within a short time he was chairman of the Chase organization, and had been joined on its list by Ohio senator John Sherman and the congressman-general, James Garfield. By February 21, the *Cincinnati Daily Enquirer* correspondent in Washington was reporting no fewer than twenty-seven senators in the expanded group.[16]

Word of this Chase conspiracy, with Pomeroy as one of the "head devils," had been filtering back to John Hay as early as December 13.[17] Word had also filtered as far west as Joseph Medill in Chicago, who wrote in the *Tribune,* "I presume it is true that Mr. Chase's friends are making for his nomination, but it is all lost labor; Old Abe has the inside track so completely that he will be nominated by acclamation when the convention meets."[18]

What did Chase himself know of all this, and when did he know it? Probably everything, and probably from the beginning—but he wasn't letting on he had anything to do with it. John Hay was likely writing with his tongue in his cheek when he reported something Chase told him in early January. "It is singularly instructive," Chase had confided to Hay in a philosophical moment, "to meet so often as we do in life and in history, instances of vaulting ambition, meanness and treachery failing after enormous exertions and integrity and honesty march straight in triumph to its purpose." Hay, in reporting this to his diary, wrote wryly, "a noble sentiment, Mr. Secretary."[19]

On January 18, five days after his fifty-sixth birthday, Chase wrote a friend and major supporter in Ohio: "At the instance of many who think that the public interest would be promoted by my election in the chief magistracy, a committee, composed of prominent Senators and Representatives and citizens, has been organized here for taking measures to promote that object." He explained that the committee, through a subcommittee, had conferred with him and that he had explained to it all the objections that seemed to him to exist against such use of his name. But, he said, "they have taken these objections into consideration, and assure me that they think I ought not to refuse its use; and I have consented to their wishes. . . ." The modest and reluctant candidate then went on to say that "it is a source of real gratification to believe that those who desire my nomination, desire it on public grounds alone, and will not hesitate, in any matter which may concern me, to act upon such grounds and on such grounds only." Of course, he added, "under these circumstances, I desire the support of Ohio."[20]

Chase had by now elevated to a fine art form this talent for not seeming to run while actually moving ahead at full speed. On January 26 he wrote another Ohioan, "Some friends are sanguine that my name will receive favorable consideration from the people in connection with the Presidency. I tell them that I can take no part in anything they may propose to do, except by trying to merit confidence where I am."[21] Two days later he wrote yet another friend: "So far as the presidency is concerned, I must leave that wholly to the people. Those of them who think that the public goodwill be promoted by adherence to the one-term principle, and by the use of my name, are fully competent, and far more competent than I am, to bring the matter before the public generally; and the people will dispose of the case according to their own judgment. Whatever disposition they make of it, I shall be content."[22]

Even as he wrote those words, the people who were more competent than he to bring the matter before the public were about to do it. They had produced a document called "The Next Presidential Election," and were already sending it out. By early February, 100,000 copies were in the mails under the frank of several sympathetic senators and congressmen, including Senator John Sherman. The document opened by deploring the rash of legislative and committee endorsements of Lincoln, and got meaner as it rambled along through six closely printed pages. It said many things, but its main message was that the president's vacillation and indecision had been "the real cause why our well-appointed armies have not succeeded in the destruction of the rebellion." It called Lincoln unfit for reelection and insisted that a better man must be found. It didn't suggest a specific replacement, but merely tried to convince the public that a change was clearly necessary.[23]

The document went out to leading Republican politicians and newspapers around the country. The Democratic press, of course, got it, and the rankly Democratic *Cincinnati Daily Enquirer* published it on February 10, "to show the workings of a portion of the Republican mind."[24]

"The Next Presidential Election" was, however, only a forerunner for something more explicit. Even as it was blanketing Ohio and boomeranging against Senator Sherman, who denied he had had any idea of its true contents when he had lent his frank to it, something more sensational yet was in the works.

A second document, labeled "strictly private," began circulating on the heels of the first, and had been sitting in newspaper offices for some time. On February 20 the *Washington Constitutional Union* reprinted it in full, and it became strictly public. Two days later, on Washington's birthday, it went out widespread over the Associated Press wire and was being published everywhere. This second document, signed by Senator Pomeroy, and therefore known as the Pomeroy Circular, was the other shoe dropping. It brought the pot to a furious boil and probably made Chase wonder whether his friends were as fully competent to bring the matter before the public as he thought they were.

The Pomeroy Circular was a shorter broadside than "The Next Presidential Election," and less brutal. It made virtually the same arguments—with one key difference. After again calling Lincoln unfit and his reelection "practically impossible," the circular went on to say that it found the qualities needed in a president during the next four years united better in Chase than in any other man. It said that a central organization was even now in place to bring about this happy substitution, and called on the "hearty cooperation" of all like minds.[25]

To quote Lincoln's backwoods inventor, there was a "rekyle," and it wasn't "forrid."

When Gideon Welles read the circular in the newspaper, he predicted that "it will be more dangerous in its recoil than its projectile"—i.e., it would hurt Chase more than Lincoln.[26] The "White House little ones," Nicolay and Hay, had been aware of its existence for several days. The former had written the latter on February 17 that "corruption intrigue and malice are doing their worst, but I do not think it is in the cards to beat the Tycoon."[27] And it was unlikely that any of this was going to improve Pomeroy's chances for a bigger bite of the patronage pie in Kansas.

Chase was aghast and mortified. He immediately sent Lincoln a total disclaimer: he had known nothing of the circular's existence until he read it in the paper like everybody else, and here was his resignation.[28] Lincoln, who had not read the circular, but to whom the whole affair had doubtless begun to look like the declining he had had in mind, answered the secretary a few days later. "I find there is really very little to say," he wrote blandly. "My knowledge of Mr. Pomeroy's letter having been made *public* came to me only the day you wrote; but I had, in spite of myself, known of its *existence* several days before. I have not yet read it, and I think I shall not. . . . I have known just as little of these things as my own friends have allowed me to know. They bring the documents to me, but I do not read them—they tell me what they think fit to tell me, but I do not inquire for more." As for Chase's offer to resign, "I do not perceive occasion for a change." Lincoln also assured Chase, "as you have assured me, that no assault has been made upon you by my instigation, or with my countenance."[29]

By this time, however, an assault had very definitely been made. Even as Chase was writing his disclaimer on February 22, Frank Blair, of the family that went in for a funeral whenever it went in for a fight, was figuratively staring at Chase and sharpening his knife.

Frank was old man Blair's youngest son, at age forty-three, and the pride of the family. He was a Princeton graduate and an alumnus of the Transylvania law school, a congressman from Missouri since 1856 and a general in the army since 1862—and good at both. Generally credited with saving his state for the Union when secession came, he was picturesque in looks as well as action, a wiry and well-built five feet eleven inches and 175 pounds, which he carried arrow-straight. He had a head of rugged force with a sorrel-colored mop of hair and a long, drooping red mustache. His eyes were steely gray, of great depth and light and mirroring exactly his kaleidoscopic emotions and mood swings. He loved his liquor, but carried it well. He was western and one of a kind.

He had a high-pitched voice that gradually descended to a lower register as it screeched along, with a speaking style that flowed easily with it, hurling out fire and brimstone all along the way. He was recklessly brave, both as a politician and a soldier, ardent, impetuous, heroic, audacious, and dominating—but also wholly forgiving. He attacked whatever needed attacking with death-dealing ferocity, but never, after it was done, did he hold a grudge. He therefore never understood why political foes, gutted by him, continued to resent his scorching philippics long after he had delivered them. Some thought him magnetic; others thought him monstrous. Friends idolized him, foes hated and feared him. He had a flaming temper, which often careened out of control. Then cusswords would fly, followed in the soothing course of time and second thought by a contrite and heartfelt apology.[30]

He was the pride and despair of his beautiful sister, Elizabeth Blair Lee, who said of him, "Frank will not let even a great man set his small dogs on him without kicking the dog, & giving his master some share of his resentment. . . ."[31] He didn't flinch at calling men "traitors," "maniacs," or "nincompoops," if that was what he thought they were.[32]

But Frank's temper was unsettling to the family. "Our only real trouble," Elizabeth confessed, "is Frank will give vent to some of his wrath which will only hurt himself & help his foes." And when that invariably happened, she would fret and write, "I confess to some nervousness about the outrageous insult F gave his colleague." Bad temper, this gentle sister thought, is "so very unprofitable," anger "the poorest of counsellors."[33]

Lincoln said of the Blairs that they had "to an unusual degree the spirit of the clan. Their family is a close corporation. Frank is their hope and pride." Frank had often been Lincoln's hope and pride as well. Except for Frank, he once said, he "hardly knew how he could have managed successfully the affairs of the Government in Missouri."[34]

Indeed, Lincoln's fondness for the Blair clan disgusted Count Gurowski, who called the president "Blairized."[35] But Lincoln used the Blairs at least as much as they used him.

What do you wish my brother to do, Postmaster General Montgomery Blair had asked Lincoln in late November 1863, before the Thirty-eighth Congress convened: occupy his seat in Congress or remain in the field?

"My wish . . . ," Lincoln had answered, "is compounded of what I believe will be best for the country, and best for him. And it is, that he will come here, put his military commission in my hands, take his seat, go into caucus with our friends, abide the nominations, help elect the nominees, and thus aid to organize a House of Representatives which will really support the government in the war. If the result shall be the election of himself as Speaker, let him serve in that position; if not, let him re-take his commission, and return to the Army. . . ."

"He is young yet," Lincoln told Montgomery. "He has abundant talent—quite enough to occupy all his time, without devoting any to temper. He is rising in military skill and usefulness. His recent appointment to the command of a corps, by one so competent to judge as Gen. Sherman, proves this. In that line he can serve both the country and himself more profitably than he could as a member of congress on the floor." That, Lincoln told Montgomery, is "what I would say, if Frank Blair were my brother instead of yours."[36]

Frank had done what Lincoln advised. He had come to Washington, put his commission in Lincoln's hands, and taken his seat in Congress. But unfortunately he had not come until the second week in January, too late to be a factor in organizing the House, as Lincoln had hoped.

But now he was still there, and glaring at that turncoat Chase. The secretary's trade clampdown on the Mississippi had put Chase in Frank's bad graces to begin with. Since early January, Frank had been trying to get the House to investigate the Treasury Department, but without success. Chase's courtship of the radical anti-Lincoln Charcoals in Missouri, with an eye to controlling the state's delegation to the Union National Convention, had ratcheted the celebrated Blair temper up near the breaking point. Now here came the Pomeroy Circular. That cut it. Warfare with the Blairs, as Welles explained to his diary, is "open, bold, and unsparing."[37] And warfare was what Chase was about to get from Frank.

On Friday, February 26, the wind and dust were about as intolerable as Washington had ever seen—a miserable prelude to the weekend. It wasn't as bad the next day, Saturday, but fine dust still filled the streets and obscured the sky even when the wind wasn't blowing. On that day, Frank Blair stood up on the floor of the House and began to read from a prepared speech.

"A more profligate administration of the Treasury Department never existed under any Government . . ." Frank said. The whole Mississippi valley, he charged, "is rank and fetid with the fraud and corruptions practiced there by his agents. . . . 'Permits' to buy cotton are just as much a marketable commodity as the cotton itself. . . . The practice of taking bribes on the part of these Treasury agents for permits to trade, and for conniving at violations of law, is so common that it has almost ceased to attract attention or excite comment. It is the most corrupting and demoralizing system that ever was invented, and has become a public scandal." No wonder, Frank raged, that General Grant said, "No honest man could do business under such a system."[38]

It was a speech to turn politics on its ear—and it did. But even then Frank wasn't through. Two days later he reintroduced his resolution for an investigation of the Treasury Department, which Chase's friends in the House sidetracked into committee and diluted with added power to investigate other departments as well. Even worse, Frank said he wasn't through talking and would be back with more in a few days.

The damage had already been done. The "rekyle" of the scorching Pomeroy manifesto had done it even without Frank's screed. Three days after the circular hit the newspapers, pro-Lincoln Union Party members in the Ohio legislature passed a resolution unanimously endorsing Lincoln's renomination. This was treachery in Chase's own house, Brutus stabbing Caesar. Once again in his political career, Chase found himself a presidential candidate without even the support of the delegation of his own home state.

The end of his candidacy was at hand. "It seems clear to me," said James Garfield, Chase's Ohio friend and chess partner, "that the people desire the reelection of Mr. Lincoln and I believe any movement in any other direction will not only be a failure but will tend to disturb and embarrass the unity of the friends of the Union." He advised Chase, perhaps over the chessboard, that he ought to withdraw from the contest.[39]

Chase had since read Frank Blair's speech and was steaming, threatening in letters to friends not only to resign from the cabinet, but to withdraw his name from the canvass unless the Blairs were muzzled. He had already offered to fulfill the first threat, and was soon fulfilling the second. A grudging letter went out from him on March 5 to Ohio state senator James C. Hall, and through him to his friends in Ohio, asking that his name no longer be considered for the nomination.[40]

"I am trying to keep all Presidential aspirations out of my head," he sadly wrote his friend A. G. Riddle.[41] The disbelieving said they would believe that when they saw it. Virtually nobody believed they had really seen the last of Chase and his presidential ambitions. His partisans had by no means stopped working for him, and his name was still out there as a contender in the public mind.[42] David Davis, Lincoln's old circuit-riding friend from Illinois, now a Supreme Court justice, told Thurlow Weed that Chase's withdrawal was "a mere sham, and very ungraceful at that." Another Lincoln partisan, Senator Edwin D. Morgan of New York, wrote Weed that "Mr. Chase will subside as a presidential candidate after the nomination is made—not before."[43] James Gordon Bennett, the acid-tongued and dubious editor of the *New York Herald,* wrote, "The salmon is a queer fish, very shy and very wary. Often it appears to avoid the bait just before gulping it down."[44]

But it probably didn't escape Lincoln—or his friend Alexander McClure, either—that Chase had at last been declined. His candidacy had gone up in flames as surely as Lincoln's stables had burned down. Or, as George B. Lincoln (no relation) put it to the president in a letter on February 26, "What is the matter? Friend Pomeroy's yeast don't make the Chase pudding rise!"[45]

10

LET HIM HAVE THE PRESIDENCY

IT IS THE NATURE OF POLITICS THAT WHEN ONE MAN'S PUDDING isn't rising, another man's is.

It is also the nature of politics that in times of war and national upheaval, generals who become heroes also become candidates for president. Lincoln understood those twin axioms of politics as well as anybody. And even as Chase's presidential pudding was collapsing, the president was carefully watching a general whose political pudding was plainly on the rise.

Ulysses S. Grant was clearly a man to watch. He was the most successful general the Union had produced. He was a veteran of twenty-seven battles in his forty-two-year lifetime, from Palo Alto in Mexico to Lookout Mountain in Tennessee. And he had never been in one that was lost. As a Union general he had captured two Confederate armies and utterly defeated a third.

He wasn't much to look at—slouchy and commonplace—but he fought and won battles. In October, after Grant captured Vicksburg, Lincoln elevated him to command of all Federal operations from the Mississippi east to the Alleghenies. And Grant had rewarded the president's faith by saving Chattanooga and breaking Confederate power in Tennessee. Governor Thomas E. Bramlette of Kentucky called him "the first Gen'l of the age," and many in the North agreed.[1]

Grant's philosophy of war was as direct and down-home as he was. "The art of war is simple enough," he said. "Find out where your enemy is. Get at him as soon as you can. Strike at him as hard as you can and as often as you can, and keep moving on."[2]

Lincoln had never met Grant personally. But the president liked him. Grant was Lincoln's kind of general. In 1862, after the epic two-day battle at Shiloh, which Grant won on the second day, but almost lost on the first, the general endured a firestorm of criticism. There were charges that he was an incompetent drunkard and ought to be sacked. Lincoln said then, "I can't spare this man; he fights."[3] At the time the president had but few generals who fit that description.

Lincoln liked him because not only did he fight, but he made do. "General Grant is a copious worker and fighter," the president said, "but a very meager writer or telegrapher." Lincoln liked especially that this general "doesn't worry and bother me. He isn't shrieking for reinforcements all the time. He takes what troops we can safely give him . . . and does the best he can with what he has got"[4]—all in all, "a very determined little fellow."[5]

There was a perception in the North that the Union Army of the Potomac, despite its victory at Gettysburg, was a feckless fighting machine. When it was said to be on the move again in late February, George Strong in New York wrote in his diary, "If so, its movement is probably *andante maestoso*—slow, and destined to cause mourning."[6]

For some time, Lincoln had wanted to bring Grant east to see if he could do something with that army—even take Richmond. If Grant can take Richmond, the president had been heard to say, "let him have the Presidency."[7] Grant was also, in this presidential election year, a tempting prize for restless radical party politicians seeking to replace a president whom they didn't want.

They were not alone in favoring Grant. Since the middle of December the editor of the *New York Herald,* James Gordon Bennett, had been wearing out type pumping Grant for the presidency.

"It is evident . . . ," the editor wrote in December, when he began nominating Grant daily in the *Herald,* "that our next President must be a military man, of tried experience and acknowledged capacity. . . . We have had quite enough of a Civilian Commander-in-chief during the past four years." Bennett believed the next president must also be free of political taint, independent of all political factions and influence. "In General Grant," he said, "we have all these qualifications, combined with many others almost equally indispensable."[8]

For weeks, without letup, Bennett's drumbeat for Grant resonated daily from the *Herald*'s editorial pages. Horace Greeley at the neighboring *Tribune* read them and called them the kiss of death. Having "boxed the compass with its old favorites, and run their names up and down the scale till they grate upon the ears of its readers," Greeley grumbled, the *Herald* was now taking Grant as its latest victim. There were some things that even Ulysses S. Grant could not survive, Greeley said, and that was six articles per day by Bennett in favor of his nomination and election to the presidency.[9]

The Democratic congressman from Ohio, Sunset Cox, believed he had the Grant candidacy figured, just as he had the McClellan candidacy pegged. Over their dinner together in Washington, John Hay had asked Cox, "You don't agree with the *Herald* on Grant?"

"Grant belongs to the Republicans," Cox answered. "We can't take him. . . ." But then he said, "The Republicans won't take him either. They have got his influence and have no further use for him."

"If I were a soldier," Hay said, "I should much prefer commanding the U.S. Army for life to four years in the executive mansion. I think Grant would."

"So would McClellan, I know," said Cox.[10]

Lincoln wasn't so sure about any of this. He thought he knew where McClellan stood. But he wasn't so certain of Grant. And he had to know. Grant as a general pleased him; Grant as a political candidate worried him. It wasn't so much that Grant might run against him. What worried Lincoln was that Grant might be so diverted by running that he might not be up to fighting.[11]

The president went first to Elihu Washburne to see what he could learn. Washburne was Grant's congressman from Illinois, and the general's most consistent and visible champion in Washington. Navy Secretary Welles didn't think much of Washburne, and wouldn't have advised Lincoln to consult him on any matter. Welles thought him the meanest man in Congress, "whose honesty and veracity I know to be worse than indifferent."[12] But Lincoln knew Washburne well, and he said to him:

"About all I know of Grant I have got from you. I have never seen him. Who else besides you knows anything about Grant?"

"I know very little about him," Washburne admitted. "He is my townsman, but I never saw very much of him. The only man who really knows Grant is Jones. He has summered and wintered with him." That was J. Russell Jones, a close friend of Grant's who had spent time with him in Mississippi in the winter of 1862–63.[13]

Lincoln knew Jones, too. He was the U.S. marshal for Illinois, named to the job early in Lincoln's administration. So Lincoln sent for Jones.

Though Jones knew Grant well, he didn't know whether Grant wanted to be president. Indeed, Jones had been trying to find that out himself. Just a few weeks before, he had written Grant at Chattanooga saying he didn't wish to meddle in his business, but he could not restrain himself from advising Grant to resist all enticements to run for president.

Jones knew that the Congress was considering reviving the lofty rank of lieutenant general, and conferring it on Grant. The measure, introduced by Washburne, was even then before the House. Grant's friends, he and Washburne among them, were concerned that even the slightest stir of political ambition in Grant's breast might ruin his chances for that coveted promotion.[14]

As Jones headed to catch the train for Washington in answer to Lincoln's summons, Grant hadn't yet answered his letter. But neither had Lincoln in his telegram said what business he wished to transact with Jones. Jones had no idea and no information on which even to base a suspicion—on either subject.

On the way to the station, he stopped by his office in the post office building in Chicago and found several letters. He stuffed them all in his pocket without looking at them, and proceeded to the depot. As the train rattled out of Chicago eastward, he took out the letters. One of them was from Grant.[15]

Grant had been batting away urgings that he run for president at least since December. Early that month he had received a letter from Barnabas Burns, the chairman of the Democratic Central Committee in Ohio, asking if he could put Grant's name before the convention of the war Democrats in that state as a candidate for president.

"The question astonishes me," Grant had replied to Burns. "I do not know of anything I have ever done or said which would indicate that I could be a candidate for any office whatever within the gift of the people." Grant told Burns that "nothing likely to happen would pain me so much as to see my name used in connection with a political office. I am not a candidate for any office nor for favors from any party. . . ." Furthermore, Grant wrote Burns, "I wish to avoid notoriety as far as possible, and above all things desire to be spared the pain of seeing my name mixed with politics."[16]

Since then, nonetheless, the pressure on him to get mixed up in it had quickened. "I am receiving a great deal of that kind of literature," Grant wrote in the letter Jones was now reading on the train to Washington, "but it very soon finds its way into the waste basket. . . . Nothing would induce me to think of being a presidential candidate, particularly so long as there is a possibility of having Mr. Lincoln reelected."[17]

Lincoln opened the conversation with Jones at the White House by saying he had called him to Washington as somebody from the West with whom he could talk about the general situation. Nothing whatever was said of Grant. Lincoln was plowing around the stump again. Jones had been there but a few minutes, however, when he realized that it was really Grant whom Lincoln wished to talk about.

"Mr. President," Jones said, "if you will excuse me for interrupting you, I want to ask you kindly to read a letter that I got from my box as I was on my way to the train."

When Lincoln reached the part in the letter where Grant said it would be impossible for him to think of the presidency as long as there was a possibility Lincoln would run again, he read no further, but arose and laid a hand on Jones's shoulder.

"My son," he said, "you will never know how gratifying that is to me. No man knows, when that presidential grub gets to gnawing at him, just how deep it will get until he has tried it; and I didn't know but what there was one gnawing at Grant."[18]

Elihu Washburne had introduced the bill to revive the rank of lieutenant general in the army early in the session in December, after Grant's victory at Chattanooga. Only George Washington had ever held that exalted rank permanently, and then for only a short time before his death. It had been discontinued, put in retirement, until it was conferred in 1847, by brevet only, on Winfield Scott, the hero of the War of 1812 and the Mexican War.

It wasn't easily resurrected now. Many in Congress feared that so high a rank conferred on anyone was threatening to the liberties of the republic. But there was still a war to be won, and the House, after some wrangling, passed the bill, eighty-six to forty-one. On February 26 the Senate followed with a majority of six votes and with little debate. In the process, Grant's name, attached to the bill by Washburne, had been dropped. But it was distinctly understood all around that the rank was intended for him. Lincoln, by now persuaded that Grant had no presidential ambitions, signed it three days later and immediately nominated Grant to fill it. The Senate confirmed the appointment on March 2, and the next day the secretary of war ordered Grant to report to Washington.

The North's new generalissimo caught a train out of Nashville the next day, accompanied by his chief of staff, John A. Rawlins, his engineering officer, Cyrus B. Comstock, and his oldest son, fourteen-year-old Frederick.

Grant hoped this wouldn't take too long. Washington was the last place he wanted to go. His second-in-command, Maj. Gen. William T. Sherman, who had been to Washington many times and had a brother there who was a U.S. senator from Ohio, had warned him about the place. Sherman, in fact, viewed Grant's promotion as an "almost dangerous elevation." Above all, Sherman advised him, do not remain in Washington. "Come out West," Sherman urged, "take to yourself the whole Mississippi Valley, let us make it dead-sure, and I tell you the Atlantic slope and Pacific shores will follow its destiny, as sure as the limbs of a tree live or die with the main trunk." Leave Henry Halleck, the general-in-chief of the armies until Grant had been promoted, to deal with the intrigue and politics of Washington, Sherman urged; he's used to it and better qualified. "For God's sake and for your country's sake," Sherman pleaded, "come out of Washington." And that was what Grant intended to do, as soon as he could get his third star and leave. Grant and Sherman had what Nicolay and Hay would later describe as "a not very intelligent dread of Washington and its political influences; something of the feeling which sailors have towards lawyers."[19]

Grant arrived in Washington about dusk on March 8, travel-beaten, rumpled, and unmet—plans to meet him at the station had gotten snarled. It had been dreary and rainy all day in the capital, a cheerless welcome for the first soldier of the land, who had never been in Washington for more than a day in his entire life. So he found his way unattended to Willard's Hotel, that "centre of Washington, whence come the rumors and epidemics of excitement," and where everybody who was anybody stayed.[20]

His weatherbeaten major general's uniform, needing ironing, was half hidden under his linen duster as he approached the registration desk at Willard's. Grant was never too pushy, and major generals were not an unusual phenomenon in Washington. So when he modestly asked for a room, the clerk replied, "I have nothing but a room on the top floor."

"Very well; that will do," said Grant, and signed the register, "U. S. Grant and son, Galena, Ill." The astonished double take by the registration clerk when he looked at the signature would be only the first of many that evening.[21]

U. S. Grant was not the sort of man who usually caused a stir. Navy Secretary Welles thought him "without presence."[22] "There was nothing marked in his appearance," agreed Richard Henry Dana. "He had no gait, no *station,* no manner"; he was an "ordinary, scrubby-looking man, with a slightly seedy look, as if he was out of office on half-pay, and nothing to do but to hang round the entry of Willard's, cigar in mouth. . . ."[23] He looked more a mechanic, a businessman, a country storekeeper, or a farmer than a soldier. He was an extraordinary man who looked ordinary.[24]

In motion, Grant appeared to get across the ground quickly. Dana thought he moved queerly doing it, however, not quite walking, definitely not marching, but pitching along as if the next step would bring him flat on his face. Standing or walking, he generally carried his left hand in his trousers pocket, with an unlit cigar clamped tight in his mouth, which he chewed restlessly. He was of middle height, five feet eight inches tall, of a spare, strong build with sloping shoulders. His eyes were clear blue—one riding a little lower than the other. His forehead was high, his nose aquiline. His hair was light brown, and he wore a close-cropped beard of foxy tinge. His jaw was square-set, but not sensual. His face was generally immobile, his eyes being the most expressive of his features. A reporter who saw him thought that his features, when at rest, appeared as if carved from mahogany. Another, who had many occasions to study the face up close, said that when it did move it had three expressions: deep thought, extreme determination, and great simplicity and calmness. He had what one of his staff called a somewhat careworn look that was never absent from his countenance. He also had a musical voice—though he had no gift for music. Indeed, he admitted he was tone deaf and knew only two tunes—one was "Yankee Doodle" and the other wasn't. Having no ear for music or rhythm, he never kept step to the military airs played by his bands, no matter how vigorously their drums beat time. When he walked in company, there was never any semblance of keeping step with others.[25]

Grant needed a horse to bring out his true grace. As a rider he was elegance incarnate. It was generally agreed that he was the finest horseman ever to attend West Point.

But afoot or horseback, there was something about him. Elizabeth Blair Lee thought it was "the same quiet, resolute bearing which denotes a man of Will."[26] Even Welles, who didn't like him and deplored his lack of soldierly dignity and bearing, thought there was about him the suggestion of "latent power."[27]

Theodore Lyman of Meade's staff, who was soon to meet him for the first time, thought him "the concentration of all that is American. He talks bad grammar, but he talks it naturally. . . . His writing though very terse and well expressed, is full of horrible spelling. In fact, he has such an easy and straightforward way that you almost think that he must be right and you wrong, in these little matters of elegance." Lyman thought him a man of rough dignity, rather taciturn, who "habitually wears an expression as if he had determined to drive his head through a brick wall, and was about to do it."[28]

After a hasty toilet in their room at the Willard, Grant, with Frederick in tow, went down to the dining hall for dinner. At first there was no stir. Then a gentleman nearby stared at him and asked a neighbor: "Who is that major-general?"

"Why that is Lieutenant-General Grant!" the neighbor exclaimed.

The jig was up. The news flew from table to table. Pennsylvania congressman James K. Moorhead, present at the occasion and always ready with a few remarks, stood and announced publicly: "Ladies and Gentlemen: The hero of Donelson, of Vicksburg, and of Chattanooga is among us. I propose the health of Lieutenant-General Grant." The diners were instantly on their feet, huzzahing, waving handkerchiefs and napkins, and pounding on tables, making silverware and crockery dance. A few diners danced wildly themselves, in reckless disregard of furniture and decorum.

Much astonished and painfully embarrassed, Grant stood, dabbed awkwardly at his mustache with his napkin, bowed stiffly about him to the four points of the compass, shook hands with those few near enough to clutch at him, then vainly presumed to sit down again to his dinner. No use. It was Grant's first levee. For nearly a quarter of an hour it roared on before the hero of Donelson, Vicksburg, and Chattanooga could beat one of the few retreats of his military life.[29]

It was the day of the week for the regular Tuesday-evening levee at the White House, and the night was raw and rainy. Word had spread that Grant would be present, and the White House was mobbed. Lincoln had been busy at the pump handle for nearly an hour and a half when Grant arrived at about nine-thirty with former secretary of war Simon Cameron. There was a stir at the door of the Blue Room as he entered, and Lincoln broke off and strode forward to meet the man of the hour.

"This is General Grant, is it?"

"Yes," Grant confessed.[30]

The two men talked briefly, and Lincoln gave Grant over to Secretary of State Seward to present to Mary, and told John Nicolay to send for Secretary of War Stanton. After paying his respects to Mrs. Lincoln,

Grant was hustled into the East Room by Seward, where pandemonium set in. Cheer after cheer rose to the chandeliered ceiling. The
crowd pressed in to get a closer look at his face and form. Women were
caught up and whirled into the torrent that swept through the East
Room. Laces were shredded, crinoline mashed. People stood on sofas
and tables to take sightings or get out of harm's way.[31]

Grant himself retreated to a sofa, his back to the wall, caught up
against his will in what he would call his "warmest campaign during
the war."[32] After a while, flushed, heated, and perspiring, and with
Mary on his arm, he promenaded the East Room behind the president
and Mrs. Seward.[33]

When the official party at last retired to the Blue Room, the president excused himself for a moment and went upstairs, returning in a
short while to take a seat near Grant, Stanton, and John Nicolay. Lincoln said to Grant, "Tomorrow, at such a time as you may arrange with
the Secretary of War, I desire to make to you a formal presentation of
your commission as Lieutenant General. I shall then make a very short
speech to you which I desire you to reply for an object; and that you
may be properly prepared to do so I have written what I shall say—
only four sentences in all—which I will read . . . as an example which
you may follow. . . ."

Lincoln was being considerate again, concerned that Grant might
not be accustomed to public speaking, and wanting him to be not only
prepared, but at ease. Lincoln was also being political. "There are two
points that I would like to have you make in your answer," he told
Grant. "[First], to say something which shall prevent or obviate any
jealousy of you from any of the other generals in the service, and sec-
ondly, something which shall put you on as good terms as possible with
the Army of the Potomac."

Grant asked at what time the presentation should take place.

"The Secretary of War and yourself may arrange the time to suit
your convenience," Lincoln said. "I am all ready, whenever you shall
have prepared your reply."

"I can be ready in thirty minutes," Grant said.

Lincoln didn't have anything that soon in mind. One o'clock the next
afternoon was agreed on, and Grant left, accompanied by Stanton, glad
the hectic day had finally ended.

By the next day the rain had lifted and the weather was pleasant. At
one in the afternoon, in the cabinet room, with the cabinet present, Lincoln opened the ceremonies with his four prepared lines, saying the

nation appreciated all Grant had done, put its trust in him for what was left to be done, and promised to sustain him in all he must do. Lincoln added that with all he said for the nation went his own hearty personal concurrence. He then presented the commission.

Grant had hastily written out his reply in pencil the night before. And now he was having trouble reading it. He began, then stopped, caught his breath, and proceeded. He said: "Mr. President, I accept this commission with gratitude for the high honor conferred. With the aid of the noble armies that have fought on so many fields for our common country, it will be my earnest endeavor not to disappoint your expectations. I feel the full weight of the responsibilities now devolving on me; and I know that if they are met, it will be due to those armies, and above all to the favor of that Providence which leads both nations and men."

It was not exactly what Lincoln had intended him to say, but it was more than appropriate.

After the presentation, Grant asked Lincoln what special service was requested of him. Lincoln replied that the country wanted him to take Richmond. Nobody had yet been able to do it. Could he? Grant said without hesitation that he could if he had the troops. Lincoln assured his new general-in-chief he would have them.[34]

The next day, March 10, Grant was formally assigned command of all the Union armies. As if to give meat to Lincoln's pledge that the nation would sustain its new general-in-chief, the order for 500,000 more men to be drafted under the conscription act took effect.

Grant immediately beat it out of town. He went first, that day, to Brandy Station to visit Meade, whom he had not seen since the Mexican War, and the Army of the Potomac, which he had never seen. The next day Grant headed for the train, intending to get out of the East altogether. But, Lincoln told him, Mrs. Lincoln was planning a military dinner at the White House in his honor. Twelve other prominent generals were invited.

No, sir, Grant said, I'm leaving.

"I don't see how we *can* excuse you," Lincoln replied. "It would be Hamlet with the Prince left out." Lincoln had just seen the actor Edwin Booth as Hamlet at Grover's Theatre.

"I appreciate fully the honor Mrs. Lincoln would do me," insisted Grant, his resolution as unyielding as ever, "but time is precious; and— really—Mr. President, *I have had enough of the show business.*"[35]

The dinner came off, but without Hamlet, who had returned to the West. But Grant wasn't to stay there, despite Sherman's urgent warnings and his own personal inclination. He had decided that events demanded he move east for good, and headquarter with the eastern army. He had merely returned west to put Sherman in charge and come back.

On March 23 he did come back. The day before, winter, lingering in the lap of spring, had set in motion a fiendish reprise. As Brooks wrote, all day "it blew and at night it snew," burying the nascent springtime jonquils, crocuses, roses, and posies under a suffocating white shroud—"the envious sneaping frost biting the firstborn infants of the spring," as Shakespeare described such things.[36] By bedtime, five inches of snow had fallen. The next morning, the day Grant returned, there were ten inches on the ground in Washington. It had been the biggest snowstorm of the entire winter.[37]

But by evening the snow had mostly melted, and Grant went out to Culpeper Court House, a few miles south of the headquarters of the Army of the Potomac, and pitched his own tents.

Lincoln had finally gotten what he wanted, someone competent who he believed would take responsibility for running the army and only expect from him what help he needed, and which he would gladly give.[38] In the process, Lincoln had also ensured that the most potent potential political opponent in the country would be otherwise occupied in 1864.

On Orange Mountain in New Jersey, another general not so fully occupied, who, but for fate and other reasons, might have been in that military pantheon where only Washington, Scott, and now Grant had ever been, was writing his mother a letter.

"Time flies so rapidly and so quietly in this out of the way place," George McClellan wrote, sounding wistful, "that I really have nothing new to tell—unless I would commit to paper the wise sayings and new pranks of the baby."[39]

But for McClellan, as for Grant, unquiet days and important battles—on strikingly different battlefields—still lay ahead.

11

THE EDITOR GENERALS

———

I<small>T WAS THAT TIME OF YEAR IN</small> W<small>ASHINGTON WHEN</small> "<small>THE GLORY OF</small> spring was over all, the dogwoods were shining with their milk-white blossoms, the Judas trees and the sassafrases were purple and cold, and the magnolias were opening."[1]

It was the season of renewal. The new campaign with the new lieutenant general was about to begin on the battlefields south of Washington. The nation awaited that new clash of arms with mixed feelings of anticipation, optimism, and dread.

But on Capitol Hill, Congress was looking for renewal and not finding it. For Thaddeus Stevens, in particular, little was changing or renewing this spring. It was business as usual. Attorney General Bates commented on that fact in his diary, quoting a report in the *Baltimore Clipper* of an evening session of the House in which Stevens had introduced a bill to disenfranchise the seceded states. "Uncle Thad," Bates clucked disapprovingly, ". . . always full of whims and oddities. He is, at once ignorant and careless of the constitution. He thinks of it only as a bar of Juniata Iron—that may be forged into any shape, and cut into any pieces, to suit the fancy of any [Pennsylvania] blacksmith." But, wrote Bates, seeking mitigating circumstances, it was an evening session, "when no one can guaranty the sobriety of the House."[2]

The voice of one member of this sometimes not-so-sober body had been silenced forever this spring. Owen Lovejoy, Lincoln's radical friend, had been desperately ill since early in the year. He had been gaining slowly, but, as he said, "it is hard work drawing the sled uphill."[3] On a trip to Brooklyn on March 25, the sled became too heavy to pull any longer, and he died. He was fifty-three years old.

The funeral services, opening with a solemn dirge, were read at Henry Ward Beecher's Plymouth Church in South Brooklyn on March 28. The tabernacle was filled long before the ceremonies began at two o'clock in the afternoon. Beecher read the eulogy. "Dead," he said, "he yet speaketh. Young men will be inspired by his words and works."[4]

Lincoln grieved quietly at yet another ruinous loss. Lovejoy had been a radical he could always count on in the crunch, and he was gone. The president was to say of his longtime friend that "throughout my heavy and perplexing responsibilities here, to the day of his death, it would scarcely wrong any other to say he was my most generous friend."[5]

James Gordon Bennett at the *New York Herald* marked Lovejoy's passing in his typically irreverent fashion. Noting that several newspapers and congressmen were "exhausting the English language" in eulogies to Lovejoy, Bennett said, "We see no reason why people should begin to tell flattering falsehoods about a man the moment he is dead." Dead, he yet speaketh, Beecher had said. That's the trouble, Bennett said. Lovejoy, the blunt old editor wrote unlovingly, was "one of those radical men . . . who do a great deal more harm than good in the world, and whose epitaph should be 'The evils they have done live after them.' "[6]

Bennett's ungracious and aweless comment on the dead could scarcely have surprised Lincoln. There wasn't much to be done about the country's "newspaper Generals," as somebody called them.[7] Many times through the past three years they had said the same, and worse, about Lincoln.

Lincoln had been a dedicated newspaper reader in his Springfield days. His law partner, Billy Herndon, remembered how Lincoln sprawled on the sofa in their office to read them; how he splayed his long legs out in two directions, one foot on the chair, the other on the table, and read the papers aloud, absorbing them through both the eye and the ear to better remember them. It nearly drove Herndon crazy.[8]

As president, Lincoln only had time to read the papers hit-or-miss— "to skirmish" with them, as he put it.[9] He was no longer the careful reader he had been, depending on the papers to help him shape and distill his concept of the times. He now had other sources, and so little time. Francis Carpenter, the young artist virtually living in the White House that spring while he painted the signing of the Emancipation Proclamation, could only remember a single instance when he had seen

Lincoln reading a newspaper.[10] It was much more painful reading them now.

Having no responsibility for the government, the editor generals were free with advice, and when it was disregarded, they were just as free with denunciation. Lincoln came in for more than his share of nagging, scolding, calumny, and worse. The violent criticism, attacks, and denunciations rarely seemed to ruffle him, if they reached his eyes at all. But Lincoln knew how important these editors and their newspapers were in shaping opinion in the North. They were the nation's conduits for communicating fact, near-fact, opinion, and outright lies in the country. They all had strong opinions, and they were plentiful, contradictory, widely read, and often believed or disbelieved according to their political biases. Lincoln understood their capacity for mischief. He knew they mattered.

Occasionally he would joke about them. Inspecting a new repeating gun that prevented the escape of gas, he said, "Well, I believe this really does what it is represented to do. Now have any of you heard of any machine, or invention, for preventing the escape of 'gas' from newspaper establishments?"[11]

No newspaper in America leaked more gas than Horace Greeley's *New York Tribune,* and none had more influence. The *Tribune*'s weekly edition had the widest circulation of any paper out in the American heartland, among Lincoln's common men. The daily edition had equal clout in the big cities. Throughout the war, Greeley had been perhaps the most aggravating of all the New York editors, a major headache for Lincoln. He was a pest, unwilling to temporize, willing always to meddle, ready with advice—wrong as often as right. But he was an able writer, able to reach readers in their own language, and therefore somebody who had to be dealt with. He had the ear of the country as no other editor did. Scores of thousands turned to his *Tribune* daily or weekly for news and opinion. What they often heard was an uncertain trumpet sending out strident and inconsistent blasts. But that hardly mattered. It was their paper and he was their editor.

That editor was one of a kind, fifty-three years old, tall and gawky, with what might be called a badly set frame. He draped this irregular body daily in clean but disheveled linen. Everything he wore seemed to trail after him rather than go with him. He often wore a long white duster, the pockets stuffed with newspapers and one pantleg or the other snagged on a boot-top. On his head he wore a broad-brimmed white straw or felt hat, and generally carried a fat umbrella.

Under the hat rested a nearly perfectly ball-shaped head—rather too large for his vital organs, one observer thought—with a childlike and clean-shaven face and a deceptively sweet and earnest smile. His eyes, sunk in a dumpling forehead and strikingly nearsighted, were small and crystal blue, peering out owl-like through round, gold-rimmed glasses. His complexion was pale and white. Atop his head, thin, flaxen hair curled halfheartedly, and under his cherubic face swooped a collar of flaxen throat hair, giving him something of the appearance of a sunflower. He was a man of wayward whims and eccentric manners, stooped and myopic, with a shrieking voice to match his pen.[12]

Greeley worked in his office on the third floor of the *Tribune* building, called the Old Rookery. There this rare bird sat at a desk nearly as high as his chin, his myopic eyes crowding the paper, with nothing audible but the relentless scratch of his busy pen, churning out almost illegible editorial prose at furious speed. As he finished each sheet, he either perched it momentarily on his knees or let it flutter to the floor, already thickly strewn with papers.[13]

This output was scooped up by a copy boy and rushed to the composing room, where it was met with blank and puzzled stares. Fortunately, Greeley had in his employ one man, John C. Robinson, who was preternaturally gifted at reading this hen-scratching. Time and again, when Greeley himself was unable to read what he had just written, he took it to Robinson, who would examine it steadily for a minute, then read it off as if it were in print. Minus this translator, his typesetters admitted to taking the undecipherable text for what they thought it ought to be rather than what it seemed to be.

In his writing mode, Greeley, notoriously absentminded, became oblivious. His office boy recalled one day watching him write at his desk, absorbed in his editorials, and utterly unconscious of water dripping steadily down on him from a leaky pipe above.[14]

It was Greeley's practice to go to church to sleep. Arriving early, he generally took his seat and nodded off immediately. He went to church one day with his friend Oliver Johnson, to hear the Reverend William Henry Channing preach. On the way, Greeley begged Johnson to try to keep him awake so he could report what Channing said in the newspaper the next day. The two sat in a pew within six feet of the pulpit, directly under the eye of the preacher himself. Johnson did his best to keep Greeley awake, tugging repeatedly at his elbow and "playing a by no means soft tattoo upon his ribs." But it was no use. Greeley was "nid-nodding," as Johnson put it, through the entire discourse, not a little to Channing's annoyance. After the service, Greeley and Johnson returned together to the Old Rookery, where Greeley perched at once at his desk and began scratching out a report of what the preacher had said and nobody figured Greeley had heard, filling somewhat less than a column.

When Channing read the report in the *Tribune* the next morning he was utterly astonished, and asked Johnson afterward if it was possible Greeley had actually written it. Johnson attested it was indeed the work of the editor.

"Why," Channing said in wonder, "I could not myself have made so accurate an abstract of my own discourse. . . . He has not only given the substance of what I said, he has followed my line of thought, and remembered not a little of my language."[15]

Despite his absentmindedness, Greeley had what one of his staff described as a memory for facts and information "as retentive as Pascal's."[16]

He also had a kindhearted, philanthropic streak as gargantuan as his absentmindedness. He was a soft touch for a handout or a loan to almost anybody. But he had his limits. Solicited one day to subscribe to "a cause which will prevent a thousand of our fellow-beings from going to hell," Greeley snapped, "I will not give you a cent. There don't half enough go there now."[17]

Gideon Welles thought Greeley a scheming busybody.[18] Lincoln's political friend from Pennsylvania, Alexander McClure, thought him, despite his boundless generosity and philanthropy, "one of the best haters I have ever known," capable of holding tremendous grudges.[19] The celebrated preacher Theodore Parker said of him that "he is *capricious, crotchety, full of whims, and wrong-headed*" (emphasis in original). Joseph Medill, his counterpart on the *Chicago Tribune,* said of him that he was another of those "sore-headed politicians."[20]

Greeley said of himself that "I should have been a farmer."[21] But Medill was right. He also wanted very much to be a politician, but had to settle for being what he saw himself actually to be—an "ink-slinger."[22]

He slung more than ink. He slung havoc, and a lot of it in Abraham Lincoln's direction.

Greeley and Lincoln met personally for the first time in December 1848, when they were fellow congressmen in the Thirtieth Congress.

Greeley was already a famous editor and was filling a temporary vacancy in the House. Lincoln was an unknown westerner who had been in Congress but a year. The editor was a powerful and bitter enemy of fellow New Yorker William Seward, and in the Republican national convention in Chicago in 1860, he played an important role in defeating Seward and nominating his fellow ex-congressman for president.

Like many other Republicans, Greeley had since come to view Lincoln's elevation to the presidency as a terrible mistake. He had taken to calling him "half a statesman and half a horse jockey."[23]

Greeley was always in a hurry. Lincoln wasn't; indeed, Lincoln refused to be rushed. Greeley had prodded him impatiently and relentlessly toward emancipation of the slaves, and Lincoln had eventually gotten there, but he had taken his own time doing it. In other ways as well, Greeley, who thought the president's heart was in the right place but his policies weren't, grew more and more impatient and agitated as the war raged on.

By the spring of 1864, Greeley was in the front ranks of those Republicans opposing Lincoln's renomination. Indeed, he had been working tirelessly to find a workable alternative since early 1863, looking everywhere for another man, any man, who might replace the president as the Union Party's nominee. Greeley was looking for both a stronger president and a more pliant one. He wanted a chief executive who would resist any compromise in the conduct of the war, but would follow his unsolicited advice.[24]

Greeley's first choice in the spring of 1863 had been Maj. Gen. William S. Rosecrans, the most successful and popular general in the public eye at the time. Greeley sent his friend James R. Gilmore, who wrote radical propaganda pieces under the pseudonym of Edmund Kirke, to feel out Rosecrans. Greeley's idea was to find out first if Rosecrans was "sound on the goose"—Greeley's euphemism for a strong antislavery policy. If so, would he consider the nomination? Rosecrans turned out to be sound enough on the goose, but not interested in the nomination. It was just as well, for by September Rosecrans had lost the battle of Chickamauga in Tennessee, and both his military and political suns had set.[25]

Greeley had then swung his support to Salmon Chase. But the Pomeroy Circular had just cut the ground out from under that alternative. Now, in the spring, Greeley was casting an inquiring eye toward John C. Frémont, the famed western explorer, fired general, and favorite of many radicals. Frémont had been the Republican nominee for president in 1856, the first in the young party's history. Talk had started this spring of pushing him forward again in this canvass, and Greeley, again without a horse, was interested.

Another editor ever-interested, and just as unhandy to deal with—perhaps more so—was busy this spring hurling his own thunderbolts from the editorial offices at the *New York Herald*.

The *Herald* was the spiciest paper in America, laced with sex, scandal, and James Gordon Bennett's erratic opinions. Bennett's pen, someone said, "burns at the nib, and its strokes are like the stings of scorpions."[26] His paper had the largest circulation of any newspaper in the country, even greater than Greeley's, and was nearly as potent as the latter in shaping public perceptions in the North. It cut a wide swath across the readership of the country, reaching out more than most other big-city papers to all classes of readers, covering subjects other papers largely neglected. Former president James Buchanan, who had often been its victim, called it "the most powerful organ in the country for the formation of public opinion." Not only was it widely read in America, but it was more talked about in Europe than any other American newspaper.[27]

Bennett had a nose for news that some believed bordered on the supernatural, and a stable of good, well-paid reporters to report it. Sprinkled amid the sensationalism were columns of solid reporting of the news of the nation and the war. The *Herald* was cast in the image of its editor and founder: it was risqué, piquant, often outrageous, and full of odd surprises. But it was also mortared with solid chunks of good information. Above all, it was readable. Indeed, it was hard not to read.[28]

Bennett himself was lean and gnarled, rough-hewn and bony, a bit over six feet tall—a lonely crag of a man with a clustering crown of curling white hair, a florid complexion, and a prominent aquiline nose. He was always well dressed, quick and nervous in his movements. Out of him when he talked came a voice harsh and strident, sounding like one of his editorials, charged with sharp colloquialisms and full of sting. His mind teemed with ideas, which escaped daily out onto the pages of his paper, to the chagrin of his many victims.[29]

Bennett, one who knew him said, "threw arrowy glaces"—in at least two directions.[30] For, like Ben Butler, Bennett was irremedially cross-eyed, "so terribly cross-eyed," another who knew him said, "that when he looked at me with one eye, he looked out at the City Hall with the other."[31] When his enemies made fun of him for this peculiar defect, he snapped back that it stemmed from trying to follow their political movements.[32]

Bennett's rival editors considered his sheet a newspaper from hell. Henry J. Raymond of *The New York Times* said, "It would be worth my while, sir, to give a million dollars, if the Devil would come and tell me every evening, as he does Bennett, what the people of New York would like to read about next morning."[33]

It was universally agreed that Bennett was sinful and unscrupulous. His critics called him "Old Satanic." Gideon Welles despised him, calling him "an editor without character whose whims are often wickedly and atrociously levelled against the best man and the best causes, regardless of honor and right."[34]

Bennett, who idolized Benjamin Franklin and the poet Robert Burns, liked to think of himself as the Napoleon of the press.[35] He spelled out his editorial policy from the start, in the first edition of the *Herald* in 1835: "We shall support no party—be the organ of no faction or coterie, and care nothing for any election or any candidate from president down to constable."[36] He had never strayed from that path, which took him in decidedly erratic directions and which caused him to write in what one critic called a "vein of Mephisthelean mockery."[37]

When he first started the paper he saw himself as "one poor man in a cellar against the world."[38] He had begun it all in a dingy basement on capital of $500. His desk had been a board resting on flour barrels. He had been his own editor, reporter, clerk, ad salesman, and circulation department.[39] The paper had since prospered and moved to its own building, and he had taken on help, but Bennett's stance against the world hadn't changed at all. He was Scottish, stubborn, a muckraker—and he was proud of it all.

This burr under the national saddle had no use for Abraham Lincoln, and never had. After Lincoln was nominated for president in 1860 and as the secession crisis deepened, Bennett goaded him to step down even before he was inaugurated. "A grand opportunity now exists," Bennett wrote then, "for Lincoln to avert impending ruin, and invest his name with an immortality far more enduring than would attach to it by his elevation to the Presidency. His withdrawal at this time from the scene of conflict, and the surrender of his claims to some national man who would be acceptable to both sections, would render him the peer of Washington in patriotism." However, Bennett warned, "if he persists in his present position, in the teeth of such results as his election must produce, he will totter into a dishonoured grave, driven there perhaps by the hands of an assassin, leaving behind him a memory more execrable than that of Arnold—more despised than that of the traitor Catiline."[40]

Bennett's overriding cause was preservation of the Union, and his early objection to Lincoln was fear that his party would destroy it. He wanted Lincoln out of the way in 1860 for those reasons. Now, in 1864, he still wanted him out of the way—and still for the same reasons. He believed Lincoln was a captive of the abolitionists, whom he despised. Bennett was something of a Southern-leaning war Democrat, who wanted the Union restored as it was, and was a bitter foe of Republican attempts to broaden the conflict into an emancipation crusade. He viewed Chase as a dangerous radical and tended to favor McClellan, whom he had always liked. The man he liked now, however, was Grant, whom he had been plugging without letup for president since mid-December.[41]

In this new election year, Bennett was saying this of Lincoln: He "is a joke incarnated. His election was a very sorry joke. The idea that such a man as he should be the President of such a country as this is a very ridiculous joke. . . . His intrigues to secure a renomination and the hopes he appears to entertain of a re-election are, however, the most laughable jokes of all."[42]

Lincoln viewed Bennett warily, but not without humor. "Too pitchy to touch," John Hay had said of him, and Lincoln agreed. A patient man, the president had tried to stay on the cross-eyed editor's good side, if there was one. He had said, "It is important to humor the *Herald.*" Bennett was not somebody you ought to ignore, even if you wanted to. And Lincoln knew it.[43]

There was another New York editor general who, with Greeley and Bennett, formed something of an upper triumvirate in the press hierarchy of the North.

Unlike the other two, Henry J. Raymond, the editor of *The New York Times,* looked normal. He was bewhiskered, with a shapely head and trim, well-dressed figure. His height was about the American average, five feet six inches, his eyes were hazel, his hair was black, and his complexion was swarthy.[44]

Raymond was a prodigy of sorts. He had begun reading at age three, and had delivered his first speech at five, and his first political speeches on the stump in a presidential campaign at twenty, when he was still too young to vote.[45]

Raymond was one editor Lincoln could be grateful for. He liked the president, supported him, defended him, wheeled his big, high-toned newspaper along the same policy path—and understood politics so well that he was a leader in Lincoln's own Republican party, a prominent figure in its birth in 1856. He had held office himself—as speaker of the New York House of Representatives and lieutenant governor of the state in the 1850s. In the early months of 1864 he was writing a history of the president's administration, scheduled to be published in May and designed to promote Lincoln's nomination and reelection.

Raymond had a quality rare among journalists of the day: an ability to see both sides of a question and discuss it without misrepresentation, rancor, and poisonously barbed epithets. Nobody was certain whether this was a virtue or not, because it often caused him to temporize, or, as fellow journalist George Alfred Townsend put it: "He was always ditching and diking with his untiring pen"—rather like McClellan on a battlefield or Lincoln in politics.[46]

Gideon Welles didn't like him. Welles, an editor himself before he became secretary of the navy, didn't like any of these New York editors. He called Raymond's *Times,* even though it supported Lincoln, "a profligate Seward and Weed organ, wholly unreliable," and he called Raymond himself "an unscrupulous soldier of fortune," a political vagabond. Welles's view was perhaps colored by the fact that Raymond often had the Navy Department under bombardment.[47]

Raymond had apprenticed in the newspaper business under Greeley at the *Tribune* in the early 1840s. But they had had a falling-out, and Raymond had jumped to the *Morning Courier and New York Enquirer,* before founding the *Times* in 1851. He had since built it into one of the premier newspapers in the country. By 1864, with its excellent news service, its coverage of foreign affairs, and its stable editorial policy, general sobriety, and high moral tone, the paper had attracted a growing army of readers in and around New York.[48]

There were other editors throughout the North who possessed heft and weight. Manton Marble, at the viciously anti-Lincoln, anti-Republican, pro-Democratic *New York World,* stood only a notch below the big three in the pantheon of New York journalism. His paper had become, in its two years of existence, the bible of the Democrats in the country, widely read and seconded by all shades of opinion within the party.

In Chicago were two powerful papers staffed by enterprising reporters and with editors who couldn't have been more different. Joseph Medill at the *Chicago Tribune* had given the Republican party its name and had helped nominate Lincoln in Chicago in 1860. By and large, he still supported his old friend. However, he was a radical in his convictions, tenacious in his policies, active and industrious on behalf of causes dear to him, and often maddened by Lincoln's hesitant, plodding approach to matters Medill thought urgent. Medill was an intense Republican who put the party above Lincoln in his scale of priorities. Occasionally he berated the president editorially, but he was convinced that God meant him to be reelected and there wasn't anything that could be done to prevent it.[49]

Medill's polar opposite in Chicago was Wilbur F. Storey, editor of the *Chicago Times*. Storey and his paper lived on the ragged edge of sedition. The acting assistant provost marshal general of Illinois was to call the paper chief among the instigators of insurrection and treason during the war, "the foul and damnable reservoir which supplied the lesser sewers with political filth, falsehood, and treason. . . . The pestilential influence of that paper in this State has been simply incalculable." But Storey was committed to getting the news. He is alleged to have advised one of his war correspondents: "Telegraph fully all news you can get, and when there is no news, send rumors." Storey was also a harder hitter in the Democratic cause even than Manton Marble at the *World* or William Prime at the *Journal of Commerce* in New York. When Lincoln signed the Emancipation Proclamation in 1863, Storey went ballistic. He got so virulent after Vallandigham's arrest later that year that Maj. Gen. Ambrose Burnside, who had arrested Vallandigham, also shut down Storey's paper. Burnside had acted without sanction from Washington, and the paper wasn't closed long—less than a day. After that, Storey became even more seditious. His paper became known as "Old Storey's Copperhead Times," and was so often threatened by patriotic townsmen that he kept loaded muskets and hand grenades in his editorial rooms, and had the place rigged to release scalding steam on invaders. Storey was of powerful physique and commanding presence, armed, and mad as hell most of the time. One didn't attack him without courting a certain amount of bodily risk.[50]

The three main editor generals in New York waged an incessant, ongoing, violent editorial war of words against one another. Greeley and Raymond used their papers as mouthpieces for party principles. Bennett was a loose cannon beholden to no principles whatever, and apt to fire in any direction—more often than not at his rival editors. He called Greeley "Old White Hat" or "Old White Coat," and not infrequently opened an editorial salvo in this way: "Greeley, with his usual stupidity. . . ."[51] Greeley called Raymond the "little villain."[52] Bennett called Raymond "the monkey editor, chattering and skipping about, and playing the very mischief among the crockery."[53] Bennett dismissed his chief rivals in New York as "the tardy *Tribune,* the tattling *Times* [and] the wicked *World.*"[54]

Into this caldron of insult, Marble lobbed his own grenades. And insult and counterinsult whistled in regularly from as far away as Chicago. Joseph Medill believed he had both Greeley and Bennett figured out. They "hunt in couples," he said. "They pretend to hate each other, but the hatred is a sham. . . . They are as 'thick as two thieves,' behind the rose-bush." Medill pointed out that Bennett had broken ground against Lincoln's reelection and brought Grant to the front as his candidate, "be-slavering" him with adulation and puffery and castigating Lincoln pitilessly in the process. Greeley soon followed, Medill pointed out, and was now looking everywhere for anybody but Lincoln. So here they were again, "hunting in couplet to hound down our noble and patriotic President."[55]

Greeley's method of hounding had come down by the spring of 1864 to getting the Union Party nominating convention postponed. It had been called for June 7 in Baltimore. With virtually all delegates by now instructed for Lincoln, it was clear to Greeley and others that the only chance to stop him now was somehow to get the meeting time put off— by at least two months.

The nub of Greeley's pitch for postponement was this: no man can doubt that much will happen before July Fourth—"very important events certainly, decisive events probably." Let us see how they work out, Greeley urged. Let us see if the great army we have marshaled and the gallant new lieutenant general we have put at its head cannot first crush the rebellion. Let us meanwhile postpone all presidential discussion—at least until September. Any opening of the canvass before then would be "unwise and premature."[56]

Greeley was happy to pitch this to anybody who would listen. "I mean to keep the Presidency in the background until we see whether we cannot close up the war," he wrote a prominent Connecticut Republican. "I am terribly afraid of letting the war run into the next Presidential term; I fear it will prove disastrous to go to the ballot-boxes with the war still pending. Let us have peace first, then we can see into the future."[57]

Or, as he wrote his good friend Rebekah M. Whipple: "As to the Presidency, I am not at all confident of making any change; but I *do* believe I shall make things better by trying. There are those who go so far as they are pushed, and Mr. Lincoln is one of these. He will be a better President, if reelected, for the opposition he is now encountering."[58]

Greeley was "in the sulks," as a fellow Republican put it, had been for a long time, and would probably remain so. And there was no telling meanwhile what would be coming out next from the illegible pile of pen-scratchings on the floor of the Old Rookery. On April 1, Greeley ran three and a half columns of arguments in the *Tribune* from six other papers, for and against postponement of the Union Party convention. He had the pot boiling and intended to keep it boiling, hoping to buy time and keep the field open, hoping somebody would surface with enough support to unhorse Lincoln.[59]

Many radicals were in the sulks this spring, and agreeing with Greeley. In late March, William Cullen Bryant, the editor of the influential *New York Evening Post,* signed a petition with several other prominent New York radicals, including sixteen New York state senators, urging postponement of the convention. They wanted to wait, to let opinion jell, at least until September. They did not consider the pro-Lincoln endorsements already in from nearly every state in the Union jelled opinion. The problem was, it hadn't jelled to their taste.[60]

All of this was putting Edwin D. Morgan in a quandary. Morgan, the U.S. senator from New York and chairman of the Republican National Committee, was getting petitioned in such volume that he was not only annoyed, but alarmed. He wrote Gideon Welles about it, asking him what he thought. He sent similar letters to every member of the party's executive committee. Every member but one had answered back urging no postponement, Welles among them. Delay, Welles snorted, would only give the malcontents, the intriguers, and opponents of the president weeks more to assail, misrepresent, and divide. Get the thing over and done with as soon as possible.[61]

Raymond agreed. Postponement, he argued, would bring three more months of wrangling and division in the party, an intestine war that could only promote discord in the Union ranks and do infinite mischief. "The sooner the candidate is selected," he wrote in the *Times,* "the sooner shall we have that united and hearty support which is so important to the country and the cause."[62]

Any hope that Bennett at the *Herald* would stay out of this wrangle was wishful thinking. He weighed in early in April with his own unique proposal. Better even than a postponement, he suggested, was to do away with the conventions altogether, and replace them with a caucus of the pro-war and pro-Union members of the Congress of both houses. The caucus would then name a candidate—anybody but Lincoln. Why wait, Bennett argued, on "that self-constituted and irresponsible gathering of vagrant politicians known as the National Party Convention?" We have had twenty-eight years of convention-nominated presidents, he said, and every one of them has been a failure. And what has it led to? The most terrible war in the history of mankind.[63]

Nobody else wanted to get near that idea: too pitchy to touch.

It was a time when a man on horseback had compelling political appeal. War was everywhere, the motif for everything. Lincoln had worried about Grant until he talked with Jones. Bennett had been plugging Grant's candidacy without mercy and without his approval.

Even not-too-successful generals couldn't be counted out. Indeed, one was at that moment the leading Democratic contender. And his name came soaring into public view again at a monster mass meeting in New York in mid-March.

The Cooper Union was lit up on the seventeenth for the giant McClellan rally organized by his New York backers. The general himself had no part in this; he was still leading the quiet life of the reclusive noncandidate on Orange Mountain. But this big gathering was billed as the meeting to place his name for president before the country. The large hall was jammed, standing room only. And when a curtain at the rear of the speaker's platform was dropped to reveal a far larger-than-life portrait of the general, there was bedlam. Cheer after cheer shook the hall for Little Mac, lasting several minutes. Behind the portrait, stretching across the entire center arch, was a magnificent Union flag, flanked on either side by the city and state banners. Over the portrait hung the motto, "McClellan and Liberty," and on either side of the portrait were words of wisdom from the would-be candidate himself, fiery words from the Harrison's Landing letter. Flags hung everywhere, and enthusiasm rocked the hall as speaker after speaker stepped up to praise McClellan and denounce the tyrant in Washington.[64]

The very next evening a much quieter meeting for a yet less successful candidate-general convened at the Cooper Union. John C. Frémont, like McClellan, had been sacked earlier in the war by Lincoln. Not only had Frémont not forgiven the president, but neither had the radicals, particularly the big German-American element. They loved Frémont, because he was "good on the goose." Indeed, no man was better on freeing the slaves than Frémont. He had in fact done it in his military jurisdiction, Missouri, in late 1861, wholly without presidential approval and far before Lincoln thought it politically appropriate. When Frémont had refused to rescind the order, Lincoln had done it himself and then removed the general and assigned him to another command, in the mountains bordering the Shenandoah Valley. Frémont, who had won fame and political luster as a western explorer in the 1840s and 1850s, and had been the first Republican presidential nominee ever in 1856, turned out to be an inept general, whatever the command. Lincoln had fired him for good in 1862, and had earned not only Frémont's everlasting enmity but the rancor of the German-American radicals as well.

Now, in this uncertain time when the radicals were ready to seize on any candidate who might unseat Lincoln, Frémont looked attractive. He was perfect on the issue that counted—emancipation. As Manton Marble at the *New York World* pointed out, he had unquestioned priority as the leader of the emancipation movement. Marble said he was an emancipationist from principle and not, like Lincoln, an emancipationist from policy, a longtime favorite of the German Republicans and the uncompromising abolitionists. Marble predicted that these elements were certain to rally to the Frémont standard now, and were just the kind of men to hold fast to their convictions and preferences in defiance of party discipline. Frémont was therefore a potentially dangerous foe for Lincoln. And now that Chase had been politically beheaded, the field was clear for him as the anti-Lincoln candidate in the Republican party. He was more acceptable to the "thick-and-thin" radicals than anybody else. He had experience running for president, and he was, as Marble said, "neither timid by nature nor restrained by position." Marble predicted he would "make a bold headway" against Lincoln.[65]

For once Bennett agreed with something another editor said. "General Frémont, with the radical black republican and red republican German legion devoted to his advancement," Bennett wrote, "is really a more dangerous rival to President Lincoln than Mr. Chase."[66]

Many radicals agreed. By early March a rump nominating convention had already been called for Cleveland on May 10 with the idea of nominating Frémont, subject to withdrawal from the race only if somebody other than Lincoln was nominated in Baltimore in June. On

March 18, the day after the big McClellan meeting, Frémont's supporters in New York met in the rooms of the Women's Loyal League in the Cooper Union to get things rolling. Among those present were members of Frémont's staff. A Frémont Campaign Club was organized, and Greeley, like Demosthenes with a lamp looking for any viable candidate, dropped by, said a few words in favor of postponing the Union Party convention, and assured the meeting that theirs was "not a factious movement."[67]

Whatever it was, it was rising in the political wings and would likely emerge soon onto the main stage of the canvass.

12

THE CONFEDERATE CONNECTION

S PRING WAS LATE COMING TO RICHMOND. A NORTHWEST GALE
dropped several inches of snow on the second day of April. But by
the twenty-second, the weather had turned, and the days were
bright and beautiful and the cherry trees were in bloom.

No number of bright and beautiful days could erase the unrelenting
winter of hard times that defined life in the Confederate capital this
spring. In three years of war, Richmond had tripled from its peacetime
population of forty thousand—and changed dramatically. There was
melancholy talk now of "the coarse vices of the street," and the town's
growing reputation as "the wickedest city" in the Confederacy, with its
"shops of female infamy."[1]

But it wasn't sin that was devastating Richmond; it was scarcity and
its handmaiden, inflation. A buyers' panic had visited the city in February and never left. A grim joke was going around: Whereas one once
took money to market in a purse and carried the purchases home in a
basket, one now needed a basket to carry the money and only a purse
to carry the purchases.[2]

"This is the famine month," John Jones, a clerk in the rebel War
Department, wrote in his diary in March. Every commodity in the
market was "up, up, up." By mid-March, bacon was bringing $10 to
$15 a pound, meal $50 per bushel. Flour ran $300 a barrel, fresh fish
$5 a pound. It cost another $5 for half a pint of snap beans to plant
in the ground. A large wild turkey was going for $100 on the open
market.[3]

"My daughter's cat is staggering to-day, for want of animal food,"
Jones reported on March 18. "Sometimes I fancy I stagger myself. We

do not average two ounces of meat daily; and some do not get any for several days together."[4]

There had been no relief in April. Tea was bringing $22 a pound, coffee $12, brown sugar $10, milk $4 per quart. A pair of boots cost $200, a coat $350, trousers $100, shoes $125. Meal was going for $60 to $80 a bushel, white sugar $900 a barrel. A pair of chickens was bringing $35. Pet pigeons were mysteriously disappearing from their cages overnight around the city. Thefts of stock were common. Live poultry, hogs, cows, present the evening before, were gone in the morning.[5]

The Jones family's meat ration had shrunk even further—to an ounce a day—and on April 8 a pet parrot stole the cook's ration and bolted it down before it could be snatched back. "This is famine," Jones lamented. And it was becoming more brutal every day. "Soon," he predicted, "no salary will suffice to support one's family."[6]

The last half of 1863 had been a nightmare for Jefferson Davis's Confederacy. The currency had become nearly worthless. A rail system, inadequate to begin with, could no longer be depended on to move armies and supplies. Scarcity and discontent were everywhere. Conscription had reached out and swept every able-bodied southerner between the ages of eighteen and forty-five from his hearthside. Slavery, the South's labor system, was threatened by Lincoln's edict of emancipation. Rebel strongholds had been seized, its territory divided, and its armies thrown back at Gettysburg and Chattanooga. Vicksburg had fallen, and the South was cut in half at the Mississippi. And there seemed to be no hope of help from the outside. No nation had yet recognized the Confederacy, and probably never would, barring independence. Thousands of its soldiers had been killed or captured, and there seemed no way to replace them.[7]

Nobody knew better than Jefferson Davis, the Confederacy's worn and weary president, that the South was on the ropes. It no longer had the military or economic resources to win peace and independence on its own. It had to look elsewhere. And ironically, it had to look northward. Nowhere was the presidential election of 1864 in the North more important in this difficult year than it was in the South.

That had been apparent for months now. There was talk of bitter unrest in the western states of the North—in Illinois, Indiana, and Ohio. Reports were drifting into the South of a general debilitating war-weariness in the North that was driving more and more people toward the peace-minded Democrats. Rumor had it that secret societies were organizing revolt. There was talk of a violent breakaway, and of a Western Confederacy.

Whether it was true or not, the South wanted to believe it. It was the one remaining ray of hope on an otherwise bleak landscape. A Western Confederacy was the best that could happen, but almost as good would be a Republican defeat in the coming presidential election. If an anti-war Democrat won the presidency in the North, the South wouldn't have to win the war. It would probably get by ballot what it had fought for all these bloody years to get with bullets: independence, with slavery intact.

Everybody in the South believed this. The editor of the *Richmond Enquirer* believed it. "That canvass," he wrote in early March, "will be more important in its ultimate bearings upon the present war than the military campaign of the ensuing Spring and Summer."[8] The editor of the *Augusta Constitutionalist* in Georgia believed it. He wrote in January: "Every bullet we can send . . . is the best ballot that can be deposited against his [Lincoln's] election. The battle-fields of 1864 will hold the polls of this momentous decision."[9]

Joseph Medill at the *Tribune* in Chicago was amused. "The realm of Dixie," he wrote, "care more about our next President than we do ourselves. . . ."[10]

Jefferson Davis, the ruler in that realm, cared a great deal. He was entirely in tune with Lincoln's political enemies. Like Greeley, like Bennett, like the radicals, like the Democrats, he wanted somebody else at the helm in the North. He knew that while Lincoln held power in Washington, there would be no letup in the war against his Confederacy, nor any compromise toward independence. Lincoln had never admitted there was a Confederate nation, but only that there was a rebellion. He would brook no Southern independence—and no peace, either, without an end to slavery.

Only in the triumph of a peace Democrat—or of a war Democrat on a peace platform—did there seem any real hope, and Davis knew it. He also knew that it would be in the best interests of the Confederacy, as the election campaign progressed in the North, to see that the war went hard for the Union. Another massive invasion of the North, as there had been during the election campaigns in 1862 and at Gettysburg the following year, appeared unlikely; the South now simply lacked the resources for any such drive. But if the Confederates on the battlefield could cause the fighting to go against Northern arms right up to election day, Lincoln might lose and the South might have peace on its terms. Even if the North could simply be checked, not beaten, on the battlefield, that might be enough. But if the Union armies started to win—and the coming spring campaign under the North's new lieutenant general was ominous—then Lincoln would likely be reelected and hope for the Confederacy as a separate nation would be gone for good.

Robert E. Lee, from his vantage point close to the North, had been looking beyond its army to its politics at least since the summer of 1863—and seeing opportunity, perhaps the only opportunity left the Confederacy. In a memorandum to Davis on June 10, even before Gettysburg, Lee conceded that the South was outnumbered and outgunned, and that the gap between the North and South in strength was widening steadily.

"Under these circumstances," Lee wrote, "we should neglect no honorable means of dividing and weakening our enemies that they may feel some of the difficulties experienced by ourselves. It seems to me that the most effectual mode of accomplishing this object, now within our reach, is to give all the encouragement we can, consistently with truth, to the rising peace party of the North. . . . Should the belief that peace will bring back the Union become general, the war would no longer be supported, and that after all is what we are interested in bringing about."[11]

It was now the spring of 1864, the election in the North loomed, and Davis agreed with Lee. Political developments in the North, he believed, were now ripe, the prospects of the peace party encouraging. The moment favored some action to tip popular sentiment against Lincoln.[12]

There was no lack of ideas on how to do this, some of them gratuitous. The advice coming from Georgia was like that. Georgia was a seedbed of dissent, home to Davis's unhappy vice president, Alexander Stephens, and a maverick-minded governor named Joseph E. Brown. They both detested Davis, but, like him, longed for peace and believed the key to it was Lincoln's defeat in November. Their mouthpiece, the *Augusta Chronicle & Sentinel,* put it this way: "It is unquestionably our policy to do everything in our power to increase the number of unconditional peace men at the North. We believe this can be done by carrying the sword in one hand and the olive branch in the other."[13]

Uncompromising states'-rights men, they also believed it could be done from Georgia. Governor Brown had his own plan for peace, which he had introduced earlier in the year in his state legislature. It called for a separate peace with the North, and it was not kindly received in Richmond. The *Richmond Examiner* blasted it as an "absurd project," and called it the "heresy of a separate peace," and "a monstrous treason."[14]

Davis had what he thought was a better idea: sedition, a covert and indirect approach through agents in Canada to undermine Northern public opinion, and if that didn't work, to incite and bankroll open revolution. He had begun that spring to look for commissioners he could send there to do the job. By the end of April he had found them.

Davis's wife, Varina, was worried about her husband. She saw as well as anybody that the Confederacy was threatened on every hand and encompassed "so perfectly" that "we could only hope by a miracle to overcome our foes." She also saw how it was getting to her husband. His health had eroded from loss of sleep, and he was forgetting to eat. She had resumed a former practice of carrying something to him at one o'clock every afternoon that they could eat together. Often in the night she heard him fervently humming his favorite hymn:

> *I'll strengthen thee, help thee, and cause thee to stand*
> *Upheld by my righteous, omnipotent hand. . . .*[15]

In Washington in late April, Lincoln casually picked up a copy of a *Richmond Examiner* and read there a raking attack on Davis.

"Why," Lincoln remarked to John Hay, "the *Examiner* seems about as fond of Jeff as the *World* is of me."[16]

These two presidents were not alike in most things, but they were alike in the enemies they seemed to make. Like Lincoln, Davis was under a firestorm of criticism at home. The fourth session of the First Confederate Congress had adjourned on February 17 in grumbling discontent with his administration and the progress of the war. Like Lincoln, Davis was denounced for want of capacity. Like Lincoln, he was praised for his personal qualities and vilified for his public ones. The editor of the *Richmond Examiner* praised his literary abilities, his spruce English, his ascetic morals, the purity of his private life, and the extraordinary facility of his manners, but denounced his statesmanship and his leadership.[17]

Like Lincoln, Davis's enemies within, particularly the renegades from Georgia, thought him a disaster—a tyrant, usurper, and traducer of civil and states' rights. Northern copperheads detested Lincoln for his draft law, for his suspension of habeas corpus, for his incompetence.

Davis's own nest of Southern copperheads detested him for all of the same reasons.[18]

There was yet one other way in which these two dissimilar men were similar—a very personal way. Both had boys, more than one. Lincoln had his Tad—and, before he died in February 1862, Willie. Davis had his boys too, particularly Joseph Emory, his favorite.

Everybody called Joseph Emory "Little Joe." Barely five years old, he was considered the "good child of the family." His mother described him as "the most beautiful and brightest of my children" and "Mr. Davis's hope, and greatest joy in life"—as Willie had been Lincoln's.[19]

And because of Joe and Willie, these two men were about to be linked in yet another way.

Davis had been all morning at his desk in the executive mansion on April 30. He had visited one last time for a final word with the commissioners he had picked to incite Northern discontent from Canada. It was a warm spring day, and at one o'clock in the afternoon, Varina left her children playing in the room off the second-floor piazza, and, with her basket lunch, went to her husband's office.

She had just uncovered the basket and begun to serve the meal when a servant came running for her. Little Joe, in play, had climbed over the connecting angle of the bannister on the high veranda and fallen the twenty feet to the brick pavement below. The Davises sprinted to where he had fallen, and took the boy in their arms. But he was insensible, and within a few minutes he was dead.[20]

One of the first to reach the mansion, where Varina was shrieking uncontrollably, was Mary Eulalia Semmes, the wife of the Confederate senator from Louisiana, an accomplished harpist and leading Richmond hostess. There she found another of Davis's sons, Jeff, kneeling by his dead brother's side.

Crying out, he said, "Mrs. Semmes, I have said all the prayers I know how, but God will not wake Joe."[21]

Throughout the afternoon, friends streamed to the house to stand vigil and to try to comfort Varina. They found Davis at his wife's side, murmuring over and over, "Not mine, oh, Lord, but thine." A courier came with a dispatch. Davis took it, held it open for some moments, and looked fixedly at Varina. He tried to write an answer, and then cried out in protest, "I must have this day with my little child." Somebody took the dispatch to Samuel Cooper, the Confederate adjutant general, and left the grieving Davises alone with their agony.[22]

The melancholy watch continued on into the night. Every window and door of the mansion seemed to be flung open, as if venting its anguish with its human occupants. The wind blew the curtains, and every gaslight flared.

Mary Chesnut, Varina's close friend, came as soon as she could. Mary was the wife of former U.S. senator James Chesnut, now a Confederate brigadier, whom Davis had just that morning assigned the duty of organizing the reserve forces in South Carolina. As she sat in the drawing room at midnight, "numb—stupid—half-dead with grief and terror," Mary could hear Davis pacing endlessly in the room above. The whole house otherwise was as still as death itself.

The funeral procession wound up the hill among the tall white monuments of the Hollywood Cemetery. The James River tumbled below, over rocks and around islands. Hundreds of Richmond children, each with a green bough or a bunch of flowers, came and threw them on Joe's grave. The boy's body was soon buried under a mass of white flowers and crosses. For Mary Chesnut, the dominant figure in that wrenching tableau was "that poor old gray-haired man," standing bareheaded, as straight as an arrow, beside his little son's open grave. Varina stood back in her heavy black wrappings, her tall, sorrowing figure drooping. Mary remembered it a month later in her diary: "two dark, sorrow stricken figures . . . they rise before me now."[23]

But for the president of the Confederacy—as for the president of the Union—grief, like everything else, had to give way to the business of war and administration. The Second Confederate Congress was about to convene. Life goes on.

On May 6, Jacob Thompson was on his way to catch a steam packet called the *Thistle,* a sleek-hulled Confederate blockade runner. Thompson was Canada-bound, the head of Davis's newly named commission charged with swaying the election in the North. It had all happened so quickly. Less than a month before, on April 7, Davis had sent Thompson a telegram, care of Mississippi governor Charles Clark. "If your engagements will permit you to accept service abroad for the next six months," the wire read, "please come here immediately."[24]

Thompson had not been Davis's first choice; others had already turned down this thorny assignment. But Thompson would do. He had been around the block. Like Davis, he was a Mississippian, and Davis had politicked with him—sometimes been at political odds with him— in Washington in the years before the war. A man with a slightly slippery reputation, Thompson had been secretary of the interior in the Buchanan administration, and in that post had done all he could, even then, to foment division. An ardent secessionist, he had been for a long time unfaithful to the Union.

His co-commissioner to Canada, Clement C. Clay, would be joining him on the *Thistle*. Clay was an Alabaman, a former U.S. and Confederate senator, who had also politicked with Davis in the antebellum years. He was closer to Davis than Thompson was, indeed he was a close friend and ally, a man of culture and refinement. But he was also in delicate health, frail and sickly, a chronic asthmatic. Partly because of this, he was peevish, irritable, and suspicious.[25]

As Thompson made his way to the rendezvous with the *Thistle*, waiting on the river, he was carrying drafts for a million dollars in gold, issued him from a $5-million fund that had been quietly appropriated by the Confederate Congress in mid-February for secret service operations. The commissioners were going to Canada solely as agents of the Confederate president. Their nominations to any mission had never been communicated to the Congress. Most rebel congressmen knew nothing of it.

Davis had written Thompson and Clay identical letters on April 27 and 29:

"Confiding special trust in your zeal, discretion and patriotism, I hereby direct you to proceed at once to Canada, there to carry out such instructions as you have received from me verbally, in such manner as shall seem most likely to conduce to the furtherance of the interests of the Confederate States of America which have been entrusted to you."[26]

That was it. Only the most indistinct of orders had been put in writing. Their instructions had all been entirely verbal and were elastic at best, but Thompson could see a general outline. He knew what had to be done.

He saw it as his job to do everything he could to afford the Northwestern states every possible opportunity "to throw off the galling dynasty at Washington and openly to take ground in favor of States' rights and civil liberty."[27]

He knew that to do this he must try to judge public sentiment and feeling in the North, and as far as possible to turn any existing or potential pro-peace prejudices to the interest of the Confederacy. He was authorized to negotiate with or buy anybody who might help to that end. He had been urged and authorized to make wise use of any political opportunity that surfaced. He was to try to buy influence with key newspapers in the North that might be counted on to turn their presses to the cause. He knew it would be difficult; the newspapers of the North were hardly united on any subject, but most of them generally supported the war effort, if not Lincoln's way of running it.[28]

The Northern will to continue the war must somehow be undermined. If negotiation and peaceful means didn't work, then force was an option. That was what the million dollars was for, in part—to buy rebellion, if willing and rebellious peace-minded men could be found to foment it. Indeed, the best possible scenario in Thompson's mind, what would please him the most, would be a civil war in the Northwest, a conspiracy leading to a second Confederacy. He intended to promote that idea wherever possible.[29]

The job called for improvisation. Since Thompson was leaving Richmond with no clear plan or operational doctrine, he would be winging it. It would be up to him and Clay, and a third member of this commission, James P. Holcombe, already in Canada, how to pull it off.

There was also the matter of the prisoners. An army of Confederate prisoners as numerous as the army Lee had armed and waiting this spring south of the Rapidan was locked up in Northern prison camps, doing the man-starved South no good. The North had cut off all prisoner exchanges, to press its numerical advantage. If those thousands of veteran rebel soldiers could be released and either returned or organized in the North to augment a Northern conspiracy, it would be literally worth an army gained to the beleaguered Confederacy.

Davis grasped at this outside chance to replenish the dwindling ranks of the rebel armies. Conscription had not been enough, and there seemed to be no other existing source. In March he had therefore sent two men, Holcombe, a scholar, and Thomas Hines, an adventurer, to Canada on separate missions to see what could be done.

Holcombe was a romantic—thin, ascetic, and always dressed in a black suit and tie that made his pale face appear deathly. As befitted a scholar—he was the South's leading legal authority, a teacher of law at the University of Virginia—he carried with him a slender, red leather-bound book of poetry, which he read in lagging moments. Davis had sent Holcombe north to help get escaped prisoners returned south.

Hines was at least as thin and at least as romantic as Holcombe. Where Holcombe was a scholar, however, Hines was an incendiary. Where Holcombe carried poetry, Hines toted a gun and a disposition to use it. Hines may have looked the ascetic, with his slender 130-pound body and sleepy-eyed appearance. But his mind was rapier-quick, his body as graceful as Apollo's and whipcord-hard. A Kentuckian, and only in his twenties, he had been an officer in John H. Morgan's Confederate cavalry division, an outfit that specialized in raids and near-scrapes behind enemy lines in the Northwest. Hines was sweepingly mustachioed, with thick, curly black hair, slanting eyebrows, and an instinctive appreciation for beautiful women, good music, and fine horses. On top of all this he was absolutely fearless—the perfect paradigm of the swashbuckler. He had persuaded Davis to send him to Canada in March not just to help escaped prisoners return south, but to organize them for escape and use them in a Northern uprising.

At Hines's side was John B. Castleman, another Morgan alumnus, also from Kentucky and also in his twenties and fully Hines's equal in fearless abandon and heedless desperation—two men who lived their lives on the edge.[30]

Already hatching in the seditious heads of Davis, Thompson, Hines, Castleman, and other shadowy figures waiting in Canada were schemes for uprisings in the half-dozen prison camps in the North—all of them improbable in concept and even more improbable of execution. Plans were afoot for a raid on Camp Douglas in Chicago during the Democratic national convention, and a plan to capture the lone Union gunboat on the Great Lakes and use its fourteen guns to break Confederate inmates out of the prison camp on Johnson Island. And this wasn't the extent of it. There were plans to interfere and disrupt in other ways through Ohio, Illinois, and Indiana—all across the Northern border. There was even a plot to burn New York City.[31]

Thompson was open to all of this and more as he, Clay, and their young commission secretary, William W. Cleary, another of Hines's Kentucky friends, boarded the *Thistle* the morning of May 6 and steamed down the Cape Fear River to Fort Fisher on the North Carolina coast. The blockade runner was a swift, narrow, knifelike sidewheeler lying low in the water and painted gray-white to make her difficult to see at night. Her machinery was polished, glistening, and in perfect working order; it had to be. Arriving at Fort Fisher at about four in the afternoon, she dropped anchor and silently waited for night to fall. At about eight o'clock, phantomlike, she crossed the bar and crept cautiously out in the dark toward the open sea.

Running with every light extinguished, and burning virtually smokeless anthracite coal in her hooded furnace, she began to thread through what Cleary described as the "towering hulls" of the Northern blockading squadron. Through this gauntlet of thirteen looming superstructures the *Thistle* slid as silent as a fish, her engines softly throbbing. She went unnoticed until dawn, when she was sighted breaking hellbent for the open sea, and the chase began. For the next five hours, departing for a time from its charted course, the *Thistle* ran the race with its pursuer, finally drawing ahead and putting in, panting but safe, at the port of St. George in Bermuda.[32]

Thompson, Clay, and Cleary sailed from there for Halifax on the British mail steamer *Alpha,* arriving on May 19. Clay, ill again, was forced to lay over. But Thompson and Cleary were anxious to be on with it, and set out for Montreal, arriving there on May 29, where Thompson put his million dollars into an account in the Bank of Ontario. He was soon in Toronto, where he set up permanent headquarters and began immediately on his errand of sedition.

He soon discovered that it wasn't going to be easy. As things then stood, only days before the Union Party's national convention, Thompson saw that Lincoln was bound to be nominated and, unless something drastic was done, reelected. He quickly shifted to the drastic, traveling to Windsor, Ontario, to meet with Clement Vallandigham. Vallandigham, never without his own visions of peace, told Thompson that if Grant failed before Richmond, and if Sherman stalled before Atlanta, a peace candidate might yet be nominated and elected.

But just in case, Vallandigham acquainted Thompson with the secret Sons of Liberty organization, of which he was supreme commander, a pro-peace movement based on state sovereignty, states' rights, and individual freedom—causes close to both Thompson's and Vallandigham's hearts. Vallandigham estimated Sons of Liberty numbers at about 170,000 in Illinois, Indiana, and Ohio alone, with large and growing memberships in Kentucky and Missouri—and everywhere animated by hostility to the war. The organization, semimilitary in structure, was not necessarily pro-Confederate. There was little sympathy for the South in its makeup; it just wanted the war to end, the armies to withdraw, and individual liberties to be left alone. Its members were unhappy with the Lincoln administration and wanted a peace man elected president.

They were not, however, Vallandigham suggested, above using insurrection, rebellion, and force to reach those goals—to set up a Western Confederacy, if necessary. That was what Thompson wanted to hear. He was ready with his million dollars to bankroll just such a thing, and was eager for the ball to begin—if Vallandigham and the Sons of Liberty were ready to dance.[33]

1 3

AN UNQUIET SPRING

⟡

"THE PRESIDENTIAL EXCITEMENT APPROACHES," A FRIEND WROTE Manton Marble in early May.[1] And nobody was more disgusted by that fact than the Polish count, Adam Gurowski. "The re-election!" Gurowski snarled into his diary. "The re-election overawes and submerges everything, even sound common sense."

Two weeks later he was still disgusted and incendiary. "As the Washington winds raise clouds of dust filled with atoms of offal putrefied in the streets and alleys," he growled, "so in all parties, among copperheads as well as among Republicans, election and re-election fill the air with all kinds of foetid miasma. All the worst and meanest passions are stirred, and they rise like gases to the surface."[2]

Gurowski was right about both the election and the wind. Both had been blowing strongly as April ended, and John Nicolay, Lincoln's young secretary, was as disgusted as the count. Late in the month he wrote his fiancée, Therena Bates, in Pittsfield, Illinois, that it was warm and sunny in Washington, but windy and very dusty. He was resigned to it now after three years. "So Washington weather goes," he told her, "rain or dust—cold or heat—always a disagreeable extreme. . . ."

It was also after Lent, and the social season was over, and that didn't help Nicolay's disposition. As for the election excitement, he dismissed it as a few malcontents in the Republican party "stewing around, trying to make Butler, Frémont, or anybody they can get the nucleus of a little faction in opposition to Lincoln, but there is not the remotest prospect that their eggs will hatch."[3]

Noah Brooks also had his pince-nez in position tracking the political signs as spring turned toward summer. Wise men were telling him that if the coming military campaign in Virginia succeeded, Grant would be the next president; if not, neither Grant nor Lincoln could be elected. The more reasonable scenario, Brooks suspected, was that Grant's success would very likely elect Lincoln, and his lack of success would elect any man put up by the Democrats in Chicago.[4]

An overwhelming majority of the delegates to the Union Party's national convention scheduled for Baltimore in June were now instructed for Lincoln. New York, Ohio, and Illinois had all just held their state conventions and declared unanimously for his renomination. They were the last. The party's commitment to Lincoln throughout the loyal states was now complete, save for mulish Missouri and its nest of grumpy radicals.

There was also what Henry Raymond at *The New York Times* called "the little squad of bolters" about to meet in Cleveland in the last days of May to nominate John C. Frémont. But Raymond saw a positive side even to that prospect. "We like this," he wrote. "A political campaign with a foregone conclusion would naturally be a dull one. Something to lighten it up is needed; and this convention promises to be 'as good as a play.' " Raymond foresaw it as a meeting of malcontents who were dissatisfied with Lincoln's policy, but who would find it impossible to agree on any positive policy of their own. "No practical result can come from it," Raymond predicted, "and the country will have an excellent laugh for nothing."[5]

Raymond's book about Lincoln had just come out, 496 pages of the president's speeches, letters, addresses, proclamations, messages, and a brief sketch of his life. It was being reasonably well received. Even Horace Greeley, who had no love for Raymond and very little for Lincoln, was calling it "a real service" to the American public. A few facts were questionable, Greeley cautioned his *Tribune* readers, but he said that on the whole it was "a well-arranged, readable, interesting book."[6]

It seemed that everybody but Lincoln was agreed that his renomination was a foregone conclusion, that it was impossible for any conceivable combination to undo it now. Even Count Gurowski had bowed to the inevitable. The people were for reelection, the count muttered grudgingly into his diary, even though the majority in Congress were still against it.[7]

But Lincoln wasn't fully convinced. Alexander McClure, visiting the White House from Pennsylvania, assured him that his nomination was wrapped up, that nothing could conceivably reverse it now. "Well,

McClure," Lincoln said, thinking of 1860, "what you say seems to be unanswerable, but I don't quite forget that I was nominated for President in a convention that was two-thirds for the other fellow."[8]

As Lincoln fretted over renomination, anxiously awaited the opening of the spring military campaign, and tried to get his reconstruction plan on track without further offending the radicals, he had also been dealing with his "leg cases."

One of the things the war had brought more of than he cared to think about were death sentences for deserters. And he had to review them all. His kind heart tilted toward forgiveness. He was given to commuting them one after another—"trying to evade the butchering business," as he put it.[9] His softheartedness was well enough for his conscience, but sometimes hard on discipline, often disgusting the military commanders who had done the sentencing.

It all reminded Lincoln of the story of the Irish soldier who, when asked why he had deserted, replied, "Well, Captain, it was not me fault. I've a heart in me breast as brave as Julius Caesar; but when the battle begins, somehow or other these cowardly legs of mine will run away wid me!"[10]

So Lincoln called these death-sentence convictions for cowardice and desertion, which he must approve or disapprove, his "leg cases." He would set aside the more difficult ones, and come back to them later, explaining meanwhile to impatient generals that "they are still in soak."[11]

Since the end of February he had given up saving deserters on a case-by-case basis, and had simply issued a general order, directing that the death sentences of all deserters, which he had not otherwise acted on, be reduced to imprisonment at the Dry Tortugas, in the Gulf of Mexico, west of the Florida Keys.[12]

This softhearted approach had particularly outraged Ben Butler, who would never think of such leniency himself. In February, Butler decided that a sudden attack on Richmond, perhaps taking the city and ending the war, would make him a hero and coincidentally a daunting candidate for the presidency in his own right. He launched his masterstroke early in the month, but was met by a surprising and unexpectedly large Confederate force ten miles from Richmond. His own force was thrown back in confusion. Butler had blamed this setback on a "leg case" whose death sentence had been lifted by the president and who had then escaped and warned the Confederates.

"You may see how your clemency has been misplaced," Butler wired Lincoln in a huff. "I desire that you will revoke your order suspending executions in this department. Please answer by telegraph."[13]

Lincoln never answered. But the president was thinking a good deal about Butler this spring. The general was politically popular. A laudatory book about his military regime in New Orleans had just come out and was a big seller. Chase's candidacy had crashed, and the radicals, looking for any likely replacement for Lincoln who was "right on the goose," were finding Butler an increasingly attractive election year option. And Butler was doing nothing to dampen speculation. He was watching squint-eyed and with great interest from Fort Monroe as the election-year drama continued to unfold.

It was no secret that Butler wanted to be president. And others shared that wish. Ben Wade and Thaddeus Stevens both favored Butler, too. Greeley was anointing him editorially, and Wendell Phillips, the abolitionist orator, was keen on him. "Lincoln drifts," Phillips said in a speech in Massachusetts, "Butler steers."[14]

Many radicals besides Wade, Stevens, Greeley, and Phillips also liked Butler. They liked his style. They liked it that he didn't hesitate "to take advanced steps," as Lincoln did. They expected he would be "a vigorous ruler," not afraid to hurt rebels, as Lincoln seemed to be. Butler wouldn't be afraid to "hang traitors, confiscate their property, do justice to loyal men, and retaliate the wrongs even of negroes."[15]

In March, Simon Cameron, the Republican political boss of Pennsylvania, visited this traitor-hanging politician at Fort Monroe. Some say Lincoln sent him.

Cameron and Lincoln were another of those odd couples that politics occasionally produces, to the wonderment of all. Cameron was a political insider of the slickest kind. For helping nominate Lincoln in Chicago in 1860, Lincoln's floor managers had promised him a cabinet seat. Lincoln had honored the promise and appointed him secretary of war.

Cameron was a slight man with a thin, calculating mouth, deepset, keen gray eyes, and gray hair. But he was a political heavyweight, the shrewdest of the Pennsylvania politicians. He turned out to be a far better politician than an administrator, and in January 1862 Lincoln had eased him out and replaced him with Edwin Stanton, who was a far better administrator than a politician.

There had been no hard feelings on either Cameron's part or Lincoln's, and the president had continued to value the Pennsylvanian's

political acumen, while taking into account his less-than-spotless reputation. Cameron's political integrity was widely suspect. It was said
that he believed an honest politician was one who when bought stays
bought.[16]

Cameron liked Butler—indeed, they were two of a kind. What they
talked about at Fort Monroe is a matter of some speculation and considerable skepticism, even to this day. The two would later say that
Cameron had come at the president's behest to offer Butler the vice
presidency on the Union Party ticket, which Butler, with an eye on the
bigger prize, refused.[17]

In April, Lincoln decided to visit Butler himself, for what reason
nobody knows. "Mrs. L and I think we will visit Fort Monroe some
time next week . . ." Lincoln wired Butler on April 7. "Please do not
make public our probable visit." But four days later, the president
wired again: "Mrs. L is so unwell that I now think we will not make
the contemplated trip this week." He chose not to come without her,
and whatever he might have had in mind, and whether it had to do
with politics or war or both, went out with the trip.[18]

It would not appear unreasonable that Lincoln, even if he didn't
want Butler as a vice president, did want a war Democrat such as Butler to strengthen the ticket and widen its appeal. He surely at least
wanted to know what the unpredictable general's intentions were.

Richard Henry Dana, the celebrated writer-lawyer, was in Washington in late April at Willard's inquiring about his luggage. As he
waited, a short, round-shouldered man in a tarnished general's uniform
approached the desk and asked after a General Dana. Try as he might,
Dana couldn't place this nondescript officer. But a staring crowd had
begun to form around him. Two other generals came up and were
introduced. Still Dana didn't catch his name. It wasn't Joe Hooker.
Dana knew what Hooker looked like. Whom could it be? Dana asked
the doorkeeper.

"That is General Grant," said the doorkeeper. Dana then joined the
starers. It wasn't the first time Grant had invited a puzzled double take.

The next morning Dana was introduced to Grant over breakfast. As
the general was leaving the table to return to his army, Dana said, "I suppose, General, you don't mean to breakfast again until the war is over."

"Not here I shan't," said Grant, a man of few words.[19]

The country was on the brink of a great military campaign, perhaps the most important of the war—the campaign that might end the

rebellion for good. And it was all in the hands of this taciturn, nondescript general whom few seemed able to recognize on first sight.

As May opened, an attack in Virginia against Lee's army seemed
imminent. Exactly how, where, or when, only Grant knew, and he wasn't
saying. The nation did know that any day now was to bring renewed
war on a widespread scale. A closely coordinated movement from Virginia to Tennessee to Georgia to Alabama seemed likely. Grant would
probably move on Richmond from Culpeper, Butler from the James,
Maj. Gen. Franz Sigel by the Shenandoah Valley, Sherman from Chattanooga toward Atlanta, and perhaps there would even be a long-
awaited attack on Mobile—all in one grand consort. Not in the history
of modern scientific war, Henry Raymond at *The New York Times*
would soon write, had there been anything at once so colossal and so
complex.[20]

The Union's Army of the Potomac, more than 120,000 strong,
waited between the Rappahannock and the Rapidan. On April 9, preliminary orders went out to General Meade. Lee's Army of Northern
Virginia was to be the objective. "Wherever Lee goes," Grant wrote
Meade, "there you will go also."[21]

Lincoln had no more idea what Grant's plans were than any other
citizen. Anxious but confident, he wrote his general on April 30: "Not
expecting to see you again before the Spring campaign opens, I wish to
express, in this way, my entire satisfaction with what you have done up
to this time, as far as I understand it."

The particulars of your plans, Lincoln wrote, "I neither know, or
seek to know. You are vigilant and self-reliant; and, pleased with this,
I wish not to obtrude any constraints or restraints upon you." But Lincoln couldn't help being apprehensive. "While I am very anxious that
any great disaster, or the capture of our men in great numbers, shall be
avoided," he wrote Grant, "I know these points are less likely to escape
your attention than they would be mine. If there is anything wanting
which is within my power to give, do not fail to let me know it."

He closed, "And now with a brave Army, and a just cause, may God
sustain you."[22]

Lee waited below the Rapidan with his ragged little army, half the
size of Grant's, depleted in numbers and vastly inferior in resources.
But it appeared as ready as it was possible to be under the circumstances. The same anxious feeling was in the air throughout the Confederacy. John Jones, the war clerk in Richmond, reported to his diary
in the closing days of April that troops were passing through day and

night, concentrating under Lee to the north. They were coming hither from all quarters, he wrote, "like streamlets flowing into the ocean." The great battle, he predicted, couldn't be much longer postponed.[23]

On May 3, Jones wrote in his diary that it was rumored Grant's army was in motion.[24] It was a prophetic entry. Orders had gone out that day from Grant that the army was to move across the Rapidan that night, march around the right flank of Lee's army, and wedge itself between him and Richmond.

Soon after midnight on May 4, Grant's army was moving toward the three fords of the Rapidan. It was the most silent of movements— "without call of bugle or beat of drum," one soldier said.[25] Maj. Gen. Phil Sheridan's two cavalry divisions led the two infantry columns across Germanna and Ely's fords, six miles apart. The wagon trains began crossing at Culpeper Mine ford and following the column across Ely's.

For the seventh time in the war, a Union army was marching on Richmond. Abraham Lincoln could tell a story about that, too. Earlier in the war, a petitioner who had waited for three months in vain for a pass to Richmond, applied as a last resort to the president. "My dear sir," Lincoln told him, "I would be most happy to oblige you if my passes were respected, but the fact is I have within the last two years given passes to more than 250,000 men to go to Richmond, and not one of them has got there yet in any legitimate way."[26]

May 4 dawned clear, warm, and beautiful, and by late in the afternoon the Union cavalry and infantry had crossed the river. The wagon train would take longer, for it was sixty-five miles long, long enough to reach from the Rapidan to Richmond. It wouldn't finish crossing until the afternoon of the fifth.

Lee watched and waited. As Grant's army filed into what was called the Wilderness, near Chancellorsville, he began setting his own army in motion. He ordered the two corps of A. P. Hill and Richard S. Ewell up from Orange County Court House, Ewell down the turnpike and Hill down the plank road, the two parallel throughways intersecting Grant's line of march. At the same time he called James Longstreet's corps up from Gordonsville, forty miles away.

That night, Grant's army bivouacked on the Chancellorsville battlefield. It was for many of his soldiers a grisly trip back in time. The field was still strewn with the haunting reminders of the year before— weatherbeaten remnants of decayed clothing, rusted gun barrels, and bleached bones. "The dead were all around us," wrote Private Frank Wilkeson, "their eyeless skulls seemed to stare steadily at us."[27]

The Wilderness was a dense, tangled undergrowth of low-limbed and scraggly pines, stiff and bristling chinkapins, scrub oaks, hazel, sweet gum, and cedar. It was, one reporter said, a "thick chaperal, through which no artillery could play," a region of dark hollows, "of gloom and the shadow of death."[28]

Well known to Lee, it was *terra incognita* to Grant, akin to what one of his privates called "a voyage of discovery made in unknown lands, among warlike enemies lying in ambush."[29] It was an equalizer of armies of unequal size, the last place Grant wished to meet Lee, the one place Lee wished to meet Grant.

Both armies entrenched the night of May 4, east of the Germanna Ford Road, and awaited the dawn of a new day. That day, the fifth, dawned beautiful and springlike, far too serene for the bloody, hellfire work that lay ahead.

What happened next was not so much a battle as what a reporter described as "the fierce grapple of two mighty wrestlers suddenly meeting." It was, in his words, the "strangest of battles ever fought—a battle which no man could see, and whose progress could only be followed by the ear," in which a massive concentration of 300 cannons could only stand silent and useless. It was a sightless surging through a "horrid thicket" in which "lurid fires played." Out of its impenetrable depths came "the crackle and roll of musketry like the noisy boiling of some hell-caldron."[30]

"The work was at close range," yet another reporter said. "No room in that jungle for maneuvering; no possibility of a bayonet charge, no help from artillery; no help from cavalry; nothing but close, square, severe, face-to-face volleys of fatal musketry." The wounded "stream out, and fresh troops pour in," the reporter wrote. "Stretchers pass out with ghastly burdens, and go back reeking with blood for more."[31]

The fighting raged through the twilight hours, ending only at about eight in the evening, when darkness fell and when, the private wrote, "the sad shadows of night, like a pall, fell over the dead in these ensanguined thickets."[32]

But it wasn't over. The next morning the battle continued and the Wilderness was soon ablaze. The soldiers fought the enemy and flames and suffocating smoke at the same time. As the fighting surged through its second day, Grant waited at his headquarters, coolly smoking a cigar and whittling on a piece of wood. Sometime during the fighting, Meade said to him that the enemy seemed inclined to make a

Kilkenny-cat fight out of it. And Grant said, "Our cat has the longest tail."[33]

Lee rode among his soldiers, so close to the fighting that his alarmed army shouted him, almost as one voice, to the rear.

At the end of the second day, Friday, May 6, the fight in the Wilderness ended. It was a draw, and decided nothing. But the casualties were staggering. Grant had lost more than 17,000 killed, wounded, and missing, the Confederates more than 7,500. Thousands, blue and gray, still lay dead and wounded, some bodies charred beyond recognition in the thick, smoldering woods.

But, surprisingly, no Union retreat back across the Rapidan followed this rebuff, as had happened in every other such engagement of the Army of the Potomac in the past. In mid-evening on May 7, Grant, instead of retiring, began shifting his army southeast along the line toward Spotsylvania Court House, probing for another opening around Lee's right flank. Lee moved sideways to block him. The two armies then began another bloody two-week shootout around Spotsylvania, some ten miles from the Wilderness battlefield. It was yet another standoff, and on May 21, Grant again shifted his front, moving south from Guiney's Station toward the North Anna River, Lee moving with him. The fighting had developed a pattern. One Confederate described it as "a succession of death grapples and recoils and races for new position." There was a slide to the east, and another, and another.[34]

The cavalryman Charles Francis Adams Jr., son of Lincoln's ambassador to Britain, wrote, "No one knows whether tomorrow the Army is to fight, to march, or to rest." In late May, marching seemed to be the order of the day.[35]

After three days of sporadic fighting on the North Anna, Grant shifted his front yet again, and pulled up on the first day of June at Cold Harbor, near the site of the Seven Days battles in 1862. There Lee dug in and Grant prepared to deliver another blow.

As Grant was sidewinding toward Richmond, Butler was on the James, getting in trouble. The steeples of Petersburg were but seven miles away. Richmond lay but fifteen miles to the north, a seemingly easy target. But within days Butler, demonstrating his inept generalship, found his army of 39,000 ingloriously bottled up in the Bermuda Hundred, a triangle of ground between the James and Appomattox rivers, by 10,000 Confederates. The soldiers began to call Butler's operations the "stationary advance."[36] The disappointed Grant said it was as if

Butler's army, now completely sealed off from further operations in front of Richmond, was "in a bottle strongly corked."[37]

On the other main front in the West, Maj. Gen. William Tecumseh Sherman began his march south on May 7. He marched that day out of Chattanooga toward Atlanta with a force of nearly 100,000, against some 60,000 Confederates dug in at Dalton, Georgia, under Gen. Joseph E. Johnston.

The North was in an anguish of uncertainty and concern. The "painful suspense . . . the intense anxiety is oppressive, and almost unfits the mind for mental activity," Navy Secretary Gideon Welles confided to his diary.[38] Noah Brooks wrote that unlike at any other time, all other news and conversations were being swallowed up and lost sight of in the speculation about what was happening with Grant's army between the Rapidan and Richmond. People went about the streets with their hands full of newspaper extras. Every messenger from the front, or from any source of news, was mobbed with questions. News reports from the front were read aloud from the desk of the presiding officers of both houses of Congress, bringing business to a halt, distracting everybody. The Senate at one point adjourned for three days at a time—its constitutional limit—to digest the news from the front and to consider the controversial House bill to increase the internal revenue. The House skipped its Saturday session to ponder the news, to try to sort out what it meant.[39]

For three days after Grant crossed the Rapidan and plunged into the Wilderness, Lincoln heard nothing. He hadn't slept all night on Friday, May 6, as the army fought across the rivers. The next day the weary and anxious president walked again to the telegraph office to take up the vigil.

"Nothing, Mr. President," the operator on the desk told him. "Nothing that amounts to anything."

But then the young cipher operator told him of a man who had come to the telegraph office at Union Mills, a little Virginia settlement twenty miles from Washington, on the road to Culpeper. The man claimed he had left the army early that morning. He had asked for Deputy Secretary of War Charles A. Dana. He said he wanted to send a dispatch to the *Tribune*. But he had gotten Stanton instead of Dana, and Stanton had accused him of being a spy and ordered him held to be shot the next morning.

"Ordered him shot?" Lincoln repeated, perhaps thinking, Oh, God, another leg case.

"Yes, Mr. President."

"He is at Union Mills?"

"Yes."

"Ask him if he will talk with the President."

Henry E. Wing, the prisoner ordered shot in the morning, lay on a cot in the telegraph office at Union Mills. This was an unfair and ungrateful predicament for a former soldier who had been wounded in the leg fighting for the Union at Fredericksburg. Since he was now crippled and couldn't fight anymore, he had become a newspaper correspondent for the *Tribune*. He looked disreputable enough just then to be shot. His slight, 130-pound frame was clad in the rough butternut garb of a plantation hand, heavy brogans on his feet, a faded cap on his head, and covered head to foot with Virginia mud.

A message clattered in over the wire from Washington.

"The President wants to know if you will talk with him," the operator at Union Mills told Wing. "He wants to know if it is true that you have come from the army."

"Tell him yes."

"He wants to know if you will tell him what news you bring."

"Tell him if he will first send one hundred words to the *Tribune*, I will tell him."

The answer came back: "Write your hundred words and we will send it at once."

Wing hurriedly scribbled his hundred words, and within moments Lincoln had them on the wire, not only to the *Tribune*, but to the country.

Back on the line to Wing, the president telegraphed: "If I send an engine for you, will you come to Washington?"

Between one and two o'clock in the morning—it was now Saturday, May 7—Wing found himself in a cabinet meeting in the White House. In his muddy and disheveled outfit, he made less than a glittering impression. Stanton perhaps believed he ought to go ahead with the execution. Nor did this vagabond tell them much beyond what was in his dispatch to the *Tribune*.

However, when the cabinet members left, more than a little disappointed, Wing held back, as if there was something more he wished to tell Lincoln.

"You wanted to speak to me?" the weary president asked.

"Yes, Mr. President. I have a message for you—a message from General Grant. He told me I was to give it to you when you were alone."

Lincoln was instantly all attention.

"Something from Grant to me?"

"He told me to tell you, Mr. President, that there would be no turn-ing back."[40]

Lincoln must have thought at that heartening moment what the rest of the country thought shortly afterward, when Grant said, "I will fight it out on this line if it takes all summer."[41] This Grant was different from all past commanders of the army. He just wouldn't let up. Any other commander would have been back upon Washington by this time, as Noah Brooks wrote, "with the whole rebel army thundering at his heels." As reinforcements kept flowing through Washington to the front by the thousands, Brooks wrote that people were wondering: "Can Lee stand all this?"[42]

It wasn't until May 9 that the first dispatches directly from Grant began arriving in the telegraph office. But it was clear from the first of them that his strategy was simple and direct: "continuous hammering," or what the Duke of Wellington, half a century before, had called "hard pounding."[43]

The next night, sometime after midnight, even the elements seemed to echo this hard pounding. A heavy, black raincloud, which one observer said "appeared to embrace the earth," suddenly gathered over Washington. The darkness was complete, the density of the cloud almost palpable to the senses. When the rain began to fall, it came down in merciless cascades. Thunder roared and lightning flashed con-tinuously, illuminating the black sky with a steady, electrifying light. All objects were sharply illuminated and brought into bold relief. The thunder, the observer said, came in crashes rather than in rever-berations.[44]

Something else was also coming to Washington with crashing effect. Grant's continuous hammering had its fearful price. The fighting from the Wilderness to Spotsylvania had been murderous. And the conse-quences, wounded and dying, were now pouring into Washington.

About twilight one evening, Lincoln was riding in his carriage slowly toward the Soldiers' Home. As he stopped at a streetcorner for a word with Illinois congressman Isaac Arnold, a line of wounded men filed past. "Look yonder at those poor fellows," Lincoln exclaimed. "I can-not bear it. This suffering, this loss of life is dreadful."[45]

Casualties were arriving each day at the wharves on the Potomac by boatloads. The twenty-one hospitals in the city and vicinity were jammed. Thousands of strangers from the North had filled Washing-ton, friends and relations seeking their own among the maimed and dying. The country was appalled, and there was dark talk that Grant, although dogged, was also a butcher who harbored too little regard for human life.[46]

"Was the whole of Grant's army being sent back wounded to Washington?" one horrified observer asked himself. It appeared so.[47]

On May 28 the weather was lovely, cool, calm, and clear, perfect, Noah Brooks thought, in every way. It would have made every heart glad, he believed, had not the air, so "heavy with summer blooms and fresh with young life," not been even "heavier with woes from the fringed edge of battle." He described the scene in the dispatch to his newspaper that day: Every night, when the glowing hues of evening were gilding the waters of the Potomac and softly lighting the green of the riverbank, the boatloads of wounded soldiers arrived at the wharves and discharged their precious freight. Long trains of ambulances waited to take them away. There were the anguished faces of the spectators, who stood in long lanes through which the sad processions moved from each boat. Many women, and even men, wept from sympathy and could not see the silent suffering unmoved. "The long, ghastly procession of shattered wrecks," Brooks wrote, the tearful, sympathetic spectators, "the rigid shapes" of the already dead, the "smoothly flowing river and the solemn hush in foreground and on distant evening shores," made, in his mind, the saddest sight of the war.[48]

It appeared to Gideon Welles that these wounded being sent in waves back to Washington were living witnesses to the country's agony. "This almost innumerable host," he wrote, was "an affecting spectacle that grieved the hearts of all, and of none more than the president, who was blamed and held responsible for the killed and wounded by a large portion of his countrymen."[49]

The grieving Lincoln had been much taken with young Henry Wing of the *New York Tribune*. When Wing prepared to return to the front, the president told him that whenever he returned to Washington he was to come and "tell me all you hear and see." On one of his returns after their briefing session, Lincoln talked to him of politics, and of the canvass of 1864, and of his own personal predicament—things he might not have confided to another politician.

"There's many a night, Henry," the president said, "that I plan to resign. I wouldn't run again now if I didn't know these other fellows couldn't save the Union on their platforms, whatever they say."

"I can't quit, Henry," Lincoln said sadly. "I have to stay."[50]

Lincoln was like his soldiers. He seemed trapped in the war for the duration.

14

THE CLEVELAND 400

—✦—

HIS HAIR WAS DARK, HIS SKIN OLIVE, HIS EYES BLUE AND riveting. His features were chiseled and handsome. His mind was agile, his body catlike, his nature brimming with ardor and heedless impetuosity. His was the face and form of adventure and romance, and his name was John Charles Frémont.

He had been an American legend and a household name for nearly two decades—for ten years at least before Abraham Lincoln emerged from obscurity into the popular psyche. He was a romantic and a dreamer, a wanderer and adventurer. No one knew the American West better than Frémont. As an army officer he had surveyed, explored, and charted more pure western wilderness than any other living man. He had lived his life on the abyss of physical peril in dark, unmarked, Indian-infested regions. He had left his name written large across the geography of a third of the continent, and carved out immortality as "the Pathfinder of the West."[1]

Frémont was such a larger-than-life character by 1856 that he became the newly founded Republican party's first presidential nominee. He knew next to nothing about politics, but he had also known next to nothing about the West when he began that career. He was exploring unknown ground politically just as he had explored it geographically. He lost the race in 1856, one of the few adventures in his life up to that time at which he had ever failed. He had since also failed as a Union general.

Politics and war, as it turned out, both required a different kind of talent than he possessed. But now, in the spring of 1864, he was nonetheless being pressed to explore the enigmatic region of politics yet again, to answer its call once more. For a band of unreconcilable radicals and abolitionists were bent on making him president instead of Abraham Lincoln.

From birth, Frémont had been cut from different cloth—the product of a love affair between a romantic French émigré and the beautiful young wife of a wealthy and prominent Virginia nobleman. The illegal lovers had run away together in 1811, leaving Richmond reeling in the scandal of the decade. Later, still together, they created young John Frémont, giving him life in Savannah, Georgia, on January 21, 1813.

Frémont was born out of wedlock, for his parents could not legally marry until his mother's husband died. That didn't take long, however. Twice her age, old enough to have fought in Washington's army, and not half as romantic as her Frenchman, the husband died soon after young Frémont was born. The French father was also soon dead, and the mother raised her young son alone in Charleston, South Carolina. Despite her flair for the romantic, Frémont's mother was devout, and began early angling her young son's education toward the Episcopalian ministry.

No son ever held more promise, with his wiry, agile body, his brilliant and active young mind. He was more handsome than he needed to be, and everybody called him Charley. From an early age, although he loved his mother and was an obedient son, he found courting adventure and physical peril far more interesting than the scriptures.

One such peril he courted, when he was old enough and it came time to fall in love, was the beautiful Jessie Benton, daughter of the formidable Thomas H. Benton, United States senator from Missouri, who frowned on the match. Frémont was by this time a young army officer, and he and Jessie, as desperately in love as his mother and father had been, decided to elope.

The couple married secretly, without Benton's consent or knowledge, on October 19, 1841, in a ceremony in the parlor of Gadsby's Hotel in Washington. They subsequently confessed in an emotional encounter with the outraged Benton, who ordered young Frémont from his house, shouting dramatically, "Never cross my door again!" and adding emphatically that "Jessie shall stay here!"

To that, Jessie clutched Frémont's arm ever tighter and, borrowing from the biblical Ruth, said, "Whither thou goest, I will go; and where thou lodgest, I will lodge; thy people shall be my people, and thy God my God!"[2]

Knowing his headstrong daughter meant every word of it, and being a politician and accustomed to compromise, Benton backed down.

Jessie stayed, as her father ordered, but so did Frémont, contrary to Benton's orders, moving in with his new bride. Benton was soon won over, for the son-in-law was worthy, and this was a marriage made in heaven. Jessie was in every way a match for her explorer groom, and did as much as he himself did to make him what he was by 1864.

Frémont was an excellent topographer, surveyor, and mathematician, with a true scientist's reverence for his calling. This talent, together with his inclination to wander and explore and his poetic appreciation of the American West, carried him into his life's work. He soon became the officer everybody thought of when there was an expedition to lead in the unsurveyed West. He went on to become one of the pioneers in the winning of California, and eventually its governor, then its U.S. senator.

He was not however, an unalloyed hero, or universally beloved. He had some impure metal in him. He was impetuous, with erratic judgment, particularly of men, and a dreamlike side that made him often less than practical. Gideon Welles, who had an opinion of nearly everybody, had a low one of Frémont. Welles had supported him in 1856 for president. But now, in the war, he viewed him as "reckless, improvident, wasteful, pompous, purposeless, vain, and incompetent. . . . On all occasions he puts on airs, is ambitious, and would not serve under men of superior military capacity and experience."[3]

Frémont held a position not many pegs above Beast Butler in the estimation of the South. The *Augusta Chronicle & Sentinel* viewed him as an "unprincipled adventurer," and his supporters as a "mongrel herd of Northern fanatics." Alexander Stephens, the vice president of the Confederacy, thought him "as unprincipled as Cicero represented Catiline to be." In Stephens's view, even Lincoln was better for the South than Frémont.[4]

At the war's beginning, Lincoln thought well of Frémont. "Even now," he had said, as late as December of 1863, "I think well of his impulses. I only think he is the prey of wicked and designing men and I think he has absolutely no military capacity."[5]

When the war broke out, Frémont was in Europe. He had hurried home, and Lincoln had made him a major general and given him command of the important Western Department in Missouri. There he was soon in trouble, first with the powerful Blairs, then with Lincoln himself. Early in his assignment, in August 1861, Frémont took it on himself to free the slaves of all Missouri secessionists. That pleased the radicals and abolitionists enormously, but set Lincoln's teeth on edge. Though this might be a good idea someday, it wasn't one whose time had yet come in 1861. It invaded the political arena, impinged on presidential authority, and threatened to loosen Lincoln's tenuous hold on a critical border state early in the war, when he could little afford it.

Lincoln asked Frémont to modify the order to bring it in line with current policy Union-wide. Frémont refused. So Lincoln rescinded the order, and within weeks relieved Frémont, reassigning him to command of the new Mountain Department in western Virginia. There, in the Shenandoah Valley in the early summer of 1862, Frémont was outmaneuvered by a Confederate general even more daring and impetuous than he, Stonewall Jackson. When Lincoln put another general over him, the proud Frémont asked to be relieved. He had not since been reassigned.

Frémont was the darling of many radicals and abolitionists, particularly of the Germans in St. Louis. They had never forgiven Lincoln for firing him. Nor had Frémont. As early as May 1863 it became known to a small group of his supporters that Frémont was willing to present himself again as a presidential candidate. By March 1864 a campaign was actively under way by a coterie of those supporters to make it happen.

There were two main centers of anti-Lincoln, pro-Frémont discontent in the country: in St. Louis, among the Germans, and in New York. All had a pro-Frémont, anti-Lincoln bias tracking back to the original cause of the quarrel between the two in Missouri. The pro-Frémont radicals had two favorite descriptions of Lincoln's policies: "imbecile" and "vacillating." They favored the immediate extinction of slavery throughout the country by congressional action, absolute equality of all men before the law, and a vigorous execution of the laws confiscating rebel property. And they shared a powerful hatred of the president.[6]

The movement to put Frémont forward began in Missouri, that hotbed of anti-Lincoln radicalism. It had since spread to the German enclaves in Illinois, Iowa, Wisconsin, and Indiana. A Frémont movement emerged openly in New York City in February. In March a Frémont journal, the *New Nation*, was launched. A New York Frémont club was organized on March 18 in the meeting at the Cooper Union at which Greeley had spoken. There had also been an early fluttering of Frémont activity in those other two main pockets of abolitionism in the country, New Jersey and New England.

Calls for a convention to nominate Frémont for president began going out into the country in early May. The main call urged "all independent men, jealous of their liberties and of the national greatness," to meet in Cleveland on the last day of May for consultation and concert of action in the coming presidential canvass. The idea was to "resist the swelling invasion of an open, shameless, and unrestrained patronage which threatens to engulf under its destructive wave the rights of the people, the liberty and dignity of the nation." The call urged that the one-term principle be written inflexibly into the law. It blasted the coming Baltimore convention as not truly national—too far from the geographical heart of the nation and therefore not likely to represent the true will of the people. Besides, they believed it already pre-rigged for Lincoln.[7]

Reaction followed the calls as night follows day. Manton Marble at the *New York World* called it "a political flank movement." He relished any likely divisive scrub race among the detested Republicans that might derail Lincoln, and predicted a teeming of delegates to Cleveland that would be "immense in numbers."[8]

James Gordon Bennett at the *New York Herald* advised them to convene, by all means, but nominate Grant and make Frémont his vice-presidential running mate instead. Such a coupling, Bennett predicted, would be a "powerful ticket" on which conservatives, black and red Republicans, and Democrats could all cordially combine. But when the Frémont clubbers in New York came out ten days later emphatically reaffirming that this was a convention to nominate Frémont, Bennett wrote that he was beginning to suspect they were going to make of it "only another radical abolition *fiasco*."[9]

Henry Raymond at *The New York Times* called it "the bolters' convention." Others saw it as a convention of "ultra patriots, sore-heads and cranks." Thurlow Weed called it a "slimy intrigue."[10]

Elizabeth Cady Stanton, the assertive female crusader who was for, among other things, women's right to vote, invited herself. "To your call 'to the radical men of the nation,' taking it for granted you use 'men' in its largest sense," she wrote the Central Frémont Club of New York, "I desire to append my name."[11]

Wendell Phillips, the flame-breathing abolitionist, smiled benignly on the whole idea of this unauthorized convention. Phillips was a volatile mixture of the nation's most gifted orator and its most extreme radical. Bennett conceded he was "undoubtedly the best public speaker on this continent. His eloquence is as classical as that of Cicero, and as effective as that of Demosthenes." Manton Marble called Phillips "that first of orators and worst of fanatics and disunionists." Henry Raymond believed he was made only to be "a gadfly to the body politic."[12]

Whatever he was, Phillips rarely missed an opportunity to slap at Lincoln. He had been doing it since the day the president was elected in 1860. Lincoln, he had said then in a speech in Tremont Temple in Boston, is but "a pawn on the political chessboard, his value is in his position; with fair effort, we may soon change him for a knight, bishop, or queen, and sweep the board."[13]

Phillips had been trying to trade him in for a different chess piece ever since, and here was another opportunity. He hailed the bolters' convention and outlined a proposed platform: subdue the South as rapidly as possible. The moment Confederate territory falls under Federal control, confiscate and divide the lands of the rebels. Immediately extend the right of suffrage as broadly as possible to blacks as well as whites. Let the Federal Constitution outlaw slavery throughout the Union and forbid any distinction in any state on account of color or race. Above everything, he urged, nominate "a statesman and a patriot," not a Lincoln. Frémont, he said, would do just fine.[14]

On the morning of May 31, in answer to the call, the delegates began drifting into Chapin Hall in Cleveland. The *World* was still predicting great things for it and calling it "the People's Convention." It was a rump session if ever there was one. There was no slate of delegates as such. No credentials were asked for. Anybody with nothing else to do could stray in, take a seat, make a speech, and cast his vote.[15]

The *World* reported that the "gentlemen whose hair is brown, and long, and parted in the middle" were there in force. These were, in Marble's definition, the radical theorists, who "are not, never have been, and never will be politicians, nor can they be made such by any sort of process. Not one of them ever had an opinion worth entertaining upon the subject of the government of a nation." But the one great end and aim of their dreams was to destroy the hated Lincoln, an objective shared by Marble. The *World* noted that the miscegenationists were also present, but fewer in number than one would have expected in such an abolition-tinted gathering. It was a convention heavy with German accents.[16]

The unsympathetic *Cleveland Herald* looked at the crowd and called it a convention of "sly politicians from New York, impetuous hare-brained Germans from St. Louis, abolitionists, and personal friends and parasites of Frémont." The equally unsympathetic *Cincinnati Daily Commercial* called it a collection of "long-haired radicals" who had called a meeting at Cleveland because they couldn't afford to go to Baltimore.[17]

Elizabeth Cady Stanton was there as advertised, so one wit said the convention was composed "of the gentler sex of both genders." Welles, looking on from Washington, snorted and called it "a heterogeneous mixture of weak and wicked men."[18]

It all reminded the *Cleveland Plain Dealer* of the Spirits in Shakespeare's *Macbeth*:

> *Black spirits and white,*
> *Blue spirits and grey,*
> *Mingle, mingle, mingle, mingle,*
> *You that mingle may.*[19]

The innumerable host Manton Marble had predicted hadn't materialized. Chapin Hall had a capacity of five hundred. The reporter from the *Chicago Tribune* could never count at any time more than two hundred. The attendance figure generally agreed on was about four hundred.[20]

In the telegraph office, Lincoln heard that figure and summoned a Bible. When it arrived, he read aloud from 1 Samuel 22:2, the story of David at the cave of Adullam: "And every one that was in distress, and every one that was in debt, and every one that was discontented, gathered themselves unto him; and he became a captain over them; and there were with him about four hundred men."[21] Lincoln took his stories from anywhere he could get them.

Tall, beardless, handsome Edward Gilbert, the president of the New York Frémont Club, called the meeting of the Adullam 400 to order at eleven in the morning, then passed the gavel to the temporary convention president, ex-governor William F. Johnston of Pennsylvania, who soon passed it on to the permanent president, John Cochrane of New York.

Cochrane was what the *Plain Dealer* called a man of "fine parts," a former congressman, an eloquent stump speaker, a skillful organizer, and a soft, persuasive leader. He had a good presence and a clear, penetrating voice, which came out in round, rhetorical periods in a fine, finished style. He had it in him to stir men's emotions, even if they didn't always guide reason in a straight line. Until Fort Sumter and the outbreak of the war he had held strong Southern sympathies—like many another prominent New Yorker. But when Sumter was shelled, he went to war for the Union and was for a while a brigadier general until forced to resign with a physical disability.[22]

Wendell Phillips, who had so favored the convention, hadn't come. He had sent a message instead. It was read, and his oratorical power seeped through even in the written word. He blasted Lincoln once more, calling his administration "a civil and military failure, and its avowed policy ruinous to the North in every point of view." He then hailed Frémont, whose "thorough loyalty to democratic institutions, without regard to race, whose earnest and decisive character, whose clear-sighted statesmanship and rare military ability justify my confidence that in his hands all will be done to save the State that foresight, skill, decision, and statesmanship can do."[23]

Endorsing Frémont was getting a little ahead of the convention agenda, but not by much. Resolutions were passed in the afternoon embodying several of Phillips's earlier recommended planks. A call for a constitutional amendment prohibiting slavery nationwide and assuring absolute equality before the law became a plank. So did a demand for an amendment setting the one-term principle in concrete. Another plank said that reconstruction belonged to the people through the Congress, not to the president. And finally there was a plank calling for confiscation of all rebel lands and their distribution among Union soldiers and settlers—as "a measure of justice." A plank that didn't get passed was a suggestion that members of the convention not accept any offices of trust, honor, or profit from the administration in power during the next presidential term. That was going too far.[24]

When it came time that evening to name a candidate, there was an eleventh-hour effort by a knot of Grant supporters to stop the Frémont stampede by postponing the nominations. It failed, and Frémont was nominated by acclamation. Chapin Hall erupted in clamorous cheering that continued for fifteen minutes. The delegates swayed to and fro, howling and screaming. The *Chicago Tribune* correspondent wrote, "I never before supposed that one hundred men—not even Missouri border ruffians—could raise such a yell."[25]

John Cochrane became the vice-presidential nominee, also by acclamation, a choice that raised at least two sets of eyebrows in Washington. Welles told his diary that Cochrane was "wayward and erratic."

He had been at one time and another, Welles noted, a Democrat, a Barnburner (a New York Democrat who opposed the extension of slavery to the territories in 1846), a conservative, an abolitionist, an anti-abolitionist, a Democratic Republican, and now a radical Republican. "It will not surprise me," the navy secretary wrote, "if he should change his position before the close of the political campaign, and support the nominees of the Baltimore Convention. There is not a coincidence of views and policy between him and Frémont."[26]

John Hay also was astonished. Cochrane had just been to the White House telling the president that he intended to go "up to Cleveland to try to forestall and break up that bolting institution." Now look what he had done instead.[27]

So, in twelve hours on May 31, the convention had met, listened to speeches, passed its resolutions, and nominated its ticket. Only one last task remained. What should the party, with its new candidates, call itself? A committee was appointed, and after what the *Chicago Tribune* described as "many sittings and conferences among the wet nurses and old ladies of the Convention," came the name "Radical Democracy." It was adopted, and the convention adjourned that evening.[28]

The press began pointing out after it was over that the convention had done something illegal: it had nominated two New Yorkers. That would disenfranchise the entire state of New York, for the Constitution barred electors from voting for citizens of their own state for both president and vice president. But the delegates had discussed that point and concluded that Frémont was still a resident of California, although presently living in New York. The army register still listed him as a Californian. So they had gone with "the two Johns from New York."[29]

On June 4, Frémont accepted the nomination. But he rejected the confiscation plank as too vindictive, taking some of the sheen off his candidacy for some of the radicals. He also laid down a large caveat: if the Baltimore convention, to convene in three more days, nominated any man who would uphold "our cardinal principles"—that is, nearly anybody but Lincoln—Frémont would support him. If the convention nominated Lincoln, however, it would be fatal to the country and there would remain no other alternative but to organize against him, "to prevent the misfortune of his re-election." With that, Frémont accepted the nomination and announced he had resigned his commission in the army.[30]

What had it all amounted to?

Bennett wondered, "What are they driving at?" Not the election of Frémont, he reasoned, not with a platform and a ticket such as that. Nobody imagined such a thing. No, Bennett believed, their object was not Frémont's election, but Lincoln's defeat. They should have nominated Grant instead as he had advised—and was still advising. Grant's nomination at either Baltimore or Chicago now, he suggested, would cause the whole Frémont thing to go away—and Lincoln with it.[31]

Henry Raymond at *The New York Times* saw the Cleveland affair as a form of "mental hallucination" by a set of "witless fellows." "What a precious piece of foolery it all is," Raymond wrote. Not since the meeting of the three tailors on Tooley-street, who took action "in the name of the people of England," had there been anything so droll. He called the whole thing "simply a flank movement against the Administration" that had no hold whatever on public confidence or public sympathy. He called Frémont a "lost leader," stamped by his nomination unmistakably as a political adventurer of the most dangerous sort— buying revenge or success at the price of liberty, striking "a base alliance" with the peace Democrats and the haters of equal rights.[32]

Raymond was speaking for most Lincoln men. They confidently believed—or at least hoped—that the 400 at Adullam had just baked another pudding that would fail to rise.

15

WHAT! AM I RENOMINATED?

GRANT'S ARMY WAITED BEFORE COLD HARBOR ON THE FLAT lowlands of the Chickahominy River. Not far beyond lay the outskirts of Richmond. Two summers before, in 1862, George McClellan and Robert E. Lee had fought the Seven Days battles along this line from the Chickahominy to Harrison's Landing on the James River.

Grant had arrived at Cold Harbor on the first day in June 1864, to find Lee already digging in. The Army of Northern Virginia was shielded behind strong natural fortifications stretching from the Chickahominy on the south to the swamps of the Totopotomoy on the north.

After nearly a month of trying to slip around Lee's right flank, Grant had decided to attack him head-on at Cold Harbor, hoping that a powerful surprise blow now would split the rebel army, crush it, and make Richmond his. It was to be a smashing attempt to ram through.

Grant's army wasn't quite ready on June 1, and the attack was put off that evening, and again the next day. It was set finally for the morning of the third. The evening before, many of the Union soldiers stared at the rebel works they were to assault the next morning, and began making crude name tags to pin to their clothing so their dead bodies would not find anonymous graves.

Rain began to fall. It rained all night, ending only as dawn approached. A gray, somber mist still overhung the lowlands. The fields all around were green, fragrant, and wet. The birds had begun their morning song, oblivious to what was about to happen. At four-thirty a sudden outburst of cheering and the din of musket fire erupted along the Federal line.

"Line followed line," reported a Union officer, "until the space inclosed by the old salient became a mass of writhing humanity. . . ." A reporter from *The New York Times* wrote later that "the dark hollows between the armies were lit up with the fires of death."[1]

Lincoln's reporter, Henry Wing, watched, appalled by what he saw. The marching lines, he wrote, "went against those heights without a waver. There wasn't a chance of success. They knew it, but they went on just the same, dropping in their tracks as they came; and those behind rushed over the dead and wounded and fell. You could not believe so many men could die in twenty minutes; and that is all the time it took."[2]

In those twenty minutes Grant lost some 7,000 killed and wounded, three times Lee's losses. It had been a slaughter pen, one of the worst of the war. The cost had been horrendous, and there had been no breakthrough, no crushing of Lee's army, no conquest of Richmond. It had been worse than futile. "It was not war," a Union officer said, "it was murder."[3] One Union soldier said what many others doubtless thought: "There isn't much science in a bull-headed attack along a six-mile line; and if there isn't any science, what's the use of generals?"[4]

No further assault, by either side, seemed feasible. The two armies, numb and exhausted, continued to wait entrenched side by side, that day and the next and the next—only yards apart at places, with the dead and wounded lying between them.

A hundred miles to the north, Washington was swarming with life, even as Cold Harbor was shrouded by death.

"Washington is overrun with politicians, with contractors, and with busy-bodies of all kinds and sizes," hissed Adam Gurowski to his diary. "The Baltimore Convention is at the door, and the ravens make due obeisance to the White House." Elizabeth Lee, the sister of the Blair brothers, wrote her admiral husband on June 6 that "the delegates are flocking & there seems no doubt of Lincolns renomination."[5]

For several days the delegates to the Union Party's national nominating convention had been stopping by the White House. "Patriots on the way to Baltimore," John Hay described them, "who wish to pay their respects & engrave on the expectant mind of the Tycoon, their images, in view of future contingencies." The news from Cold Harbor, still sketchy and incomplete, was a troubling note darkening the prospect. But the air nonetheless was charged with expectation.[6]

Hay took note of visiting delegations, and found some of them bogus and irregular. There was even a delegation from secessionist South Carolina wanting an audience with the president.

"Let them in," said Lincoln.

"They are a swindle," said Hay.

"They won't swindle me," said Lincoln.[7]

Florida had sent two delegations, each attacking the other as unprincipled tricksters. Missouri had also sent two dueling delegations, in line with that state's split personality, one conservative and one radical. The convention would have to decide which one to seat.

"The Radicals are here in great force . . . ," Attorney General Edward Bates confided to his diary. "Some of them I think, are in an awkward quandary." They were nearly all instructed to vote for Lincoln, and many of them hated to do it.[8]

But also present in force were Lincoln's friends and allies—Simon Cameron, Thurlow Weed, Leonard Swett, Alexander McClure, Henry Raymond. They were an impressive array of shrewd political operators, skilled at every brand of maneuver an election campaign required. They had been at work for the president since January, sewing up the nomination. And now they would be in Baltimore to finish the job.

"What a crowd of sharp-faced, keen, greedy politicians!" was Count Gurowski's curse on all of them, on both sides.[9]

Gurowski wasn't the only grumpy one. There was a subterranean grumpiness underlying everything. It was a radical grumpiness, an anti-Lincoln, anti-Blair, anti-Seward, anti-cabinet bias, a feeling that Lincoln and all the things they detested about his administration were being crammed down their throats. The swallowing was made even harder by the fact that they knew they had been outsmarted and outmaneuvered again. Since the snows had begun to melt, it had been evident to the most narrow and malignant of Lincoln's foes in his own party that nothing could now prevent his nomination. For the party's radicals it was a galling fact of life.[10]

On June 5, two days before the convention was scheduled to convene, John Nicolay left for Baltimore in the company of Simon Cameron. There, Whitelaw Reid, the reporter from the *Cincinnati Daily Gazette* and an energetic anti-Lincoln man, told Lincoln's young secretary that the radicals conceded the president's nomination. Their present game was to shape a radical platform for him to stand on.[11]

Horace Greeley was as unhappy as ever, still wishing for a postponement, taking one more shot at it. On the day before the convention opened, he wrote, "We could wish the Presidency utterly forgotten or ignored for the next two months, while every impulse, every effort of the Loyal Millions should be directed toward the overthrow of the armed hosts of the Rebellion."[12]

But nobody was listening.

By Monday, the sixth, Baltimore was groaning under a torrent of delegates, political hangers-on, and excitement-seekers. Every arriving train was jammed. The hotels were filled to capacity. Monday was fearfully hot. Even a tremendous downpour at about sunset had failed to cool either the weather or the fever heat of the convention-goers. The corridors and passages of the hotels swarmed with sweaty and steamy crowds, anxious for something or another. The delegations were scattered in various hotels, but mainly in the Eutaw House on Baltimore's upper side, and in Barnum's City Hotel, farther downtown. There was caucusing everywhere; everybody was being buttonholed by somebody.[13]

At the Eutaw House, where the New York delegation was housed, that ultimate Republican political insider and tactician, Thurlow Weed, hovered about the hallways and caucus rooms. He ambled about the hallways with his soft, catlike tread, his head inclined to one side as if in great haste, talking in low, confidential tones. He was not a delegate to this convention, but was a looming presence nonetheless.[14]

The radical Lincoln-haters were not done yet. A meeting of the Grand Council of the Union League had been called in Baltimore for Monday night. The Union League was a strong force for the Union and for the war. Among its members were senators and congressmen and other leading Republicans and war Democrats. But it also contained what Lincoln's young third secretary, William O. Stoddard, called "hot-headed and free-tongued representatives of every faction of the Republican party inimical to Mr. Lincoln."[15]

One pro-Lincoln politician called it "a terrible body in its malignity towards the President." Everybody expected that this meeting of its Grand Council on the night before the convention was where all the anti-Lincoln steam would be let off.[16]

As the evening warmed up, the meeting was fulfilling all expectations. One senator rose to assault Lincoln with a raking fire, arguing against his nomination, talking darkly of his administration's malfeasance, tyranny, corruption, illegal acts, abuse and misuse of power, favoritism, fraud, timidity, inertness, oppression, and willful neglect. A congressman followed with a similar litany. Other speakers joined in.

"Another and another," Stoddard grieved as he listened, "all on the same side! Has Lincoln no friends left?"

Then a lank, cadaverous figure with long and reckless hair and a hint of Mephistopheles about him, rose and said: "Mr. President—Gentlemen of the Grand Council."

Oh God, thought Stoddard, it was Jim Lane. Stoddard remembered how Lane, the United States senator from Kansas, had assailed Lincoln so bitterly the year before at the meeting of this same Grand Council in Washington. Here he was again, a delegate not only to the convention but to this meeting as well.[17]

Lane had been coming a great deal lately to the White House. He was likely to show up at any time, gaunt, tattered, uncombed and unshaven, his neck innocent of a collar and guiltless of a necktie, his thin hair standing fretful on his crown like a porcupine's quills. He seemed to John Hay to be coarse, mean, and ignoble, with "the sad, dim-eyed, bad-toothed face of a harlot." Yet he also had a certain easy bonhomie that made him instantly at home anywhere.[18]

James Gordon Bennett at the *New York Herald* thought him merciless and cunning, "a jayhawker only anxious for plunder . . . him and his horde of harpies. . . ."[19] The description was apt, for Lane appeared something of a harpy himself, with his bent for sarcasm and invective, his harsh, raspy voice, his crude gestures, and his long, bony forefinger.[20]

He chewed tobacco when he could borrow it. He was divorced and didn't pay his debts and he often took the name of the Lord in vain— and in stride. He was said to worship at the shrine of Venus, altogether the kind of man that clergymen, as a class, shunned and tried to forget.[21] Just this past May he had been seen in a public street in Washington having a disagreement with a woman of the town. She had handed him a note. He had torn it up insultingly. She had knocked off his hat, then grabbed it, and for several minutes had beaten him about the head and ears with it. The scene had caused considerable excitement and comment.[22]

Lane's voice could be a bugle blast—or a lullaby. He was, to say the least, a vivid, electric kind of man, though a bit on the sinister side.

He had taken of late to calling himself a "vindictive" friend of the president—meaning vindictive against all enemies, his as well as Lincoln's. John Hay thought the adjective "especially felicitous."[23] It was said that patronage had put him on the Lincoln bandwagon. And now here he was, rising in the meeting of the Grand Council of the Union League to say something. Stoddard had seen him at the White House only the day before, closeted with Lincoln. But the secretary had no feel for what he was about to say or do now.

Lane paused for an uncommonly long time, looking along the benches, peering into face after face, as if searching for meaning. Stoddard thought his voice, as he began, could smash through a wall.

"For a man to stir up sore and wounded hearts to bitterness," Lane began, "requires no skill, no power of oratory. For a man to address the minds of men sickened by disaster, wearied by long trial, heated by passion, bewildered by uncertainty, heavy with grief, and cunningly to turn them into one vindictive channel, into one blind rush of senseless fury—that requires no great power of oratory. It may be the mere trick of a charlatan."

That's Lane, thought Stoddard, with that peculiar facility of his for saying an offensive thing in a most gallingly offensive and insolent manner. Stoddard noted that a hundred faces in the hall flushed with wrath.

"For a man to address himself to an assembly like this," Lane continued, "goaded almost to madness by long suffering, sorrow, disaster, humiliation, perplexity, and now aroused by venomous art to an all but unanimous condemnation of the innocent, and to turn them in their tracks and force them to go the other way—that would indeed be a feat of transcendent oratorical power."

Lane then said, "I am no orator at all" (which was a lie), "but that is the very thing I am now about to do" (which was the truth).

Sentence by sentence, piece by piece, he began pulling apart the indictment against Lincoln. Those in the audience leaned forward and listened, swept along despite themselves until they were soon believing, with him, that any other nomination the next day but Lincoln's would amount to the nomination of McClellan by the Republican convention and his election by the Republican party; that it would sunder the Union, make permanent the Confederacy, reshackle the slaves, dishonor the dead, and disgrace the living.

After Lane's fierce closing shout, a resolution favoring Lincoln's renomination was adopted with but a handful of dissenting votes. Thought Stoddard admiringly: "There is hardly steam left in the opposition boiler to blow one last, hoarse whistle of a perfunctory vote for a candidate named Grant."[24]

The radicals had launched their last preconvention shot, exhausted their ammunition, and been undercut by the senator from Kansas. They had misfired yet again, and the convention was about to convene.

The Front Street Theatre in Baltimore was a fallback site. The radical malcontents, with the reported treachery and connivance of that prince of radical malcontents, Maryland congressman Henry Winter Davis, had prebooked Baltimore's big convention hall, leaving convention planners scrambling at the last minute for another meeting place. The Front Street Theatre was also large, but quite inadequate to the occasion and very poorly appointed for a political convention. It was going to be a can of sardines. But spruced up a bit and festooned with flags, it might be made to do.

The parquet on the main tier, intended for the some five hundred delegates, was floored over and elevated to a level with the stage. The dress circle on the first balcony was arranged and set aside for the alternates. The second balcony was appropriated for the vast bevy of ladies expected to grace the hall. The "masses," that miscellaneous crowd of spectators representing every political party and all shades of acceptable and questionable society, would tenant that part of the theater known as the "celestial regions" or "nigger heaven."

The president of the convention would preside from an elevated platform at the extreme end of the stage, with a canopy of flags at his head and the press corps at his feet. The curtains and scenery were removed and the back of the theater thrown open to let in the outside air. For it was summer, the heat was withering, and the theater was an oven. The open back would also let in the noise from the street, and this was one of the busiest, noisiest corners in Baltimore.[25]

It would be a convention loaded with eminent politicians, more than were ever assembled as delegates in any convention before. No less than six Republican governors would be attending.[26]

At eleven o'clock on Tuesday morning, June 7, the doors to the theater were thrown open and there was a rush to the stairways leading to the upper tiers. The delegates and alternates began entering by the side doors. As the crowd waited—every available seat was now filled—the Second United States Artillery band from Fort McHenry tuned up and "discoursed" what the *Baltimore Sun* described as "most delightful music," a medley of national airs that animated the crowd.[27]

At noon the band broke into a rousing grand overture, and New York senator Edwin D. Morgan, the Republican national chairman, mounted the podium.

Morgan was the first and only national chairman in the Republican party's young eight-year life. In 1860, after his first four years in the job, he had agreed to serve again for another term, even though his candidate, William Seward, had not been nominated and he was deeply disappointed. Since then he had become reconciled to Lincoln—even liked the president now, indeed had consulted him just before coming to Baltimore from Washington.

Morgan was a big man physically, of massive frame, more than six feet tall, and in his mid-fifties. His face was clean-shaven but for sidewhiskers, now turning gray. His eyes were blue and deep-set. He was grave, somewhat rigid in bearing, but solid, able, quiet, and forceful, inspiring confidence. He had started out as a merchant, then had made his mark in politics, first as a governor of New York and now as a senator.[28]

He was not known as a good platform speaker. But after gaveling the convention to order, he said something in his opening remarks that brought the delegates to their feet with three rousing cheers. Lincoln had put him up to it.

"It is not my duty nor my purpose to indicate any general course of action for this Convention," Morgan said, "but . . . in view of the dread realities of the past, and of what is passing at this moment—and of the fact that the bones of our soldiers lie bleaching in every State of this Union, and with the knowledge of the further fact that this has all been caused by slavery, the party of which you, gentlemen, are the delegated and honored representatives, will fall short of accomplishing its great mission, unless, among its other resolves, it shall declare for such an amendment of the Constitution as will positively prohibit African slavery in the United States."[29]

Next to the name of Lincoln, this was what the delegates most wanted to hear: the call for an amendment to end slavery everywhere. It was Lincoln's gift to them, delivered by Morgan. Thirty miles away, in Washington, the president was sending healing balm to the rabidly radical antislavery wing of his party. He was trying to mend the party and cement all of its parts to his candidacy.

Having dropped this word, Morgan nominated Robert J. Breckinridge of Kentucky for temporary chairman of the convention, handed him the gavel, and returned to Washington where the Senate was still in session.

They called Breckinridge the "Old War Horse of Kentucky." He was ancient, a preacher, indeed one of the most venerated and distinguished divines of the Presbyterian ministry. He was known for his piety, his learning, his eloquence, and his great skill in pouring oil on troubled waters. He was also the only one of the distinguished Breckinridges of Virginia and Kentucky to have remained true to the Union in this war of brothers. The father of two secessionist sons, both high-ranking officers in the Confederate army, he was tall and thin, with a voice perhaps too weak to chair a convention, but with a heart and a brain that fully compensated for that lack.

It is doubtful that any political convention ever assembled on the American continent represented so many different and divergent political faiths, all drawn together by that one central cause—union. The aged theologian from Kentucky saw this perhaps as clearly as anybody there. "I see before me," he said, "not only primitive Republicans and primitive Abolitionists, but I see also primitive Democrats and primitive Whigs—primitive Americans, and, if you will allow me to say so, I myself am here, who all my life have been in a party to myself."

But, like everybody else there, Breckinridge had his limits. "As a Union Party," he told the delegates, "I will follow you to the ends of the earth, and to the gates of death! But as an Abolition party—as a Republican party—as a Whig party—as a Democratic party—as an American party, I will not follow you one foot."[30]

His peroration was caught up in a whirlwind of applause—"cheered to the echo," as Noah Brooks put it.[31]

Then Simon Cameron stood and started the trouble with a motion for a roll call of states to present credentials. That simple motion quickly became entangled in a maze of parliamentary procedure and a confusing welter of amendments and countermotions. Temporary Chairman Breckinridge, his faint voice outshouted in the uproar from inside and out, soon became bemused.

At this point Henry Raymond, a delegate at large from New York and editor of the *Times*—hence accustomed to shouting out editorial opinions from both the printed page and the platform—began rising to fill the lulls of despair with his strong voice. At first he attempted to explain the latest motion or amendment. Finally he defined what was going on as a "mass meeting," which needed to be turned into a convention if anything was to get done. First, Raymond reasoned with his fellow delegates, we must decide what states have sent delegates, next what delegates they have sent, and third, by what authority they have come. So, Raymond argued, we must first get the credentials of each state before we can have delegates. Then we can appoint committees, and then our mass meeting will become a convention. He made the appropriate motion to get things moving in that direction. The derailed convention was soon back on track with committees, including one on credentials, appointed and ordered to report the next day.[32]

This matter of credentials was critical. Some dozen states needed their status clarified. Several of them had warring contingents seeking seats; others weren't certain they would be seated at all, and, if seated, whether they would have full voting rights on the floor. Tennessee was in this category, a fact that brought Horace Maynard, head of that delegation, to his feet.

Maynard was a tall, angular, commanding, almost fear-inspiring figure. He had a harsh, high voice that carried to the outermost fringes of the largest of outdoor crowds. Indoors it was a trumpet. Maynard had long, deep black hair, a high brow, a straight, prominent nose, and an eye lit with fire. There was not a drop of Indian blood in him, but he brought savagery to mind. He was in fact called the "Narragansett Indian."[33]

He began to speak. He said of himself and his delegation, "We represent those who have stood in the very furnace of the rebellion, those who have met treason eye to eye, and face to face, and fought from the beginning for the support of the flag and the honor of our country." He told the delegates of how outnumbered and often outlawed by Confederate Tennesseans, they had fought on and endured and survived. He told the convention delegates they must not "pass us by, or forget or ignore our existence." Tears welled in his eyes, and many in the audience sobbed. It was a moving speech. But the fate of his delegation was in the hands of the newly appointed credentials committee, which wouldn't report its recommendations until the next day.[34]

In the session that evening before adjournment, the convention got its permanent chairman, the ex-governor of Ohio, William Dennison. He was escorted to the podium, followed by great applause and two huge bouquets of flowers. Dennison looked like a chairman. He was tall and handsome and gubernatorial. But he also had a hoarse voice and, Brooks thought, not much vigor of manner. Brooks wished the convention would put a little more starch on the podium. But he conceded that Dennison gave a short and sensible speech.[35]

The next morning at ten o'clock, Dennison reconvened the convention. The Reverend M. P. Gaddis, a delegate from Ohio, addressed the throne of grace, then the jockeying for seats began. Tennessee, Arkansas, and Louisiana, the three states undergoing Lincoln-driven reconstruction, were seated with full voting rights. So were the three territories that had sent delegates: Nebraska, Colorado, and Nevada. Florida, Virginia, the territory of New Mexico, and the District of Columbia were seated without the right to vote. The aspiring delegation from South Carolina was excluded altogether; it hadn't swindled the convention any more than it had swindled Lincoln. Only this last denial made the relentless Thaddeus Stevens truly happy. Ever honed and hungry for vengeance, he objected to seating any delegates from any seceded state.

And then there was Missouri. Two delegations had come to Baltimore claiming to represent the state, a pro-Blair conservative contingent and an anti-Blair radical contingent. Lincoln, browbeaten over the months by both sides, saw the problem more clearly than most. The Missouri radicals represented the rapidly developing radical sentiment nationwide. The conservative delegation could not be seated without perhaps fatally offending that powerful element. The very practical president clearly knew that the radicals had to be assuaged.[36]

When Nicolay, believed to reflect Lincoln's thinking, began a soft sell for seating the radical delegation, the message began to dawn.

Clark E. Carr, an Illinois delegate, had come to Baltimore a strong champion of the Missouri conservatives. But he caught the drift quickly—and reluctantly bowed to its wisdom. "The proper and wise thing for Republicans to do," he came to admit, "was to bring together all the elements of the Republican party—including the impracticables, the Pharisees, the better-than-thou declaimers, the long-haired men and the short-haired women—and continue to prosecute the war with vigor until the last enemy should lay down his arms."[37]

Not everybody, however, was as immediately pliable and willing as Carr. Even the venerable Breckinridge, a conservative seeing what was about to happen, called it a shameless cave-in to Lincoln's enemies and denial of his friends.[38]

But the natural bent of this basically Blair-hating convention, which was about to nominate a candidate many of them really didn't want, was to seat the radicals. Lincoln's subtle promptings cinched it. The vote was a lopsided 440 to 4. The convention cackled and shrieked its approval. As the pro-Blair conservative delegates left the hall, one correspondent wrote, "the roof of the theatre lifted."[39]

Henry Raymond, head of the powerful New York delegation, biographer of Lincoln, convention pacifier, and an old hand at drafting political statements, had been the logical choice to head the platform committee. He and his committee soon had eleven resolutions ready, with something for everybody. The suave editor, in his mid-forties and looking ten years younger, came to the podium with his monocle and gold-headed cane and laid the package before the convention.[40]

He ticked the planks off one by one:

1. Quell the rebellion and punish the rebels who caused it.
2. No compromise or peace without the unconditional surrender of the Confederacy.
3. A constitutional amendment ending and forever prohibiting slavery in the United States—a necessary plank to mollify the radicals.
4. Thanks to the soldiers and sailors fighting for the Union, and special provision for the disabled and wounded among them.
5. Praise to Lincoln for the job he had done so far to save the Union, and support for what he must yet do.
6. A purge of any cabinet member who did not support these principles—another plank for the radicals.
7. Full protection for all soldiers, regardless of color, and redress for violations of laws of war enforcing such protection.
8. Encouragement, by a just and liberal policy, of foreign immigration and asylum for the oppressed.
9. Speedy construction of a transcontinental railroad.
10. Economy and responsibility in public spending, and a vigorous and just system of taxation.
11. Vigorous implementation of the Monroe Doctrine and strict opposition, by force if necessary, to any foreign monarchies trying to get new footholds in the New World.[41]

That was it, in short. As the more sacred of these planks were read, delegates leaped to their feet with rousing cheers. In the end everybody applauded, the resolutions were unanimously approved, and Raymond was praised. Noah Brooks hailed the platform as "complete, concise, and ringing with patriotic fire."[42]

That sixth resolution—purging the cabinet—raised a few eyebrows. Never before had a political convention put a plank in the platform condemning the cabinet of a president seeking a second term. The resolution was generally viewed as aimed at Montgomery Blair in particular, whom the radicals desperately wanted to get rid of.[43] What Lincoln might do about it, nobody knew.

So now the convention had come to the main order of business, what they were all there for: to renominate the president.[44] Simon Cameron was first out of the box again, with another motion to confound the convention. He moved that Lincoln and Vice President Hamlin be declared the choice of the party by acclamation and have it done with. Chaos followed immediately. Shouts of "No, no!" rocked the hall.

Soon it was pandemonium, what Brooks called a "tempest-tossed assemblage," filled with stentorian voices rising above the din.[45]

William M. Stone of Iowa leaped to his feet to try to get Cameron's motion laid on the table. Thaddeus Stevens shouted for a roll call and a vote by states, but the chairman failed to hear him above the tempest. Burton C. Cook, chairman of the Illinois delegation shouted, "I move that Abraham Lincoln, of Illinois, be declared the choice of this Convention."

Stone insisted again on his motion, and Jim Lane's trumpet voice was heard above the uproar, "Stand your ground, Stone! Stand your ground! Great God, Stone, Kansas will stand by you!"[46]

Gazing on the pandemonium, Brooks saw Simon Cameron standing in the midst of it with arms folded and smiling grimly, regarding the uproar he had caused with quiet composure.[47]

Stevens tried again: "I called for a vote by states before the result was declared."

"The Chair did not hear the gentleman from Pennsylvania," the chair admitted.

"I supposed so," said Stevens, "for there was a universal yell everywhere."

The universal yell thundered on.

Now Raymond rose again, the pacifier, with a suggestion. Lest it appear that Lincoln's nomination was railroaded through, he proposed a roll call of the states—rather than nomination by acclamation—"by clamor," as one delegate put it. In the end, Raymond reasoned, it would lead to the same result: a unanimous vote for the president. What he didn't say was that his procedure would also take Hamlin out of the picture, which he wanted, because there were other plans afoot for the vice presidency.

What Raymond was suggesting was what Stevens was proposing and what Stone and Lane and just about everybody else wanted. Cameron graciously accepted the idea, for, as it would become evident long after, he really didn't favor what he had just proposed any more than they did. It had all been a diversion.

After Raymond's suggestion was adopted, Cook leaped to his feet again: "Mr. President, the State of Illinois again presents to the loyal people of this Nation, for President of the United States, Abraham Lincoln. God bless him."

"In the name of the great West," Stone of Iowa shouted, with Lane and Kansas doubtless standing by him, "I demand that the roll be called."

Then Thompson Campbell of California rose and said, "I rise, sir, to second the nomination by the honorable gentleman from Illinois." This was an important point, for Campbell was an old personal friend of Lincoln's from Springfield, and it had been agreed within the Illinois delegation that he would be allowed to nominate his old friend.

But the impatient delegates didn't want to hear any more speeches. "Vote, vote," they shouted. "No speeches, call the roll, order, get down." It was apparent, as John Hay noted in his diary, that the delegates were remorselessly bent on coughing down the crack orators of the party, expressing the wish of the people, and going home.

Campbell was a tall, spare man with a saturnine visage and tremendous lung power. He kept on, trying to be heard above the hoots, striving to do his duty to the president, gesticulating wildly. But nobody was listening, despite his booming voice. Finally he threw up his hands in exasperation and sat down, his visage more saturnine than ever.[48]

The secretary of the convention called for the roll and Maine answered first, casting her entire fourteen votes for Lincoln. So it went, peaceably down the roll, past New Hampshire and eleven other states to Arkansas, all unanimous for Lincoln. Then came Missouri.

John F. Hume, the chairman of Missouri's newly seated radical delegation, rose with orders from home. Sorry, he said, but we have come instructed and can't on the first ballot "give our votes in unanimity with those who have already cast their votes." That meant Missouri wasn't voting for Lincoln. There was a disbelieving silence followed by more pandemonium.

"Order, order!" the cry went up.

"I appeal to the Convention," shouted the irrepressible Jim Lane, "to hear Missouri."

A motion to that effect was passed, and the tumult subsided.

It is a matter of much regret, Hume apologized. In the end, he promised, the radicals of Missouri intended to fight for and emphatically support whoever the nominees were, but for now they were instructed to cast their twenty-two votes for Ulysses S. Grant, who was at that moment staring at the stubborn Confederate army dug in at Cold Harbor.

The convention erupted again. Such a storm of disapproval A. C. Widdicombe, of the Missouri delegation, had never seen in any convention he had ever attended. Delegates and onlookers howled in protest, and Widdicombe believed his hair actually stood on end. After Hume sat down, Widdicombe said later, "there we were, as solemn and determined as men could look," with the mob all around demanding they change their vote. "I hadn't any doubt for a few moments," said Widdicombe, "but that we would be picked up, every man of us, and thrown out into the street."

Jim Lane stood up in the tumult to vouch for the Missourians again, saying they were his neighbors, that they had come to the convention with proper credentials and been admitted legally as delegates. That being the case, they had the right to vote for whomever they pleased, and it was not Republicanism to try to prevent them. That calmed the crowd some. Then Stone of Iowa, as irrepressible as Lane, sprang to his feet once more to say the Missourians were neighbors of his, too, and he didn't like to see them treated that way. That calmed the convention still more, and the roll call went on with occasional scattered grumbling.[49]

When the last delegation, Nevada, cast her votes for Lincoln, making it 484 to 22, Hume rose again, asked that the nomination be made unanimous, and switched Missouri's vote to the president.

Wild confusion, nothing new to this convention, followed. Men hurrahed, embraced, threw up their hats, jumped on benches, danced in the aisles, waved flags, yelled, and, reported Brooks, viewing it all through his pince-nez, "committed every possible extravagance." The band broke out into a rousing "Hail Columbia." Horace Maynard, the "Narragansett Indian," was seen alternately hugging and shaking hands with Henry Raymond, the distinguished editor of *The New York Times*. The racket was so intolerable that Brooks involuntarily looked up to see if the roof had been blown away. When quiet was half restored, the band struck up again, this time with "Yankee Doodle," the only tune Grant would have recognized had he been there, and the celebration started again. Order was a long time returning.[50]

In Washington, Lincoln had no idea what had transpired. But he had business at the telegraph office, where he met Major Eckert, who congratulated him on his nomination.

"What! Am I renominated?" Lincoln exclaimed.

When assured it was so, he said he was gratified and asked Eckert if he would send word to the White House when a vice president had been agreed upon.[51]

Vice President Hannibal Hamlin, like Lincoln, expected to be renominated in Baltimore.

He had been nominated to run with Lincoln in 1860 because he was a representative Republican fresh from the Democratic party and from a state, Maine, where an election in September was considered the "finger-board" of victory or defeat in that presidential canvass.[52]

Hamlin had been a congressman, governor, and senator from his state. He was about five feet ten inches tall, with an olive complexion, deep-set eyes, a broad, full forehead, and stooping shoulders. He invariably wore a rust-colored suit of broadcloth, a swallowtail coat, a low vest, and black trousers with side pockets into which his hands were everlastingly thrust. He seldom, if ever, wore an overcoat, no matter how bitter the weather.[53]

After the election in 1860, Hamlin had drifted away from Lincoln, Zionwards, into the radical wing of the party. However, he expected to be renominated in Baltimore.

But even as he entertained this comforting notion, the stars were realigning themselves. It was being reported by some that Lincoln himself wished to trade Hamlin in for another—for Governor Andrew Johnson of Tennessee, a strong war Democrat. Lincoln had nothing against Hamlin, even though his vice president held strong positions opposed to his—Lincoln seldom held anything against anybody. It was suggested that Lincoln simply believed, as many did, that a war Democrat would help the ticket in what looked like a very close election. It was a matter of practical politics.

The idea that Lincoln now preferred Johnson had been surfacing for months, and by convention time, many seemed to know it firsthand.

Jim Lane knew it. Earlier in the year, half a dozen Kansans were talking together. The subject of the vice presidency came up. "Oh, Hamlin, of course," all of them said. But Lane said, "No—Andrew Johnson. Mr. Lincoln does not want to interfere; but he feels that we must recognize the South in kindness. The nominee will be Andy Johnson. . . ."[54]

Alexander McClure, Lincoln's sometime confidant from Pennsylvania, seemed to know it. He was to write years later that Lincoln called him in on the eve of the Baltimore convention, told him his choice was Johnson, and then sent McClure to the convention to work for his nomination. McClure said that Leonard Swett also knew it, and so did Simon Cameron.[55]

McClure also testified that Ward Lamon, the marshal from the District of Columbia and Lincoln's old friend and bodyguard, knew it. Lamon was later to claim in a letter to McClure that he had gone to the convention bearing a letter embodying Lincoln's pro-Johnson position, to be used only if absolutely necessary.[56]

A young Republican partisan named Abram J. Dittenhoefer, who had met with Lincoln about ten days before the convention, also knew it. He later wrote, "I had known from the President's own lips, at my last interview, that he desired the selection of Andrew Johnson."[57]

Andrew Johnson must have known it. His private secretary, Benjamin C. Truman, later wrote, "I saw and handled all his correspondence during that time, and I know it to be a fact that Mr. Lincoln desired the nomination of Johnson for Vice-President, and that [William G. "Parson"] Brownlow and [Horace] Maynard went to Baltimore at request of Lincoln and Johnson to promote the nomination."[58]

Johnson had been a U.S. senator from Tennessee in March 1862, when Lincoln persuaded him to take the thankless, life-threatening job of military governor of that part of the state which had remained loyal or been wrested from Confederate hands. Being military governor of Tennessee, a seceded state, was the toughest and most disagreeable job in the country, like being behind enemy lines in the war zone.

Johnson and Lincoln had never fit under the same umbrella except on one issue: the Union. They both believed the Union must be preserved. They had met for the first time in 1847 when both were young congressmen, Lincoln a Whig from Illinois and Johnson a Democrat from Tennessee. They had both voted on the Wilmot Proviso, a bill to forbid the extension of slavery into newly acquired territory, every time it came up. And every time, Lincoln voted for it and Johnson against it. Andrew Jackson was Andrew Johnson's idol. Lincoln's was Henry Clay, Jackson's bitter enemy.

These two seeming political polar opposites did have a few personal things in common, besides devotion to the Union. Both were born poor, to mudsill working fathers in log cabins, less than a year apart. Johnson's father died when he was only four years old, and his mother raised him in near poverty, far down on the social scale. Lincoln's mother died when he was only nine. Also well down on the social scale, Lincoln had a year of formal schooling; Johnson had none, but had apprenticed to a tailor when he was in his early teens.

Although he had no education, Johnson had a talent for politics. He rose from the tailor's profession to become a congressman from Tennessee in the 1840s, governor in the 1850s, and finally a U.S. senator by the 1860s. He was of medium height, broad-shouldered, deep-chested, and slightly swarthy. His eyes were dark, deep-set, and piercing. He was a jut-jawed nonsmiler who never had much time for levity. He even dressed seriously, in a black frock coat and waistcoat, black doeskin trousers, and a high silk hat. He was habitually calm, reserved, and unflappable.

He had been a firm-handed, courageous military governor in Tennessee, often physically threatened, but backing down to nobody. Senator Charles Sumner called him that patriot, "faithful among the faithless, the Abdiel of the South."[59]

"Parson" Brownlow of Tennessee began paving the way for a Johnson takeover of the vice presidency the night before the nominations in Baltimore, in the last speech of the evening. There were no two deadlier political enemies in Tennessee than Brownlow and Johnson. For years they had been venomous foes. But like Lincoln and Johnson, they agreed on one thing: the Union. Brownlow had stirred imaginations when the war began by vowing, as secessionist leaders took Tennessee out of the Union, that he would fight them "till Hell froze over, and then fight them on the ice."[60]

When Lincoln named Johnson military governor of the state, Brownlow said, "I have battled against Andrew Johnson perseveringly, systematically and terribly, for a quarter of a century. He has blasted me on every stump in Tennessee. We have given the other as good as he sent. . . . [Now] we are hand-in-hand fighting the same battle for the preservation of the Union. We will fight for each other against the common foe. He is now at the head of our new State Government; and I take pleasure in saying that he is the right man in the right place."[61]

Brownlow told that story again to the convention the night before the nominations. The stage was set.[62]

The mighty political triumvirate from New York—Seward, Weed, and Raymond—also had powerful reasons for backing Johnson. They also believed him to be Lincoln's choice. But even more urgent in their thinking was the fact that Daniel S. Dickinson, another New Yorker, was being pushed for vice president. Dickinson was a man of fine talents, extensive accomplishment, and great legal learning. He was one of the country's most distinguished political speakers, noted for his wit and repartee. He was so apt with anecdotes and biblical allusions that everybody called him "Scripture Dick." He was a man of commanding presence, with long, silvery locks, he had the backing of half of the New York delegation, and he was willing.

The Seward-Weed-Raymond combine was, of course, unwilling. They knew that if Dickinson was elected vice president, Lincoln couldn't keep Seward as secretary of state; it would be politically unseemly to have two New Yorkers occupying the second two most powerful offices in the country. The struggle between the Dickinson and Johnson camps in New York had been raging behind the scenes for weeks as the moment to nominate a vice president arrived. It was now splitting the delegation down the middle. It was also a radical-conservative split; almost everything was.

Burton C. Cook, chairman of the Illinois delegation, was confused. He had come to the convention expecting Hamlin to be renominated, and expecting to vote for him. But now there was all this Johnson talk. And his fellow Illinoisan, Leonard Swett, who was close to Lincoln, was now declaring his support for Judge Advocate General Joseph Holt. What did this mean? Cook wanted to do the right thing, meaning he wanted to do what Lincoln wanted. But what did Lincoln want? He appealed to John Nicolay, Lincoln's personal secretary, who was monitoring the convention. Nicolay must surely know.

But Nicolay didn't know either. If Lincoln indeed favored Johnson for vice president, he knew nothing of it. The president had been very selective about whom he told. He had not told Nicolay or Hay. Nor had he told his reporter friend, Noah Brooks. Lincoln had been hounded by Brooks and others in recent weeks to say whom he did prefer. He seemed to Brooks, who favored Hamlin, always to dodge the question, sometimes saying, "It perhaps would not become me to interfere with the will of the people." He was, Brooks thought, maddeningly vague.[63]

On June 5, at Cook's request, Nicolay wired Hay from the Eutaw House to learn whom Lincoln favored. Hay didn't know either, but he would ask. The next day Hay wired back that "the President wishes not to interfere in the nomination even by a confidential suggestion. He also declines suggesting anything in regard to platform or the organization of the Convention. . . . He is, and intends to be absolutely impartial. . . ."[64]

That wasn't much help to the befuddled Cook. On June 8, as the moment to decide approached, Lincoln's wishes were still unproclaimed. But his preference was "in the air." Nearly everybody perceived it was Johnson and had bowed to that fact.[65]

On the floor, Indiana nominated Johnson. Stone, who seemed to be seconding everything, seconded the nomination. Tennessee's Horace Maynard made a speech in favor. Cameron nominated Hamlin as instructed by the Pennsylvania delegation, but without a speech. Lyman Tremaine, Dickinson's floor manager, nominated his man on behalf of a portion of the New York delegation.

On the first ballot, Johnson had 200 votes, Hamlin 150, and Dickinson 108. Sixty-one votes were scattered among seven other candidates.

As the secretaries were computing the vote, states began switching wholesale. Cameron switched Pennsylvania's vote to Johnson, and the very disgusted Thaddeus Stevens turned to McClure and said, "Can't you find a candidate for Vice-President in the United States, without going down to one of those damned rebel provinces to pick one up?"[66]

Lane made Kansas solid for Johnson. Even Maine was finally obliged to throw its votes from Hamlin to Johnson. Illinois followed, then Missouri. New York at last united behind Johnson. Tremaine then moved that the nomination be made unanimous. The motion carried, to resounding cheers.[67]

The convention suddenly found itself with little else to do. Committees were named to notify the two nominees, and the gavel came down. At four-thirty in the afternoon of that busy day, the convention adjourned *sine die.*

Ah, said the *Richmond Examiner* from behind the Confederate lines, so we have the "Illinois rail-splitter" and the "Tennessee tailor."[68]

Yes, agreed Andrew Johnson, the mudsill worker's son from the furnace of the rebellion. "What will the aristocrats do," he asked, with what must have been a smirk on his generally serious face, "with a rail-splitter for President and a tailor for Vice-President?"[69]

The point wasn't lost on Manton Marble at the *New York World,* either. "The age of statesmen is gone," he complained editorially. "The age of rail-splitters and tailors, of buffoons, boors and fanatics has succeeded. . . . In a crisis of the most appalling magnitude, requiring statesmanship of the highest order, the country is asked to consider the claims of two ignorant, boorish, third-rate backwoods lawyers, for the highest stations in the government. . . . God save the Republic!"[70]

"The Republican convention nominated Lincoln just as was expected," sighed a Democrat in Washington. "We must now beat him or the country is ruined."[71]

"The politicians have again chosen this Presidential pigmy as their nominee," fumed James Gordon Bennett in the *New York Herald* on

June 10. For the radicals, he wrote the next day, Lincoln is "a bitter pill to swallow; but if there is no help for it they will try to gulp him down."[72]

So said the Lincoln haters. The Lincoln supporters, however, saw his nomination as a beacon.

"[The] Convention, in thus unanimously nominating you for reelection," said William Dennison the next day, when the committee of one delegate from each state met Lincoln in the White House, "but gave utterance to the almost universal voice of the loyal people of the country. To doubt of your triumphant election, would be little short of abandoning the hope of a final suppression of the Rebellion and the restoration of the Government over the insurgent States."[73]

"I will neither conceal my gratification, nor restrain the expression of my gratitude," Lincoln replied.

When the National Union League that same day presented him with a copy of its resolutions approving and endorsing the convention nominations, Lincoln said he did not permit himself to conclude that he was the best man for the job in the country. But it reminded him of the story of an old Dutch farmer, who had once said to a friend that "it was not best to swap horses when crossing streams."[74]

As the president was saying that, U. S. Grant was preparing to cross a stream of his own. On Sunday, June 12, at about dark, he began moving his army across the James River. Lee knew nothing of it until the next day, and when he heard, he immediately began shifting his own little army southward one more time. Even as he moved to counter yet another shift, Lee was unaware at first of the magnitude of this new change of base, or that it would open a whole new phase in the war.

Six days later, Lee found himself behind the trenches in Petersburg, Grant digging in at his front. The overland campaign had ended. In six weeks of marching "in blood and agony from the Rapidan to the James," Grant had covered some sixty miles and lost nearly 60,000 men—a thousand per mile, 2,000 a day, three for every one of Lee's losses, a number equal in size to the entire Confederate army he faced. Now, after all that, the war in the South had come down to a siege.[75]

That could well be what the election campaign in the North would also come down to before it was over. The coming summer would tell.

16

WAR WEARINESS

———

THE NORTH, SO BUOYED WITH HOPE IN THE SPRING, WAS plunged deep in gloom by early summer. The expectation of an early end to the war had been dashed and frustrated in those sixty miles from the Wilderness to the James.

"Grant the Hammerer" was on hold before Petersburg. Gideon Welles was disgusted, believing Grant had "perseverance and obstinacy, and but little else." Many in the disenchanted North seemed now to agree with him.[1] In the West, Sherman's army seemed stalled as well on the road to Atlanta.

There was no good news anywhere. The national debt was approaching $2 billion, an incomprehensible sum. The national credit had sunk to its lowest ebb, and the treasury was nearly empty. The war was costing $2 million a day with little to show for it. The president had called for half a million more volunteers, and another draft seemed certain.

Worst of all, the wounded and dying were still landing at the wharfs on the Potomac, and making their agonized way through Washington's streets huddled in their ambulances—their "procrustean boxes," as Count Adam Gurowski called them.[2]

Looking at the summer, Lincoln, perhaps better than anybody, understood how elusive victory was—and how distant still.

"I wish when you write and speak to the people," he told his reporter friend Noah Brooks, "you would do all you can to correct the impression that the war in Virginia will end right off victoriously." Lincoln had been too often disappointed to be optimistic.

"To me the most trying thing in all of this war," the president told Brooks, "is that the people are too sanguine; they expect too much at once. I declare to you, sir, that we are today further ahead than I thought one year and a half ago we should be, and yet there are plenty of people who believe that the war is about to be substantially closed. As God is my judge I shall be satisfied if we are over with the fight in Virginia within a year. I hope we shall be 'happily disappointed,' as the saying is, but I am afraid not—I am afraid not."[3]

John Nicolay, the president's young secretary, knew Lincoln in all his moods. He had often seen that mobile face run the "long gamut of expression from grave to gay, and back again from the rollicking jollity of laughter to that serious, far-away look that with prophetic intuitions beheld the awful panorama of war, and heard the cry of oppression and suffering."[4]

Lincoln was seeing the awful panorama of war and hearing the cry of oppression and suffering perhaps more plainly and more painfully than ever in this early summer of 1864. And Nicolay was writing the *Chicago Tribune,* trying to get across the idea of the magnitude of the job Lincoln faced. "The President's task here is no child's play," he wrote the *Tribune.* "If you imagine that *any man* could attempt its performance, and escape adverse criticism, you have read history in vain, and studied human nature without profit."[5]

On the morning of June 16, Lincoln, with Mary, Tad, Judge Thompson Campbell, who had tried so hard in vain to second the nomination of the president in Baltimore, Cuthbert Bullitt of New Orleans, and J. R. Macartney of the *Daily Morning Chronicle,* boarded two cars bound for Philadelphia. There was to be an important meeting of the Great Central Sanitary Fair that day, and Lincoln had been invited to speak.

Sanitary fairs were local agencies that raised funds to administer to the needs of the soldiers. Lincoln knew the Union would suffer terribly without them, and he had accepted the invitation. Edward Everett was also to speak.

Brig. Gen. Lew Wallace, commanding in the region, joined them in Baltimore. In Philadelphia, Broad Street from Chestnut Street to the depot was lined with people as Lincoln's train arrived shortly after noon. The waiting crowd watched him step down and cheered his barouche as its two gray horses pulled it slowly up the street toward the hotel. It was a beautiful, sunny day and flags were flying everywhere.

Later, at the fair, Lincoln spoke of war. "At the best," he said, "[it] is terrible, and this war of ours, in its magnitude and in its duration, is one of the most terrible. It has deranged business. . . . It has destroyed property, and ruined homes; it has produced a national debt and taxation unprecedented. . . . It has carried mourning to almost every home, until it can be said that the 'heavens are hung in black.' "

Then Lincoln said, "It is a pertinent question often asked in the mind privately, and from one to the other, when is the war to end? . . . We accepted this war for an object, a worthy object, and the war will end when that object is attained. Under God, I hope it never will until that time. . . . General Grant is reported to have said, I am going through on this line if it takes all summer. This war has taken three years; it was begun or accepted upon the line of restoring the national authority over the whole national domain, and for the American people, as far as my knowledge enables me to speak, I say we are going through on this line if it takes three years more."[6]

On the last day of May a correspondent from Pennsylvania sent George McClellan this bit of hopeful verse for the sorrowing times:

> The Boreal storm that rages now,
> Is but the harbinger of spring,
> And if we brave its furious blast,
> The vernal hours more joy will bring.[7]

It was June, and McClellan was about to step into the eye of the political storm. He was to return to West Point to deliver the oration for the dedication of the site of a battle monument to the officers and men of the regular army killed in the war.

By noon on June 15, the day of the dedication, a crowd of about 3,000 had converged on the academy grounds, arriving by overland train and by steamer up the Hudson River. At about one o'clock McClellan arrived on the flower-decked dais with the chief marshal for the occasion, the hero of Fort Sumter, Major—now Brigadier General—Robert Anderson.

The famous Anderson introduced McClellan as "one who is better known to you than I who introduce him," and McClellan stood to a thunder of cheers. He spoke at length of the "clang of arms" and of its "sacred brotherhood." He began with a soaring review of how the dead had been commemorated in memory down the centuries, from Old Testament times to the plain of Marathon to the pass at Thermopylae to the hills of Palestine to the present moment.

Then he spoke of the rebellion, called it "gratuitous and unjustifiable," and, in so doing, made a political statement.

"Rebellion against a government like ours," he said, "which contains within itself the means of self-adjustment, and a pacific remedy for evils, should never be confounded with a revolution against despotic power, which refuses redress of wrongs."

This rebellion of ours, McClellan went on to say, "cannot be justified upon ethical grounds, and the only alternatives for our choice are its suppression or the destruction of our nationality. At such a time as this, and in such a struggle, political partisanship should be merged in a true and brave patriotism, which thinks only of the good of the whole country. It was in this cause and with these motives, that so many of our comrades gave their lives, and to this we are all personally pledged in all honor and fidelity.

"Shall such devotion as that of our dead comrades," McClellan demanded, "be of no avail? Shall it be said in after-ages, that we lacked the vigor to complete the work thus begun? that, after all these noble lives freely given, we hesitated, and failed to keep straight on until our land was saved? Forbid it, Heaven, and give us firmer, truer hearts than that!"[8]

Such words could not have gone down well in the Confederacy, or with the peace wing of McClellan's own party. They were militant words that spoke to the necessity of maintaining the Union and promised no peace until the rebellion was crushed. Did the Democrats' probable candidate intend not peace, but more war? This was no better than the gall and wormwood Lincoln and the Republicans were promising.

A Confederate soldier in Arkansas wrote in anger and disappointment: "I don't want such an intensely Union man, as he seems to be, to be their nominee."[9]

The reaction to the oration in the North ran mainly along party lines. That ultimate Democratic partisan, Manton Marble, the recently wed young editor of the *New York World,* wrote him, "I do not hesitate to say that it is far superior to Mr. Everett's Gettysburgh address in all essential aspects—if the object of oratory is to touch the hearts & move the minds of men."[10] Lincoln's short Gettysburg oration was apparently not even in the running, in Marble's mind.

James Gordon Bennett, who didn't like much of anything most politicians were saying, did like what the general said at West Point. Calling it "truly eloquent," a "great discourse," he compared it to the immortal funeral oration of Pericles at the public interment of Athenian warriors who had fallen in one of the Peloponnesian campaigns. It was a masterpiece, Bennett said.[11]

Then there was the Republican reaction. Joseph Medill at the *Chicago Tribune* called it "a neat, wordy, pointless speech . . . a very smooth, glossy, slick piece of gab."[12]

Whether it was a masterpiece or simply a slick piece of gab, the speech worried some of McClellan's friends. One of them believed that it had caused some supporters to doubt that he would accept the nomination if offered. "Your W. P. speech," Sunset Cox wrote him, "will give you the election, but it does not help to the nomination."[13]

There was much speculation by mid-June about just when that nomination might occur. The Democratic convention had been set for July 4 in Chicago. But there was now pressure to postpone it. The gloom of the summer and the military bog-downs everywhere had buoyed Democratic hopes—so much so that August Belmont called a top-level party conference in the middle of the month to consider the changing political landscape and Democratic tactics in the light of that shifting landscape. Several in the meeting urged that the convention be postponed until September to give the party more time to iron out its platform differences and to await the course of events. By then, decisive changes in Union military fortunes might have swung a mass of the party rank and file decisively either to a war or a peace position. Others opposed delay, fearing it would be fatal to an effective organization for the coming national election campaign.

Governor Horatio Seymour and the New York Democratic strategist, Dean Richmond, vigorously urged postponement. Belmont himself was uncertain, so he asked McClellan's friend, S. L. M. Barlow, to sound out the general on the subject.[14]

McClellan was listening and saying nothing publicly. He was inclined against postponement, however. Sunset Cox had written him in early June suggesting that the push for postponement was fueled by the belief that Grant would fail in Virginia. Cox argued that this hope gave impulse to the peace men hoping either to control the nomination, if it was put off, or at least to divide the convention. Cox's own view was that if the Democrats were to win in the fall, they ought to be getting on with uniting the divided elements of the party now, the sooner the better.[15]

McClellan wrote Cox from Saratoga, New York, on June 20 that Seymour had lobbied him on the question, but had not convinced him.

McClellan told Cox that "the coolest, most disinterested, men I have seen" favor holding to the original schedule.[16]

Marble was one of those cool and disinterested men against postponement. He wrote McClellan on June 13 calling the postponers "Ishmaelites," as much outcasts in nineteenth-century party politics as Ishmael had been in Old Testament times.[17]

But the drive for postponement was too compelling. By June 25 it had been done. The convention was put off for eight weeks, to August 29. McClellan wrote Marble, washing his hands of the whole business, telling him, "I feel now perfectly free from any obligation to allow myself to be used as a candidate. It is very doubtful whether anything could now induce me to consent to have my name used."[18]

Cox was no happier about it than McClellan. He wrote Marble that he was mortified, vexed, and discouraged, believing the postponement only afforded the radical peace men in the party a chance to dump McClellan—if he didn't dump himself first.[19]

Another Democrat, Earl Goodrich of St. Paul, Minnesota, wrote Marble between trains in Mansfield, Ohio, on June 27. He also deplored the postponement. "This is not the old Democratic way of doing," he wrote. "Micawber [Charles Dickens's Micawber, always waiting for something to turn up] is a character to be laughed at, but not imitated. This is not a time for fault-finding, however; but for hoping all things, and believing all things, which are against this Administration and its continuance."

Goodrich wrote Marble that "there is no enthusiasm among the Republicans at the West; and even the Democrats are lifeless just now, as if stunned by the late change of programme. They don't comprehend it; each faction fears it may be a movement in the interest of the other; so they are 'all silent, and all damned'—nonplussed."[20]

The Republicans took satisfaction from this Democratic angst. James C. Conkling wrote his senator, Lyman Trumbull, from Illinois in late June, saying, "The postponement of the Chicago Convention we regard as an indication that the elements of the Democratic party are too hostile at present, to enable them to work harmoniously and it is very doubtful whether any thing can possibly occur within two months which can reconcile their discordant views. As far as I can judge our Union party are 'waiting and watching' in a *solid body* and will be ready to act vigorously whenever the campaign opens and an opposition ticket shall be presented."[21]

A female friend of Manton Marble, who discreetly signed her letters "Chateau 64," may have been closer to the target than anybody, when she wrote him in July, in another context, "But we never know how to understand you Democrats."[22]

Somebody else having trouble understanding Democrats this summer was Jacob Thompson, the Confederate agent in Canada. Thompson was still hoping for and expecting a spontaneous uprising in the Northwest of the thousands of Sons of Liberty his old prewar friend, Clement Vallandigham, had told him about.

Before the war, Vallandigham had evoked the chilling image of a secessionist West. "But, gentlemen of the North," he had said in a speech on the House floor in 1859, "you who . . . are hurrying this Republic to its destruction . . . did it ever occur to you that when this most momentous but most disastrous . . . event . . . shall have been brought about, the West, the great West, which you now coolly reckon yours as a province, yours as a fief of your vast empire, may choose, of her own sovereign goodwill and pleasure . . . to set up for herself? Did you ever dream of a Western Confederacy?"[23]

Jacob Thompson surely had. He dreamed of it daily. But it wasn't happening. There had been a plan for such an uprising in June. The signal was to be Vallandigham's rearrest. The Ohio copperhead had decided to return home from exile. He was certain that when he did he would be arrested again. The Confederate agents in Canada, therefore, watched expectantly in mid-June as he crossed the border in Canada and headed for Ohio.

But there was no arrest, and no uprising. Vallandigham began speaking again, saying every incendiary thing he had said the year before to warrant his arrest, and worse. He openly invited trouble and got none. Lincoln simply left him alone.

The disappointed insurrectionists set another date, July 20. Their plan was ambitious: to move on the prison camps at Chicago, Columbus, Indianapolis, Alton, and Rock Island; seize the arsenals at those points; free and arm the Confederate inmates; commandeer the telegraph lines and railroads; move as small armies southward, rendezvousing at Louisville and St. Louis, drawing the disaffected to their ranks as they marched; overthrow the state authorities as they went, organizing provisional governments in their stead; and so threaten the Union cause in the Northwest as to turn the tide of the war and force a favorable peace.

But it didn't happen. The Sons of Liberty weren't ready. The uprising was postponed again, to coincide with the newly postponed Democratic convention in Chicago in late August. Things weren't going as fast as Thompson had hoped they would. He was seeing too much waffling by his would-be Northern allies.

Thomas Hines, Thompson's fiery co-conspirator, described him as a man of sterling integrity, undoubted ability, and large political experience. But Hines also believed that Thompson was "inclined to believe much that was told him, trust too many men, doubt too little, and suspect less."[24]

Thompson's hopes had been reborn in the summer of Northern discontent. He began to believe that if Lee could hold his own in front of Richmond, and if Joseph Johnston could frustrate Sherman in Georgia in the weeks prior to the election, Lincoln might yet be beaten.[25]

He also continued to believe that there was going to be that uprising in the Northwest leading to a western Confederacy. He was addressing every energy to that end, liberally bankrolling the Sons of Liberty and lobbying Richmond for a Confederate invasion of Kentucky and Missouri to abet and encourage rebellion. He continued trying to tip public opinion in the North toward peace with the South and making discreet contributions to the political campaigns of Democratic peace candidates. He was also participating in schemes to further fuel Federal financial instability.

There were grounds for Thompson's hope. There was a longstanding bond between the South and the Northwest. Southern leaders had cultivated support in the nonslaveholding region north of the Ohio for at least two decades before the Civil War. There were strong sympathetic and demographic ties between the two regions as well. The 1860 census showed that 475,000 residents of Ohio, Indiana, and Illinois had been born in the slave states. Four of every ten northwesterners in 1860 were of Southern birth or parentage. Those tens of thousands made up the core of the Democratic party in the Northwest.

The South and the Northwest had traditionally been tied together economically by their shared dependence on the Mississippi River. That tie had loosened somewhat by 1860 with the westward march of the railroads linking the Northwest to the Northeast. But the South-Northwest economic bond was still binding. The pro-Southern bent in the Northwest was not predominant, but it was definitely there. "Doughfaces"—Northern men with Southern sympathies—and copperheads abounded.[26]

In this reasonably friendly climate, a pro-Southern secret organization called the Knights of the Golden Circle had taken root by 1862, mainly in Ohio, Indiana, and Illinois. In time it had become the Order of the American Knights, then, by 1864, the Sons of Liberty. Each of these clandestine organizations was mainly military in character. Loyal Unionists called its members "midnight traitors" and "dark-lantern knights."[27]

They were seen by loyal northerners as intensely treasonable and revolutionary. There was evidence that they were undermining the North in many ways short of rebellion. They were helping Union soldiers desert, and protecting them when they did. They were discouraging enlistments and openly resisting the draft. They were circulating disloyal and treasonable publications and passing intelligence to the enemy. They were recruiting for the rebels or helping them recruit within Union lines, and supplying Confederate forces with arms and ammunition. They had abetted Southern raids and invasions of the North. They had destroyed government property and persecuted loyal northerners, and were thought not to be above assassination and murder.[28]

Lincoln himself called all this incendiary activity "the fire in the rear."[29] Judge Advocate General Joseph Holt, who was studying it in detail, called the secret society behind it "this infamous league of traitors and ruffians," with "its capacity for fatal mischief."[30]

Little of this fire and fatal mischief was escaping notice in the North. The governors of Indiana and Illinois, Oliver P. Morton and Richard Yates, were both reporting conspiracy and subversion in their states. Reports from other sources were also flooding Washington with demands for more arrests to stifle the treason that was clearly afoot. Morton visited Washington in person to impress on the national leadership the seriousness of the threat and to demand its suppression. He urged the arrest of the Indiana leaders of the Sons of Liberty as essential to "the success of the National cause in the autumn elections."[31]

Lincoln was as sensitive as any man alive to anything that might affect the elections. But he was also skeptical. "Nothing," he told one senator, "can make me believe that one hundred thousand Indiana Democrats are disloyal."[32]

None of this was helping dispel Lincoln's own personal melancholy. He was a man with a naturally sorrowful bent. Sadness was evident in his eyes—all who had ever met him had seen it. And it had only deepened in the fourth summer of this war between brothers. He was as disappointed as the rest of the country that Grant's spring campaign in Virginia had ended in a siege at Petersburg instead of the destruction of the Confederate army. And on June 20 he left Washington by river steamer to visit Grant's army for a little reassurance. It was his first visit to the Army of the Potomac since Grant had become general-in-chief in March.

The Chesapeake was choppy, giving the steamer a hard overnight ride. The presidential stomach was still churning a bit when he arrived at Grant's headquarters at City Point the next day about noon.

Lincoln reviewed the army astride Grant's big bay horse named Cincinnati. A figure on horseback dressed in civilian clothes always looks strange and out of place in the midst of a great army. But Lincoln in his frock coat and high black silk hat, with his long legs dangling downward and his trousers gradually working upward above his ankles, looked more absurd than most. One of Grant's staff officers thought he looked more the country farmer on the way to town in his Sunday best than the president of a great republic.[33]

Lincoln returned to Washington on June 23, sunburned and tired but refreshed and somewhat cheered. As he told Ben Butler during the trip, "When Grant once gets possession of a place, he holds on to it as if he had inherited it."[34] That tenacity comforted Lincoln. It promised victory in the future. It might take a while yet, Lincoln knew, and the summer was hot and discouraging, but the prospects were heartening.

Lincoln and his cabinet. Some thought them an ill-assorted and heterogeneous body of men. *(National Archives)*

Lincoln with his secretaries, Nicolay and Hay—"the White House political little ones." *(Library of Congress)*

George B. McClellan in 1864. *(Fessenden Collection, Special Collections, Bowdoin College Library)*

Salmon Portland Chase. The presidency was glaring out both of his eyes. *(National Archives)*

Kate Chase and William Sprague. She was ambitious and he was in love. *(National Archives)*

Charles Sumner. *(National Archives)*   Thaddeus Stevens. *(Library of Congress)*

Two who faced Zionwards.

Secretary of the Navy Gideon Welles. He wore a wig and kept a diary. *(National Archives)*

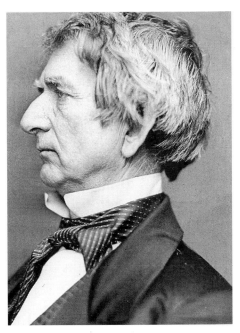

Secretary of State William S. Seward. He smoked a cigar and threw clanging oracles into the night. *(National Archives)*

Mary Lincoln—in her "trotting harness." *(Ostendorf Collection)*

August Belmont. The Democratic National Chairman. *(Library of Congress)*

THE COPPERHEAD PARTY.—IN FAVOR OF *A VIGOROUS PROSECUTION OF PEACE!*

Above: A White House levee.
(National Archives)

Left: How Republicans viewed copperheads.
(Library of Congress)

Bottom left: Ben Butler. Not much of a general but a potent political player.
(National Archives)

Below: Horace Greeley. Inkslinger who yearned to be a politician.
(National Portrait Gallery)

Ulysses S. Grant. It was said he could be silent in several languages. *(National Archives)*

John C. Frémont. The candidate of the Cleveland 400. *(National Archives)*

James Gordon Bennett. The editor who thought himself the Napoleon of the Press, and who Lincoln thought too pitchy to touch. *(Library of Congress)*

Henry J. Raymond. Lincoln's lieutenant general in politics. *(National Archives)*

Left: Hannibal Hamlin. He was out.
(National Archives)

FRANK LESLIE'S ILLUSTRATED NEWSPAPER.

JEFF DAVIS'S NOVEMBER NIGHTMARE.

Above: Jeff Davis's November nightmare.
(Library of Congress)

Left: Andrew Johnson. He was in.
(National Archives)

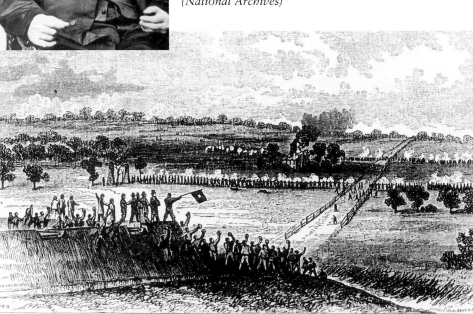

Fort Stevens under Confederate fire. Where Lincoln watched as the bullets flew.

Ben Wade.
(National Archives)

Henry Winter Davis.
(National Portrait Gallery)

The two radical architects of congressional reconstruction.

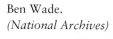

Above: Marvelous Democratic equestrian performance. *(Library of Congress)*

Left: Clement Vallandigham. Architect of the war failure plank.
(National Archives)

Left: Pro-Lincoln cartoon.
(Library of Congress)

Below: Pro-Lincoln cartoon.
(Library of Congress)

Above left: Pro-McClellan
cartoon.
(Library of Congress)

Left: Sojourner Truth.
She came to see the president for
herself.
(National Portrait Gallery)

Right: Lincoln four years longer.
(Library of Congress)

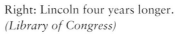

17

SHOWDOWN AT THE CAPITOL

———

T HE LAST WEEK IN JUNE WAS HOT—FEARFULLY, WILTINGLY HOT. The thermometer had hovered above ninety degrees nearly every day since Lincoln had returned from City Point. Nearly everybody in Washington was carrying a fan, trying to conjure a compensating breeze from the still, hot air.

The face of nature, Noah Brooks complained, was as parched and dry as a desert. "Great clouds of dust fill the fevered air," he wrote his newspaper, "choking the lungs and filling the eyes." Everywhere, he wrote, "heat, discomfort, dirt, and languid annoyance reign."[1]

In the twenty-one hospitals in and around Washington, 20,000 sick, wounded, and suffering soldiers from Grant's army reminded the city daily of the horror of war. The stench from the canal, an open sewer baked by a merciless sun, was overpowering. Washington was ill-kept, sad, noisome, stinking, and burning up.

Nowhere did languid annoyance reign more intensely than in Congress. The lawmakers were still in session long past the anticipated adjournment time. Dilly-dallying, buncombe, and gab, Brooks explained, had conspired to keep them six weeks longer than they had intended.[2] In contrast to the searing heat, the immense white dome of the Capitol loomed, as it always did, cool and austere, shining like an iceberg through the trees.[3]

Inside the icy-looking dome, it was oven-hot. Congress was meeting day after scorching day in the thinnest of clothes, with "its myriad fans in its myriad hands," fanning and fuming, a "feverish, cross, and impatient monster." In the House chamber, a very small public stared down in pity from the nearly deserted galleries. Doomed reporters—Brooks among them—clerks, and doorkeepers watched, with an anxious eye on the daily rise of both the thermometer and congressional tempers.[4]

Over in the Senate chamber, William Pitt Fessenden of Maine, chairman of the Finance Committee, was sick at heart, impatient, and ailing. He wished to be out of the unbearable heat and home again in Portland, in his house on State Street by the ocean, where he could enjoy "a sniff of salt air." More than most, Fessenden was mentally and emotionally exhausted. In April his soldier son, Frank, had lost a leg in the ill-starred Red River campaign in the Trans-Mississippi West, and was making a slower-than-expected recovery. The senator was worried, spent, and nearly prostrated by the heat.[5]

Late in the afternoon on the hot, listless Monday of the new week— June 27—a message arrived at Lincoln's desk from Treasury Secretary Salmon P. Chase. It was the nomination of Maunsell B. Field to be the new assistant secretary of the treasury at New York. Lincoln looked at the name and winced. Field's appointment would be just one more radical triumph that he couldn't afford.

The situation in New York had been muddying the political waters for a long time, fraying tempers and further stretching patience.

Earlier in the year the customhouse in New York City had become a problem. Complaints of irregularities and inefficiency were rife, causing yet more friction between Chase, who wanted to get rid of the customs officer, Hiram Barney, because he wasn't working out to suit him politically, and Lincoln, who was finding the situation a political albatross.[6]

Now John J. Cisco, the assistant secretary of the treasury at New York, remarkably able and efficient through three administrations, had resigned, effective June 30. His post was one of the most important in the country financially and politically.

Chase had always made all the important Treasury Department appointments in New York from his own pool of supporters, most of them radicals. He believed that in filling this important post, in particular, he ought not be interfered with. It was his right hand, and it was one of the richest patronage plums in the Federal government. He did not intend to have it fall into the hands of his opponents in the party. But for three years Republican conservatives in New York had endured Chase's appointees, and they were tired of it. Ever since Cisco announced his decision to quit in May, they had been putting the heat on Lincoln to name someone of their choosing.

Lincoln was concerned that Cisco not be replaced by someone objectionable to New York senator Edwin Morgan in particular. He had attempted to get Chase and Morgan together to settle on someone satisfactory to both. And they had tried. The post was first offered to two New York bankers acceptable to both sides. Both turned it down. Morgan had then suggested three other men, but Chase had rejected them all for one reason or another.

On this scorching Monday morning in late June, Chase had called on Morgan to tell him he had decided to nominate his own assistant secretary of the treasury, Maunsell Field, for the post. This had appalled Morgan, for Field was entirely without standing in the financial and political circles of New York; he would be a disaster. But Chase would have it no other way. By four-thirty in the afternoon the nomination was on Lincoln's desk.

It wasn't that Lincoln had anything against Field personally. Indeed, he rather liked him. He was a man of ingratiating presence, bug-eyed, with a bushy mustache, good education, polished manners, and a certain talent as a writer. But he was a social animal, not a political one. He had been, for some two years early in the war, deputy assistant treasurer at New York under Cisco, but had impressed few during that time, except Chase, who had made him his own assistant in late 1863.

Noah Brooks, who at one time or another had studied nearly everybody through his pince-nez, had also studied Field. He was a gentleman of ability, perhaps, Brooks had decided, but the victim of some popular prejudices that had become fixed in part because he "parts his hair in the middle, wears a white necktie and lemon colored kids." Brooks believed Field had not especially distinguished himself in the Treasury Department further than "to superintend the fitting up of Chase's private offices with Axminister carpets, gilded ceilings, velvet furniture, and other luxurious surroundings which go to hedge about a cabinet minister with a dignity quite appalling to the unaccustomed outsider."[7]

"I doubt if any one but Chase," Gideon Welles grumped into his diary, "would think of him for the place, and Chase, as usual, does not know the reason."[8]

Lincoln didn't know the reason either. He only knew that the party in New York was split into two warring wings—as so much of his party was, everywhere—that he couldn't afford to quarrel with either one of them, and that this appointment would stir up nothing but trouble.[9]

The morning after he sent Field's name to Lincoln, Chase awoke and, as was his practice, turned to the Scriptures in his daily attempt "to reach God in prayer." He read Paul's epistle to the Ephesians, and it cheered and inspired him. "May God in His infinite mercy," he thought, "send us peace with Union and freedom."[10]

Chase was to get no peace from Lincoln that day. Even as he was reading from the epistle to the Ephesians, Lincoln was writing an epistle to Chase. "I can not without much embarrassment, make this appointment," Lincoln wrote his treasury secretary, "principally because of Senator Morgan's very firm opposition to it. . . . It will really oblige me if you will make choice among these three [proposed by Morgan], or any other man that Senators Morgan and [Ira] Harris [the other senator from New York] will be satisfied with, and send me a nomination for him."[11]

Instead, Chase sent Lincoln a note asking for a personal interview. He wished to press the nomination face to face. He didn't intend that either Lincoln or Morgan should have the final say in this appointment.[12]

But neither did Lincoln intend to meet with Chase, since he didn't believe the main difficulty was between the two of them. He wrote a second note to his treasury secretary saying that, and telling him, "I do not think Mr. Field a very proper man for the place, but I would trust your judgment, and forego this, were the greater difficulty out of the way." The greater difficulty was the trouble with Hiram Barney, whom Thurlow Weed and other anti-Chase Republicans now wanted to be rid of and Chase didn't. There had also been another divisive appointment in New York since then to further fan the flames. All that, Lincoln explained to Chase, "has . . . kept me at the verge of open revolt. Now, the appointment of Mr. Field would precipitate me in it. . . . Strained as I already am at this point I do not think that I can make this appointment in the direction of still greater strain."[13]

When he received this, Chase wired Cisco, asking him to stay on for at least another quarter. He then sent Lincoln a note saying that if Cisco declined to stay, he still favored Field. Cisco eased the strain somewhat, later in the day, with a wire to Chase agreeing to withdraw his resignation temporarily.[14]

Early the next morning Chase sent Lincoln Cisco's telegram—and with it his own resignation.

Chase wielded resignations as a gunfighter wielded six-shooters, pulling them from his holster at the slightest affront to his power, position, prerogatives, or prestige. This was believed to be at least his fourth resignation as secretary of the treasury, and Lincoln remembered them all. The first time was over a cabinet crisis in December 1862, when both Chase and Secretary of State Seward resigned. Lincoln had refused then to accept either of those resignations.

The second time was over a collector of customs on the Pacific Coast, one of Chase's men. Serious charges had been brought against the collector when Chase was out of town. Lincoln, viewing the charges as just cause, removed the offender. When Chase returned and learned of it, he angrily sent the president his resignation.

On receiving it, Lincoln ordered his carriage and drove to Chase's house at Sixth and E streets. The president found the secretary in his study and, with the resignation in hand, put a conciliatory arm around his neck and said, "Chase, here is a paper with which I wish to have nothing to do; take it back, and be reasonable." Lincoln explained to Chase what had happened in his absence, and said he would be happy to appoint anybody else that Chase wished. The president had a hard time bringing him around, but he finally did, and nothing more was heard of that resignation.

But there was soon another one, as Lincoln remembered it, this time over Barney in New York. Lincoln had refused that resignation too, mollified Chase, and, against his better political instincts, kept Barney on.[15]

Now Lincoln, in June 1864, was staring at resignation number four. Chase never expected his resignations to be accepted, and he had no reason to expect this one would be. But Lincoln had now had one too many of them.

"He knows that the nomination of Field would displease the Unionists of New York, would delight our enemies, and injure our friends," Lincoln told Register of the Treasury L. E. Chittenden. "He knows that I could not make it without seriously offending the strongest supporters of the government in New York, and that the nomination would not strengthen him anywhere or with anybody. Yet he resigns because I will not make it. He is either determined to annoy me, or that I shall pat him on the shoulder and coax him to stay. I don't think I ought to do it. I will not do it. I will take him at his word."[16]

The next morning, the last day of the month, Lincoln called John Hay into his office.

"When does the Senate meet today?" he asked his young secretary.

"Eleven o'clock."

"I wish you to be there when they meet. It is a big fish. Mr. Chase has resigned and I have accepted his resignation. I thought I could not stand it any longer."

"Is it about the Field matter?" Hay asked.

"Yes."

"Who is to be his successor?"

"Dave Tod. He is my friend, with a big head full of brains."

Hay had his doubts about David Tod, the former governor of Ohio, a Youngstown capitalist and prominent war Democrat. "Has he the skill and experience necessary for such a place?" Hay asked the president.

"He made a good Governor, and has made a fortune for himself. I am willing to trust him."[17]

Hay set out for the Capitol, and Lincoln wired Tod in Ohio: "I have nominated you to be Secretary of the Treasury in place of Gov. Chase who has resigned. Please come without a moment's delay."[18]

Hay arrived at the door of the Senate chamber while the chaplain was delivering the opening prayer. When the praying ended and the politicking was about to begin, Hay threw in the president's bombshell and returned to the White House.

At that moment Salmon Chase was in William Pitt Fessenden's office at the Capitol, discussing the gold bill and a proposal for a tax increase. A messenger appeared at the door and the finance chairman excused himself a moment to speak privately with him. When Fessenden returned to his desk he asked Chase:

"Have you resigned? I am called to the Senate and told that the President has sent in the nomination of your successor."[19]

Nobody was more surprised by this news than Chase himself. Hurrying back to his office, he found Lincoln's note awaiting him. "Your resignation of the office of Secretary of the Treasury . . . is accepted," Lincoln's note began. "Of all I have said in commendation of your ability and fidelity, I have nothing to unsay; and yet you and I have reached a point of mutual embarrassment in our official relation which it seems can not be overcome, or longer sustained, consistently with the public service."[20]

"So my official life closes," Chase confided that evening to his diary. Later he was to write his friend Simon Cameron, "My feelings upon going out of office are of a mixed sort—regret that I leave great works half done—satisfaction in relief from cares and manifold annoyances. Sometimes one of these feelings predominates—sometimes the other."[21]

Chase's avowed enemies, the Blairs, had no such ambiguous feelings about it. Good riddance, old man Blair said, in effect, to his son Frank: "Chase, you see, hung on as long as possible, and dropped off at the last like a rotten pear, unexpectedly to himself and to everybody else. He supposed he could bully Lincoln by threatening to resign unless he was permitted to make the Treasury appointments without control."[22]

Congress, meanwhile, was in turmoil. The *New York World* reported that Chase's resignation was "so entirely unexpected as to cause the greatest commotion everywhere." From the mutterings he heard, the *World* correspondent predicted that if Montgomery Blair didn't also now resign or wasn't removed, " 'Rome will howl' " with "a fearful echo at the November ides."[23]

James Gordon Bennett at the *New York Herald,* always ready to oblige with a sardonic comment, wrote, "The charm of the Happy Family is broken." He then suggested, Why stop there? Make a clean sweep of it. Get rid of "the bungling and blundering Secretary of War, Stanton, and that incompetent old sleepy head, Grandmother Welles, of the navy." Why not them, too?[24]

Within an hour of receiving Tod's nomination, the Senate Finance Committee, in a body, followed Hay down the hill to Lincoln's office, led by Fessenden, who only wanted to be home in Maine, sniffing the salt air. They protested the change, and objected in particular to Tod, who they believed too little known and too little experienced. Lincoln told them he could not, in justice to himself or Tod, now withdraw the nomination.[25]

The correspondent of the *New York World* as usual put a far less elegant spin on it. He explained that Tod was known in Washington for "a jolly fellow and a good story-teller, one after Mr. Lincoln's own heart, but who knows as little of finance as a cow does of arithmetic."[26]

Tod also knew he wanted no part of the job. By nightfall he had wired Lincoln pleading ill health and refusing the nomination. Hay hurried to the Hill to tell Fessenden this, and noted that the reaction was universally favorable: Tod was "not such a fool as I thought he was," they all said. "Shows his sense."[27]

The next morning, the first day of July, Hay went in to see the president at ten-thirty, and Lincoln told him, "I have determined to appoint Fessenden himself."

Hay told Lincoln that Fessenden was at that moment in his room waiting to see him.

"Send him in [and] go at once to the Senate," Lincoln urged Hay.

The unsuspecting Fessenden had come to the White House that morning to press the appointment of his friend, Hugh McCulloch, the comptroller of the currency, as the new secretary of the treasury. Much to Lincoln's amusement, Fessenden sat down and began first to talk of other matters. At length he brought up McCulloch's name.

"Mr. Fessenden," Lincoln said, interrupting him, "I have nominated you for that place. Mr. Hay has just taken the nomination to the Senate."

Fessenden was horrified.

"But it hasn't reached there," he exclaimed. "You must withdraw it—I can't accept!"

"If you decline," Lincoln said, "you must do it in open day, for I shall not recall the nomination."

By the time Fessenden reached the Capitol, Hay had already put the nomination in. The Senate, going into executive session and deliberating for less than a minute, had confirmed him. The stunned senator staggered into his office to begin writing his letter refusing the appointment. All he wanted to do—had been looking forward to for weeks— was to get out of Washington and home to Maine. And now this!

Back at the White House, Lincoln mused to Hay, "It is very singular, considering that this appointment of F.'s is so popular when made, that no one ever mentioned his name to me for that place." As the time ticked by and still no refusal had yet come from Fessenden, Lincoln said, "I hope from the long delay, that he is making up his mind to accept. If he would only consent to accept [and] stay here and help me for a little while, I think he would be in no hurry to go."[28]

Fessenden was definitely in a hurry to go. But he couldn't even get his letter written. His office was swarming with one visitor after another, urging him to accept the nomination. Telegrams with the same message were pouring in from around the country.

Fessenden was a spindle of a man, not over five feet ten inches tall and weighing less than 130 pounds. Noah Brooks described him as "one of your narrow-chested, thin men who have not much vitality nor physical endurance."[29] Fessenden's thin face matched his thin disposition—Yankee bleak, sour, crabbed, and dyspeptic. His carriage, one observer noted, was "on the old-time ministerial order—slow, precise, deliberate, sedate, senatorial."[30] Maunsell Field called him "a martyr to dyspepsia,"[31] which caused him to be somewhat unsociable, often irritable. His friends called him "Pitt."

It was generally conceded that Fessenden was the best all-around debater and practical legislator in the Senate, who took a special delight not in flaming oratory, but in dry details. He was essentially a financier, good with numbers, cool, methodical, intelligent, immovable. Field knew of no senator who could stand up successfully against him in

free-for-all debate on the floor. Charles Sumner had often been his vic-
tim in such clashes, and hated him for it. It was said that before the war
Jefferson Davis, then also a U.S. senator, feared to cross swords with
Fessenden more than with any other member.[32]

Fessenden was numbered among the Senate radicals, though he didn't
share their vindictive natures. He moved among them without being
completely one of them. Thaddeus Stevens found him suspect, contam-
inated with "too much of the vile ingredient, called conservatism,
which is worse than secessionism."[33]

By late in the afternoon, with his letter of refusal still unwritten, Fessenden fled the Capitol and went to Chase's house, only a block from
his own home on E Street. There too he met with pleas to take the job.
When Chase heard Fessenden's name had been sent to the Senate and
confirmed, he thought it "a wise selection." A year and a half before,
Chase had told Fessenden that "you have the brain of a statesman and
the heart of a patriot"—both in short supply and never more urgently
needed, he said.[34]

Now Chase was telling him he ought to accept the appointment, that
all of the great work of the department was now fairly blocked out and
under way. The most difficult part of the job would be to raise money
to keep the war going.[35]

Fessenden, momentarily wavering, asked if he could count on Chase's
help and advice. It was unlikely he would need it, Chase told him, but all
he could give was at his service.[36] Fessenden, still in torment, rode back
as far as the Capitol with Chase in the former secretary's carriage. By ten
o'clock in the evening, however, he was more resolved than ever to reject
the nomination, and was at home beginning to write out his refusal.

"I have reached a point where my physical powers, already much
impaired, can only be restored and sustained by a period of absolute
repose," he wrote. "I feel that to undertake, at this time, the duties and
responsibilities of an office involving labor and interests so vast, would
be an act of folly on my part, and certain to result in speedy failure."[37]

Rushing over to the White House with this late-hour document, he
found Lincoln already retired for the night. He would have to wait
until the next morning to refuse the nomination. He returned dejectedly
home, calling this day "one of the most miserable of my life."[38]

Early the next morning he was again at the White House, telling Lincoln he had a letter for him that he deemed must be presented in person. If it was a letter declining to accept the Treasury job, Lincoln told
him, he would not receive it.[39]

Fessenden was in a quandary. He talked to Stanton, but got no sympathy there either. "You can no more refuse than your son could have refused to attack Monett's Bluff," Stanton told him, "and you cannot look him in the face if you do."

That hurt. But "it would kill me," Fessenden protested.

"Very well," said the unsympathetic secretary of war, "you cannot die better than in trying to save your country."[40]

It was that idea—that he must accept the job to save the country, thrown at him from every direction—that finally caused Fessenden to cave in. Later that day he told Lincoln he would accept the job, and then told his close friend and fellow senator, James Grimes of Iowa, that "it may result in the destruction of all the reputation I have gained."[41]

The country heaved a sigh of relief. Everybody but Fessenden was delighted. The *Washington Chronicle* praised him, calling him "a Senator who never left his post, never made a speech without a purpose . . . a positive, daring statesman . . . of purity and whiteness." Even Manton Marble at the *New York World,* not given to praising either radicals or Republican cabinet members, called him "unquestionably the fittest man in his party for that high trust."[42]

"Never," said Maunsell Field, who would now stay on to work for Fessenden, "did a man more reluctantly accept office."[43]

Henry Winter Davis was what Noah Brooks would call "a singularly alert and singularly violent politician."[44] He was a congressman from Maryland, an ultraradical protégé of Thaddeus Stevens, and chairman of the House Committee on Foreign Affairs—an apt position, since he considered the South a foreign nation that needed subjugating. He was slight but tall—about six feet—looking younger even than his youthful forty years. He was light-complexioned, with a round, boyish head and sandy hair and mustache. He was compellingly handsome, with an aristocratic bearing and manner.

He possessed oratorical gifts almost beyond reason. His voice, one observer said, was silvery, "as seductive and winning as a morning thrush."[45] "Clear and cold like starlight," another said.[46]

But, peering at Davis though his pince-nez, Brooks saw "a political charlatan . . . insatiate in his hates, mischievous in his schemes, and hollow-hearted and cold-blooded."[47] And there was no one Davis disliked more than Abraham Lincoln. He had hoped to be in Lincoln's cabinet, but his archenemy, Montgomery Blair, had been appointed instead. Davis had never forgiven the president and had offered him nothing but venom since.[48]

This gifted, eloquent, proud, vengeful politician had emerged by the summer of 1864 as Lincoln's chief opponent on reconstruction, chairman of a House select committee appointed to draft a counter program. Davis believed Lincoln incapable, but safe "if managed by the radicals—not otherwise."[49]

Since his December message, Lincoln had been anything but safe, by Davis's standards. The president had been pushing ahead on his own reconstruction plan in Louisiana, Tennessee, and Arkansas—to mounting radical anger and alarm. Lincoln's program had to be wrecked, and Davis, working swiftly, had a bill ready to report by late January.

Not every congressman, however, was as driven as Davis, and the bill was controversial. It wasn't until March 22 that it finally reached the floor for discussion, and Davis had risen then to unleash his starlight voice on Lincoln and his policies. Lincoln's Emancipation Proclamation, Davis argued, was of dubious validity. It had not ended slavery everywhere, and might not ever—particularly in loyal states and territories. That was what reconstruction was all about in Davis's mind—the end of slavery everywhere. It was a paramount part of the reconstruction bill he had crafted.

Davis and his allies in the Congress had viewed Lincoln's plan of reconstruction as a ruse to assure himself a majority of the delegates to the nominating convention—"a political trick," New Jersey's Nehemiah Perry said, "worthy of the most adroit and unscrupulous wire puller." Lincoln, in the radical mind, was hurrying these reconquered states back into the Union to pad his reelection prospects in 1864. It was little more than a scheme to steal the election.[50]

Here was the one thing on which the radicals and the Confederates agreed. The *Richmond Examiner* at about this time was sounding just like the champions of the Davis bill. Lincoln's ten-percent plan for pirating Louisiana, Arkansas, and Tennessee back into the Union, the *Examiner* fumed, was "one of the vilest cheats of the war," designed for "the lowest and vilest party purpose," a black Republican method of "stumping the South."[51]

It wasn't until May 4 that Davis's bill came to a vote in the House, and was passed 74–59. It was not an impressive majority. And even some of Davis's friends were dubious. William B. Hill wrote to John

A. J. Cresswell, Davis's fellow congressman from Maryland, that "Davis I see has been kicking up a dust in the House. I fear the chase he has entered upon will only serve to discover his grave."[52]

There were more similarities than differences between the Lincoln and Davis plans. But the differences, such as they were, were sharp: Lincoln would leave the reconstructed states to abolish slavery themselves; Davis's bill would compel immediate emancipation in all of the states. Lincoln would allow ten percent of the voters to set up new state governments; Davis would require a majority. Lincoln would bar only a few of the leading Confederates from voting and holding office; Davis would bar a vast number. Lincoln said nothing about repudiating the South's war debts; Davis would repudiate them all. Lincoln would have the Executive manage reconstruction; Davis would wrest it from his hands and make it a congressional process from beginning to end, subject to congressional control at every step.

Even so, the bill did not go as far as many radicals intended reconstruction to go. The Davis bill restricted suffrage to whites only. The radicals eventually intended it to be extended to blacks as well, to ensure the growth and dominance of a native Republican party. The bill admitted that the seceded states were still entitled to some rights under the Constitution. The ultimate Republican program envisioned a conquered-provinces approach. The bill didn't call for confiscation of rebel property. The radicals eventually intended to seize the Southern plantations and distribute the land among the former slaves. The purpose now was to get the best bill possible at the moment to forestall Lincoln from bringing back the rebellious states unpunished and unrepentant. A more thoroughgoing and vindictively satisfying reconstruction measure would come later.[53]

There was no mistaking what this bill, however limited, intended to do immediately. It was meant to undo Lincoln's program and put reconstruction into congressional hands. Its aim, as Lincoln's secretaries, John Nicolay and John Hay, saw it, was to "put a stop to the work which the President had already begun in Tennessee and Louisiana, and to prevent the extension of that policy to other Southern States." Gideon Welles believed, knowing Davis, that its object was as much to pull down the administration as to reconstruct the Union.[54]

There were two other compelling reasons radicals desperately wanted this bill. First, there was no reconstruction plank in the Union Party platform. As things now stood, the party would go to the electorate in November on Lincoln's plan, not theirs. The presence on the ticket of

Johnson—that living tool of the president's policy in Tennessee—made this even clearer. If this bill was passed and signed into law, however, the congressional plan, and not Lincoln's, would then stand as the party's statement on reconstruction. Second, the recent failure to pass a constitutional amendment prohibiting slavery in the states meant that the Davis bill was the sole antislavery measure that had a chance now of passing before Congress adjourned. And it was already July, and Congress was about to adjourn.[55]

Davis's bill had been in the Senate since May, and nothing had yet happened. Davis was getting nervous and edgy. The bill had gone to the Senate committee on territories, chaired by Benjamin Franklin Wade, as unbending a radical as existed. But what was Wade doing with it? Time was slipping away.

In any cow pasture, Ben Wade would have been the bull. They called him "Bluff Ben" for a reason. He was stout of figure, a block of a man, not quite five feet nine inches tall, 185 pounds. He was manly, courageous, vehement, and earnest. Noah Brooks said of him that he had a bulldog obduracy that was "truly masterful."[56]

"Stamped all over with honesty and fearlessness," as another observer said of him, Wade was armed with a powerful voice capable of passionate invective and irony, a voice that "quivered in all the octaves of eloquence." The invective tended to profanity. "Damn it," he said, "I can't be emphatic without swearing; I don't mean any disrespect to the Deity or to my hearers." As he warmed to his theme his hair, perhaps offended by what his mouth was saying, became ruffled and stood up like bristles. He would unbutton his vest, shove up his coat sleeves, tear off his cravat, and yank off his collar. In his most earnest moments he would rise on his toes, hold aloft his hands at arm's length, and, as he brought them down, jump onto his heels.[57]

Gideon Welles saw him as a man with "a good deal of patriotic feeling, common sense, and a strong, though coarse and vulgar, mind."[58] He dressed in black and wore a shrewd, sour, nervous face with dark, melancholy eyes that burned with a deep, smothered fire. He could be a good friend but also a gifted enemy, not given to hedging his opinion of either men or measures. Behind his bluff-faced exterior, however, lurked something of a tender heart. He was gracious, even lovable, in private life. But publicly he was the living embodiment of the vengeful radical. Not infrequently his intense radicalism betrayed him into outbursts of flaming temper. In the antislavery cause he was said to wield "trenchant weapons." Nobody, not even Thaddeus Stevens and Henry

Winter Davis, burned more to remake the South than Ben Wade. Nobody believed more ardently that the right to do so belonged to the Congress. And nobody resented Lincoln's attempted "usurpation" of that right more than he.[59]

Wade had entered the Senate from Ohio the same year Charles Sumner had entered it from Massachusetts—in 1851—and, like Sumner, was a veteran of the antislavery old guard. As the present Congress staggered toward adjournment in the final scorching days of June 1864, this radical veteran of the antislavery wars was having trouble getting the reconstruction measure to the Senate floor.

As in the House, not all in the Senate shared his flaming interest in it. Everybody just wanted to get done, get out of the heat, and go home. The chambers and the conference and anterooms were sweltering; the Capitol was a furnace. It wasn't until June 29, only five days before scheduled adjournment, that Wade got a hearing for the bill. Only on July 1 did he succeed in getting it to the floor. He finally rammed through a Senate-House compromise measure, called the Wade-Davis bill, on July 2 by a narrow 18–14 vote. Seventeen senators were absent, doubtless in cooler places.

On July 4, Independence Day, many in Washington awoke to the thunder of cannon, ringing of bells, and what Salmon Chase described as the "whiz-whiz snap-snap" of firecrackers.[60]

Fireworks were also about to whiz and snap at the Capitol. Adjournment was expected at noon, and Lincoln was there, in the president's room off the Senate chamber, signing the many bills being "pitchforked into shape" in the chaotic closing hours of the session.[61]

The president's room was a square apartment with windows looking to the north. It was elegantly appointed, with tasteful curtains; its floor was richly carpeted and its furnishings were simple but costly. A vaulted ceiling was magnificently frescoed with scenes from the young nation's history. The walls were adorned with large mirrors and portraits in fresco of Washington and his first cabinet. A superb chandelier shed a soft light throughout the room.[62]

There Lincoln sat as time ticked on, signing the eleventh-hour legislation, attended from time to time by members of his cabinet. On the House floor a secretary was mindlessly reading aloud from the Declaration of Independence, over Sunset Cox's vigorous protest that it was an insurrectionary document that would give aid and comfort to the rebellion.[63]

As the clock continued to tick, word started to spread among the radicals that the president hadn't yet signed the all-important Wade-Davis bill. Speculation began to course through the two chambers that he didn't intend to sign it, that he would simply let it die with a pocket veto. This was an unexpected turn of events. Nobody had seriously believed the president wouldn't sign the bill at this late hour, despite his objections to it. And a pocket veto had rarely been used by any president.

Nobody was more appalled by this prospect than Zachariah Chandler, the radical senator from Michigan, who gave nothing away to his friend, Ben Wade, for bluffness. Chandler was a man of huge frame, with a large mouth that drooped at the corners in a perennial look of disapproval and which also gave nothing to Wade in the production of cuss words. He was another of the earnest men, intensely radical, with a blustering presence and a strong menacing voice.[64]

Chandler had greeted the Civil War as a rather gratifying turn of events. "Without a little blood-letting," he had said in early 1861 as the war approached, "this Union will not, in my estimation, be worth a rush." He had been known ever since as "the Blood-letter."[65]

And now, exceedingly anxious for the fate of the Wade-Davis bill, a measure near his heart, he was lumbering into the president's room in his stooping, shuffling gait, his Prince Albert coat flared open with a large expanse of shirt bosom showing, and bloodletting on his mind.[66]

He demanded bluntly of the president whether the bill was signed. Lincoln told him no, and Chandler argued that if it wasn't signed, it would make a terrible record for the party to run on in November.

"Mr. Chandler," Lincoln told him, "this bill was placed before me a few minutes before Congress adjourns. It is a matter of too much importance to be swallowed in that way."

"If it is vetoed," Chandler insisted, "it will damage us fearfully in the Northwest. It may not in Illinois; it will in Michigan and Ohio. The important point is that one prohibiting slavery in the reconstructed States."

"That is the point on which I doubt the authority of Congress to act," Lincoln replied.

"It is no more than you have done yourself," objected Chandler.

"I conceive that I may in an emergency do things on military grounds which cannot be done constitutionally by Congress," Lincoln said.

"Mr. President, I cannot convert your position by argument, I can only say I deeply regret it," Chandler said, and left the room.

But Lincoln continued talking without Chandler, explaining his reasoning to the room in general: "I do not see how any of us now can deny and contradict all we have always said, that Congress has no constitutional power over slavery in the States."

It was the core problem laid bare: the question of who was to control reconstruction.

Now Lincoln was the lawyer again, presenting his case to the jury: "This bill and this position of these gentlemen seems to me to make the fatal admission [in asserting that the insurrectionary States are no longer in the Union] that States whenever they please may of their own motion dissolve their connection with the Union. Now we cannot survive that admission, I am convinced."

The president continued addressing the room: "If that be true, I am not President, these gentlemen are not Congress. I have laboriously endeavored to avoid that question ever since it first began to be mooted and thus to avoid confusion and disturbance in our own counsels. It was to obviate this question that I earnestly favored the movement for an amendment to the Constitution abolishing slavery, which passed the Senate and failed in the House. I thought it much better, if it were possible, to restore the Union without the necessity of a violent quarrel among its friends, as to whether certain States have been in or out of the Union during the war: a merely metaphysical question and one unnecessary to be forced into discussion."[67]

That said, Lincoln pocketed the Wade-Davis bill. It was a few minutes past noon. Time had run out, and Congress had adjourned.

"God be thanked!" sighed Attorney General Edward Bates into his diary that night.[68]

"If they choose to make a point upon this," Lincoln mused to John Hay as they left the Capitol together, "I do not doubt that they can do harm. They have never been friendly to me [and] I don't know that this will make any special difference as to that. At all events, I must keep some consciousness of being somewhere near right: I must keep some standard of principle fixed within myself."[69]

The two men most likely to make a point on this and do harm, Henry Winter Davis and Ben Wade, were stunned and incensed. As the House adjourned and members headed for the doors all around him, Davis continued to stand at his desk, pale with wrath, wildly waving his arms and denouncing the president into the emptying chamber.[70]

Four days later, Lincoln tried to blunt the harm he sensed was coming. He had pocket-vetoed the bill partly because he believed it unconstitutional, but mainly because it threatened his reconstruction policies in Louisiana, Tennessee, and Arkansas. But now he must try to defuse the anger, try to maintain party harmony in the face of the coming election, try to keep reconstruction from becoming an issue. On July 8 he issued a proclamation explaining his veto.

In it he acknowledged that the Wade-Davis bill had expressed the sense of Congress on the subject. He said he was flexible, unready to be chained to any single plan of restoration. But he was loath to see the free-state constitutions and governments already installed in Arkansas and Louisiana set aside and held for nought, thereby repelling and discouraging the loyal citizens who had set them up. He said he believed the system for restoration contained in the bill was one very proper plan, however, and if any state did choose to adopt it, he would support it.[71]

Instead of appeasing the leaders of congressional reconstruction, Lincoln's proclamation only further outraged them. Having stuck the knife in, he now seemed to them to be turning it.

"What an infamous proclamation!" Thaddeus Stevens fumed. "The idea of pocketing a bill [and] then issuing a proclamation as to how far he will conform to it, is matched only by signing a bill and then sending in a veto. . . . But what are we to do? Condemn privately and applaud publicly?"[72]

It was doubtful that Lincoln had heard the last of the subject from these unhappy, hot-blooded, and steaming congressional radicals, either publicly or privately.

18

Get Down, You Fool!

O N July 2, Union Maj. Gen. Franz Sigel, commanding the
Reserve Division in the Department of West Virginia at Martinsburg, hurried off a telegram to Washington.

"There are strong indications," he wired, "of a movement of the
enemy in force down the Valley."[1]

It was that unguarded back door to Washington again. Often in this
war, the rebels had come along that natural alleyway of the Shenandoah Valley of Virginia behind the Blue Ridge to the south and its con-
tinuation, South Mountain, to the north. Twice under the sheltering
cover of those mountain ranges they had come through the backyard
and "carried devastation with fire and steel" to the quiet rural hamlets
of Pennsylvania and Maryland. Robert E. Lee had done it in force in
the fall of 1862 and again in the summer of 1863. Stonewall Jackson
had driven to the banks of the Potomac by that same open alleyway in
the spring and early summer of 1862, before receding back up the valley. Now another Confederate commander was approaching along this
"race track of rushing armies"—and in an election year.[2]

"We always have big scares from that quarter," Gideon Welles wrote
in his diary, "and sometimes pretty serious realities."[3]

It was still too early, on July 2, to tell whether this was just another
scare or a pretty serious reality. The only solid information coming into
Washington was that a considerable Confederate force had moved down
the valley and reached Winchester, only sixty miles from unguarded
Washington. What its intentions were, and where it was headed,
nobody in the North knew.

Robert E. Lee knew. It was his idea.

Sitting in Petersburg under siege by Grant's army, Lee had found Washington's unguarded rear an irresistible attraction; it looked to him to be a way to take pressure off his beleaguered lines. A raid down the Shenandoah Valley threatening Washington might force Grant to part with so much of his army to protect the Northern capital that the siege would have to be lifted. If the venture succeeded, it might also rearrange Lincoln's reelection prospects in November.

Lee had two targets in mind for the expedition: a demonstration against the Union capital and, if possible, a cavalry dash on Point Lookout in Maryland to support a plan then afoot to liberate Confederate prisoners there.

What was there to lose? On June 12, as he was leaving Cold Harbor to follow Grant to the James, Lee detached a force under Lt. Gen. Jubal A. Early, with orders to head for the valley, clear it of Union Maj. Gen. David Hunter's marauding Union force, and, if plausible, proceed to Washington.

Jubal Early was a Confederate hard case if there ever was one, and a good choice for this kind of assignment. Although he was a West Pointer, he didn't look much like a general. His shoulders were stooped and rounded, bent by rheumatism, which gave him the look of a man old beyond his years. He wore a bushy, gray-streaked beard. His eyes were small, dark, deep-set, and glittering, his nose aquiline. His step was slow, shuffling, almost irresolute.

"I never saw a man who looked less like a soldier," said one Confederate. Nor did Early sound like a soldier. His voice was a piping treble that snaked out of him in a long-drawn whine or drawl, and was capable of the vilest profanity in the Confederate army. He was in many ways personally objectionable, of a snarling, rasping disposition. His opinions were undiluted, emphatic, and denunciatory. His dislikes went unhidden, his views were bitter, his conversation racy and pungent. He was an unregenerate Confederate who had at first opposed the war, but when it came, had thrown himself into it body and soul. And he was a fighter, bold without being rash.[4] Lee liked him and called him "my bad old man."[5]

Early was not without flashes of humor. When his onetime commander, Stonewall Jackson, sent him a query after a hard march, asking why he had seen so many stragglers in the rear of his division that day, Early had answered that Jackson "saw so many stragglers in the rear of my division to-day, probably because he rode in the rear of my division."[6]

Early had left Lee's army near Cold Harbor at about two o'clock in the morning on June 13 with about 10,000 troops and twenty-four pieces of artillery, later increased to forty. His army was a collection of veterans, many of them survivors of Jackson's old "foot cavalry," men trained to march long, fight hard, and not straggle—and who knew the valley intimately. To them it was going home.

Early's army passed into the valley at Lexington, Virginia, and marched through the cemetery where Jackson was buried. Jackson's veterans marched slowly and silently past the sacred grave with their hats off, their arms reversed, and tears in their eyes. Not a man spoke, not a sound was uttered. Only the muffled tramp of feet told of their passing in review.

"Alas," sighed Henry Kyd Douglas, one of Jackson's former staff officers, "how few of them were left."[7]

The valley everywhere showed the scars of war. And the little rebel army moved through it down the beaten track it knew so well, marching hard, as it had when Jackson drove them there. Joined by a division of 2,000 men under Maj. Gen. John C. Breckinridge, Early batted Hunter's smaller force aside, driving it into West Virginia, then started rapidly down the valley. On Saturday, July 2, he entered Winchester, triggering Sigel's telegram to Washington. On Sunday he seized Martinsburg and occupied Bolivar Heights, above Harper's Ferry. Up to then there had been nothing to stop him.

But the Union force under Sigel now occupying Maryland Heights across the two rivers that joined at Harper's Ferry was too strong to dislodge. So Early simply skirted it and began crossing the Potomac into Maryland at Shepherdstown on Tuesday, July 5. By the next day he was across the river. On Thursday the seventh, his advance began passing through the gaps on South Mountain west of Frederick. On the eighth, his whole army was on the move through the passes. That night he reached Cotoctin Mountain. Within easy marching distance before him now lay Frederick and just beyond it the Monocacy River. Across the river lay the open roads to Baltimore and Washington.

Maj. Gen. Lew Wallace, commanding the Union Middle Division, headquartered in Baltimore, had rushed toward Frederick when he got the word. Now he stood on the banks of the Monocacy, a crooked little river running in a southerly direction into the Potomac. Where he was standing, the turnpike to Washington and the B&O rail line to Baltimore both crossed the river, some three miles east of Frederick. This marked the western limit of Wallace's department. Beyond was

Hunter's responsibility. But Hunter was out of the picture, and something had to be done.

The son of a former governor of Indiana, Wallace was one of those generals who owed his rank and position to political connections. Before he went to fight in the Mexican War in the 1840s, he had been a lawyer and a newspaper reporter. After the war he was elected to the Indiana legislature and was active in the state militia.

Now he was standing at Monocacy Junction, gazing out to the west. There he saw all the gateways of the Shenandoah Valley—its roads, passes, gaps—standing wide open, with Washington exposed, "its very nakedness," Wallace thought, "inviting attack." He saw it all "with shuddering distinctness."[8]

Where Wallace stood, the river flowed lazily below, over a rocky bed. Beyond, to the west, stretched a valley as level as a prairie for ten miles, to the wall of blue mist that was Cotoctin Mountain. The fields were golden with wheat ready for the reaper, and dotted with great brown-painted barns. It was a scene Wallace found "so smilingly Arcadian that the thought of war coming to mar it sent a shock through me."[9]

Looking from Monocacy Junction toward the east, Wallace could see a farm of extensive reach, a succession of meadowlands and corn-fields, lushly green with summer growth. A stately mansion house to the southeast dominated the farm, and between it and the river rose rough, dark-wooded hills into which the Baltimore & Ohio rail line plunged over the iron bridge and was speedily lost to sight. It was altogether a beautiful vista, front and back. As a soldier who would soon be fighting there said, "If we must make war, it might be where every prospect pleased."[10]

Here, in this Arcadian setting, Wallace intended to make a stand against an invading Confederate army of a size and strength still unknown, lying now at the foot of that wall of blue mist only ten miles away.

Lt. Gen. U. S. Grant, at Petersburg, had found the reports that began reaching him only five days before hard to believe. A Confederate army of force, marching toward Washington? He had no indication that any part of Lee's army had been detached. He did not know that Early's little force had left three weeks before. By July 6, however, Grant was persuaded. Immediately he had detached Maj. Gen. James B. Ricketts's division from the veteran Sixth Corps and sent it toward Baltimore. Two days later he detached the remainder of the corps and set it steaming for Washington.

Ricketts arrived in Baltimore on the eighth, as Early was marching through the South Mountain passes, and found Wallace gone. He put his division aboard a train and set out immediately for Monocacy Junction. Wallace got word that day that Ricketts would be there by one o'clock the next morning. With those 3,000 veterans, Wallace would have a force of about 7,000 men to try to hold Early's army at bay. By now he knew that all he could hope for was to delay its march long enough for help from Grant to reach Washington, for Wallace was certain now that the Confederate objective was the capital itself.

He caught his first sight of Early's army moving toward Frederick, against the "purpling face" of the mountain, at about 4:00 P.M. on July 8. There it was, three long, continuous, yellow lines, apparently on as many roads, inching serpentlike into the valley. Wallace fancied, watching first one and then the other of these yellow streaks through his glasses, that now and then he could see flags gleaming faintly through the rising dust clouds. What he saw were columns of infantry with trains of artillery. How hopeless of victory his effort was, he thought. He could not stop it. He could only hope to delay it. But could he delay it long enough?[11]

Saturday, July 9, began as a beautiful, cloudless summer day. The smell of new-mown hay hung in the air. The sun was bright and hot, but a breeze was blowing as Early's marching army passed Frederick. One Confederate soldier marveled at the sights and sounds and smells. "The air," he wrote, "was laden with the perfume of flowers; the birds were singing in bush and tree; all the fields were green with growing crops. The city, with its thriftiness, looked as if it had just been painted and whitened. A few floating clouds added effect to the landscape. It was a day and an hour to impress all."[12]

Wallace waited across the river with his little pickup force of mostly inexperienced, unfought, untrained short-term men, reinforced by Ricketts's veterans, who had arrived in the night. To get on the road to Washington, the Confederates must cross the river against this waiting force. Early's army, passing Frederick, heard the first crack of muskets on the road ahead and knew what it meant: the Yankees intended to dispute their crossing of the river.

It was about seven o'clock in the morning when the battle was joined. By eleven o'clock the sun was beating down fiercely, the heat was oppressive, and the thin Federal line was still holding stubbornly. Ricketts's veterans, the main line of defense, were giving as good as they got. Wallace looked at his watch then, and again at noon, and at one and at two, and at 2:45. "Nearly eight hours now!" he thought. For eight hours he had delayed Early at the Monocacy.

At three o'clock he dictated a telegram to Grant at City Point: "I have been fighting General Early here since seven o'clock. With General Ricketts' aid have repulsed two attacks. A third and heavier is making ready. It is evident now he is aiming at Washington. Has been fighting us with eighteen or twenty thousand men. . . . If you have not already strengthened the defensive force at Washington, I respectfully suggest the necessity for doing it amply and immediately."

At four o'clock Wallace stared apprehensively at Ricketts's thin line, which had taken such a pounding and had held so well. He thought it looked for the most part like a far-stretched blue thread about to break. At 4:20 the shadows of the sun were lengthening, suggesting to Wallace the coming of evening, of the day almost gone.

He was finally beaten. The Confederates were now across the river and on Wallace's little force in overwhelming numbers. The retreat began, up the pike toward Baltimore. Wallace had lost a fourth of his men killed, wounded, or missing, but he had delayed the Confederates nearly ten hours—a full day. He had been at the right place at the right time and had done the best he could.[13]

With the stubborn Federals at last pushed aside, the road to Washington lay open. Early was also aware of that day lost, also aware that he must hurry before Grant could reinforce Washington from City Point. But it was too late in the day, now, to start for Washington. His battle-weary little army needed rest. He would start first thing in the morning.

By daybreak—it was Sunday, July 10—he was on the march again. The day was hotter even than the day before. For twenty grueling miles he drove his army, hastening, one of his soldiers said, "as fast as men could travel." In the evening he pulled up four miles from Rockville, only fifteen miles from Washington, virtually at the gates of the capital.[14]

Washington by now was in a dither. Suddenly, on this hot Sunday morning, it had dawned that a rebel army was but miles away, with nothing now standing in its path. Everybody of course had been aware that Early's force was advancing down the Shenandoah Valley, and had been watching nervously since Sigel's warning telegram. But now the scare had become a reality.

And nobody seemed to be doing anything about it. Welles fumed darkly into his diary on July 8 about the "dunder heads at the War

Office," suggesting they were in a fog, or scare, and not knowing what to say or do. "Halleck," Welles complained, "is in a perfect maze, bewildered, without intelligent decision or self reliance, and Stanton is wisely ignorant." Welles was inclined to believe that the ignorance this time was profound, that the War Department knew absolutely nothing of Early's army—its numbers, where it was, or where it was going.[15]

Where it was going was painfully evident by Sunday. Washington was gearing up to repulse this invasion and to appear as calm under the circumstances as possible. The *Chicago Evening Journal* correspondent, Benjamin F. Taylor, wired his paper: "Bands of music, bodies of infantry and little clouds of cavalry begin to pass across the city; hard riders dash through the streets; engines are harnessed to the trains; steamers draw heavy breaths and give symptoms of waking; the treble of the newsboys flaunting their second extra, and singing out, 'rebels a marchin' on to Washin'ton!' again startles you, and at last the city brushes the poppy leaves off its eyelids and is broad awake. It leans out of windows; it comes fairly out of doors; it ties itself in knots on street corners; it buys 'extras' and reads them; it hears rumors and believes them; it whistles a little and tries to look unconcerned."[16]

Washington, although now nervous and apprehensive, was not wholly unready. It was garrisoned by a pickup force of "hundred days men," the invalid corps, District of Columbia volunteers, and a few dismounted cavalry. As the enemy approached, Quartermaster General Montgomery C. Meigs hastily organized his force of some 3,000 employees and marched them toward the forts ringing the city. Every available man was being armed and put into the trenches. A force of about 20,000 men of all sorts, but mostly raw, undisciplined, or otherwise handicapped, had been scraped together. It was a scarecrow army, but it would have to do. In overall charge was Maj. Gen. Christopher Columbus Augur, the commander of the Department of Washington, a forty-three-year-old West Pointer. Still missing was real military muscle, hardened veteran fighters. But they were on the way, from Grant's army.

The city's main defense was its fortifications, which had been carefully constructed and tied together in such a fashion that a comparatively small force of disciplined troops could hold them indefinitely against a sizable force. But this pickup defense hardly met that description.

Through all of this, Lincoln had remained calm. Even on Sunday, with the rebels thundering toward the gates, he didn't fear that Washington was about to be seized. His main fear was that an opportunity to trap and bag a large Confederate army might be wasted. On Sunday, at about two o'clock in the afternoon, he wired Grant.

"Now what I think," he told his general, "is that you should provide to retain your hold where you are certainly, and bring the rest with you personally, and make a vigorous effort to destroy the enemie's force in this vicinity. I think there is really a fair chance to do this if the movement is prompt." But Lincoln did not make this an order. It was up to Grant, and Grant had already dispatched one of his best army corps.[17]

Lincoln also had a panicky Baltimore on his hands. To an urgent call from that city for reinforcements, he wired his reply: "I have not a single soldier but whom is being disposed by the Military for the best protection of all. By latest account the enemy is moving on Washington. They can not fly to either place. Let us be vigilant but keep cool. I hope neither Baltimore or Washington will be sacked."[18]

Stanton, more excitable by nature, was now alarmed. On July 2 the Lincolns had taken up their summer residence at the Soldiers' Home. But in the middle of the night on the tenth, Stanton sent a carriage out to the residence with orders for the Lincolns to return immediately to the White House. The enemy was simply too close for comfort. Lincoln, irritated and against his will, came. When he learned later that a small vessel was tied up on the Potomac, ready to whisk him out of Washington if that became necessary, he was further annoyed.[19]

There had been no rain around Washington for weeks, and the heat overnight had been oppressive. It was already hot and dust-blown when Early started his army up again at daylight on Monday morning, July 11.

At the War Department telegraph office, a wire from Grant arrived at about seven in the morning, telling Lincoln he wasn't coming himself, but that he had sent an entire corps and over 3,000 other troops, under "an excellent officer," Maj. Gen. Horatio G. Wright. Grant had also ordered the Union force in the Shenandoah Valley, under Hunter, whom Early had driven into the mountains on his march toward Washington, to come up on the rear with another 10,000 troops. "I have great faith," Grant wired the president, "that the enemy will never be able to get back with much of his force."[20]

The officers at Grant's headquarters were not taking it all very seriously. They were calling it the "little scare."[21]

At eight o'clock Lincoln wired back. Fine, he said. The enemy will learn of Wright's arrival and then the trick will be to unite Wright and

Hunter south of Early before he can recross the Potomac. The prospect pleased the president.[22]

As Lincoln was writing this, he could hear firing between Rockville and Washington. "Rebels are upon us," Gideon Welles wrote in his diary. "Having visited upper Maryland, they are turning their attention hitherward." Welles had earlier ordered three navy gunboats to Washington from the Havre de Grace, Gunpowder, and Bush Rivers.[23]

Refugees were now streaming into the city in the path of Early's advance, flying in wild disorder down Seventh Street, hauling their household goods with them. The motley force defending the city waited. In Georgetown Heights, blue-coated mounted guards of the invalid corps had been watching over Maj. Gen. Henry Halleck's house, blowing "peas on a trencher," the dinner call, nightly. There were wags in Washington who were suggesting the rebels might be found guilty of petty larceny should they march down Rock Creek and seize Halleck.[24]

Now in the Washington suburbs, Early wheeled his infantry to the left and began advancing on the city by Seventh Street through Silver Spring. A cloud of cavalry covered either flank, and a cloud of dust covered all. One of his foot soldiers believed it was even hotter than the day before, and they were marching even faster.[25] Confederate raiding parties had by now severed all rail communications between Baltimore, Washington, and the North. By afternoon the last remaining telegraph link would be cut. The only communication with the rest of the Union was now by steamer from Georgetown to New York.[26]

Shortly after noon, Early, riding in the front, arrived with his army before Fort Stevens on Seventh Street. He raised his glasses and peered intently at the fortification. From all he could see, it appeared but feebly defended. But as he prepared to assault, he saw a cloud of dust rising in the rear of the fort and a column of blue-clad soldiers beginning to file into the works. Skirmishers were quickly thrown out from the fort, and artillery opened on the Confederates. The prospect now looked less promising to Early. He decided to reconnoiter. That would likely take the rest of the afternoon, and the idea of it was making him crankier than usual.[27]

Maj. Gen. John C. Breckinridge, Early's second-in-command, was on familiar ground. Washington had long been his home away from Kentucky. He had been President James Buchanan's vice president, and in 1860 he had been the South's candidate for president, heading a third-party ticket that had broken away from the main Democratic party. When the war came, he went with the Confederacy and had been fighting in its armies with distinction ever since, a rare politician with military aptitude.

At about five o'clock in the afternoon he and Early rode together onto the grounds of the Blair mansion. Breckinridge knew that house intimately. He had spent endless enjoyable hours there in his Washington years, in the 1850s. Indeed he was a cousin of the Blairs, and had been a frequent guest at this Silver Spring home.

Now it was abandoned, and he was appalled. Rebel soldiers were inside, rummaging and robbing and creating havoc. Seeing this, Breckinridge flew into a rage.

Early also flew into a rage, but for a different reason.

"You have ruined our whole campaign," Early shouted, dressing down the officer commanding at the mansion. "If you had pushed in the Forts this morning at 8 o'clock we could have taken them—Now they have reinforcements from Grant and we can't take them without immense loss perhaps 'tis impossible."

As Early was angrily reprimanding this derelict officer, Breckinridge was cursing soldiers carrying things out of the house. The piano cover was just leaving, which a soldier intended to convert into a horse blanket. Breckinridge ordered it returned and the soldier clapped in irons. He sent off for a regiment to guard the house.

Early, still disgusted, turned to Breckinridge. " 'Tis no use to fret about one house when we have lost so much by this proceeding."

"This place," Breckinridge replied, "is the only one I felt was a home to me on this side of the mountains."

From one end of the room, a voice piped up and said this was his home, too.

Breckinridge turned to see Jim Byrne, a son of a former nurse at the Blair mansion. Jim had been sent to the house by his mother that morning to find and fetch his younger brother Ned, a deaf boy of thirteen, who was Elizabeth Blair Lee's gardener. He hadn't found Ned, Jim told Breckinridge. Instead he had been taken prisoner himself, and now he would like to return to his mother, who was left alone and unprotected in the path of this invasion.

Breckinridge began asking Jim questions. How were the Blairs and Lees? Where were they?[28]

The Blair men were away from the Silver Spring mansion on a fishing excursion in Pennsylvania, and the women of the house had hastily run off to Cape May, leaving the premises empty. Welles had told his diary on July 9 that this seemed a singular thing to do, in light of what was going on.[29]

"That accounts for their leaving everything exposed in this way," Breckinridge said.

Later that night Breckinridge put Jim on a donkey belonging to one of the young Blair children, and sent him home to his mother. By then Breckinridge and Early had made the mansion their headquarters and settled in. Breckinridge once more bedded down in the only house he had ever felt at home in this side of the mountains.[30]

There were some who saw an ironic humor in this sudden attack in the north, after all available Union troops had been sent south.[31] Redemption, however, had begun arriving at the docks on the Potomac at about noon on the eleventh, just as Early was pulling up before Fort Stevens. The two divisions of the famed Sixth Corps had arrived at last. Steaming close in their wake was the Nineteenth Corps, a unit from New Orleans, which had come to join Grant at Petersburg after the failure of the Red River campaign. This corps had put in earlier at Hampton Roads to join Grant's army. Without debarking, it was ordered to Washington to help the Sixth Corps put down the little scare.

Lincoln was at the wharves to meet this salvation, striding joyfully among the debarking soldiers in his high-topped hat, buoyed by their cheers. Hurriedly they formed and began marching through the streets of Washington toward Fort Stevens. These were the troops that Early had seen, prompting his reconnaissance.

In the early afternoon Lincoln went out to where the action was. More curious than worried, intent on seeing the rebel army he intended to bag, he stood on the parapets at Fort Stevens, oblivious to the sniper fire whistling about him. It was a first. Never before in the nation's history had its president been under enemy fire. Nobody in the fort was thrilled with this historical benchmark. A soldier suggested he ought to get down before he got his head knocked off.[32]

The reconnaissance had depressed Early. The works now appeared quite formidable. What looked to him like seasoned fighters had arrived and markedly beefed up Fort Stevens, more than equalizing the odds. Despite this, he resolved to attack the next morning, unless it was meanwhile shown to be wholly impracticable.

In the night, reports reached him at the Blair mansion that what he had seen the day before were two corps arriving from Grant's army. He decided to delay his attack, planned for daylight, until he could examine the works personally one more time. As soon as it was light enough to see, he rode to the front and found the parapets lined with troops. An attack now seemed suicidal. At that moment, with the sun glinting from the Capitol dome—his prize so near, yet so far—he gave up all hope of capturing Washington. Nonetheless, he decided he would stay awhile before turning back, and give the Yankees as much hell as he could.[33]

July 12 was a beautiful day—"bright and glorious," a surgeon from the Union Sixth Corps described it. It belied the vicious skirmishing going on in front of the fort throughout the morning.[34] In the afternoon Wright sent out a brigade to clear the area along the Silver Spring Road, and Lincoln was there again, standing tall on the parapets, watching the action, sniper fire again singing all around him.

Standing beside the president was General Wright, who was horrified by the prospect that Lincoln might be shot if he remained where he was. He explained to the president that the parapets were entirely too dangerous a place for him.

Lincoln, who had once confessed to a friend that under fire he would probably cut and run like any serious leg case, replied calmly, "It is not more dangerous for me than it is for you."

"But," Wright reasoned with him, "it is my duty to be here while it is your duty not to expose yourself. Your position requires this, and I particularly request you to remember it."

Just then a surgeon standing three feet from the president dropped to the ground, shot through the left thigh.

More alarmed than ever, Wright said firmly, "Mr. President, you must really get down from this exposed position. I cannot allow you to remain here longer and if you refuse I shall deem it my duty to have you removed under guard."

Just then a young lieutenant colonel of Wright's staff, Oliver Wendell Holmes Jr., who had been busy with other matters, suddenly glanced up and saw the towering figure, a civilian, standing spectacularly exposed to the sniper fire. He was appalled. "Get down, you fool!" he shouted.

Now that was an order Lincoln could appreciate, a soldier who knew how to talk to a civilian. Perhaps amused by the absurdity of being threatened with arrest by one of his own generals and called a fool by one of his officers, Lincoln finally, if reluctantly, stepped down to a safer vantage point. But even from there he continued to bob up and down, peering over the ramparts at the action unfolding before the fort, still exposing himself, still making everybody nervous.[35]

Navy Secretary Gideon Welles arrived at Fort Stevens in the afternoon with Senator Ben Wade, who was perhaps still more put out with the president for vetoing his reconstruction bill than with the rebels for invading Washington. They found Lincoln sitting calmly in the shade by then, his back against the parapet, an occasional rifle bullet whistling over his head.

The day was winding down; the rebel skirmishers had been driven back and were showing signs of withdrawing. The talk of all the soldiers at Fort Stevens was of Jim Byrne's little brother Ned, Elizabeth Blair Lee's deaf thirteen-year-old gardener. Ned had finally been found. The reason Jim hadn't found him earlier was that he had run off, as the rebel army approached, with old man Blair's rifle. Ned was reported to have killed five or six rebel sharpshooters with it since then.

When Elizabeth Lee heard of this, she wrote her husband, "I do not like to think of anybody so young taking the lives of so many men. . . . But this young gardener of mine is no common boy & has shown marked character from infancy."[36]

After dark on July 12, Early said to Henry Kyd Douglas in his falsetto drawl, "Major, we haven't taken Washington, but we've scared Abe Lincoln like h———."[37]

That night the rebel sharpshooters were replaced by cavalry pickets in front of Fort Stevens. By next morning the cavalry was also gone. Early's soldiers had vanished before both Washington and Baltimore, as quickly as they had come.

To Lincoln's chagrin, there had been no immediate pursuit. Assistant Secretary of War Charles Dana saw the problem clearly: nobody was pursuing because nobody was in charge. Augur could command only the defenses around Washington. Halleck wouldn't give orders except as he received them from Grant. Lincoln wouldn't interfere, as impatient as he was. Not until about noon on July 13 did Grant put Wright in overall command.[38]

On the evening of the thirteenth, Wright marched out of Washington in pursuit, with about 15,000 men. Early had been reported at about three o'clock that morning passing through Rockville, headed for Poolesville and White's Ford on the Potomac, some twenty-six miles away. Wright arrived at Poolesville on the evening of July 14 to find that Early had crossed the river that morning. He had slipped the noose. Wright stopped at the riverbank and wired Washington, advising against further pursuit. That day, communication was again opened with the North.

Elizabeth Blair Lee, still at Cape May, was sick at heart, but relieved. Her admiral husband, Samuel Phillips Lee, the commander of the North Atlantic Blockading Squadron, had without orders sailed partway up the Potomac from Hampton Roads on the thirteenth when he thought Washington endangered, and had been reprimanded for his trouble.

"It is very hard," Elizabeth wrote him that day from the Atlantic Hotel, "but as long as God spares our dear ones & covers their precious heads in battle I cannot grieve even for a home where everything is as dear to me as at Silver Spring. each bush & tree—having had my care & watching in that lawn—Still if our Capitol is not dishonored—My Husband & Brother brought safe thro all these hardships & battles—I shall be thankful—& will try let no other feeling come in my heart."[39]

A note had been left on the mantel in the library at the Blair mansion, below the picture of Maj. Gen. John Dix. It read, "A confederate officer, for himself & all his comrades, regrets exceedingly that damage & pilfering was committed in this house, before it was known that it was within our lines, or that private property was imperilled—Especially we regret that Ladies property has been disturbed, but restitution has been made, & punishment meted out as far as possible. We wage no ignoble warfare for plunder or revenge, but for all that men hold dearest." On another photograph was written, "A confederate officer has remained here until after eleven—to prevent pillage & burning of the house . . . who found in this home good & true friends—"

The hand of John Breckinridge was in all this, and Elizabeth recognized it. "Thus," she wrote Admiral Lee on July 16, "bread cast upon the waters came back to us. . . ."[40]

If his sister was grieved but grateful, Montgomery Blair was steaming. His house, standing not far from his father's in Silver Spring, had not enjoyed Breckinridge's personal protection. It had been burned to the ground. The postmaster general was not as angry with Early as he was with Halleck and Stanton, neither of whom he liked—a feeling that was mutual. "Nothing better," Blair is reported to have said, "could be expected while poltroons and cowards run the War Department."[41]

This in turn set a fire of indignation under Halleck, who protested to Stanton, who protested to Lincoln, demanding Blair's dismissal from the cabinet. Lincoln replied to Stanton on July 14, "I do not consider what may have been hastily said in a moment of vexation at so severe a loss, is sufficient ground for so grave a step. Besides this, *truth* is generally the best vindication against slander." Lincoln said he would continue to be the judge of when a member of his cabinet would be dismissed.[42]

Another cabinet member, Gideon Welles, was mortified by the raid. He called it "our national humiliation." The rebels, he wrote in his diary, had been defiant and insolent, and Union soldiers had been resolute and brave. But the War Department and the generals had been alarmed and ignorant and had made themselves and the administration appear contemptible.[43]

As the newspapers in the North began to piece together all that had happened, many were finding it difficult to disagree with Welles. Bennett at the *New York Herald* talked of "the great noodles who mismanage our military and all other matters at Washington." As usual, he had a suggestion. To take care of any such future raids, he advised that a new military department be created encompassing the country for a hundred miles around Washington, and that George McClellan be put in command. He began recommending this daily in his editorial columns.[44]

Henry Raymond at the pro-administration *New York Times* tried to put as good a face on the affair as possible. The important thing to remember, Raymond wrote, was that this raid had little importance militarily. The key thing to keep in mind, he advised, was what was happening behind Richmond and before Atlanta—two other cities then under siege. That was what really mattered. "These alone," Raymond wrote, "will tell the story."[45]

Raymond called the raid the "annual 'scare.' " Another proadministration paper, the *Chicago Tribune*, agreed: "Just as we have Annual School Examinations and Annual Horse Shops," so we have annual invasions.[46]

Nobody was quite sure what effect this annual invasion might have on the election in November. The *Richmond Examiner* in the South believed it likely to have some political fallout. It wrote: "Early is stumping the States of Maryland and Pennsylvania for the peace party."[47] Some in the Confederacy believed it all a gigantic mistake, that instead of killing off Lincoln it would kill off the peace party just beginning to show some head of strength, and return the administration to popularity and power.[48]

Lincoln was just plain put out. The rebels had gotten away again. On the fourteenth, as he was starting out to the Soldiers' Home for the night—Stanton had said it was safe to return—he told John Hay, "Wright telegraphs that he thinks the enemy are all across the Potomac but that he has halted [and] sent out an infantry reconnaissance, for fear he might come across the rebels & catch some of them."

Said Hay to his diary, "The Chief is evidently disgusted."[49]

If Lincoln was disgusted, the excitable Count Gurowski, as usual, was apoplectic. He had been locked up in a station house for attempting to discipline the Washington fire department. The count, who had been figuratively drawing pistols on generals now for three years, had actually drawn a real one on the firemen to force them to run faster.[50]

Gurowski was fined five dollars and soon released from confinement, and all of Washington was freed from anxiety. Nobody knew for certain what it all added up to, or what effect, if any, it would have on the election. But at least life would return to normal in the capital, and little Ned Byrne could lay down old man Blair's smoking rifle and go back to his gardening.

19

THE PEACESEEKERS

ORACE GREELEY WAS IN A BLUER THAN USUAL FUNK THIS summer. There had been the Chase collapse, which had carried off his candidate for the presidency and the only friend he had in the Lincoln circle. Grant had bogged down in front of Petersburg. And now, in early July, there was a rebel army marching on Washington.

The erratic, advice-doling editor was particularly war-weary, the summer was a hot one, and he was undergoing dramatic mood swings. He was emotionally drained. He ached for an end to this entire unending, distracting civil war. In the buoyant days of early spring, before Grant's bloody Virginia campaign began, he had predicted that the whole thing would be over by now.

Instead Lee, lying in at Petersburg, was looking perennially unbeatable. Richmond was looking impregnable, and a Democratic victory in November was looking more and more probable. Greeley saw nothing ahead but ruin for the country. It would be far better, he believed, to make the best peace possible now with the Confederacy, before that happened.

Greeley had longed for peace since the summer of 1861, when the Union army had suffered its shocking defeat at the first big battle of the war, at Bull Run. Before that, he had been the loudest voice in the country shouting, "On to Richmond." But Bull Run had sobered him and downsized his expectations. Ever since, he had lobbied Lincoln to work out a negotiated peace with the South. In virtually every letter he had written to the president since then—and there had been many—he had urged Lincoln to seek a negotiated end to the bloody strife. He was convinced the South would lay down its arms if properly approached, and the whole thing could be over.

He had been disappointed when Confederate Vice President Alexander Stephens had made peace overtures in the summer of 1863 and been rebuffed by Lincoln. Stephens had sought to come to Washington to talk terms. Lincoln had said no, mainly because Stephens's overtures assumed independence for the Confederacy. For Lincoln that was a nonnegotiable issue.[1]

It had come to Greeley's notice in the early summer of 1864 that Confederate commissioners were now operating in Canada, and had been having confidential interviews with various peace men and Democrats. He had learned that there might be a possibility of negotiating a peace through them. There were intimations—Gideon Welles called them "vague & indefinite rumors"—that peace was desired by the rebels, but that the administration would not listen to overtures or receive propositions that might lead to an adjustment. Greeley, whom Welles described as "often credulous and always ready to engage in public employment," wanted desperately to believe the rumors true.[2]

In this mood, the editor remembered his friend, William Cornell Jewett, who was said to be in close touch with the rebel commissioners in Canada. Jewett was a former promoter of gold mines in Colorado, and was now mining peace. He had been to Europe three times attempting to persuade the leading powers to intervene between the two warring sides. Failing that, he had returned to promote a scheme for an armistice and a convention of states. Clement Clay, one of the rebel commissioners in Canada, described Jewett as "a man of fervent and fruitful imagination and very credulous of what he wishes to be true"—rather like Greeley.[3]

Manton Marble at the *New York World* called Jewett "that dancing wind-bag of popinjay conceit," and an "overweening rogue."[4] Attorney General Edward Bates called him "that meddlesome blockhead . . . a crack-brained simpleton (who aspires to be a knave, while he really belongs to a lower order of entities)."[5] Photographs of Jewett showed a face with the look of a wild-eyed arsonist, ringed entirely by bushy black hair, the eyes staring out intense and incendiary behind little steel-rimmed glasses.[6]

Henry Raymond of *The New York Times* said of him: "No business man in the country would trust any commission to a head with so many screws loose."[7]

Greeley would. He wrote Jewett, better known as "Colorado," and got an immediate answer. The Confederates considered Greeley a very desirable opportunity. They believed from his past actions and utterings that he was a sincere friend of peace, even peace with separation if necessary. They figured they could hardly do better.[8]

Jewett eagerly advised Greeley that he was authorized by George N. Sanders to say that there were "two ambassadors" of the Confederate government in Canada "with full and complete powers for peace" and ready to negotiate. He suggested that Greeley come at once to Niagara Falls for a private interview or, if not that, send the president's pledge of protection, and Sanders and the two ambassadors would meet Greeley in New York City. The whole matter of this war might be consummated "by you, them and President Lincoln." The next day Jewett followed up with another urgent telegram: "Will you come? Parties have full powers."[9]

George N. Sanders was a perfect collaborator for Jewett and Greeley. He was a Kentuckian and a visionary—a vessel of "wild and impractical thoughts." He was widely viewed as a man of imposing personality and audacious presumption, with few if any principles and little regard for right or wrong—and strictly pro-slavery. He was a freelance in politics, known in Democratic circles since the early 1850s as a hotheaded meddler. He was of striking appearance, with a pleasant smile and speech. He had a massive head, powerful features, an abundance of disheveled hair, and radiant blue eyes. One of his associates in Canada described him as a man of "active brain and tireless scheming." He appeared now to be Jewett's main contact, the go-between linking him to the rebel commissioners.[10]

Jubilant in the belief that the end of the slaughter might at last be near, Greeley sent an urgent message to Lincoln:

"Our bleeding, bankrupt, almost dying country . . . longs for peace—shudders at the prospect of fresh conscriptions, of further wholesale devastations, and of new rivers of human blood. And a widespread conviction that the Government . . . are not anxious for Peace, and do not improve proffered opportunities to achieve it, is doing great harm now, and is morally certain, unless removed, to do far greater in the approaching Elections. . . ."

Greeley told Lincoln that here was another opportunity that must not be missed. "I entreat you, in your own time and manner," he urged the president, "to submit overtures for pacification to the Southern

insurgents which the impartial must pronounce frank and generous."
The sooner the better, Greeley urged—"at once."

Greeley pressed Lincoln to give the safe conduct required by the
rebel envoys at Niagara. But if not that, something else. "Do not, I
entreat you, fail to make the Southern people comprehend that you
and all of us are anxious for peace. . . . Mr. President, I fear you do not
realize how intently the people desire any peace consistent with the
national integrity and honor. . . . I do not say that a just peace is now
attainable, though I believe it to be so. But I *do* say, that a frank *offer*
by you to the insurgents of terms . . . will . . . prove an immense and
sorely needed advantage to the national cause; it may save us from a
northern insurrection. . . . I beg you to invite those now at Niagara to
exhibit their credentials and submit their ultimatum."[11]

Lincoln couldn't count the times Greeley had written him advice,
big advice, urgent advice, advice sometimes contradicting the earlier
advice, since this war began. Here he was doing it again. As Lincoln
told a friend from Illinois, young Shelby Cullom, "While Mr. Greeley
means right, he makes me almost as much trouble as the whole Southern Confederacy."[12]

There was, in this war-weary summer, what Lincoln's personal secretaries, Nicolay and Hay, called "this unreasonable and abnormal
craving" for peace negotiations of some kind.[13] Lincoln suspected they
could lead nowhere, given the unbending positions of the two sides.
There seemed to him to be little to gain in negotiation now, and perhaps much to lose. But politically he could not ignore the craving. He
had to deal with it. He had to deal with Greeley.

But if he had to make a peace overture, it would have to embody certain strict requirements. He replied to Greeley on July 9, the day Wallace was fighting Early at Monocacy Junction, that if the editor could
find anybody professing to have any proposition from Jefferson Davis
in writing for peace embracing the restoration of the Union and abandonment of slavery, whatever else it embraced, then he should bring
him or them. At the very least they would have their safe conduct.[14]

Greeley didn't like it that Lincoln was laying down unbending terms
at the outset—restoration of the Union and abandonment of slavery.
He wouldn't mention that to the Confederates, fearing it might kill
negotiations before they began.[15]

Moreover, Greeley found in Lincoln's message another disturbing suggestion he hadn't counted on: that Greeley himself bring the negotiators

to Washington. Editors didn't do things, they suggested things, which others were then supposed to do. He answered Lincoln the next day, as Early was marching from the Monocacy toward Washington, that he had "neither purpose nor desire to be made a confidant, far less an agent in such negotiations." He suggested to Lincoln again the harm done by rebuffing Stephens the summer before, forgetting that he had himself approved the rebuff in an editorial in the *Tribune*. He again urged the president to reassure the South somehow that any offer of peace and reunion would not be spurned in the North, but favorably received and considered.[16]

Three days later, as Early was retreating from Washington, Greeley wrote Lincoln again. He advised the president that two persons commissioned and empowered to negotiate peace waited at Niagara, ready to meet with Lincoln or his representatives. He said he hoped to hear back that Lincoln had done something about it.[17]

Instead Lincoln wired back, "I . . . am disappointed . . . I was not expecting you to *send* me a letter, but to *bring* me a man, or men." He told Greeley he was sending John Hay to New York with a more complete response.[18]

Hay arrived in New York on Saturday, July 16, at six o'clock in the morning, and checked into the Astor House. While he was washing his face in his room, up came Greeley's card, and Hay went down to the parlor and handed him Lincoln's letter.

It read, "I am disappointed that you have not already reached here with those Commissioners, if they would consent to come, on being shown my letter to you of the 9th. Inst. Show that and this to them; and if they will come on the terms stated in the former, bring them. I not only intend a sincere effort for peace, but I intend that you shall be a personal witness that it is made."[19]

Greeley didn't like anything about this message. He remonstrated with Hay, saying he thought himself the worst possible choice for such a job, that as soon as he arrived at Niagara the newspapers would be full of it and he would be abused and blackguarded. However, he told Hay that if the president insisted, he would go. But he must have an absolute safe conduct for four persons, arguing that the president's earlier letter was not enough.

This seemed a reasonable request to Hay, and at nine o'clock the secretary wired Lincoln to that effect, suggesting appropriate language for the safe conduct. At about noon a wire came back from Lincoln approving Hay's language and ordering him to write it. Hay did so, and took it to Greeley at the Old Rookery.

Hay had left the names of the Confederates blank, expecting Greeley to fill them in. "I won't write a word," Greeley protested in his peculiar querulous manner. "I expect to be pitched into everywhere for this; but I can't help it."

Hay finally got the safe conduct fixed in a way satisfactory to Greeley, and the editor, still reluctant but stuck with it, said: "I will start tonight. I shall expect to be in Washington Tuesday morning if they will come."[20]

The next day Hay wired Lincoln: "Gave the order yesterday. He promised to start at once and I supposed did so." Hay himself started back to Washington that evening, arriving the next morning, Monday the eighteenth.[21]

That same day Lincoln issued a call for 500,000 more volunteers to replenish the ranks of his army depleted by the severe early summer of fighting in Virginia. It wasn't the most peaceful of gestures. The president wasn't counting on Horace Greeley to bring peace at Niagara.

At Niagara, Greeley engaged rooms on the American side of the falls, at the International Hotel, and opened communications immediately with Colorado Jewett. Through Jewett he apprised the commissioners that he had arrived to talk. He told them he had a safe conduct for them, if they were duly accredited, and propositions for peace. If they wished to go to Washington, he would go with them. He still did not mention Lincoln's preconditions.

The commissioners he was writing to were Clement Clay and James Holcombe. The chief commissioner, Jacob Thompson, was not there and was not going to be there. He approved of none of this. And both Clay and Holcombe were embarrassed. Neither of them was an accredited representative empowered to commit the Confederacy to anything, and they had to admit it. They assured Greeley, however, that if they were given a safe conduct to Washington and thence to Richmond, they could secure the necessary official authority.[22]

Greeley was disappointed. This wasn't all he had thought it might be. He wired Lincoln again, saying he was in communication with the peace emissaries, but didn't find them empowered as he had been led to believe. However, he told the president, they were in the confidential employment of the Confederate government and entirely familiar with its wishes and opinions on the subject of peace. If the circumstances

were communicated to Richmond, they or others would be immediately empowered to negotiate.[23]

John Hay had been back in Washington only a few hours when this
message came from Greeley, and he took it to Lincoln. The president
read it and told Hay to be ready to travel again if necessary. That afternoon, after a word with Secretary of State Seward, Lincoln handed Hay
another note and told him to take it immediately to Niagara Falls.

Hay left that evening and arrived in New York City the next day,
Tuesday, the nineteenth, too late to catch the evening train to Niagara.
He caught the first train on Wednesday morning, arriving at eleven-
thirty, and went immediately to see Greeley at the International
Hotel.[24]

Greeley frowned again as he read this new message from the president, this time addressed to "To Whom it may concern." It repeated
that Lincoln would entertain any proposition from any source that controlled the armies at war with the United States and that embraced "the
restoration of peace, the integrity of the whole Union, and the abandonment of slavery." It once more guaranteed safe conduct both ways
to any would-be negotiators.[25]

Greeley again remonstrated with Hay. This refusal to enter into
negotiations without conditions, the editor told him, was a great mistake. Hay argued that Lincoln's preconditions were perfectly proper,
indeed indispensable, that the president could not deal with emissaries
with no powers, that he could do no more than what he was doing.

Greeley looked across the roaring abyss toward Canada and said he
wouldn't go. He had all along declined to see these people himself and
didn't want to see them now. He thought Hay ought to go over alone
and deliver the letter. Hay said he thought so too, but that he believed
Lincoln and Seward thought otherwise, and insisted Greeley must go
with him as a witness. So the two got into a carriage and drove across
the falls to the other side.

At the Clifton House, they were met by Sanders, a seedy-looking
rebel, Hay thought, with grizzled whiskers and "a flavor of old clo' [old
clothes]." Hay wrote Greeley's name on his own card and sent it up to
Holcombe, the only commissioner present. Clay was out of town.

A crowd began to gather as Greeley, Hay, and Sanders stood at the
counter in the barroom talking. Greeley's famous and bizarre figure
had been recognized. The barroom began to fill and the hall outside to
bloom with—Hay noted with some pleasure—"wide-eyed and pretty
women."

Ushered upstairs, Greeley and Hay found Holcombe in his room taking tea. He was "a tall, solemn, spare, false-looking man," Hay noted, "with false teeth, false eyes, and false hair." Hay delivered Lincoln's letter, added a few words Lincoln and Seward had told him to add, and said he would await any message they cared to send back to Washington.

Holcombe said, "Mr. Clay is now absent at St. Catherine's. I will telegraph to him at once, and inform you in the morning."

As Greeley and Hay were about to step into the carriage to return to the other side of the falls, Greeley told Sanders, "I expect to be blackguarded for what I have done, and I am not allowed to explain. But all I have done has been done under instructions."[26]

Indignation was not long in coming from the would-be rebel negotiators. In a letter to Greeley—with a copy to the rest of the Northern press—they raked Lincoln's "To Whom it may concern" letter as an infamous about-face from what they had earlier understood. It bore no resemblance to what was originally offered—safe conduct with no strings. This, they raged, "precludes negotiation and prescribes in advance the terms and conditions of peace. . . . It returns to the original policy of no negotiations, no truce with the rebels until every man shall have laid down his arms . . . and sued for peace."[27]

What Greeley feared greatly was soon visited upon him; within days he was being blackguarded. Welles entered into his diary that the scheming busybody had found himself caught in "the meshes of his own frail net."[28]

That was nothing compared to what Greeley's rival editors began saying. "Peace negotiations have again broken out . . . ," Bennett wrote, "that shuffle-gaited peripatetic, old Greeley, has gone on a peace mission to Niagara. . . ."

For the next several days Bennett blackguarded the shuffle-gaited victim, always in high glee. "Let it never be said again that there is nothing new under the sun," Bennett wrote. "Read the reports which we publish to-day, of the proceedings of these peacemakers at Niagara Falls, with the mighty river roaring, foaming, rushing and tumbling below them like this awful rebellion, and be satisfied that wonders will never cease. Niagara itself is cast into the shade. . . ."

Bennett called the performers in the fiasco "desperate adventurers, noisy charlatans and political donkeys." He wrote that Colorado Jewett might be a nincompoop, but at least he was a nincompoop with genius. Greeley, Lincoln, Clay, Sanders, and Holcombe, Bennett suggested, were nincompoops without genius.[29]

"Greeley and Jewett—Jewett and Greeley," Manton Marble wrote in the *New York World,* "which is Don Quixote and which Sancho Panza?" If the subject were not too serious for laughter, he wrote, "we should go into convulsions."[30]

Even Henry Raymond, Lincoln's ally at *The New York Times,* couldn't resist a disgusted sideswipe, calling the whole affair "back-door diplomacy" and "Niagara tom-foolery."[31]

Shortly after this affair, being widely hailed as a fiasco, Senator James Harlan of Iowa said to Lincoln in a conversation on the White House terrace, "Some of us think, Mr. Lincoln, that you didn't send a very good ambassador to Niagara."

"Well, I'll tell you about that, Harlan," Lincoln replied. "Greeley kept abusing me for not entering into peace negotiations. He said he believed we could have peace if I would do my part and when he began to urge that I send an ambassador to Niagara to meet Confederate emissaries, I just thought I would let him go up and crack that nut for himself."[32]

Lincoln had not only to contend in this hot election-year summer with Early making war on Washington and, worse, Greeley making peace. But there was Colonel James F. Jaquess as well, another visionary bent on bringing peace.

Jaquess was one of those oxymorons often found in this war—a fighting preacher. He was an erect, spare man, with gray hair and beard, a high, broad, open forehead, and a thin face lit with the light of unbending earnestness, strength, and benevolence.[33]

He was a Methodist clergyman, but also a colonel in the Union's western army. He had been commissioned by Governor Richard Yates to raise and lead the Seventy-third Regiment of Illinois volunteers. He was seen as a man with force of character and considerable practical talent, and he had proved a good regimental commander. But he was also ensnared by what Nicolay and Hay considered a piety and religious enthusiasm touching on the fanatical—or prophetic—depending on whether his cause, whatever it might be, failed or succeeded.

His cause, beginning in 1863, was peace, and God had driven him to it. He claimed that the Divinity had told him as early as May of that year that he ought to propose to Washington that he go into the Confederacy, from which he would return within ninety days with terms of peace that the government would accept. He proposed no compromise with traitors, but only "their immediate return to their allegiance to

God and their country." He believed this could be done with appeals to his fellow churchmen in the South. He proposed to undertake this mission in the name of the Lord, and applied to his commander, Maj. Gen. William Rosecrans, for a furlough to that end.

The thing about Jaquess was that his illusions were so strong and earnest that others half believed them. Rosecrans half believed them. When James Gilmore, the lecturer-writer with the nom de plume of Edmund Kirke, was sent to Rosecrans by Horace Greeley in the summer of 1863 to see if the general was sound on the goose and would like to run for president, Rosecrans had introduced him to Jaquess. Gilmore also half believed the fighting parson, and agreed to take his idea for a peace mission to the Confederacy to the president himself.

Even Lincoln half believed it. He said, on Gilmore's appeal, that such a mission promised good if it were free from difficulties, "which I fear it can not be." Lincoln agreed to let Jaquess try, however, and approved the furlough and the mission, without of course, any official sanction, backing, or authority. Jaquess had entered the Confederacy, but couldn't make the right connections and finally had to give up peace and return to war.[34]

But in the spring of 1864 he was back again, like Greeley, with peace on his mind, and this time in actual working partnership with Gilmore, who had continued to half believe.

Gilmore once more took a proposal to Lincoln—this time that Jaquess and Gilmore visit the Confederacy together and try to see Jefferson Davis himself. Lincoln had no illusions that any of these peace missions would come to anything as long as the Confederacy held to its idea of independence and slavery. But it was hot and it was July, and notions of peace were everywhere. As in Greeley's mission, just then beginning to develop, Lincoln saw some value in silencing these fruitless clamors once and for all. So again he gave Jaquess a leave of absence and both him and Gilmore permission to pass the lines. He still refused to give the mission any official sanction or authority or promise of protection. He wouldn't even give Colonel Jaquess a personal interview. Gilmore himself admitted they were going south with no terms, but only an appeal to the Confederacy to "lay down your arms, and go back to peaceful pursuits." It was not exactly a gold-plated bargaining chip.[35]

On July 6, Lincoln sent a telegram to Grant to let the two visionaries—the preacher and the novelist—pass his lines into the South "with ordinary baggage."[36] On July 16 they appeared at a Union outpost on the James, where they were let through the lines under a flag of truce by Ben Butler.

That evening they found themselves in Richmond, checked into the Spotswood Hotel, in what Gilmore described as "a shabby room with some fine furniture in very bad order."[37] The next morning they arose and penned a note to Confederate Secretary of State Judah Benjamin asking for an interview with Davis that might "open the way to such official negotiations as will result in restoring peace to the two sections of our distracted country."[38]

But first they had to pass muster with Benjamin. They found him in a room in the northwest corner of the old U.S. customhouse, with the words "State Department" over the door. Inside, the two peace emissaries were greeted by the Confederate secretary of state, whom Gilmore described as "a short, plump, oily little man in black, with a keen black eye, a Jewish face, a yellow skin, curly black hair, closely trimmed black whiskers, and a ponderous gold watch-chain."[39]

Benjamin's keen black eye fixed the two visitors, and he began to probe, thoroughly cross-questioning them, seeking any hint of official sanction. Although there was none, Davis was willing to receive any overtures that promised, however remotely, to lead to a peace and separation on Confederate terms.[40]

An interview was arranged for nine o'clock that night in Benjamin's office. For two hours the president of the Confederacy and the two peaceseekers boxed around the subject of how peace might be reached. In short, Davis told them it was to be either Southern independence or subjugation. He told them that he would receive peace proposals from Lincoln only on the basis of Southern independence, and that it would be useless to approach him on any other.[41]

There didn't look to be much hope for peace in that position. Outside the State Department room in Richmond after the interview with Davis, Gilmore told their escort, Robert Ould, the Confederate commissioner on prisoner exchanges, that it was to be "nothing but war, war to the knife."[42]

Navy Secretary Welles called this second peace mission of this busy July "another specimen of inconsiderate and unwise, meddlesome interference." The result, he told his diary, was "that Jaquess and his friend Gilmore . . . who went to Richmond to shear, came back shorn."[43]

Certainly both peace missions had shorn away any doubt of either Lincoln's position or Davis's. They showed how far apart the two sides really were, and how little they augured peace. As both sets of negotiations were ending this way, as Lincoln knew they would, he read an address that had come to his attention written by Clement Clay.

Lincoln saw Clay's document as the Confederacy's proposed platform for the Democrats soon to meet in convention in Chicago. It proposed that the war be prosecuted further only to restore the Union as it was, and in such a way as not to further threaten slave property. It urged that all Negro soldiers and seamen be at once disarmed and degraded to menial service, and that no additional Negroes, on any pretense whatever, be taken from their masters. It urged that all Negroes not enjoying actual freedom during the war be held permanently as slaves.

Clay wrote that "the stupid tyrant who now disgraces the Chair of Washington and Jackson could, any day, have peace and restoration of the Union; and would have them, only that he persists in the war merely to free the slaves."

Lincoln did not know which wing of the Democratic party would prevail at its Chicago convention, but he had his suspicions. "The convention may not literally adopt Mr. Clay's Platform and Address," he wrote, "but we predict it will do so substantially. We shall see."[44]

In a letter to his friend Abram Wakeman in New York, Lincoln said, speaking of Clay's intentions: "Does any one doubt that what they [the Niagara negotiators] *are* empowered to do, is to assist in selecting and arranging a candidate and a platform for the Chicago convention? Who could have given them this confidential employment but he who only a week since declared to Jaquess and Gilmore that he had no terms of peace but the independence of the South—the dissolution of the Union? Thus the present presidential contest will almost certainly be no other than a contest between a Union and a Disunion candidate, disunion certainly following the success of the latter."

The issue, Lincoln wrote Wakeman, "is a mighty one for all people and all time."[45]

20

THE WILD HOWL OF SUMMER

AUGUST ARRIVED IN WASHINGTON HOT AND CLAMMY, AND JOHN Nicolay was having trouble with bugs. They were invading even the sanctity of the screenless White House, and Lincoln's secretary was writing his fiancée, Therena Bates, about it.

"The gas lights over my desk," Nicolay wrote his bride-to-be, "are burning brightly and the windows of the room are open, and all bugdom outside seems to have organized a storming party to take the gas light."

Their numbers seemed to Nicolay to exceed the contending hosts at the gates of Richmond. "The air is swarming with them," he wrote, "they are on the ceiling, the walls and the furniture in countless numbers, they are buzzing about the room, and butting their heads against the window panes, they are on my clothes, in my hair, and on the sheet I am writing on."

They are all here, he wrote, "the plebeian masses, as well as the great and distinguished members of the oldest and largest patrician families—the Millers, the Roaches, the Whites, the Blacks, yea even the wary and diplomatic foreigners from the Musquito Kingdom. They hold a high carnival, or rather a perfect Saturnalia. Intoxicated and maddened and blinded by the bright gas-light, they dance and rush and fly about in wild gyrations, until they are drawn into the dazzling but fatal heat of the gas-flame when they fall to the floor, burned and maimed and mangled to the death, to be swept out into the dust and rubbish by the servant in the morning."

Nicolay saw a metaphor for the times in this mad concourse of insects in his office. It brought to mind the swarming in the day, every day, even in that same room, of all the "big bugs," who Nicolay saw "buzzing and gyrating round the great central sun and light and source of power of the government."[1]

On the first day of this blistering insect-ridden August, Senator Ben Wade wrote Horace Greeley a letter. Wade was hotter than the weather. He was still simmering over the president's pocketing of the Wade-Davis reconstruction bill on July 4, and outraged by Lincoln's proclamation four days later explaining the veto.

As Wade wrote the editor of the most popular and widest circulating newspaper in the North, he had on his desk a proclamation of his own, a manifesto. It actually wasn't his. His cohort from the House, Henry Winter Davis, who was, if anything, hotter than both Wade and the weather, had written it. But now Wade was about to do something with it.

"Will you please publish the enclosed, addressed, 'To the Supporters of the Government,' " Wade wrote Greeley. The request had no question mark after it. It was a statement.[2]

Greeley, still fresh from the embarrassing affair at Niagara, and steaming himself, very likely found the attached document delicious. Certainly he agreed with much that it said. Of course he would publish it.

It was a detailed, withering denunciation of Lincoln's reconstruction policy and his veto of the Wade-Davis bill. Among other malignant things, it said, "A more studied outrage on the legislative authority of the people has never been perpetrated." It charged the president with "dictatorial usurpation." It called his veto "this rash and fatal act . . . a blow at the friends of his Administration, at the rights of humanity, and at the principles of republican government." It then threatened him politically: "If he wishes our support, he must confine himself to his executive duties—to obey and execute, not make the laws—to suppress by arms armed Rebellion, and to leave political reorganization to Congress." The manifesto charged that the president, by preventing this bill from becoming a law, "holds the electoral votes of the Rebel States at the dictation of his personal ambition." He had, the manifesto charged, inaugurated "civil war for the Presidency."[3]

The manifesto, signed by Wade and Davis, was itself civil war on the president by two powerful members of his own party. Greeley, who had been waging his own civil war on Lincoln for years, ran it in two and a half incendiary columns in the *Tribune* on August 5.

It was an extraordinary document, "the most vigorous in attack," Nicolay and Hay would later say, "that was ever directed against the President from his own party during his term."[4]

It was clear to everybody what it was—a radical gambit to drive Lincoln from the presidential canvass, whether he would go or not. It fell like a thunderclap on the country, the party, and the president with lightning swiftness, staggering every politician who read it. No such bomb had ever been thrown before in American politics.

Secretary of State William Seward read the manifesto to Lincoln that evening in the White House, and Lincoln reacted as any other candidate for the presidency might react. He said, "I would like to know whether these men intend openly to oppose my election—the document looks that way."[5]

Later he complained to Noah Brooks that "to be wounded in the house of one's friends is perhaps the most grievous affliction that can befall a man." But as usual, it reminded him of a story. And he told Brooks the one about the procrustean bed. A mythical Greek giant named Procrustes built an iron bedstead on which he compelled his victims to lie. If the victim was too short to fill the bedstead, he was stretched by force until he was long enough; if he was too long, he was shortened to fit. This, Lincoln thought, was the sort of reconstruction the Wade-Davis approach called for. If any state coming back into the Union did not fit the Wade-Davis bedstead, so much the worse for that state.[6]

But Lincoln had somehow to live with Wade and Davis and their manifesto, which was out there now in public, and which reminded him of yet another story, which he told another friend. He said he felt a good deal about it as the old man did about his cheese, when his very smart son found, by the aid of a microscope, that it was teeming with maggots.

"Oh father!" exclaimed the boy, "how can you eat that stuff? Just look in here, and see 'em wriggle."

The old man took another mouthful and, putting his teeth into it, replied grimly, "Let 'em wriggle!"[7]

Not everybody reacted with such humor or resignation. Montgomery Blair, the lightning rod on which many anti-Lincoln fulgurations naturally fell, reacted violently, lumping the manifesto's authors with the Confederates. "We have Lee & his—on one side," Blair fumed, "and Henry Winter Davis & Ben Wade and all such Hell cats on the other. . . ."[8]

James Gordon Bennett at the *New York Herald* reacted in his usual sardonic fashion. In this "remarkable document," Bennett wrote, they had charged the president with "arrogance, ignorance, usurpation, knavery and a host of other deadly sins, including that of hostility to the rights of humanity and to the principles of republican government. Nothing that Vallandigham or the most venomous of the copperhead tribe of politicians have uttered in derogation of Mr. Lincoln has approached in bitterness and force the denunciations which Messrs. Wade and Davis, shining lights of the Republican party, have piled up in this manifesto."

Bennett predicted it would cause what it was intended to cause—a call for a new convention to repudiate and annul the nominations of both the Baltimore and Cleveland conventions and replace them with a single unified presidential and vice-presidential ticket of "acknowledged ability and patriotism." Bennett called for Lincoln to step aside voluntarily—by no means the first time he had proposed such self-surgery by the president. "One thing must be self-evident to him," Bennett wrote, "and that is that under no circumstances can he hope to be the next President of the United States."

How about Grant instead? Bennett suggested. If not him, then McClellan or Winfield Scott Hancock or William T. Sherman or Joe Hooker, generals all. Bennett much preferred Grant over McClellan. He had been mercilessly plugging Grant for president for months. McClellan, Bennett explained, knew how to manage an army, but didn't know how to manage the administration politicians. Grant had proved that he knew how to do both.[9]

Henry Raymond at *The New York Times* wrote stiffly that the manifesto's real object was to defeat the president's reelection and aid the Democratic party. Wade and Davis were, in effect, traitors to the cause. Raymond blasted Davis in particular, arguing that when he stabbed the candidate of his own party, he stabbed the cause.[10]

This wasn't exactly a new thing—this lashing out at Lincoln. In May, Raymond had himself lashed out at the "horrible stream of blackest crimination" that seemed constantly to dog the president. "No living man," Raymond wrote, "was ever charged with political crimes of such multiplicity and such enormity as Abraham Lincoln. He has been denounced without end as a perjurer, a usurper, a tyrant, a subverter of the Constitution, a destroyer of the liberties of his country, a reckless desperado, a heartless trifler over the last agonies of an expiring nation. Had that which has been said of him been true there is no circle in Dante's *Inferno* full enough of torment to expiate his iniquities."[11]

The overriding first reaction of Lincoln's enemies, and even of some of his would-be friends, to the Wade-Davis manifesto was that his cause and the election were lost. This was the common assumption of political insiders in Washington and New York. Whether it was shared by the people of the North at large, nobody knew. The politicians and editors were mainly talking with one another, not with the electorate.

The Confederates certainly wanted to believe it true. Manton Marble at the *New York World* reprinted an article from the *Richmond Examiner,* which to a large degree he agreed with, if not in wording, then in sentiment. "The fact . . . begins to shine out clear," the *Examiner* editorialized, "that Abraham Lincoln is lost; that he will never be President again. . . . The obscene ape of Illinois is about to be deposed from the Washington purple, and the White House will echo to his little jokes no more." The paper described the Wade-Davis manifesto as "this blow under the fifth rib . . . what almost amounts to a legal impeachment."[12]

Even Thurlow Weed, that political insider and sometime visitor and confidant to the White House, was quoted as saying, "Lincoln is gone, I suppose you know as well as I. And unless a hundred thousand men are raised sooner than the draft, the country's gone too."[13]

But almost as soon as the cries of anguish began building, so did a backlash. Gerrit Smith, an ardent New England abolitionist and ordinarily no Lincoln advocate, wrote a letter to *The New York Times* protesting the manifesto. "I regret its appearance," he wrote. "For it will serve to reduce the public good-will toward Mr. Lincoln; and that is what, just at this time, the public interest cannot afford." Smith saw "a great deal of truth in it, and generally a very forcible presentation of that truth. But . . . the eve of the Presidential election is not the time to be making an issue with Mr. Lincoln in regard to either his real or supposed errors." Smith saw clearly that it could do nothing but injure the cause, that Lincoln was clearly the lesser of two evils and must be supported.[14]

One after another, many newspapers in the Midwest sprang to Lincoln's defense. These papers had consistently supported the president in the past, and were seen by some insightful observers as accurate gauges of a strong underlying grassroots sentiment in the country for Lincoln's reelection despite what the politicians believed.[15]

It was becoming apparent that Wade and Davis had seriously miscalculated and overstepped. Their manifesto was boomeranging. It was being widely viewed as rank rebellion against the party ticket. They had clearly gone too far. Even the Union men in Wade's home county in Ohio, to his mortification, were calling the manifesto ill-timed, ill-tempered, and ill-advised.[16]

It was such a dark and howling summer in the North, what Brooks described as the darkest of many dark days in the war. It was all the more difficult to endure because it was so unexpected. There was not only this depressing Wade-Davis matter, but worse, there had been no good news from the front, any front, after the high expectations of the spring. There had been the awful butchery in the Wilderness and Spotslyvania and Cold Harbor and the stall-out before Petersburg. There had been Early's raid and the peace fiascos and the call for 500,000 more men to support what looked to be an endless war. The war was savaging the Treasury, and after three years of bloody conflict, its end was still nowhere in sight.[17]

Lincoln was absorbing the full heavy weight of this heaviest and hottest of summers. Scarcely a cheering ray had dawned upon the administration since his renomination in Baltimore in June. Despite the backlash against the Wade-Davis manifesto, his defeat in November was looking to many as not only possible but probable.[18]

Pessimism was everywhere in the Union Party ranks. And not only Wade and Davis, but many other radicals were blaming Lincoln, and proposing drastic measures. Lincoln was doomed, one of them wrote Ben Butler on August 12, "unless he shall *at once* dismiss his entire Cabinet, with the exception of Seward & Fessenden, & place, in their stead, sound, energetic, reliable men in whom the country have implicit confidence."

Butler's wife, Sarah, his chief confidante, wrote her husband that "politically, the chances are for McClellan, a strange thing when it was so clearly decided that his career was finished. Lincoln's hopes are less every day. The only hope for the radicals is that Lincoln and Frémont should yield their pretensions, unite on a new man, and give the whole strength of the Republican party in opposition to McClellan."

And McClellan hadn't even been nominated yet.

Another Butler confidant wrote the general from Rochester, New York, that "in this region the President has lost amazingly within a few weeks, and if the public sentiment here affords a fair indication of the public sentiment throughout the country, the popular suffrage to-day would be 'for a change.' "

Butler's own chief of staff, J. W. Shaffer, who was in New York testing the waters, wrote him, "I have seen and talked with nearly all the leading men in the city, and they all are of one opinion in regard to Lincoln. They consider him defeated."[19]

Nicolay looked clinically— as he looked at most things—at the wild howl all about him, and wrote Therena. He told her that the Republican party was in a condition of "disastrous panic—a sort of political Bull Run."[20]

Henry Raymond at *The New York Times,* who was feeling very shaky about things himself, again wrote sympathetically of Lincoln's plight. The president was whipsawed, damned if he does and damned if he doesn't, Raymond complained. "One denounces Mr. Lincoln because he did not abolish Slavery soon enough—another because he assumed to touch it at all. One refuses to vote for him because he keeps Mr. Blair in the Cabinet—another because he keeps somebody or anybody else. Frémont runs against him because he disregards the Constitution, and Wendell Phillips speaks against him because he recognizes that instrument at all. Some censure his lenient method of treating the people of the Southern States—others his barbarous and inhuman mode of carrying on the war. One set of politicians vilify him for not admitting the Southern States at once into the Union, and Wade and Davis, with equal malignity, brand him as a usurper for proposing to admit them at all."[21]

Lincoln's would-be friends were reacting desperately in the gloom. Thurlow Weed in New York had not only told friends that Lincoln was lost, he had told Lincoln that, too. Now Weed, whom Count Gurowski called "the prince of dark deeds," was writing to William Seward.[22]

"When, ten or eleven days since," he wrote Seward on August 22, "I told Mr. Lincoln that his re-election was an impossibility, I also told him that the information would soon come to him through other channels. It has doubtless ere this, reached him. At any rate, nobody here doubts it; nor do I see any body from other States who authorises the slightest hope of success."[23]

The other channel was Raymond himself, as party chairman, who on that same day wrote Lincoln. "I feel compelled to drop you a line concerning the political condition of the country as it strikes me," he wrote the president. "I am in active correspondence with your staunchest friends in every state and from them all I hear but one report. The tide is setting strongly against us. . . ." Raymond predicted that New York "would go 50,000 votes against us to-morrow. And so of the rest. Nothing but the most resolute and decided action on the part of the government and its friends, can save the country from falling into hostile hands."

Raymond blamed two things: the want of military success and "the impression in some minds, the fear and suspicion in others, that we are not to have peace *in any event* under this administration until Slavery is abandoned." Yet, Raymond wrote, there was a suspicion, widely held, that the country could have peace with union if it would. He argued that this belief could only be expelled by a bold act. Raymond's suggestion: a commissioner to be appointed to make "distinct proffers of peace to Davis . . . on the sole condition of acknowledging the supremacy of the constitution," all other questions to be settled at a convention of the people of all the states. If the offer was accepted (unlikely, Raymond thought), the country would want the execution kept in loyal hands. If rejected (likely), it would satisfy the widespread unrest and take the wind out of Democratic sails. Either way we win, Raymond wrote the president. The North would reunite under the Republicans. All would yet be well. Lincoln would be reelected. Without this—and at once—Raymond warned, all was surely lost.[24]

Even Leonard Swett, Lincoln's political friend from Illinois, was overwhelmed by the pessimism. He had come to New York in August and found the most alarming depression possessing all the Republicans, big and little. After seeing this, he wrote his wife that "unless material changes can be wrought, Lincoln's election is beyond any possible hope. It is probably clean gone now." He wrote her that not only had Raymond given up, but he would do nothing. Nobody, he mourned, would do anything. There was not a man doing anything except mischief. "We are," Swett wrote his wife, "in the midst of conspiracies equal to the French Revolution."[25]

It was this active panic of would-be friends and allies such as Raymond, Weed, and Swett that was cutting the deepest gouge in Lincoln's reelection prospects.

"The want of any decided military successes thus far, and the necessity of the new draft in the coming month," Nicolay wrote Therena, "has materially discouraged many of our good friends, who are inclined to be a little weak-kneed." Croakers, he told her, were talking everywhere about the impossibility of reelecting Lincoln unless something was done. But Nicolay believed it was "mainly anxiety and discouragement and that they will recover from it, after the Democrats shall have made their nominations at Chicago, and after the active fighting of the political campaign begins. The Democrats are growing bold and confident, and will be very unscrupulous, but I still [do] not think they can defeat Mr. Lincoln in any event."[26]

"There is a diseased restlessness about men in these times," Hay wrote Nicolay on August 25, "that unfits them for the steady support of an administration. . . . If the dumb cattle are not worthy of another term of Lincoln then let the will of God be done & the murrain of McClellan fall on them." In a letter a day later—a sort of postscript— Hay wrote, "Most of our people are talking like damned fools."[27]

Soon after Lincoln was nominated in June the two Pennsylvania politicians, Thaddeus Stevens and Simon Cameron, came calling. Stevens, blunt speaking always, told the president that the certainty of his reelection would ride on the vote in Pennsylvania in the state elections in October. He told the president that if he was to work there for him with a good will, Lincoln must promise to reorganize his cabinet and purge the hated Montgomery Blair.

Lincoln rose to his full six feet four inches and spoke emphatically, with gestures to match. "Mr. Stevens," he told his cantankerous and demanding visitor, "I am sorry to be compelled to deny your request to make such a promise. If I were even myself inclined to make it, I have no right to do so. What right have I to remove Mr. Blair, and not make a similar promise to any other gentleman of influence to remove any other member of my cabinet whom he does not happen to like?"

Has it come to this, Lincoln demanded, "that the voters of this country are asked to elect a man to be President—to be the Executive—to administer the government, and yet that this man is to have no will or discretion of his own? Am I to be the mere puppet of power? To have my constitutional advisers selected beforehand, to be told I must do this or leave that undone? It would be degrading to my manhood to consent to any such bargain—I was about to say it is equally degrading to your manhood to ask it."[28]

More than anybody else, Lincoln was feeling the heat, both God-sent and manmade. It was an awkward time politically. As he himself was to say afterward, it was a time when "we had no adversary and seemed to have no friends."[29] Noah Brooks said of him this summer that he was a "careworn, hard-looking man."[30]

Alexander McClure, a more friendly Pennsylvanian than Stevens, visited Lincoln in the middle of the stifling heat of August and found him more dejected than he had ever seen him. "His face, always sad in repose, was then saddened until it became a picture of despair," McClure said. McClure had seen him many times when army disasters shadowed the land and oppressed his spirit, but "I never saw him so profoundly moved by grief as he was on that day, when there seemed to be not even a silvery lining to the political cloud that hung over him." Lincoln spoke to McClure of the want of sincere and earnest support from Republican leaders. He told him he could name but one who could be relied on: Isaac Arnold of Illinois.[31]

Alexander W. Randall, the former governor of Wisconsin, and Joseph T. Mills, a judge of the Fifth Judicial Circuit, also visited the president during this dismal August. Randall saw what McClure had seen, and was concerned.

"Why can't you, Mr. P., seek some place of retirement for a few weeks," Randall asked him. "You would be reinvigorated."

"Aye, 3 weeks would do me no good," Lincoln answered, "my thoughts my solicitude for this great country follow me where ever I go."

Lincoln was in a sad but talkative mood, and Mills later wrote an account of the meeting in his diary. "I don't think it is personal vanity, or ambition," Lincoln told them, "but I cannot but feel that the weal or woe of this great nation will be decided in the approaching canvass. My own experience has proven to me, that there is no program intended by the Democratic party but that will result in the dismemberment of the Union."[32]

Perhaps the most depressing visitor Lincoln received at about this time was another of the radicals. Lincoln asked him if he would speak for him in the coming campaign. "No sir," was the answer. "As things stand at present I don't know what in the name of God I could say, as an honest man, that would help you. Unless you clean these men away who surround you, [and] do something with your army, you will be beaten overwhelmingly."

Lincoln could only shrug and say, "You think I don't know I am going to be beaten, *but I do* and unless some great change takes place *badly beaten*."[33] The gloom of the hot summer was clearly getting even to him.

Worries about that other general, aside from the one expected to be nominated in Chicago, were nagging Lincoln again this August. What about Grant? There was a revived clamor in this pessimistic month to make him a presidential candidate whether he wanted to be or not. Was Grant bending to this pressure? Was it taking his mind off his job—to defeat the rebel armies? Lincoln had to know.

Again the president turned to a friend of the general's for an answer. "Do you know," Lincoln asked Col. John Eaton, one of those friends, "what General Grant thinks of the effort now making to nominate him for the presidency? Has he spoken of it to you?"

Eaton told Lincoln he knew nothing of it.

"Well," Lincoln said, "the disaffected are trying to get him to run, but I don't think they can do it. If he is the great General we think he is, he must have some consciousness of it, and know that he cannot be satisfied with himself and secure the credit due for his great generalship if he does not finish his job. I do not believe that they can get him to run."

But Lincoln wasn't certain. He asked Eaton to go to City Point and find out what Grant was thinking.

Sitting in Grant's tent, Eaton worked his way delicately around to the subject by recounting how he had met several men on the train coming down who had asked him if Grant could be persuaded to run for the presidency as a citizens' candidate. Eaton repeated the conversation to Grant and said, "The question is not whether you wish to run, but whether you could be compelled to run in answer to the demand of the people for a candidate who could save the Union."

Grant answered emphatically. Bringing his clenched fist down hard on the strap arms of his camp chair, he shouted, "They can't do it! They can't compel me to do it!"

"Have you said this to the President?" Eaton asked.

"No, I have not thought it worth while to assure the President of my opinion. I consider it as important for the cause that he should be elected as that the army should be successful in the field."[34]

Lincoln could rest easy about Grant.

The wild howl of summer reached its apex on August 22. That was the day Henry Raymond wrote him that he couldn't be reelected. It was also the day the 166th Ohio Infantry Regiment on its way home from the front, stopped to pay its respects.

"It is not merely for to-day," Lincoln told the soldiers, "but for all time to come that we should perpetuate for our children's children this great and free government, which we have enjoyed all our lives. I beg you to remember this, not merely for my sake, but for yours. I happen temporarily to occupy this big White House. I am a living witness that any one of your children may look to come here as my father's child has. It is in order that each of you may have through this free government which we have enjoyed, an open field and a fair chance for your industry, enterprise and intelligence; that you may all have equal privileges in the race of life, with all its desirable human aspirations. It is for this the struggle should be maintained, that we may not lose our birthright—not only for one, but for two or three years. The nation is worth fighting for, to secure such an inestimable jewel."[35]

On August 25, Raymond followed his cheerless letter to Washington in person. That day Nicolay wrote Hay in Illinois that "hell is to pay. The [New York] politicians have got a stampede on that is about to swamp everything. Raymond and the National Committee are here today. R. thinks a commission to Richmond is about the only salt to save us—while the Tycoon sees and says it would be utter ruination. The matter is now undergoing consultation. Weak-kneed d——d fools . . . are in the movement for a new candidate—to supplant the Tycoon. Everything is darkness and doubt and discouragement. Our men see giants in the airy and unsubstantial shadows of the opposition, and are about to surrender without a fight. I think that to-day and here is the turning point in our crisis. If the President can infect R. and his committee with some of his own patience and pluck, we are saved. If our friends will only rub their eyes and shake themselves, and become convinced that they themselves are not dead we shall win the fight overwhelmingly."[36]

Lincoln didn't put any more stock in peace overtures to the Confederacy in August than he had in July when Greeley had gone to Niagara. Although he was affected by Raymond's pessimism, he also saw potential political disaster in sending official peace emissaries to the Confederacy at this time. Lincoln and three of the stronger-kneed in the cabinet—Seward, Stanton, and Fessenden—closeted themselves with Raymond and persuaded him that taking his advice to send a peace commission to Richmond would be worse than losing the election. It would be surrendering it in advance. Raymond returned to New York reportedly "encouraged and cheered" and agreeing with them.[37]

But in his heart Lincoln was himself less than encouraged and cheered. The gloom was palpable and very pervasive. Two days before Raymond's visit, the day of one of his regular cabinet meetings, Lincoln wrote a brief note on a slip of paper and pasted it so its contents could not be seen. In it he suggested that it seemed unlikely that he could be reelected, and proposed what he intended to do in that event. At the cabinet meeting he asked every member to sign the back of the paper, but would tell them nothing of its contents. As they wondered what they had just signed, he slid it quietly into his desk drawer.[38]

As Nicolay had suggested to Hay, hell was indeed to pay. Raymond might be reassured, but others were not. Insurrection was afoot. A handful of radicals met on August 19 at the home of the mayor of New York, George Opdyke. Opdyke and two other prominent New York radicals, John A. Stevens and David Dudley Field, were the prime movers, and the meeting's purpose was to plan a call for a new convention to force Lincoln out of the canvass and replace him with someone else. Invitations had quietly gone out to a who's-who of the discontented.

J. W. Shaffer, Ben Butler's chief of staff, wrote his boss from New York that nearly everybody he had talked with agreed that there was but one course: a call for a new convention, including war Democrats, if the Chicago Convention nominated a peace man or adopted a peace platform.[39]

Throughout the summer, Horace Greeley had continued to cling to the idea of replacing Lincoln with someone else. He was in league with this movement, but unfortunately he was to be out of town on the nineteenth. He wrote Opdyke his regrets and said, "Mr. Lincoln is already beaten. He cannot be elected. And we must have another ticket to save us from utter overthrow." He proposed Grant, Butler, or Sherman for president and Admiral David Farragut for vice president. With such a ticket, he wrote Opdyke, "we could make a fight yet. And such a ticket we ought to have anyhow, with or without a convention."[40]

Salmon Portland Chase had been invited. Neither could he be present. But he wrote Opdyke hoping that the deliberations of the meeting "may be fruitful of benefit to our country."

One of General Butler's confidants wrote him beforehand that "I think light breaks through upon us—I hope for great results from the Opdyke meeting to-night."[41]

Among those reported present were Opdyke, Field, Henry Winter Davis, Roscoe Conkling, William Curtis Noyes (Chase's pipeline to the meeting), Shaffer of Ben Butler's staff, and John A. Stevens. It was agreed that a call would go out for a convention in Cincinnati on September 28. A subcommittee was appointed to prepare the call and send it out privately but extensively for signatures—as many as possible. It was agreed there would be a second meeting, in Dudley Field's parlor on August 29.

The call for the convention went out on the twenty-second. It said the convention's aim would be to consider the state of the nation and to concentrate the Union strength on one candidate who commanded the confidence of the country. The convention was euphemistically styled a "friendly consultation."

The hope was that both Lincoln and Frémont could be persuaded to withdraw in favor of another nominee to be named at Cincinnati. Charles Sumner wrote, "It may be that Mr. L. will see that we shall all be stronger and more united under another candidate. But if he does not see it so, our duty is none the less clear to unite in the opposition to the common enemy." A letter went out to Frémont on August 20 from Boston, asking him if he would withdraw if Lincoln did.

Shaffer had a two-hour talk with Thurlow Weed, and reported to Butler that Weed thought Lincoln could be prevailed on to draw off. Shaffer reported that Swett was of the same opinion.[42]

Henry Winter Davis believed that if the call fared well in New York, it would carry the country. But the call was running into opposition.

Even Roscoe Conkling, a radical party zealot and former New York congressman, who had been listed present at the Opdyke meeting, was balking. He wrote John A. Stevens that he didn't approve of the call and wouldn't sign it or ask others to sign it.

Neither would Jacob Collamer, longtime New York Whig and Republican who had long doubted Lincoln's chances for reelection. He believed a change of front on the field now in the face of the enemy would prove "almost certainly disastrous." Daniel Dickinson, the New York war Democrat who had missed becoming Lincoln's running mate at Baltimore, also demurred; he too would continue to support the president.

Lincoln himself was well informed of the movement and of those behind it, and so was that other keen politician, Ben Butler. If there was any man who had one foot in the war and one foot in politics, equally deep, it was that politician-general. With one of his crossed eyes, Butler watched the enemy from across the James. With the other he watched the party mutiny unfolding in New York.

His name was on many a mutinous lip. There had been talk for some time that Secretary of War Stanton was about to be sacked and Butler named to replace him. But in New York there was talk of an even higher place for him—anointment by the Cincinnati convention. J. K. Herbert wrote Butler, "Every man I have met says, 'Give me Butler.'"

The day after the Wade-Davis manifesto exploded on the country, Herbert had heard one man say: "In order to save the country you must make Old Ben Butler President!"[43]

"Nearly all speak of you as the man," Shaffer wrote him from New York. But Shaffer, who issued advice as well as reports, cautioned him not to commit himself, but await developments. When the time is ripe, when a convention is called, Shaffer advised, then "will be time enough to speak of candidates." He told his boss that "all agree that it is too late for you to go into the Cabinet if offered." Certain it is, Shaffer wrote him in another letter, that "the People are in a condition to be reasoned into any kind of crazy demonstrations by excitable and devilish leaders."[44]

Being something of a devilish leader himself, Butler understood this. He wrote Sarah that as to these "other movements"—he called them that to distinguish them from the military matters he was also attending to—"we must let it drift along as it will. There is nothing else to be done than duty here." He told her, "I think Lincoln is beaten, but who can be nominated at Chicago that will not lose the country?"

There was a part of the tempestuous Butler that longed for quiet. "The political cauldron is boiling," he wrote Sarah, " 'Bubble, bubble, toil and trouble,' until one hardly cares who comes uppermost. I do wish I was quiet at home, with a certainty that I was never to leave it."[45]

If Lincoln was despondent and careworn and Butler was homesick, the Democrats were jubilant. While many of them longed for peace with the South and among themselves, they highly favored this war among the Republicans. In the lowering clouds of August the Republicans were seeing only darkness. The Democrats, however, were seeing a silver lining, a luminous likelihood of certain victory in November.

Cyrus H. McCormick, the inventor of the reaper and a dedicated Democrat, wrote Manton Marble from Chicago in mid-August: "Old Abe is quite in trouble just now. . . . I think he is already pretty well played out. The Democracy must defeat themselves if now defeated."[46]

The Confederates in Canada thought so too. Jacob Thompson wrote the rebel ministers to France and England, John Slidell and James Mason, on the same day Lincoln was penning his pessimistic note and having it signed unseen by his cabinet. Thompson told the two ministers he was seeing heartening signs, "a most wonderful change in the minds of the people of the Northern States. Politicians who three weeks ago held the opinion that nothing was left them but a struggle for liberty, even to the extent of force of arms, are now willing to await and test the virtue of the ballot-box. . . ." He told them that even one of Lincoln's cabinet officers, Stanton, was saying privately that nothing now but a favorable turn for Union armies on the battlefield could prevent the president's defeat in November.[47]

A giant pro-McClellan meeting was organized in New York on August 10—one of the largest political gatherings ever held in the city, a massive demonstration in favor of the general's nomination. Four platforms were set up about Union Square, which quaked through the evening to music, booming cannon, fireworks, flaming rhetoric, cheers for McClellan, groans for Lincoln, chaos, and confusion.[48] The throng was estimated at from 30,000 to 100,000, depending on the newspaper's political orientation.

A peddler of pictures told a friend that he now sold more portraits of McClellan than of Grant. "But," he said confidentially, "if I only had *Gen. Lee,* I could sell ten times as many of him as I can of McClellan— *and to the same men.*" The *Tribune* concluded that Lee's generalship had done more for McClellan in this "foaming Presidential canvass" than McClellan's own. "Who does not see," Greeley editorialized, "that his fortunes rise as the country sinks, and that his chances would be brightened by his country's ruin?"[49]

Manton Marble's pro-McClellan *World* gushed over the mass meeting. Subheads under the main head, THE MCCLELLAN FURORE, trailed down to the centerfold, proclaiming "The Greatest Meeting Ever Held in New York," "A Hundred Mass Meetings Rolled into One," "The Great Sumter War Meeting Outdone," "New York Has Spoken," "A Feast of Lanterns," "An Army with Banners."

The *World* even reprinted the songs that were sung, including the chorus from this one, to the tune of "Vive l'Amour":

> *He'll win the race—to the White House he'll go,*
> *Whether Lincoln and Chase are willing or no.*
> *Hurrah for the man, hurrah for the man, hurrah for the man*
> *we love.*[50]

McClellan, the man they loved, didn't attend. He was still acting as if he weren't a candidate. The summer heat was getting to him as well. On August 8 he wrote his friend and political mentor, S. L. M. Barlow, that he was getting tired of the whole business. "I don't expect to see you before the 29th unless you come to Orange. I shan't come again to N.Y. & don't send me any d——d politicians."

He repeated that sentiment to William C. Prime, the editor of the *Journal of Commerce,* two days later from his mountain hideaway in Orange: "Don't send any politicians out here—I'll snub them if they come—confound them!"[51]

By now McClellan seemed to be sorry he hadn't listened to the advice a friend had written him from Newport, Rhode Island, the month before: "If there is any one thing I should wish more than another, it would be, you avoid *all* politicians and never listen to them or put your pen to paper on politics."[52]

That is difficult to do if you are the leading candidate for a presidential nomination. Besides, it was too late. Through the summer, McClellan, whether he wished it or not, had been getting letters from both wings of the party, the peace Democrats and the war Democrats, pushing their points of view and predicting calamity if their advice was not followed.

A friend wrote him a long letter saying, in part, "I do hope you will not yield one iota to the Peace men. My reasons are, if you do, you will lose far more than you will gain. In fact if you do not yield anything you will still have the vote of the Peace men because they cannot do better. . . . The whole tribe will vote for you on your noble & patriotic platform as laid down in your Pennsylvania letter & in your West Point oration. But if the ring of battle is not in the Presidential campaign platform, if the cry is only Peace, Peace, & some Vallandigham or kin is associated with you (for Vice Pres.) then our cause is lost & A. Lincoln will be our next Prest."[53]

One politician Barlow couldn't help sending McClellan, and that McClellan couldn't help seeing, was Francis Preston Blair Sr. The Blairs had been active since late 1862 trying to pry McClellan, whom they liked, away from the New York Democrats. They had never been in favor of Lincoln firing him in the first place. Now old man Blair had an idea, a proposal.

Blair was as worried as everybody else by the schisms and weakness in the Union Party. So he went to New York in late July "to make an effort at conciliation." He later explained that he went "without consulting the President, without giving him, directly or indirectly, the slightest intimation of my object, and, of course, without his authority. I apprised no one but my son."

Blair first called on the leading editors in New York, then, through Barlow, arranged a meeting with McClellan at the Astor House. In the interview he urged McClellan to have nothing to do with the Chicago convention, with either the war or peace Democrats. He told McClellan that if he accepted the nomination he would be defeated, and pictured for him the dismal fate attending defeated presidential candidates. He urged him to make himself instead the inspiring example to the loyal Democrats of the North by writing Lincoln a letter asking to be restored to service, at the same time assuring the president that he did not seek it with a view to a bid for the presidential nomination. Blair told McClellan that if Lincoln refused the request, he would then be responsible for the consequences.

McClellan listened with his habitual courtesy; nearly everybody listened to old man Blair with courtesy. He again disclaimed any ambition for the presidency, thanked Blair for his friendly suggestions, and said he would give them some thought, but that he was called now to the country to see a sick child and regretted he could not talk with him again.[54]

Soon after the meeting, McClellan wrote Blair a letter, which apparently he never mailed. In it he repeated his conviction that no man should actively seek the presidency, or refuse it if it was spontaneously offered him. Certainly he was not seeking it. As for returning to the army, he said he so disapproved of Lincoln's policies that he could no longer in good conscience serve him.[55]

And that was that. The hot summer was winding toward an end by late August, and Democrats were wending toward Chicago. The country and McClellan would soon see whether the nomination was to be spontaneously offered him, and whether he would have to accept it.

21

THE BAND PLAYED "DIXIE"

J UST BEFORE THE DEMOCRATIC CONVENTION MET IN CHICAGO, Lincoln told Noah Brooks, "They must nominate a Peace Democrat on a war platform, or a War Democrat on a peace platform; and I personally can't say that I care much which they do."[1]

Lincoln would watch from Washington, but Brooks was preparing to go to Chicago to see for himself which they would do. On August 24, the evening before the day he left, he called on the president to say good-bye.

"Good-bye," Lincoln told him. "Don't be discouraged; I don't believe that God has forsaken us yet."

He asked Brooks to write him from Chicago, two or three letters as the convention unfolded, giving him "some of the political gossip that would not find its way into the newspapers."[2]

Other Republicans were looking toward Chicago at the end of this dreary August with cynicism and scorn. One of them, Benjamin H. Brewster, wrote Lincoln on the day the convention convened, calling it "that collection of Public vagrants."[3]

John Hay, who was on a trip home to Illinois, wrote John Nicolay from Warsaw, saying he was awaiting, with the greatest interest, "the hatching of the big Peace Snakes at Chicago."[4]

As the Democrats packed their bags to catch their trains, they were seeing the coming event in much the same light as was Lincoln himself. Everything was pointing to a nominee picked by the war Democrats to run on a platform designed by the peace Democrats. It was going to be a weird fit and a fearful prospect—"one of those unhappy marriages," the *Philadelphia Inquirer* was to write, "which lead to mutual disgust, quarrels and divorce." But it seemed inevitable—like death and taxes. Everybody knew that each side had to concede something.[5]

The war Democrats, calling themselves the conservatives and led by the New Yorkers, had their sights fixed firmly on George McClellan as the nominee. They hoped something reasonable in the way of a platform could be carved out for him to stand on. But that wasn't their main worry as they caught their trains for Chicago. Their main objective on August 29 would be to get their man nominated. They would let whatever else happened happen, and deal with it when it did.

The war Democrats had everything more or less ready. The wire-pulling and arm twisting on the general's behalf had been going on for days, weeks, months. Copies of McClellan's West Point oration and Harrison's Landing letter, stitched together in a single document called "McClellan's Platform," were ready to hand out to every delegate. Things were looking good. The war had been going poorly for the country, and unhappy radical Republicans were on the edge of mutiny against their nominee; all the signs pointed not only to McClellan's nomination, but to his certain election in November.

November was not that far away. This national nominating convention was the ninth in the history of the Democratic party, and the latest that any of them had ever convened. Waiting on the course of events appeared to be paying off. If their luck held, they figured they could win this one and be back in power again in 1865.

Sunset Cox was on his way to Chicago, feeling good about the prospects. He was to lead the fight for McClellan on the floor, and he was predicting that his fellow Democrats flocking toward the Wigwam were going to "make the 29th historic."[6]

S. L. M. Barlow was one of the few in the McClellan inner circle not going to Chicago. But he was feeling good about things, too, particularly the critical soldier vote. "The conviction now seems to be almost universal," he wrote Manton Marble on August 21, "that no one but McClellan can control any large portion of the army vote in the field and at home. . . . With any other man, we utterly lose the army vote: we lose the support of tens of thousands of honest Republicans who will support him, but will not support any other nominee, unless we take a Republican pure and simple."[7]

By the eve of the convention, Barlow had worked himself up to an overwrought emotional pitch. He wrote Marble again, saying he was "almost used up by excitement." Signing off to the editor, who was going to Chicago, he said, "Goodbye. Preserve the Union, with McClellan!"[8]

It seemed a good bet. The prognosticators in Chicago were giving four-to-one odds that McClellan would be nominated on the first ballot.

Noah Brooks caught a train on August 25 bound for Pittsburgh and "burdened with Copperheads." That night a howling gale blew a train off the track ahead, temporarily blocking the way. Weatherbound at Harrisburg, Brooks and the copperheads failed to make their connection at Pittsburgh and had to wait six and a half hours for the through train to Chicago.[9]

The cars were jammed with many distinguished and jubilant Democrats, whom Brooks called "the unterrified."[10] Among the most conspicuous was Representative Benjamin G. Harris of Maryland, a loose cannon who had been censured by the House for so-called treasonable language. It was known up the line that Harris was on the train, and whenever it stopped, which was often, the butternuts (a term that usually described Confederate soldiers, but which Brooks used to describe copperheads and all Southern sympathizers) clamored for him. Brooks found Harris very companionable, and much more ardently clamored-for the farther west the train progressed.

It had also been bruited about ahead of the train that McClellan himself, who wouldn't have been caught dead in such a crowd, was aboard. So at a stop in Plymouth, Indiana, there was a cry on the platform for "Little Mac." A Union colonel going home on furlough was readily conscripted and passed off as the redoubtable general by some of the fun-loving Democrats, who didn't want to see the crowd disappointed. The willing colonel delivered what Brooks considered a very ingenious little speech in the McClellan style, and was rewarded with thunderous cheers.[11]

On another train moving west toward Chicago rode the New Yorkers —August Belmont, Governor Horatio Seymour, Samuel J. Tilden, and others—most of them carrying their high hopes for McClellan. They boarded the train in Buffalo, where they were joined by that ultimate Democratic insider and ardent McClellanite, Dean Richmond.[12]

Eleven railroad lines emptied into Chicago, and every one was bringing swarms of delegates, onlookers, and hangers-on to the convention city. Applications for lodging were still flooding into the hotels at that late date, some of them begging for floor space to sleep on if rooms were unavailable. Private boardinghouses were filling rapidly, and private homes were being pressed into service to accommodate the overflow.[13]

The ardent *Chicago Times* predicted that the city was about to host "the largest and most enthusiastic gathering ever held upon American soil."[14] The unsympathetic *Chicago Tribune,* which insisted on calling the affair the "National Copperhead Convention," compared it to a plague of locusts. The *Tribune* wrote that the Democrats had settled down on the city "like an army of grasshoppers," swarming around the entrances of the hotels "like bees around a hive in midsummer." The paper complained that the leading thoroughfares were "black with humanity in broadcloth . . . eating up every green thing."[15]

The *Tribune* grieved that "the whisky market is dreadfully excited, and fashionable drinks at popular saloons are going up with fearful rapidity." It pointed out that "the hens sympathize with this appreciation in the price of liquids. Eggs and poultry have advanced fifty percent. . . . Are we to be afflicted," the paper demanded, "with famine as well as the National Convention?"[16]

The correspondent from the *New York World* paused in the mounting confusion to get his boots shined. He was attended to by a little bootblack who gave the gleaming boots a last parting lick and called it "a extra shine for little Mac."[17]

Daily copies of the *World* were being distributed free to convention delegates. But severe storms blowing off Lake Michigan on August 26 had so interfered with the telegraph lines that it was impossible to send dispatches through in time to meet the deadlines of the impatient New York newspapers.[18]

Brooks's train pulled into this chaos late the night of August 27. He saw a sleepless city, "all alive with flags, banners, processions, music, cheers, and butternuts."[19] The city was also alive with meetings, rallies, and caucuses of all political shades. A mass meeting for McClellan on the night Brooks arrived was reported as one of the largest political gatherings in Chicago's history. Excitement around the hotels was quickening hourly, and the correspondent from the *New York World* reported that rumors were flying "thicker than mosquitoes in a swamp."[20]

Many of the brightest lights of the party had arrived, and *The New York Times* reported that a good deal of "wire-working and thimble-rigging" was going on.[21] Behind-the-scenes wrangling over what it should take to nominate—a two-thirds vote or a simple majority—was raging in the back rooms. The ultra peace men were holding out for a two-thirds vote, believing McClellan could never get that many, would peak at full strength on the first ballot, and, if not nominated, would stall and begin to fade—be a "dead cock in the pit," as they put it. The McClellan camp was lobbying for a simple, easier-to-get majority vote.[22]

August Belmont, the chairman of the Democratic National Committee, was taking this jockeying with a comparatively easy mind. It was looking good for McClellan either way. He wired Barlow in New York, who was in close touch with McClellan in New Jersey: "All going well. Success sure."[23]

To be sure, Belmont was having occasional nagging anxieties. Horatio Seymour had surfaced as a minor irritant. Belmont had thought the governor, who harbored known presidential ambitions and had been looked on as the likely nominee before McClellan's emergence, was out of the picture. Indeed, in the days before the convention, the New York newspapers reported it as a fact. But rumors that he was still available continued to buzz and hum irritatingly in the hotel hallways and back rooms.

James Gordon Bennett, who always had one cocked eye on the lookout for political duplicity, wrote in the *Herald,* "Seymour is playing possum—he is only pretending to be dead." Bennett believed it was all a stratagem of the peace Democrats, who intended to hold Seymour offstage until McClellan's drive stalled. Then they would trot him out as their replacement candidate.[24]

Now, in Chicago, Belmont was half believing this himself. While the governor was privately denying any interest in the nomination, his friends in the New York delegation and others persisted in declaring support for him. Belmont wrote Barlow on the eve of the convention, complaining, "Seymour blows hot & cold. . . . He professes not to be a candidate & will be none if I can help it."[25] Even if the tide was for McClellan, nothing was certain until the votes were cast, and this support for Seymour that wouldn't seem to go away was a bothersome undercurrent.

An even greater nagging concern in Belmont's mind was Clement Vallandigham. The prince of the copperheads was there in the Ohio delegation, leading the peace Democrats and intent, if not on preventing McClellan's nomination, at least on shaping the party platform to his way of thinking. Barlow, at home in New York, had been cringing ever since he heard Vallandigham was going to Chicago. He had written McClellan then, predicting that "Vallandigham's advent will I fear give serious trouble."[26]

Vallandigham had made a stunning comeback from his time in exile. He was not only now wandering about unmuzzled, but was a delegate to the convention and the center of attention. No matter how his critics pictured him, this "secessionist of the darkest dye," this "banished traitor *posing* as a martyr," this "pettifogging . . . disorganizer," this mischievous troublemaker with his "youthful, rosy, and pleasant face" but "venomous, bitter, and snappish manner," was, in Noah Brooks's view, "watching cat-like for a chance to spring."[27]

One of Lincoln's favorite humorists, Petroleum Nasby, persisted in calling him "Vallandigum." And Brooks had been studying him carefully through his pince-nez for months. Brooks admired Vallandigham as a "pretty talker, smooth, plausible and polished." But that was only in repose and in civil discourse. When he made a set speech and became excited, Brooks had noticed, his face changed fearfully. His mouth widened, his thin lips drew tightly over his teeth, and a vindictive, ghastly grin replaced the pleasant smile—the devil within breaking through the fair disguise.[28] Vallandigham was Jekyll and Hyde.

In Chicago, his tongue was busy. As the *Chicago Tribune* put it, "All the hissing snakes" of copperheaddom were there, "this aggregation of all that is rank in the land, demanding peace with dishonor."[29] As their leader, Vallandigham was a much-cheered speaker at meetings and rallies all over town. His rooms in the Sherman House immediately became the informal headquarters for the avowed peace men. The door was never locked, and on the night before the convention, friends and delegates walked in and out all through the evening until long past midnight.[30]

Among those who walked brazenly in was the band of Confederates from Canada. They had arrived with the throng at Chicago, under orders from Jacob Thompson and led by the two adventurers Thomas H. Hines and John B. Castleman. With them were sixty Southern soldiers in civilian dress who had escaped from Northern prisons. They harbored dark plans. The idea, while the nation was diverted by the convention, was to carry out the much-postponed uprising in consort with the Sons of Liberty to free rebel prisoners at nearby Camp Douglas.

Hines and Castleman took rooms at the Richmond House and met there on the night of August 28 with some of the leaders of the secret order. They learned then, to their dismay, that the Sons of Liberty still weren't ready. They were present in force, but spread about the city indiscriminately, wholly disorganized, with no means of rapid communication. It was very unmilitary. Hines and Castleman met its leaders again the next night, hoping to see things better organized, only to find the Sons even less ready than they had been the night before. It was hopeless. Hines and Castleman would call the whole thing off and leave town before the convention ended.[31]

The Wigwam, where the convention was about to open, was an enormous structure sitting by the lake shore at the corner of Michigan Avenue and Park Place. It could hold up to 15,000 people. A reporter from the *New York Daily Tribune* thought it would be admirably suited to a first-class circus, which, in a manner of speaking, was about to happen.[32]

Its interior was arranged along the lines of a massive amphitheater, with a platform in the center capable of seating six hundred persons—the section reserved for the delegates. For the crowd at large there were two capacious galleries, called the pits, at the north and south sections of the building. But not even the huge capacity of the auditorium was big enough to accommodate all who wanted in. August 29 dawned bright and cool, and by early morning an immense throng not favored with tickets began to gather outside the building, all the way to the lake shore.[33]

When finally the doors to the Wigwam were thrown open, the pits quickly filled with ticket holders, and the amphitheater became a bedlam. Brooks noted that now and then a train jarring, wheezing, and screeching past on the tracks outside added to the discordant clamor within, and filled the huge barn of a building with stinking coal smoke and cinders. The crowd inside was so great that many climbed up from the pits and began to roost on the rail separating them from the delegates. The rail soon gave way under the weight, creating confusion and bringing frantic ushers and policemen racing in to restore order.[34]

At about a quarter of twelve, the band struck up "Auld Lang Syne," followed by "The Star Spangled Banner," "Dixie's Land," and "Yankee Doodle." The *New York Daily Tribune* reported that "Dixie's Land," the Southern anthem, was lustily cheered, and that "Yankee Doodle," its Northern counterpart, was also cheered, only less so. But the *Tribune*'s objectivity was suspect.[35]

At noon, August Belmont called the convention to order. Intent on saying something that might somehow unite the disparate parts of his ideologically divided party, he began to deliver the opening speech.

First he slammed the Lincoln administration, always a uniting theme among Democrats. He spoke of the "four years of misrule by a sectional, fanatical and corrupt party" that had "brought our country on the very edge of ruin." He said Lincoln's reelection would be a "calamity" that would lead to "the utter disintegration of our whole political and social system amid bloodshed and anarchy, with the great problems of liberal progress and self-government jeopardized for generations to come."

It was a good beginning, pleasing to all. The American people, Belmont continued, had at last awakened to the conviction that a change of policy and administration could alone "stay our downward course." He told the delegates that the people would rally to their candidate and their platform if they offered "a tried patriot, who has proved his devotion to the Union and the Constitution," and if they pledged him and themselves "to maintain their hallowed importance by every effort and sacrifice in our power." Everybody knew he was pitching George McClellan.

Then Belmont issued his warning. Bear in mind, he told them, that the dissensions of the last national Democratic convention were one of the principal causes that put the reins of government into Republican hands in the first place. Therefore, they must beware of making the same fatal mistake again. He said, "We are here not as war democrats nor as peace democrats, but as citizens of the great Republic, which we will strive to bring back to its former greatness and prosperity, without one single star taken from the brilliant constellation that once encircled its youthful brow."[36]

Belmont passed the gavel to the convention's temporary chairman, William Bigler, a former Democratic governor of Pennsylvania. After Bigler's speech, the nuts-and-bolts part of the day began—getting organized. Committees on credentials, permanent organization, and resolutions were named. A member from each delegation was seated on each committee, with the exception of Kentucky, which got two members on the resolutions committee, but only one vote. Kentucky had sent two delegations, which had agreed to act in harmony. Then the convention adjourned, agreeing to meet the next morning at ten o'clock after the committees had done their work.

For many of the war Democrats, one of their worst fears had already materialized. Clement Vallandigham had been named to the resolutions committee from Ohio. The committee would draft the platform; it meant certain trouble. Wearing the smooth, plausible, polished side of his personality, Vallandigham announced that the resolutions committee would meet that evening at the Sherman House, in the rooms of the New York delegation. It was going to be another night with little sleep.[37]

At ten o'clock the next morning the convention reconvened. The pits were packed long before the gavel fell. Every foot of standing room was taken. Hundreds of others without tickets milled about outside. The first order of business was to put things solidly in the hands of the Almighty. Verses were read from the Book of Psalms, followed by a Prayer For the Convention and People, followed by a Prayer For our Rulers, followed by a Prayer For our Forces and For All in Suffering, followed by a Prayer For Unity and Peace, followed by the Lord's Prayer with the delegations and galleries joining in, and ending with a benediction.[38] God had been assuaged.

The committee on credentials reported, recommending the seating of all the delegations, including the two from Kentucky. Its report was quickly adopted. The six recommended resolutions of the pro-McClellan Conservative Union, which had held its own mini-convention in Chicago two days before, were presented. The fourth plank called outright for McClellan's nomination, with his election certain and immediate peace and restoration of the government to follow. That plank brought cheers from the galleries and the delegates, interrupting the business of the convention for several minutes. The Conservative Union resolutions with that unusual fourth plank were referred to the resolutions committee.

Horatio Seymour was recommended by the committee on permanent organization as the convention president, and escorted to the chair. He was accompanied to the podium by "a grand chorus of applause," the hall darkening under a flourish of hats and handkerchiefs. For several minutes the shouts were deafening.

Seymour's speech was long and appropriately insulting to the Republicans. "This administration," he said, "cannot now save this Union if it would." But if it can't, he said, then we can. "There are no hindrances in our pathways to Union and to peace," he insisted. "We demand no conditions for the restoration of our Union; we are shackled with no hates, no prejudices, no passions. We wish for fraternal relationship with the people of the South. We demand for them what we demand for ourselves—the full recognition of the rights of States. We mean that every star on our nation's banner shall shine with an equal lustre."[39]

When he had finished, Seymour asked if the resolutions committee was ready to report.

The committee had met at the Sherman House until after one o'clock in the morning. Vallandigham had made a bid to become chairman of the committee, but had lost to James Guthrie of Kentucky by a twelve-to-eight vote. Guthrie was a distinguished railroad promoter and former secretary of the treasury under President Franklin Pierce. He was tall, huge-limbed, white-haired, and seventy years old. He had a high forehead, his complexion was florid, and his voice was well modulated. Brooks observed that he spoke clearly, but had an awkward way of gesticulating with his whole body, "as though he had learned to speak in a boat." He had the general appearance of a well-fed, well-groomed Kentucky gentleman of the old school.[40]

Now he was lumbering to the podium to tell the convention that the committee on resolutions wasn't yet ready. John B. Weller of California, who chaired the subcommittee that had been named to hammer out the details of the platform, said he was satisfied the work could be finished by four o'clock that afternoon. Vallandigham, who was also on the subcommittee, doubted it could be ready that soon. But Weller and Guthrie thought it could, and the convention adjourned to await the committee's continued deliberations. Guthrie asked the members of the committee to follow him and, with Vallandigham at his side, led the way to a room off the convention floor.

Most of the resolutions were routine and easily crafted. The snag was over the second plank, and it was dynamite. Framed by Vallandigham, it said that the Lincoln administration had failed to restore the Union by "the experiment of war," and that "justice, humanity, liberty, and public welfare" required "immediate efforts . . . for a cessation of hostilities, with a view to an ultimate convention of the States." Called the "war failure" plank, it was a watered-down version of Vallandigham's often-voiced peace-compromise-reunion views. Throughout the morning and afternoon he pushed for it in the subcommittee, and finally rammed it through the full committee.[41]

When the convention reconvened at four o'clock, the committee was ready with a strikingly short six-plank platform. William A. Wallace of Pennsylvania, the committee's secretary, began reading it, plank by plank. It said that the party would adhere to the Union in the future as in the past, with unswerving fidelity; that the war had been a failure (Vallandigham's plank); that direct interference in state elections must be resisted; that Union, state, and individual rights must remain unimpaired; that administration disregard of Union soldiers in Southern prisons was to be condemned; and that the nation's soldiers and sailors had the Democratic party's full sympathy and if the party was restored to power they would get the care, protection, and regard they had so nobly earned.[42]

As the war-failure resolution was being read, it was drowned out halfway through by cheers. When order was restored, the resolution was read again and listened to this time all the way through in silence. When the reading was finished, many in the audience burst into wild cheering, which died away and was renewed a half dozen times before the third resolution could be read.

Not all were cheering, however. As the controversial resolution was read, Noah Brooks watched the faces of two key war Democrats. He saw Sunset Cox sitting with his hands clasped in his lap, his head drooping, "a picture of despair." August Belmont also "looked profoundly sad."[43] They saw immediately that Vallandigham had won in the committee and there was probably hell to pay if the resolution was passed. Belmont had seen it coming. He had earlier written that "the Vallandigham spirit is rampant & his being placed on the Comm[ittee] of Resolutions will give trouble."[44]

But the momentum was irresistible, and the war Democrats, who might yet have defeated the plank on the floor, were so intent on nominating McClellan that they considered the platform of secondary importance. The resolutions were adopted without debate. It was an outcome as harmonious as the divided Democrats could produce. When the convention realized it had passed this rough water with scarcely a ripple of dissent, it broke into wild, relieved cheering.[45]

Evening was falling when R. Bruce Petriken of Pennsylvania said, "I now move you, Mr. President, that we now proceed to nominate a candidate for President of the United States."[46]

This was the moment Sunset Cox had been waiting for. The night before the convention he had visited delegation after delegation, cajoling members on McClellan's behalf. He had endured calumny on the floor: "Get down, you War Democrat!" had been yelled at him more than once.[47]

After John P. Stockton of New Jersey nominated McClellan, Cox seconded it. He had told John Hay that it would all come down to this. "Mr. President," Cox began, "it is said that seven cities claimed the dead Homer." Putting as much into his description of McClellan as he would into a sunset, Cox continued: "Connecticut claims the ancestry of McClellan; Pennsylvania is his birth place; New York has associations with him by many endearing relations; Illinois has loved him, for he has lived among the people of Illinois; and Ohio, I trust, will give him its support, if he be nominated; and the United States of America will claim him as a resident for four years . . . in the District of Columbia, as President of the United States." And with that Cox, for a change, was rewarded with prolonged cheering.[48]

A handful of other names followed McClellan's into nomination, including those of ex-president Pierce and the two Seymours—Thomas, the ardent Connecticut copperhead, and Horatio, who still seemed to be blowing hot and cold.

Then Benjamin Harris, the Maryland congressman and peace Democrat, rose to second the nomination of Thomas Seymour, and, as he had so often done in the House of Representatives, began to outrage his audience. Only mentioning Seymour in passing, he did an abrupt turn and lit full-bore into McClellan.

"Admit the fact that all our liberties and rights have been destroyed," Harris told the convention, "and I ask you, in the name of common sense, in the name of justice, in the name of honor, will you reward the man who struck the first blow?"

Two delegates immediately leaped to their feet with points of order. Horatio Seymour, in the name of freedom of speech, overruled them.

Harris continued, "One of the men whom you have nominated is a tyrant." A mix of hisses and cheers greeted this news.

"General McClellan was the very first man who inaugurated the system of usurping State Rights," Harris said. This statement was followed by an uproar. "Maryland," Harris continued after order was restored, "has been cruelly trampled upon by this man, and I cannot consent, as a delegate from that State, to allow his nomination to go unopposed. . . . We shall never, never consent that the State of Maryland shall be so dishonored."

There was another point of order and another ruling from the chair in favor of freedom of speech. Harris read a letter McClellan had written on September 12, 1861, as commander of the Army of the Potomac. The letter not only sanctioned the breakup of a meeting of the Maryland legislature and its wholesale arrest, but said further that care should be taken to let none escape. As Harris continued reading, three cheers were called up for McClellan.

But Harris wouldn't shut up. "All the charges you can make against Abraham Lincoln and against Benjamin Butler," he said, "I can make and sustain against this man, George B. McClellan."

The convention erupted in a storm of hisses and cheers and paralyzing confusion. But Harris wasn't finished. He had another letter, which he began to read. In it, Lincoln had ordered habeas corpus suspended in Maryland just before the November state elections in 1861,

on the plea of military necessity. The order had been carried out by
McClellan.

Harris went on to mixed cheers and cries of "No, no," to say that
besides all this, "as a military man, he has been defeated everywhere."
He was, Harris said, nothing more than Lincoln's "assassin of States'
rights."

"You ask me," he continued, "to go home to Maryland—bound and
persecuted Maryland, which has suffered every injury since the tyrant
put his iron heel upon it—you ask me to return there, and, going forward to the polls, vote for George B. McClellan, the very man who
destroyed her liberties. You ask me to go home and see my friends in
the Maryland Legislature—men who were put in prison, whose property was destroyed, and whose families were left beggars upon the
world, and by the orders of this man; and yet, remembering their
imprisonment and suffering, I am asked to walk up to the polls and
vote for him. I cannot do it. I never will do it."

That tore it. The hall erupted in loud cheers, indignant hisses, and
much chaos and fist-clenching. Another point of order, by Charles W.
Carrigan of Pennsylvania, that Harris was "not a fit member of this
convention," was hurled into the uproar. "Any man who publicly
declares . . . that he will not vote for its nominee," Carrigan shouted, is
not fit to be a member of it.

With this point of order Seymour finally agreed, and Harris, having
brought utter confusion with the falling night, stepped down, saying, "I
am free to say that I will not do it."[49]

Great excitement shook the hall. Delegates sprang to their feet and
glared menacingly at Harris as he made his way back to his seat, some
shouting, "Put him out!" "Kick him out!" Someone nearby shouted,
"You're a d——d traitor!" Hearing that, Harris turned on the nearest
delegate, a New Yorker, knocking him sprawling. For a brief moment
there was a general uproar and riotous confusion.[50]

Joseph R. Underwood of Kentucky was now on his feet, attempting
"to pour a little oil upon the troubled waters," pleading for "harmony—harmony in our councils, harmony in our actions, harmony in
everything we do."[51]

But rebuttal and counter-rebuttal were now ricocheting about the
hall. It would be some time before Underwood saw harmony again, in
any guise.

Soon a delegate seized the floor whom many stopped shouting long
enough to listen to. George W. Morgan of Ohio was a longtime per-

sonal friend and former comrade-in-arms of McClellan. They had known one another since both were cadets at West Point. "If there be one man beneath the heavens who is not a tyrant," Morgan testified, "that man is George B. McClellan." Morgan argued that the Maryland legislature had clearly been in cahoots with the rebels and had been about to pass an ordinance of secession followed by an invasion of Maryland by the Confederate army when McClellan ordered it arrested. Had McClellan acted other than he did, Morgan said, he would have himself been guilty of treason. As for the charge of interfering with the election, that was a case of acting to protect the rights of citizens of the state to vote, against threatened interference and intimidation. Several Marylanders leaped to their feet to denounce Morgan and deny that their legislature had ever been in league with the rebel army to give the state over to the Confederacy. McClellan, one Marylander argued, had acted on the word of a false witness giving false testimony.[52]

At this point, in the gathering twilight, Edson B. Olds, of Ohio, broke into the argument and moved that the convention adjourn until the next morning at ten o'clock. It wasn't that Olds was distressed by the inharmony. It was simply getting dark— too dark to see. "I wish to state to the gentlemen of the convention," Olds said, "that in fifteen minutes it will be entirely dark, and there is no way to light this building."[53]

Who needs light? His motion was voted down.

In the semidarkness, Alexander Long of Ohio, another copperhead congressman who had been censured by the House, picked up where Harris had left off. Long, whom Nicolay and Hay would later describe as "a furious advocate of peace," did not think the peace plank passed earlier was peaceful enough. He had tried to get it replaced with something more plain and unequivocal, something that demanded peace in unvarnished terms. He had been ruled out of order.[54]

Now he was on his feet again, stoking the anti-McClellan flames ignited by Harris. "What has been the burden of our complaint against Mr. Lincoln and his administration?" Long demanded. "He has abridged the freedom of speech, he has arbitrarily arrested citizens and confined them in bastilles, and he has interfered with the freedom of elections. What have you proposed in these resolutions? You have . . . vindicated the freedom of speech, you have condemned arbitrary arrests and denounced interference with the freedom of elections; and yet you propose in George B. McClellan to place upon that platform one who has gone farther in all three of these measures than Abraham Lincoln himself. George B. McClellan has not contented himself with the arrest of a citizen here and there and incarcerating him in a bastille, but has arrested an entire Legislature. . . ."

Following another point of order, Long wound it up: "He is the worst man you could put upon the ticket having the name of democrat. . . . In God's name do not place upon [your platform] a man who is pledged in every act against which your platform declares." Carrigan of Pennsylvania was instantly on his feet to read a sampling of McClellan's past statements and orders refuting Long's argument.[55]

George Fries of Ohio, peering though the darkness, now rose to take up Edson Olds's crusade. "I move that we adjourn til tomorrow morning at ten o'clock," Fries said.

He was also ruled out of order.

But Fries knew darkness when he saw it, and was not to be denied. "I would ask," he persisted, "if it is the expectation of the members of this convention that we shall be able to conclude our proceedings tonight?"

Voices shouting yes and no answered him.

"I ask the gentlemen who say 'yes,'" Fries said, "what preparation has been made to light this room. . . . I for one, now state, that I do not propose to sit here in the dark."

Seymour, at the podium, could scarcely make out in the dim light who was speaking, but whoever he was, he agreed with him. "I would call the attention of the gentlemen of the Convention to the fact that it is utterly impossible to transact business in this confusion," Seymour said. George Bigler, also unable to see anything, made a motion to adjourn, and this time it passed. The main event of the convention had been called on account of darkness.[56]

Chicago that night, however, was well lit and wild with brass bands and cheering Democrats who visited the various hotels demanding speeches from prominent delegates. For at least the third night in a row there was little sleeping in the hotel rooms in Chicago. The main business of the convention was still unfinished. There were more important things to do than sleep.[57]

The next morning the delegates came ready to vote. The wait had been long enough. They could do nothing to shorten the Reverend L. J. Halsey's benediction, for the Almighty had to be honored. Nor could they stop Charles A. Wickliffe of Kentucky from introducing a curious motion that the convention, when it did finish its work that day, not adjourn *sine die,* but stay organized and ready to meet again pending any unusual future developments. The motion was referred to the resolutions committee. The reading of the minutes from the day before was swept aside—many there had heard all they wanted to about yesterday's session—and the convention moved immediately to a roll-call vote on the nominations for president.

The two-thirds rule had prevailed, but after the first ballot George McClellan had 174 votes—more than the 151 needed to nominate. It was a *fait accompli*. The anti-McClellan delegations began falling into line. Horatio Seymour pulled his name out once and for all, and soon McClellan had 202 and a half votes. It wasn't unanimous, but it was much more than enough.

The Wigwam erupted. Shout after shout went up. A cannon outside on the lake shore boomed. Music inside swelled, and for the next fifteen minutes men behaved "like bedlamites." Delegates mounted chairs. Women in the galleries waved their handkerchiefs. A wounded soldier who had found his way into the auditorium tied his handkerchief to a crutch and waved it as tears of joy rolled down his face. As the tumult began to subside, a large banner was carried to the front behind the president's chair, and elevated amid a new outburst of wild cheering. The banner read, "McClellan, Our Country's Hope and Pride," with a heroic quote from the nominee himself emblazoned there with it: "If I cannot have the command of even my own men, all I ask is to be permitted to share their fate on the field of battle." The band saluted the banner with "Hail to the Chief," and a third wave of enthusiasm swept the hall.[58]

Clement Vallandigham stepped to the podium, and there was cheering for him. He moved that the nomination be made unanimous, and a string of other peace men who had opposed McClellan followed him to second the motion. They had wished it otherwise, but they had now to bow to the inevitable. In a series of long speeches, the convention began to unite.[59]

With his man safely nominated, Sunset Cox stepped forward to introduce a resolution to proceed to nominate a running mate. Ohio nominated its son, Representative George H. Pendleton. A clutch of other names were put in nomination, including Kentucky's James Guthrie.

Guthrie was August Belmont's choice. Still smarting from the Vallandigham plank in the platform, Belmont had been leading a fight for another war Democrat to team with McClellan. The idea of George Pendleton chilled his blood nearly as much as the peace plank did. Pendleton was a rampant copperhead. Noah Brooks considered him a champion of lightweights, "who tries to ride a warhorse as well as a peace donkey." Pendleton was about forty years old, of medium size and light complexion. He was, Brooks thought, querulous, snarling, and meddling. Belmont viewed him as a disaster who had labored hard and long to obstruct and discourage the Union war effort. Only a few months before, he had opposed a congressional resolution "that it is the political, civil, moral, and sacred duty of the people to meet the rebellion, fight it, crush it, and forever destroy it." The idea of him on the ticket with McClellan was a nightmare.[60]

On the first ballot, Guthrie led Pendleton by ten votes. But the outcome had been sealed and was written in the stars. Illinois switched to Pendleton. Belmont's own New York delegation followed, then Pennsylvania. Kentucky, at Guthrie's urging, switched. Missouri followed. The remaining states were called and each fell in line for Pendleton. It was unanimous.

It was left now only to tidy things up, go home, and gird for the campaign and probable victory in November. But there was still one little hitch: Wickliffe's motion not to adjourn *sine die,* but to keep the door and the options open. It had been accepted.

Wickliffe, a former governor and congressman from Kentucky, had been around a long time—over sixty years. He was by now crippled with chronic rheumatism, and hobbled about on a crutch with a crabbed disposition to match. He was white-haired, large-framed, and a coiling copperhead. The newspapers occasionally called him a secessionist. He had made more than one disrupting "pint of order" on the House floor in his time, and was commonly known in Washington as "Old Kentucky."[61]

Nobody in the convention was in doubt what Wickliffe's motion was all about. It had been forced on the convention by the peace men. A friend wrote McClellan later, explaining it: "Mr. Wickliffe's resolution to keep the convention in continuous session was only done in the expectation that *you would not accept that platform* and this was the only method, that the people could be driven from their enthusiasm for you, viz, to kill you and then renominate one of the Seymours."[62]

The convention, therefore, would live on in dormant suspension. There was a motion to adjourn for now, subject to the call of the national committee. Nine cheers for McClellan were enthusiastically called for and given, and it was over.

Harmony was on the surface, but trouble doubtless lay just below. As the delegates were filing out, Brooks heard one of them, a peace man from Indiana, mumble that the nominee for president was a nobody and the candidate for vice president was a "putty head."[63]

Chicago that night was drunk with political excitement, ablaze with celebration. Fireworks lit the sky. The streets teemed with people. Torchlight parades and speechmaking were everywhere.[64]

Gideon Welles had watched it all skeptically from Washington. He figured that the Democrats had likely shot themselves in the foot with their "suicidal resolutions."[65]

He noted in his diary, in the days after the convention adjourned, that "guns are fired, public meetings held, speeches made with dramatic effect, but I doubt if the actors succeed even in deceiving themselves. . . . I think the President will be reelected, and I shall be surprised if he does not have a large majority."

Welles pronounced the Chicago platform "unpatriotic, almost treasonable to the Union. . . . Those who met at Chicago prefer hostility to Lincoln rather than to Davis." This, he wrote, "is the demon of party— the days of its worst form—a terrible spirit, which in its excess leads men to rejoice in the calamities of their country and to mourn its triumphs. Strange, and wayward, and unaccountable are men."[66]

Welles also wrote in his diary that "there is fatuity in nominating a general and warrior in time of war on a peace platform."[67] Many would agree with that, and there were signs, as the Democrats began streaming out of Chicago for home, that the outcome had probably revitalized the feuding Republicans. "I am armed cap-a-pie [head to foot] for the conflict," one Republican said.[68]

Count Gurowski reacted with his accustomed disgust. McClellan, he wrote in his diary, "is taken up by the politicians as glue to catch flies, but he may prove not even good for that."[69]

Gurowski's archenemies in the Confederacy had awaited the convention and its outcome with apprehension and hope. On the day it convened, Alexander Stephens wrote, "This is Monday—the great day in Chicago. I feel a deep interest as well as anxiety to know what shall be done there. Very great events and results depend upon it."[70]

When it was done, the rebels were as confused as everybody else. "Are we to take [McClellan] for a peace candidate or a reconstruction war Democrat[?]" the *Augusta Constitutionalist* asked. After reviewing

McClellan's record on the war, the *Richmond Dispatch* editorialized, "How, then, can he be considered any better for our purposes than Lincoln himself . . . we are unable to see."[71]

So it had all been just as Lincoln predicted. His opponent was a war Democrat riding into the campaign on a peace horse. The war Democrats had gotten the candidate they wanted. But the peace Democrats had gotten their principle into the platform, and McClellan would have to run on that.

Or would he?

22

CLEARING THE TRACK

❧

THREE "STUMP SPEECHES," PERHAPS THE THREE MOST ELOQUENT
of the campaign, were delivered early in the canvass, in August
and September, by three nonpoliticians.

Union Admiral David Glasgow Farragut delivered the first of these
in early August.

The North called Farragut "the brave old Salamander," because he
took so well to the water, won victories so brashly, seemed able to live
in fire, and was so old—sixty-three. He had conquered Confederate
New Orleans with his fleet in a sheet of flame and fire in 1862, and had
long had Mobile in his sights as another rebel port in urgent need of
annexation.

On August 4 he wrote his wife: "I am going into Mobile Bay in the
morning if God is my leader as I hope he is. . . ."[1] The next day, true to
his word, he steamed toward the entrance to the bay on the deck of his
flagship, the *Hartford*. His fleet of eighteen warships, including four ironclad monitors, passed brazenly under the powerful guns of Fort Morgan
and down the narrow alleyway into the bay's bristling field of crude floating mines, attached by lines to the harbor bottom and called torpedoes.

In one cannon-rocked, smoke-veiled morning, Farragut wrenched
Mobile Bay from Confederate hands. As his flagship sailed past Fort
Morgan through the narrow channel laced with mines, Farragut lashed
himself to the port rigging of his flagship and is reported to have
shouted, "Damn the torpedoes! Four bells . . . full speed!"[2]

Farragut's feat was a burst of light in the bleakest of all months for
Abraham Lincoln. It didn't in itself turn the war around or assure victory. But it was something.

*   *   *

Maj. Gen. William Tecumseh Sherman produced the second strong political statement a month later. Early in the war, Sherman had had a nervous breakdown. The idea of the war and his role in it had been more than his sensitive, temperamental psyche could stand. Sherman's friends called him Cump, but the press then had called him crazy. By 1864 he had long since gotten hold of himself, had become U. S. Grant's valued lieutenant, and now commanded the Union armies in the West. Through the summer he had been moving relentlessly, if slowly, on Atlanta, the touchstone of the Confederacy in the deep South.

Everybody knew how important Atlanta was, both as a military and a political target. "The real campaign," James Russell Lowell had written in July, "is really in Georgia."[3] It was clear to Sherman as well how all-important Atlanta was to Lincoln's reelection hopes in November. He knew that something dramatic had to happen on the battlefield if the president was to be reelected. He suspected that his conquest of Atlanta might be it.[4]

Sherman's campaign to seize this queen city of the South began when Grant marched into the Wilderness in May. Shortly after Grant began crossing the Rapidan, Sherman began his march from Chattanooga toward Atlanta. In late August, seventeen weeks of constant skirmishing and a hundred miles later, as the Democratic convention was convening in the Wigwam, Sherman was thundering at Atlanta's doors.

On August 25 he began his movement to cut the city off completely from the Confederacy. On the twenty-seventh he had his army in position southwest of Atlanta on the Sandtown Road, ready to push farther south and swing east toward Jonesboro. In Jonesboro he had cut off Gen. John B. Hood's last remaining rail lines into the city. On the thirty-first he ordered Maj. Gen. John Slocum to enter Atlanta if he could.

By then Hood saw how hopeless it all was, and so did the lowest private in his army. "The ordeal is past and . . . Hood is gone under," one of them wrote. "It requires no military man to tell that Atlanta is gone."[5]

The first explosions rocked Atlanta beginning about midnight. Mary Rawson leaped from her bed and rushed to her window to see "a most beautiful spectacle. . . . The heavens were in a perfect glow while the atmosphere seemed full of flaming rockets[.] Crash follows crash and the swift moving locomotives were rent in pieces and the never tiring metallic horse lay powerless while the sparks filled the air with innumerable spangles." This stupendous crashing of exploding locomotives and cars had scarcely ceased when her attention was called in another direction by a bright light which proved to be more of Hood's provisions going up in self-induced demolition.[6]

Another Atlantan, Wallace Reed, described "the infernal din of the exploding shells" that sent "a thrill of alarm through the city." Many believed at first that the Union army was coming in, and that a desperate battle was being waged in the streets. It took five long hours to blow up the seventy carloads of ammunition, Reed later reported. The flames shot up to tremendous heights into the hot, stifling night, and exploding missiles scattered red-hot fragments in every direction. "The very earth," Reed wrote, "trembled as if in the throes of a mighty earthquake. The houses rocked like cradles, and on every hand was heard the shattering of window glass and the fall of plastering and loose bricks. Thousands of people flocked to high places and watched with breathless excitement the volcanic scene on the Georgia Railroad."[7]

"The great struggle is over," the private in Hood's army wrote. "Atlanta is being incinerated."[8] Hood was vacating the city, destroying anything that might be useful to the Yankees as he left.

Sherman was pacing the night away in Jonesboro, twenty-six miles to the south, restless, impatient, and sleepless. He saw nothing, but he heard the muttering thunder. The next morning, September 1, Slocum marched into Atlanta and found it empty of an army, its mayor waiting to surrender the city. Slocum sent word immediately to Sherman and a wire to the War Department in Washington.[9]

Lincoln heard of it for the first time when Slocum's wire was handed to him at about ten-thirty on the night of September 2. On September 4, at about five-thirty in the afternoon, the official word finally came from Sherman himself in a telegram sent nearly thirty-six hours before.

"So Atlanta is ours," Sherman announced, "and fairly won."[10] It made a stunning political statement, the strongest possible rebuttal of the war-failure plank in the just-adopted Democratic platform.

"Union men!" shouted Joseph Medill from his editorial page at the *Chicago Tribune.* "The dark days are over. We see our way out. . . . Thanks be to God! The Republic is safe!"[11] He was speaking for nearly every Union-loving man in the North.

Two weeks later in the Shenandoah Valley, Maj. Gen. Phil Sheridan, only thirty-three years old and a bandy-legged five feet five inches tall— but much taller in the saddle—made the third statement. On September 19 he drove Jubal Early's army out of Winchester. Three days later

he beat him again at Fisher's Hill, pushing him up the valley to New
Market and beyond. No Confederate army would threaten Washington
again through the back door.

Sheridan had been handpicked by Grant to command the Union
Army of the Shenandoah after Early's raid on Washington. His orders
were to rid the valley of Early and all Confederate forces and turn it
into a wasteland.

On the evening of September 19, Sheridan wired Washington, "We
have just sent them whirling through Winchester, and we are after them
to-morrow."[12] It was also a stirring political pronouncement.

These three "stump speeches" from the battlefields had turned the
dismal summer into a sunny autumn for Abraham Lincoln. He wired
Sheridan, "Have just heard of your great victory. God bless you all,
officers and men. Strongly inclined to come up and see you."[13]

If the North was buoyed by these three key military victories by an
admiral and two generals, the South was devastated. The news from
Atlanta was particularly numbing. "We have suffered a great disaster,"
the *Augusta Chronicle & Sentinel* said on September 8. "We cannot conceal from ourselves the magnitude of the loss we have sustained. . . ."
The *Charleston Courier* the next day said, "The prospect of an early
termination of hostilities has suddenly become darkened. The hope of
receiving deliverance from our crushing woes has been abandoned, and
at the beginning of another season we are admonished to prepare to
pass through more months of blood and tears and suffering."[14]

For Mary Chesnut, the diarist in Charleston, it looked worse than
that. She wrote in her diary, "Atlanta gone. Well—that agony is over.
Like David when the child was dead, I will get up from my knees, will
wash my face and comb my hair. No hope. We will try to have no
fear."[15]

For seven days after he was nominated in Chicago, and while Atlanta
was falling, there was only silence from George McClellan.

Suddenly everything Democratic depended on him. The convention
had acted, and he was at that moment a political oddity—a warrior-
general standing on a peace platform. The country clearly knew that
until he spoke, the other shoe hadn't dropped. And George McClellan
was having trouble finding voice.

Nobody else was, though. Letters were pouring in to him on his
mountaintop in Orange, New Jersey, telling him what he must now do,

and they were the voices of Babel. August Belmont, his party chairman, and the other war Democrats knew that McClellan must somehow find a way to undo the platform damage done at Chicago, paper over the division, and make everything right—in short, work a political miracle. Belmont knew it would be a delicate thing. For the sake of unity, McClellan's acceptance letter must appear to repudiate the spirit of the Vallandigham plank without seriously alienating the peace men and the copperheads.[16]

A blizzard of conflicting advice was rolling in. McClellan's friend James Laurence wrote him from Boston on the day he was nominated and said, "Now we must go to work and elect you. I take it for granted that you do not wish to be defeated." Laurence said the first need was "an expression of your sentiments in favor of putting down the rebellion by force of arms, and repudiating all armistices or peace doctrines until the military power of the rebels is crushed." This meant out-and-out renunciation of the war-failure plank. "With the resolutions as they are, without different sentiments from you," Laurence predicted, "your defeat is as certain as that the sun will continue to shine. . . . Give us strong words, General, and we will roll up majorities for you even here at the hub of radicalism."[17]

George Ticknor Curtis, another friend, wrote, "[H]ow bitterly I am disappointed by the want of wisdom manifested at Chicago. Their second resolution looks as if it had been concocted to destroy their candidate." That they should wish McClellan to stand on it astonished Curtis. "Allow me, dear general," urged another friend, "to suggest, that you stand firmly on the noble platform constructed by your own hands, rather than step off on the one constructed for you at Chicago." From a West Point classmate, Brig. Gen. Truman Seymour, came this blunt advice: "Throw these infernal politicians overboard—and come out distinctly and unqualifiedly on the war platform. . . . I believe firmly that you will act rightly—but the world will be in doubt until you do so."[18]

The *New York Evening Post* spoke for many Democrats when it said bluntly, "It is impossible to vote for General McClellan, or any other candidate . . . on that Chicago platform."[19]

Just as blunt came advice, laced with threat, from the party's peace wing. From Vallandigham himself came this: "For Heaven's sake, hear the words of one who has now nothing so much at heart as your success. Do not listen to any of your Eastern friends who in an evil hour, may advise you to *insinuate* even, a little war into your letter of acceptance. . . ." Around the advice was wrapped an unveiled warning: "If anything implying war is presented, two hundred thousand men in the West will withdraw their support & may go further still."[20]

This was the bombardment McClellan was under as he sat down to agonize over a letter of acceptance.

The country waited. The *New York World,* to keep spirits up, ran the headline, "Victory Certain."[21] A grand McClellan ratification meeting was held in New York. One paper reported it with a cascading column of headlines: "A Hundred Thousand Patriots in Convention," "A Sea of Humanity," "Everybody for 'Little Mac,'" "The Tocsin of Doom for the Shoddy Party," "Lincoln's Knell Rung," and "The Beginning of the End." Another headline reported the meeting, "The Most Brilliant Scene Ever Witnessed on Manhattan Island," and called McClellan the "Star of Our Hope." Poetry and song rang from the ratification platforms.[22]

Still the time ticked by and nothing from McClellan. One of his defenders, a cavalry colonel, said, "People think 'Mac' is d——d slow, if he don't eat 1,000 rebels every morning for breakfast."[23] Lincoln, asked what he thought could be causing the delay, said, "Oh, he's intrenching."[24]

By September 6, McClellan was into the sixth draft of his letter. There were signs of tortured wrestling with language scattered everywhere about him on irregular-sized scraps of paper, written on, scratched out, written on again. But now he was reasonably satisfied. That night he wrote his wife, Nelly, "I think I have it now in an admirable shape & am not afraid to go down to posterity on it." He had found thirty-two more letters awaiting him—all but four on the subject and all agreeing in sentiment. "There can be no doubt," he told Nelly, "as to the feeling of the people in this part of the world—they are with me."

To William H. Aspinwall on that same day he wrote of his last draft, "It is true to the country & to myself & in entire consistency with my record. I will either accept on my own terms . . . or I will decline the whole affair."[25]

The letter was finally released to the country at midnight on September 8, addressed to the members of the committee from Chicago who had advised him of his nomination.

"It is unnecessary for me to say to you that the nomination comes to me unsought," it began. McClellan wanted to make that perfectly clear. "The existence of more than one government over the region which once owned our flag," it continued, getting into the meat of the message, "is incompatible with the peace, the power, and the happiness of the people. The preservation of our Union was the sole avowed object for which the war was commenced. It should have been conducted for that object only. . . . The reestablishment of the Union in all its integrity is, and must continue to be, the indispensable condition in any settlement."

Those last were words that Jefferson Davis, with his insistence on independence, would find unacceptable. But within that one indispensable condition McClellan said every resource of statesmanship must be bent to secure peace. "The Union is the one condition of peace—" he reiterated, "we ask no more."

Then he forswore the war-failure plank: "I could not look in the face of my gallant comrades of the army and navy who have survived so many bloody battles, and tell them that their labors and the sacrifices of so many of our slain and wounded brethren had been in vain; that we had abandoned that Union for which we have so often periled our lives."

With that understood, McClellan wrote, "I accept the nomination."[26]

There it was at last, a ringing call for the Union and a repudiation by the candidate of his party's platform—an act virtually unprecedented in American political life.

The reaction to this explosive letter depended on the political orientation of the reader. "Your letter . . . is all that conservative men desire," one jubilant war Democrat wrote McClellan. It "gives us an invulnerable position," said another. "It will do much to retrieve the follies of Chicago," said a third. It "relieves us from the stunning effect of the salient points of the platform," said a fourth.[27]

However, it raised "tall cussing" among the peace men of the party. When Vallandigham heard of it in Ohio, he canceled his speaking tour on behalf of the ticket and refused to give further support.[28]

The Confederates were disgusted. "It effectually destroys the hopes that we had begun to entertain of an early termination of the war," said the Confederate envoy to France, John Slidell, "and renders the success or failure of his [McClellan's] candidature a matter of comparative indifference." "The wolf . . . has rejected the skin of the lamb," said another disappointed rebel.[29]

Whatever he said, McClellan would have disgusted *The New York Times*. "Well, we see at last Gen. McClellan practices his favorite strategy—with bold front he fights shy," Henry Raymond wrote. Raymond pictured McClellan as "calculating, whiffling, mousing, hopping here a little way and there a little way, full of consequence and yet ever trying to hide in his own little shadow; all ambition and no courage, all desire and no decision. . . ."[30]

The peace Democrats began to talk immediately of doing more than canceling speaking engagements. New York congressman Fernando Wood called for the convention to be reconvened "either to remodel the platform to suit the nominee, or nominate a candidate to suit the platform," since it was going to be hard to have it both ways. James Gordon Bennett's advice—not that anybody had asked for it—was for Belmont to call the convention back and turn the copperheads adrift "bag and baggage."[31]

McClellan was pleased and relieved. He wrote Nelly the day after the letter hit the press, "The effect thus far has been electric—the peace men are the only ones who squirm—but all the good men are delighted with it." He told his friend Sunset Cox that "I could not have run on the platform . . . without violating all my antecedents—which I would not do for a thousand Presidencies." Besides, he didn't think he would have had any chance of carrying Pennsylvania and New York on it, two states critical to any hope of victory in November.[32]

On September 19, Patrick O'Reilly wrote to McClellan. O'Reilly was an Irish blacksmith from New York who not only had a way with a fiery furnace, but the gift of song. He pledged to McClellan, "I will leave my anvil and let my forge fire go out, and give voice and heart, with the strength and what talents it has pleased God to bless me with, for the cause of truth, the country, and their standard bearer."[33]

That was more like it. The party might be riding two horses straining in different directions, but there were those now ready and willing to try to shoe them.

As the Democrats were leaving Chicago, Lincoln's party was still having trouble with its own two unruly steeds, and Zachariah Chandler was more than a little worried.

The senator from Michigan was another of those radicals who chafed under Lincoln's plodding policies and reconstruction heresies. But he and the president were on a good personal footing. And as far as Chandler was concerned, Lincoln was far and away the lesser of the two evils. Chandler had never been able to stomach McClellan, whose name he persisted in spelling McLelland, when the general's hand was guiding the Union armies. The thought of McClellan's hand on the national tiller was unacceptable to him.

Even as the Democratic convention was meeting, Chandler was already hard at work at the equivalent of shuttle diplomacy, trying to reknit the separated pieces of the Union Party and put the patchwork firmly behind Lincoln. He believed the track must be cleared, and that it was up to him.

He began with a visit to his friend Ben Wade in Ohio. In Wade's living room, Chandler talked and coaxed. The two agreed that for the radicals to come around, something had to be done about the cabinet and the men in it who were so "obnoxious" to them. This mainly meant Postmaster General Montgomery Blair, the most obnoxious of all.

From Wade, Chandler returned east and went first to see Lincoln to try to persuade him of the logic of getting rid of Blair to appease the radicals and bring them actively into the canvass. Finding some cause for hope there—Lincoln seemed conscious that Blair could not be kept in the cabinet much longer in the face of such strong radical opposition—Chandler next visited Henry Winter Davis to get his pledge of support with Blair gone. He then went to New York to see Charles Frémont, who, Chandler believed, was key to any deal. He must be persuaded to withdraw from the race.[34]

These negotiations were taking time, but Chandler was persisting. On August 27 he wrote his wife in Michigan that he was "more & more of the opinion that the Election of Mr. Lincoln & the salvation of the country may depend upon my mission, whether anything will come of it or not. God knows, I do not. I shall leave no stone unturned to ensure success. . . . If traitors rule this land it is no place for me. . . ."

After nearly a month of shuttling back and forth between Washington and New York, Chandler wrote his wife again on September 18 that he was back in the capital. He hadn't met with Frémont again, but was scheduled to do so on the twenty-first, and then to finish up again with Lincoln.[35]

With Lincoln it was a case of what a difference a day made. The first day of September was one of the bleakest of his presidency. The melancholy of August still hung black in the air. The Democrats, now with candidate, were assailing him, members of his own party were plotting his overthrow, and the war was stalled. But the next day the news came from Atlanta and suddenly the leaden skies lifted.

Lincoln had for some time been making deals behind the scenes and calling up help in critical places. The two errant New York newspapers,

Bennett's *Herald* and Greeley's *Tribune,* had to be brought in line behind his candidacy—if such a thing was possible. He had started with Bennett. In July he sent a confidential feeler to the editor through his friend Abram Wakeman in New York. It was an offer of an unspecified post of dignity in return for his support in the canvass. Bennett, after some moments of silence, said to Wakeman that "it did not amount to much." Wakeman supposed Bennett would expect something more specific, and said so to Lincoln. What Lincoln had in mind was the mission to France. But Bennett wasn't biting. Nothing had come of it—at least not yet. He was as insulting as ever in his editorials.[36]

Lincoln wrote Greeley in August suggesting he come see him. Greeley hadn't come and didn't intend to. But when his friend George G. Hoskins offered to serve as a go-between with the president, Greeley agreed. Hoskins went to Washington and asked to see Lincoln as Greeley's representative. Lincoln told Hoskins he intended, if reelected and reinaugurated, to appoint Greeley postmaster general. It was no secret that Greeley had long coveted a high political position. Hoskins took this electrifying news back to Greeley that evening.

The editor, in his high-key tone, said, "Hoskins, do you believe that lie?"

Hoskins told Greeley that he very much did—Lincoln had pledged it on a vow.

"I don't," snapped Greeley.

"I will stake my life upon it," Hoskins replied.

Greeley fell silent, his eyes fixed on the floor as if in deep thought. After some moments, Hoskins quietly retired, leaving the editor to whatever it was he was thinking.[37]

Whatever might come of all this, Lincoln at least had the lines out.

In late August and early September he was also calling in key help for the hustings. Lincoln was worried in particular about his home state, Illinois. The most potent help he could call in there was John A. "Black Jack" Logan, a war Democrat who happened also to be a corps commander in Sherman's army. Besides being one of the most potent of western politicians and campaigners, Logan was one of the ablest of the political generals. After Atlanta fell, Lincoln asked Logan if he would campaign for him in Illinois.

Many believed the general intended to back McClellan. But Logan's wife, Mary, bet her brother-in-law two mules that her husband would support Lincoln instead. The result of this wager seemed to point up a moral: never bet with a man's wife. When Logan reached Illinois, he decorated Mary's new-won mules in gay streamers of red, white, and blue, and, with them pulling, hit the stump for Lincoln.[38]

By September 22, Zachariah Chandler figured he had an agreement. It at least appeared that way. He had just seen Frémont again and was hurrying down from New York to Washington to see Lincoln one more time.

Whether because of Chandler's deal-making or not, Frémont was about to pull out of the race. He had been under pressure from many others to do so—from his old friend the poet John Greenleaf Whittier, for one. Whittier was ardent for Lincoln's reelection and afraid Frémont's third-party candidacy would fatally split the Union Party vote. He had visited the general in August, pleading with him to stand aside for the common good of the country. Frémont's wife, Jessie, would later say that it was Whittier's appeal that had been the deciding word.[39]

Whether it was or not, on the twenty-first Frémont withdrew his name, shooting a parting arrow as he left. He was withdrawing, he wrote, "not to aid in the triumph of Mr. Lincoln, but to do my part towards preventing the election of the Democratic candidate," who, in his book, stood for the reestablishment of the Union with slavery—a more heinous outcome by far than a Lincoln reelection. But he said he still considered that Lincoln's administration "has been politically, militarily, and financially a failure, and that its necessary continuance is a cause of regret for the country."[40]

When Lincoln read this Parthian volley, he scowled, then hesitated. But it was only a momentary tick. The next day he wrote a note to Montgomery Blair.

Blair had seen it coming for a long time. He had read the sixth plank of the Union Party platform like everybody else. It had said in effect that only those who "cordially endorse the principles proclaimed in these resolutions, and which should characterize the administration of the Government," ought to be in the cabinet.[41] That had meant anybody who was not of the radical belief, and Blair knew it had been meant for him in particular.

Indeed, he had invited what was about to happen. A few days after the convention, to make things easier for Lincoln, he had offered his resignation. Lincoln had refused it. Blair then told him that it would be cheerfully placed at his disposal at any time Lincoln felt the situation demanded it.

For Lincoln in September the situation now demanded it. John Hay put it this way: Blair was a good and true man who had "stood like a brother beside the President always." But violent personal antagonisms and indiscretions—something of a Blair family trait—had done him in. He had made bitter enemies of the radicals, who had pursued him fiercely in turn.[42]

The pressure on Lincoln to be rid of Blair had been intense all through the howling summer. Massachusetts senator Henry Wilson had written Lincoln in early September, "Blair every one hates. Tens of thousands of men will be lost to you or will give a reluctant vote on account of the Blairs." Lincoln's mail was full of such appeals. He could no longer delay in complying with this heavy demand of a party that was now showing signs, however reluctant, of earnest and loyal support in the coming canvass.[43]

The letter arrived on Blair's desk the morning of the twenty-third. "You have generously said to me more than once," it began, "that whenever your resignation could be a relief to me, it was at my disposal. The time has come. You very well know that this proceeds from no dissatisfaction of mine with you personally or officially. Your uniform kindness has been unsurpassed by that of any friend."[44]

Blair replied immediately in like friendship: "I now, therefore, formally tender my resignation. . . . I can not take leave of you without renewing the expressions of my gratitude for the uniform kindness which has marked your course towards, Yours very truly. . . ."[45]

A telegram went out the next day from Lincoln to a close Blair family friend, former Ohio governor William Dennison: "Mr. Blair has resigned, and I appoint you Post-Master General. Come on immediately."[46]

That same day an exhausted Zachariah Chandler wrote his wife in Michigan, "I have succeeded in all that I have undertaken." He told her he had been running "a nightly express" between Washington and New York the past week, but now it was over.[47] An important stretch of track had been cleared.

James Gordon Bennett may have been cross-eyed, but he had seen all this coming. On August 23, when Republican despair was at rock bottom, and even Lincoln was in deepest depression, Bennett had predicted, "The republican leaders . . . may have their personal quarrels, or their shoddy quarrels, or their nigger quarrels, with Old Abe; but he has the whiphand of them, and they will soon be bobbing back into the republican fold, like sheep who have gone astray. . . ."

Whatever they might say now, Bennett prophesied, "we venture to predict that Wade and his tail; and Bryant and his tail; and Greeley and his tail; and Wendell Phillips and his tail; and Weed, Barney, Chase and their tails; and Winter Davis, Raymond, Opdyke and Forney, who have no tails, will all make tracks for Old Abe's plantation, and will soon be found crowing, and blowing, and vowing, and writing, and swearing and stumping the States on his side, declaring that he, and he alone, is the hope of the nation, the bugaboo of Jeff Davis, the first of conservatives, the best of abolitionists, the most honest of politicians, the purest of patriots, the most gullible of mankind, the easiest President to manage, and the person especially predestined and foreordained by Providence to carry on the war, free the niggers, and give all of the faithful a fair share of the spoils. The spectacle will be ridiculous; but it is inevitable."

What were the Republican grumblers to do? Bennett had asked his readers. They couldn't get another candidate with the slightest chance of reelection. They couldn't move Old Abe, who had put his foot down, and had his little political and military plans. They couldn't go for the Chicago ticket, no matter what. "No," he said, "we shall soon see them all skedaddling for the Lincoln train and selling out at the best terms they can. . . . They must sneak back to old Abe, or be left out in the cold. . . ."[48]

It was a remarkable flight of prophecy. And now in September it was all coming true.

The ground had also been shot out from under the radical movement to call a new convention in Cincinnati. One of the mutineers admitted that the fall of Atlanta "will so encourage Lincoln that he cannot be persuaded to withdraw. . . . Upon the whole I am satisfied that our movement will do no good and had better be abandoned, or at least suspended."[49]

Iowa senator James W. Grimes described the change of heart in a letter to Adam Gurowski: "One week before the Chicago convention more than one half of the republicans in the northwest wanted Lincoln defeated; one week after the convention none of them wanted him defeated by McClellan. . . ." Count Gurowski himself said, along the same line, the dilemma "makes Lincoln an anchor of salvation to escape the curse of such a lee shore as McClellan."[50]

Horace Greeley, with his tail, was one of the first to catch the Lincoln train. On August 30 he assured John Nicolay in New York, "I shall fight like a savage in this campaign. I hate McClellan."[51]

On September 6, the day after his friend Hoskins told him what

Lincoln had said about a postmaster generalship, Greeley published an editorial in the *Tribune*. "Choose ye!" it said. "For our part, we have chosen. Better a perpetual dinner of herbs, than the stalled ox. . . . Henceforth we fly the banner of Abraham Lincoln for the next Presidency, choosing that far rather than the Disunion and a quarter of a century of wars, or the Union and political servitude which our opponents would give us. . . . Let it be understood how near we are to the end of the Rebellion, and that no choice is left us now but the instrument put into our hands, and that with that we can and must finish it. . . . Mr. Lincoln has done seven-eighths of the work after his fashion; there must be vigor and virtue enough left in him to do the other fraction. . . . We MUST re-elect him, and, God helping us, we WILL."[52]

By the end of September, Greeley had warmed so to his task that he had even abandoned peace. "An Armistice!" he shouted indignantly from his editorial page. "The idea of one springs from folly or treason."[53]

Blair's resignation sent most of the other Republican radicals rushing for Lincoln's train in Greeley's wake. "*Blair* is out of the *Cabinet*," one of them said. "*Sheridan* has won another victory, and I feel like working in earnest."[54]

Ben Wade was still bitter about the "flunkies" who had failed to support him and Henry Winter Davis and their manifesto.[55] But he also had nowhere else to go, and Chandler's work and Blair's departure had heartened him.

"[Blair] has gone and I thank God for it," he wrote Chandler. "I only wish Seward was with him." He told Chandler he fully expected they could elect Lincoln overwhelmingly, that he had never doubted it. "I only wish we could do as well for a better man. . . . Were it not for the country there would be a poetical justice in his being beaten by that stupid ass McClellan. . . . I can but wish the d——l had Old Abe. But the issue is now made up and we have either got to take him, or Jeff Davis, for McClellan and all who will support him, are meaner traitors than are to be found in the Confederacy."[56]

Wade went on the stump for the Union ticket in Ohio and Pennsylvania, concentrating his heaviest firepower on damning Democrats rather than praising Lincoln.

Salmon Chase still felt wronged and hurt by the circumstances of his resignation and his own failed candidacy, but he was convinced the cause and the general interest of the country would be best promoted by Lincoln's reelection. Saying, "This seems to me the only path of patriotic duty," he hit the hustings, speaking in Indiana, Ohio, and Kentucky, and "I hope, doing good."[57]

Even the fiery girl orator, Anna Dickinson, fell into line. She had been on the stump ever since her triumphant debut in Washington in January, hurling hellfire at both Lincoln and the Democrats. But she was now coming around conditionally. "I shall not work for Abraham Lincoln," she vowed. "I shall work for the salvation of my country's life, . . . for the defeat of this disloyal peace party, that will bring ruin and death if it comes into power."[58] It was easy enough for her to do; her chief hate was not Lincoln, but McClellan and his cohorts, whom she continued calling "traitors, cowards, and ignoramuses."[59]

Radicals such as Anna Dickinson had to swallow hard. There were still diehards among them who hung back before eventually giving in. Henry Winter Davis in late September was still having trouble getting his disgust off sufficiently to make a speech.[60] Wendell Phillips was finding it even harder to swallow. He wrote Elizabeth Cady Stanton that he would "cut off both hands before doing anything to aid Abraham Lincoln's election."[61]

But, one by one, the radicals were flocking back with their tails, as Bennett predicted they would—even Winter Davis. On the Democratic side, even that defector of defectors, Clement Vallandigham, had left his sulking tent and thrown himself into the canvass. The track on both lines was now clear.

Henry Raymond, the new Republican national chairman, whom Lincoln called "my lieutenant general in politics,"[62] was now cranking up the campaign in earnest, organizing the machinery and twisting arms to get the money to keep it running. Raymond had stitched together a potent alliance with the Union Executive Committee, headed by his predecessor, Senator Edwin D. Morgan. Morgan's committee was to attend to the distribution of speakers and documents. At Raymond's other hand was the Union League, which had stepped up to its place in the canvass. Together these big Republican organizations looked to be a powerful triumvirate.

The Democratic convention, with its war-failure plank and the timely military victories by one admiral and two generals, had worked their magic. It now looked to Noah Brooks like an election campaign that would be waged "under very different auspices" from those of but a month before.[63]

However it would be waged, it was about to begin in earnest.

23

STRIKING UP A HALLELUJAH

———

THROUGH MUCH OF THE NORTH, THE DEEP GREENS OF SUMMER still lingered, but there were signs of turning. Individual trees were beginning to show the tints and hues of autumn. There was change in the air.

In New York, that teeming cauldron of excesses, the correspondent of the *Philadelphia Inquirer* was finding folly and extravagance running rampant. He supposed that an unsophisticated stranger witnessing it would scarcely believe that a great war was raging in the land, threatening the existence of the republic. "The opera and the theatres," he wrote, "are all the rage, with balls, parties, soirees, receptions, etc., innumerable."[1]

Also innumerable were the signs of a national election campaign getting under way, the twentieth in the history of the young nation. As Count Adam Gurowski had earlier written in disgust, "The quacking of politicians is audible."[2]

One of those quacking politicians, Henry Raymond, chairman of the Republican National Committee, doubling as the editor of *The New York Times,* wrote in September that the election was about "the most important of all worldly questions . . . the shape and complexion of [our] Government for ages to come."[3]

"A political campaign is before us," he wrote in his newspaper, "of more terrible moment than any military campaign. One of the latter might fail and be retrieved by another. But if this political campaign fails, it is irretrievable. There will be no subsequent opportunity to undo its effects. It would settle the war decisively, fatally, forever. . . . It is a time when more is at stake in ballots than in bullets. . . . The test is on us. The crisis summons. To your tents, O Israel!"[4]

Kirtland, Bronson & Company, manufacturers and jobbers of clothing, intimated in an ad in the *New York World* that it would have Israel
come to its establishment at 45 and 47 Chambers Street instead. There
it was having a special until-after-the-presidential-election sale, retail-
ing its large wholesale stock of suits and single garments at prices fifty
percent less than they could be made to order. But one had to hurry.
The sale would end in November.[5]

There was also a brisk business in campaign biographies. Six of them
were either out or coming out on Lincoln.[6] Two on his opponent were
being hawked in the *World* under the Kirtland, Bronson & Company
ad. *Gen. McClellan and the Conduct of the War* and *Life and Campaigns of Major-General George B. M'Clellan* could be mail-ordered in
clothback for $1.25 and $1.50.[7]

The campaign was picking up momentum daily. Hardly a night
passed now without an immense mass meeting somewhere, bristling
with patriotic political addresses by speakers recruited by either Raymond or August Belmont, the Democratic national chairman.

"Night and day, without cessation," wrote one of Raymond's recruits,
Abram J. Dittenhoefer, "young men like myself, in halls, upon street corners, and from cart-tails, were haranguing, pleading, sermonizing, orat-
ing, arguing, extolling our cause and our candidate, and denouncing our
opponents. A deal of oratory, elocution, rhetoric, declamation, and eloquence was hurled into the troubled air by speakers on both sides."[8]

Both sides were unleashing the great orators of their party, rolling
their heavy cannon into line. One Republican heavyweight hurling political shot from the stump—as he had in 1860—was Carl Schurz, the
expatriate who had quit being a Union general to plead the Lincoln
cause among his fellow Germans. John Hay liked Schurz. He called him
"the eloquent Teuton," and thought he had a certain "vigor and animal
arrogance" that helped him "bully his way through life." Schurz was an
exiled patriot, an orator, a soldier, a philosopher, and played a wicked
piano. "He has every quality of romance and of dramatic picturesque-
ness," Hay said, and he was bringing it all to the stump for Lincoln.[9]

Many other soldiers, from generals to privates, who had influence in
their communities were taking furloughs to enlist in the campaign.
Being "on duty in the canvass," one Lincoln partisan described it.[10]

The stumping was just as frantic on the Democratic side. "The
unnatural situation of four years exclusion from office," one Republican said, "seems to have produced in them a 'sacra fames,' and they are
entering into this contest like a pack of ravenous wolves."[11]

The Democrats held a giant ratification meeting for McClellan at Union Square in New York on September 17 that impressed even the jaded *New York Herald*. It was no ordinary ratification meeting, the *Herald* reporter wrote, but "a demonstration, an exhibition of numerical power, a display of force, strength and enthusiasm such as is rarely seen even in this city—the centre of accumulating wonders and excitements." At stand number three—there were ten stands, all humming at the same time—the crowd listened to a song sung by the composer himself to the tune of "We Are Coming, Father Abraham":

> *We are coming, father Abraham,*
> *Two million strong I'm sure,*
> *To drive you from the White House;*
> *Abe, your acts we can't endure.*[12]

On that same evening there was also a ratification meeting for McClellan at the City Hall in Washington that filled each of the building's three porticos. The *Herald* described it as "the largest ever assembled in Washington in opposition to any administration."[13]

Nor were the Republicans without their concords of like size. On September 22, there was a ratification meeting for Lincoln and Johnson at the Brooklyn Academy of Music. "The crush," the *Herald* reported, "was one of the greatest ever seen in those regions."[14]

The speech-making and stumping was buttressed by an outpouring of political pamphlets unmatched in any campaign before. The country was inundated. And everywhere—riding, standing, marching, stopping—people were asked how they were going to vote. There were random polls on the morning express trains in and out of the cities, and on steamboats in the rivers. Lincoln himself noted the results of a poll on the train from Pittsburgh to Harrisburg on September 13 that gave him 172 votes, McClellan 66, and Frémont 7.[15]

Virtually every regiment in the army, in the field and off, was sounded. Even Union officers in the Confederate prison in Danville, Virginia, were canvassed in a mock election. They went for Lincoln, 276 to 91.[16]

These random polls were showing a decided leaning toward the president. But the Democrats paid them no mind. They were getting their own internal messages—all favorable. In early October, Manton Marble at the *New York World* called a Democratic victory in November "assured."[17] So sanguine about the prospect of victory were the

Democrats that they were already shaping Little Mac's cabinet. The only thing that had been decided definitely was McClellan's insistence that men educated in war on land and sea, not politicians, would head his Navy and War departments.[18]

Hanging on the wall of a tavern on the Erie Railroad was this stirring banner dedicated to the Democratic candidate and to liquor sales:

V   oice of the People.
O   tard Brandy.
T   om and Jerry.
E   xtra Bourbon Whisky.

F   rench Brandy.
O   ld Ale.
R   ye Whisky.

G   in Cocktail.
E   xtra Old Wine.
N   ew Cider.

M   ilk Punch.
A   pple Jack.
C   laret Punch.
C   ognac Brandy.
L   ondon Porter.
E   xtra Old Holland Gin.
L   ager Beer.
L   ondon Brown Stout.
A   mber Ale.
N   ew Ale.

"If the cause can be preserved in alcohol," admitted *The New York Times,* "there is yet hope for it."[19]

But there was one persistent problem. The Democrats were having trouble with issues. Little seemed to be working. And what was catching fire was scorching them.

For a year, Manton Marble had been trying to hang the curse on Lincoln and the Republican party as the worst possible choice for restoring the Union. In October 1863 he accused the president of protracting the war unnecessarily as a strategy for electing a Republican president and keeping his party perpetually in power.[20]

An old preacher who opposed Lincoln's renomination in June had argued then that Lincoln didn't deserve the office because he hadn't crushed the rebellion in three long years. The Lord has not crushed the devil in a much longer time, snorted the Republicans.[21] George T. Strong, a leading New York Republican, read a Gurowski comment along the same line and demanded, "But did [the Count] ever try to gag an infuriated tom-cat? If he ever did, he would do well to remember that he found the job troublesome. . . ."[22]

Now it was autumn, and the North was deep into the campaign, and Marble was still arguing that the Democrats were the true "Union" party, that only the Democrats could make the country whole again, that the real disunion party was Republican. George T. Curtis, a strong McClellan supporter and friend, argued on the stump that there could be no question "that this administration of Mr. Lincoln stands today as a barrier against the reunion of the South and the North." The president, he said, had coupled restoration of peace with the abandonment of slavery and made it impossible. It boiled down to one thing or the other: "If slavery dies, the Union lives; if slavery lives, the Union dies." All was "cast upon this single die." If Lincoln was elected, Marble warned, a war of extermination against the Southern people would be the inevitable result.[23]

McClellan's managers—Belmont, Marble, S. L. M. Barlow, Dean Richmond—were targeting the tyranny of the Lincoln administration, the transgressions against civil liberties, the war weariness of the North. Democratic stump speakers decried the fanatical Republican abolitionism that had hold of the president, that had turned the conflict from a war for the Union into a war against slavery, and that was holding peace at bay. And they were slamming Lincoln personally. Marble called him a "buffoon" who "makes sport by low jests."[24]

There were titanic issues to be argued—reconstruction, emancipation, postwar readjustment—great questions for the ages. But they simply were not getting to the stump. It was not that the Democrats were not trying to bring them there. They were repeatedly throwing down the reconstruction gauntlet, the main issue splitting the Republicans, hoping to sunder the delicate webbing that was holding the radicals and conservatives together for the election campaign.

The Republicans weren't taking the bait. They had simply shelved the issue for the duration of the campaign. Unlike the huge stock of clothing at Kirtland, Bronson & Company, that particular article of dissension wouldn't be offered again until after the election. James G. Blaine, of Maine, explained it this way: "The . . . struggle for the Presidency demanded harmony, and by common consent agitation on the question was abandoned."[25] Besides, it was an intensely complicated and confusing subject difficult to simplify and difficult for the electorate to grasp, and nobody was explaining it clearly.[26]

Instead of being issue-driven, the campaign, as the young Republican stump speaker Abram Dittenhoefer admitted, "soon became one of great acrimony on both sides."[27]

Democrats accused the Republicans of fraud—a conspiracy to substitute Republican ballots for Democratic ones and completely skew the important soldier vote to Lincoln. The Republicans were just as outraged to discover that several thousand dry-goods boxes full of fraudulent ballots for McClellan had been seized. The Democrats insisted that Lincoln intended to control the election by force. The Republicans insisted that 500,000 copperhead Southern sympathizers in the Northwest were conspiring to overturn the government by bloody riots, and burn to the ground all Northern towns that didn't give McClellan sweeping majorities.[28]

Looking at the uproar through his own cocked eyes, James Gordon Bennett at the New York Herald wrote that it had all become a duel of "roorbacks [false or fraudulent stories told for political purposes], frauds, fabrications, delusions, humbugs and general falsehoods." More startling disclosures and wonderful discoveries happen during the two weeks before an election than during all the rest of the long year, Bennett observed. And in this one, "never were roorbacks so tremendous, frauds so plentiful, fabrications so numerous, delusions so popular, humbugs so transparent and falsehoods so generally circulated." The editor marveled that eighteen hundred and sixty-four years of Christianity did not seem to have made the world any better. "Indeed," he said, "we question whether all the ancient politicians put together could equal the politicians of New York city alone in their offenses against the moral law."[29]

Emotions, not issues, were clearly driving the campaign.

In a speech to a packed house at the Cooper Union on September 27, young Abram Dittenhoefer went so far in matching acrimony for acrimony as to call McClellan "the leader of the Confederate forces."[30] This was going way too far, but it was, in truth, the heart of the Republican campaign. Treason had somehow become the only issue that was sticking. It was the mud being flung from Republican platforms every-where, and it was clinging disastrously to the Democrats.

Republicans argued that the Democrats had "the smell of treason on their garments," that they were the party of "Dixie, Davis, and the devil."[31] The pro-Union press asked darkly why the rebellion went uncondemned by the Democrats in their Chicago platform—John Hay called it the "Chicago infamy"—but the administration trying to put it down didn't.[32]

James Russell Lowell, the ardent Lincolnite editor of the *North American Review,* wrote that the Chicago resolutions proposed only one thing: surrender. "Disguise it as you will," he wrote, "flavor it as you will, call it what you will, umble-pie is umble-pie, and nothing else."[33] A popular Republican dig at McClellan was that if he could not take Richmond with his base on Washington, he would never take Washington with his base on Richmond.[34]

Edouard Laboulaye, a not-so-neutral French journalist and politician watching the campaign, tried to put down what he thought it all really amounted to. A vote for Lincoln, he wrote, was a vote to maintain the Union with slavery abolished. A vote for McClellan was a vote to reestablish the Union with slavery intact—"to end a bloody strife and restore peace by replastering at whatever cost the old edifice of the Union, such are the promises of the General." And to uphold slavery, Laboulaye reasoned, was nothing more than the abdication of the North and the triumph of the South. Four years of war under the Democratic scenario would add up to nothing. All the millions spent, all the lives lost, all the blood poured out needlessly "on twenty battle-fields" would be for nothing. "The South," Laboulaye reasoned, "will have insanely violated the Constitution, ruined thousands of homes, after which it will come back into the Union, more invulnerable, more arrogant, and more insolent than ever. For the negroes, no hope; for the poor whites, eter-nal dependence, perpetual debasement; for the rich planters, the intoxi-cation of power and success." To vote for McClellan, Laboulaye concluded, "is to vote for the humiliation of the North, the perpetual upholding of slavery, the severance of the great republic."[35]

For Republicans, this described treason. They tried to make the country believe this also described all Democrats, copperheads and moderates alike, Vallandighams and McClellans alike—traitors all.

Nobody on the Republican side was having better success at this than Oliver P. Morton, the Republican running for reelection as gover-nor of Indiana. Nowhere were the Sons of Liberty more active, and nowhere were they more threatening to the outcome of the election, than in Indiana. In late September, Morton, with his political life at stake, moved against them, arresting several of their leaders on charges of treason and putting them on public trial. He held the trials up constantly before his electorate, hammering over and over on the theme that these traitors were all Democrats, and that all Democrats were therefore traitors.

In mid-October, Joseph Holt, the U.S. judge advocate general, released a searing study of the activities of secret seditious societies in the country, suggesting a hellish conspiracy, implicating men who were for the most part Democrats, and whipping the treason flame ever higher. His report became a powerful Republican campaign document, reprinted by the thousands and distributed from Maine to Missouri.[36]

The perception the Republicans tried to plant in the North was that McClellan was the candidate of the South. It was not a wholly invalid argument. Confederates saw little difference between Lincoln and McClellan. But it was difference enough. "One faction offers the sword alone," the *Richmond Examiner* wrote, speaking of the Republicans; "the other holds out the olive branch and the sword," speaking of the Democrats. Most southerners preferred the olive branch with a sword—at least it offered a chance for a favorable peace—and were therefore for McClellan. Not all Confederates agreed with this. Some preferred Lincoln, hoping his election would trigger that long-awaited, elusive armed uprising in the Northwest. Some feared that McClellan's election might also sow seeds of dissent in the South that would feed a dangerous and unwanted blossoming of pro-Unionism that would kill Southern independence.[37]

For the Democrats in the North, the image of the sword and the olive branch evoked yet another analogy: the albatross. That was what the traitor issue had become for them, for they seemed unable to muster an effective answer to quiet the treason charges. It was very depressing. It dampened the spirit and embittered more than one Democrat against his own kind. John Hay was telling his diary in late September that Dean Richmond, the New York war Democrat, was despondent and saying that his party were half traitors.[38]

But a new word was raising some temperatures in the campaign, and some Democrats saw in it the issue that, despite the leprous effect of the treason label, might yet beat the Republicans. The word was "miscegenation," and it had been coined by two enterprising newsmen.

David Goodman Croly and George Wakeman were two young anti-Lincoln staff members on the *New York World*. Croly, about thirty-four, was its managing editor. Wakeman, a dozen years younger, was a reporter. And in 1863, nearly a year before the presidential campaign opened, they together concocted an idea for an election-year hoax of majestic dimensions.

Croly was an Irishman who had migrated to America as a youngster, apprenticed to a Manhattan silversmith, and become a reporter on the *New York Evening Post,* then head of the city intelligence department of the *Herald*. His wife, Jane Cunningham, was herself a pioneering female journalist who wrote under the pen name Jennie June. Wakeman was from Connecticut. He had come to New York to make his way in the big leagues of journalism, working for a time for the *Ledger* before joining the *World,* and contributing to *Galaxy, Appleton's Journal,* and other periodicals on the side.[39]

Together, writing anonymously, with Croly footing the printing bill, these two Democratic journalists produced a seventy-two-page pamphlet that went on sale on newsstands in New York City just before Christmas 1863. It sold for twenty-five cents a copy, and was titled *Miscegenation: The Theory of the Blending of the Races, Applied to the White Man and the Negro*. The subtitle was crucial, for without that nobody had any idea what the new word meant.

Inside, there was no question what it was driving at. Miscegenation was simply a coupling of the two Latin root words *miscere,* to mix, and *genus,* race. The old word for it was *amalgamation*. This new term coined by the two authors had more snap, and caused more loathing.

"The word is spoken at last," the authors proclaimed. "It is Miscegenation—the blending of the various races of men"—particularly black and white, and it is not only desirable but essential. "If any fact is well established in history," the pamphlet said, "it is that the miscegenetic or mixed races are much superior, mentally, physically, and morally, to those pure or unmixed. . . . All that is needed to make us the finest race on earth is to engraft upon our stock the negro element which providence has placed by our side on this continent. . . . It is clear that no race can long endure without a commingling of its blood with that of other races. The condition of all human progress is miscegenation. . . ."

The pamphlet then got into politics. "It is idle," it said, "to maintain that this present war is not a war for the negro." It was that, and "not simply for his personal rights or his physical freedom—it is a war if you please, of amalgamation, so called—a war looking, as its final fruit, to the blending of the white and black." The authors insisted the war must go on until that "great truth" became public policy, which required that the question of miscegenetic reform be injected front and center into the approaching presidential campaign.

The authors suggested that the first movement toward this blending of the races in this country would be the merger of the Irish and the Negro. Croly, an Irishman himself, knew very well how this suggestion would sit with Irish voters. Nobody in America was more anti-Negro than the Irish.[40]

Croly and Wakeman mailed the pamphlet widely to abolitionist leaders and reformers. From everything it said, all who read it assumed it was a philippic from the pen of a fire-eating abolitionist, quite likely a miscegenationist himself. Nobody suspected it was from the artful pens of two Democratic racists on the staff of the *New York World,* aiming to stir up political trouble. That wouldn't be suspected until after the election, and neither Croly nor Wakeman would ever admit to its authorship. It would take Jennie June, after her husband died late in the century, to put their names to it once and for all.[41]

By the time of the election campaign the new word Croly and Wakeman had coined was in common currency, and curdling a lot of blood. "Lern to spell and pronounce Missenegenegenashun," Petroleum Nasby advised. "It's a good word. . . ."[42] Horace Greeley, not gifted with Nasby's sense of humor, said starchily that it was a more sensibly styled word than *amalgamation,* "tolerably accurate, although a little too long for popular and daily use." He deplored it, because the mere mention of it "fills many minds with an unspeakable wrath."[43]

With a straight face, the *New York World,* where the whole hoax was hatched, described the pamphlet in March as a "piquant oddity," but suggested that it was finding favor in abolitionist quarters.[44] That, of course, was the whole idea—that the principle of miscegenation find favor among abolitionists, be endorsed by leading Republicans, and slop out into the campaign to give the kiss of death to Lincoln's reelection.

Sunset Cox, who had some idea of the pamphlet's origin, had also taken the concept and tried to tie it to the Republicans early in 1864. In a speech on the House floor in February he had said that "the more philosophical and apostolic of the abolition fraternity have fully decided upon the adoption of this amalgamation platform." He said "these theories, which seem so novel to us, have been a part of the gospel of abolition for years." He quoted at length from the Croly-Wakeman pamphlet to show "that there is a doctrine now being advertised and urged by the leading lights of the Abolition party, toward which the Republican party will and must advance." That party, Cox said, is "moving steadily forward to perfect social equality of black and white, and can only end in this detestable doctrine of—Miscegenation!"[45]

The copperhead wing of the Democratic party eagerly embraced the issue, and it became the favorite racist campaign tool. A long, biting anti-Lincoln tract called "The Lincoln Catechism," pounded the subject, raising the specter of wholesale miscegenation under Lincoln.[46] Another copperhead pamphlet claimed that the Republican platform was

> Subjugation.
> Emancipation.
> Confiscation.
> Domination.
> Annihilation.
> Destruction, in order to produce
> Miscegenation![47]

A speaker at a McClellan mass meeting was reported by the *World* as recommending that to such a list ought to be added *polygamy,* so that "a man could have a yellow wife from China, a brown wife from India, a black wife from Africa, and a white wife from his own country, and so have a variegated family and put a sign over the door: 'United Matrimonial Paint Shop.'"[48]

Many Democratic newspapers were also picking up the new word and wielding it as a bludgeon against the Republicans.

The *New York Daily News* warned "that under its new name, a real, completely organized living monster, rears its horrible head in our midst and threatens to devour society itself."[49] James Gordon Bennett at the *Herald* called the Republicans the "miscegenation party."[50] The *World* reported that a "miscegenation ball" had been held at the New York Republican Committee headquarters at Twenty-third Street and Broadway.[51]

But like every other issue the Democrats brought to hand, this one wasn't catching on, either. The party wasn't rallying behind it. The Democratic National Committee itself did not officially push the issue.

The Republicans again didn't rise to the bait. They tended to view the whole idea of miscegenation as preposterous, and ignored it. No leading Republican endorsed it. Joseph Medill at the *Chicago Tribune* hooted at the word, and said miscegenation existed only where slavery existed, which was another good reason to vote Republican, since the Democrats wanted "the Union as it was and the constitution as it is," which meant "nothing more nor less . . . than 'slavery as it is and amalgamation, as it was.' " To most of the electorate, the word was not only too long, but the issue was too remote. Though emotionally loaded, it didn't rank with treason.[52]

The Republican radicals, now in the Lincoln fold and breathing fire from the stump, were trading the Democrats insult for insult. Ben Wade was concentrating his bilious firepower on McClellan personally. In a speech in Ohio he created a sensation by quoting a Union officer suggesting that the reason McClellan hadn't crushed Lee at Antietam when he had the chance was that "that was not in the programme." What was the program? "It was to protect the war til both parties were tired, and settle all difficulties under a Democratic Administration," the officer had said.[53]

Chase was having a good time, almost as good as if he were running himself. Republican newspapers were lionizing him as "the great statesman of the West." One of his speeches in the Concert Hall in Philadelphia in late October drew what the *Philadelphia Inquirer* called the largest crowd ever gathered for an indoor meeting in that city. "Hydraulic pressure," the paper reported, "would not have forced another individual into the vast room."[54]

Even Wendell Phillips, who had vowed to cut off both hands before saying a good word for Lincoln, was trying at least to be reasonably civil. Even less able to stomach McClellan, whom he called a dwarf, Phillips was resigned to seeing Lincoln reelected, after which he vowed he would "agitate, till I bayonet him and his party into justice."[55]

Democrats on the stump continued to be schizophrenic. Many of the most powerful Democratic orators were stumping for the Republicans. Maj. Gen. John A. Logan, home "from the tented field," was working Illinois for Lincoln behind his wife's two mules in his spread-eagle oratorical style. On two days' notice he addressed 3,000 people who slogged through rain and storm to hear him in Carbondale. In Mattoon, in Coles County, he gave another of his "high spirited and soul stirring speeches," to one of the largest open-air audiences ever congregated in that part of the state, and the *Chicago Tribune* reported it. Coles County in Southern Illinois, the *Tribune* was sorry to say, was Democratic country, "alive with snakes of all sorts." Five to six thousand people—men, women, and children, large and small—swarmed into little Mattoon in wagons, on horseback, and on foot to hear Black Jack speak. They brought music and banners and opened the meeting with a rousing version of "Rally 'Round the Flag, Boys," sung by all, and Logan was "cheered to the echo."[56]

D. S. Coddington, another war Democrat slipped from his natural political moorings and stumping for Lincoln, explained in a speech in New York how it was with his kind. "We will treat our party as a loved mistress who has jilted us," he said, "as a favorite gun that will not fire; as a match too damp with Southern tears to light. We will huddle under this Lincoln shed until democracy finds a better roof to shield us from the tempest; until better times and better men shall give us back our party, purified by defeat, and our country, relieved of the sophist and the traitor, walks forth once more among the nations of the earth, a redeemed, invincible and united commonwealth."[57]

On the other end of this schizophrenic split, the peace Democrats, as abnormal a natural fit with McClellan as the war Democrats were with the Republicans, were also huddling under the only shed available. Vallandigham, whom *The New York Times* called the "Great Banished,"[58] was out of his tent stumping without enthusiasm for McClellan. McClellan, for his part, had even less enthusiasm for Vallandigham and his kind. "I intend to destroy any and all pretense for any possible association of my name to the Peace Party," he wrote a friend.[59]

The kind of person McClellan wanted to associate with was Robert C. Winthrop, a distinguished former Massachusetts Whig congressman and senator and protégé of the great Daniel Webster. Winthrop had been speaker of the House when Lincoln was a member in the late 1840s, helped to that lofty post by Lincoln's vote. Now he was on the stump for the Democrats. A speech by him in New London, Connecticut, on October 18 electrified the party, whose Society for the Diffusion of Political Knowledge printed 200,000 copies and rushed it out into the country. The *New York World* called it "the most brilliant and effective speech of the campaign."[60]

Winthrop said in New London that he doubted that the Republicans, so riddled with radicals, were capable of applying "a wise, conciliatory, healing policy—which must follow close upon the track of military triumph in order to render it fruitful."

"Where, where," he asked, "are the men who can turn all this conflict and carnage to account, and render a repetition of it needless?
Where are the men who can save us from the reproach of having shed
all this precious blood in vain, and can originate and pursue a policy
which shall make that blood effective for the healing of the Nation?"

They were not in the Republican party, he said. A new president was
needed "to restore Union and peace to our land . . . to make way for
men, against whom the Southern heart is not so hopelessly inflamed
and embittered. . . ." Beware of men, he said, "who want guarantees
for swift, and universal, and complete emancipation, or they do not
want the nation saved." That was not a policy of unconditional Union-
ism, Winthrop argued, but of conditional disunionism. It was nothing
more than the idea that the war was not to be permitted to cease until
the whole social structure of the South had been reorganized. Besides
being an abhorrent idea, it was "utterly unconstitutional; and as much
in the spirit of rebellion as almost anything which has been attempted
by the Southern States."

The war, Winthrop said, "ought not to be prosecuted another day,
another hour, another instant, for any purpose under the sun, except
the simple restoration of the Union."[61]

McClellan was thrilled with the speech. "The country," he wrote
Winthrop, "owes you its thanks for such a calm dignified & able &
exhaustive exposition of the questions at issue. Would that the whole
contest could be conducted in the spirit with which you approach
it! . . . There is hope for our country so long as such orations can be
delivered and listened to."[62]

Like everybody else, the newspapers and their editor generals had chosen up sides. The pro-Union press was pumping the president—striking
up "a hallelujah for Lincoln," as Count Gurowski had put it.[63]

Raymond at The New York Times was shouting hallelujah louder
than anybody. He predicted a Lincoln victory, and said it would "do
more to demoralize the rebellion, than twenty National victories in
the field." It was, in fact, Raymond's "deliberate conviction" that it
would "take the heart out of the whole concern, and produce its quick
and final collapse." Raymond wanted not just a victory but an
avalanche, "a heavy majority" in both the popular and electoral vote,
to quash all doubt and suck the life out of all resistance. The twenty-
five states voting had among them 233 electoral votes. Raymond would
settle for no less than all but New Jersey and Kentucky, which he not

so cheerfully conceded to McClellan. He wanted a victory "worthy of the cause."[64]

Editors of the major newspapers were as deep in campaigning as they were in editorializing. Raymond's other job was running the Union Party campaign. Manton Marble, while stirring anti-Republican venom in the columns of the *World* by day, was high in McClellan's brain trust masterminding the campaign by night. Horace Greeley was not only an editor but a stump speaker for the Lincoln-Johnson ticket. Marble reported a speech by Greeley in Burlington, Vermont, in early October, in which he "used up two hours time, the patience of his audience, and his own wind."[65]

It was left for James Gordon Bennett at the *Herald* to walk the middle line, insulting both sides equally. He delivered summaries of what was being said. First he summarized the arguments of the Democratic press: with the reelection of Lincoln the country would get an absolute military despotism, another draft, a war of extermination against the South for Negro emancipation, a doubling of the Federal taxes, a collapse of the Federal treasury, a grand financial revulsion, universal bankruptcy, and various other catastrophes. Elect McClellan, on the other hand, and the country would get a peace offering so acceptable to the South that the rebels would instantly throw down their arms and begin to sing and dance for joy; Jeff Davis would immediately open negotiations to restore the Union on the acceptable platform of states' rights; glorious peace and brotherly love would prevail, North and South.

Just as evenhandedly, Bennett then summarized the arguments of the Republican press: with the election of McClellan the country would get rule by copperheads and traitors, a cessation of hostilities, a withdrawal of Union fleets and armies from the rebel states, a surrender to Jeff Davis, a Southern Confederacy, two or three other confederacies, a general breakup of the Union, universal anarchy and the reign of ruffianism and mob law, and repudiation and spoilation the length and breadth of the land. Lincoln's reelection, on the other hand, would "bring down the rebel coon" without firing another shot, the Confederacy would crumble, peace and reunion on the basis of human freedom would speedily follow, greenbacks would then rise above par, and everyone would be rich, virtuous, and happy.

There it was in a nutshell, Bennett said. With McClellan we would be restored to the promised land of the "constitution as it is and the Union as it was"; with Lincoln we would be ushered into the millennium of the Union "as it ought to be." As far as Bennett was concerned, it didn't matter much who won. "While we have no hopes of Paradise regained with this election," he wrote, "we have no fears of the destruction of the country with the success of either Lincoln or McClellan. Each is a failure. . . ." He believed the choice was between two evils, and he didn't believe that the defeat of one or the other would be the ruin of the country.[66]

As usual, Bennett had a better idea. His suggestion: that no matter who won the popular vote, the electors ought to cast their vote for neither Lincoln-Johnson nor McClellan-Pendleton, but for "the two best men in the country." Electors can do this, Bennett argued. It was what the founding fathers had in mind from the beginning—for independent-minded electors to choose from among the wisest and ablest men, no matter who they were. "There is nothing to prevent our recurring to this original intention," Bennett argued. Down with the "worn out humbug of the political convention system and the detestable thimble-rigging of pot-house politicians," he cried. Let the electors follow the dictates of their own better judgment and act wisely instead. So, how about Grant for president and some other such man for vice president?[67]

One had to give Bennett credit. When he settled on a candidate, as he had on Grant months before, he never let go.

The candidate Bennett had settled on was busy trying to wear out Robert E. Lee before Petersburg. Grant very likely believed that with friends like Bennett, who needed enemies? But neither had he been entirely quiet in the canvass. In the middle of August he had written his friend, Congressman Elihu Washburne, a letter saying what he thought.

"The rebels have now in their ranks their last man," he wrote. "The little boys and old men are guarding prisoners, guarding rail-road bridges and forming a good part of their garrisons for intrenched positions. A man lost by them can not be replaced. They have robbed the cradle and the grave equally to get their present force. Besides what they lose in frequent skirmishes and battles they are now loosing [*sic*] from desertions and other causes at least one regiment per day."

Given that deadly drain on their resources, Grant believed, the end was visible if we in the North would only "be true to ourselves." The only Confederate hope now was in a divided North. "I have no doubt," the general wrote, "but the enemy are exceedingly anxious to hold out until after the Presidential election. They have many hopes from its effects. They hope a counter revolution. They hope the election of the peace candidate. In fact, like McCawber [*sic*], the [*sic*] hope *something* to turn up."[68]

Grant's letter could have used a proofreader, but there was no mistaking where he stood. He was strong for Lincoln's reelection. The Republican press loved him for it. When the letter became public in early September they rushed excerpts into print.

Raymond, wearing his Republican campaign hat, and Belmont, his Democratic counterpart, wearing confidence, led their respective party organizations into the clamor. Gurowski called them Lincoln's and McClellan's "first seconds and bottle-holders."[69] Raymond spent a good deal of time marshaling speakers, raising money, and stirring the traitor issue. He had written Edward McPherson, the Republican clerk of the House, in midsummer asking him to put together a campaign document detailing how steadily the Democrats had opposed the war in Congress. "I think it could be made *very* effective," he told McPherson.[70]

Belmont was doing many of the same things and, although it was not his strong suit, also delivering an occasional stump speech. One of his speeches late in the campaign impressed even the generally unimpressible Bennett. "We had not suspected him of any oratorical aspirations," Bennett marveled. "He comes upon us like Horace's clap of thunder from a clear sky. . . . Who would have expected that Mr. Belmont could jingle words as well as dollars and make speeches as well as loans?"[71]

It developed late in the campaign that Belmont could not only jingle words and dollars and make speeches and loans, but he could also make bets. When publicly invited in the newspapers to take up a wager of two to one that Lincoln would be reelected, he replied by offering to bet that if Lincoln were reelected, the war would last through his second term, and that if McClellan were elected, there would be peace and reconstruction.[72]

It seemed the only two men in the campaign doing little and saying nothing were the two presidential candidates themselves. Both Lincoln and McClellan were closemouthed, and had been from the minute the campaign began. Everybody understood. It was generally thought indiscreet for a presidential candidate to make public speeches on his own behalf during the campaign—lest he be betrayed into saying something indiscreet. All the political dirty work and rabbit-punching were being done by others.[73]

That didn't mean that many backers wished it were otherwise. Charles Mason, the Iowa judge managing McClellan's campaign in the nation's capital, implored him to visit Pennsylvania before the critical state and congressional elections there in mid-October. Mason wrote

McClellan on October 3 that his mere presence "at some of the great political meetings which will be held next week would greatly promote their interest. . . ."[74]

"I fully appreciate the importance of carrying that State," McClellan answered, "and I would do everything in my power to aid in securing that result, but I have made up my mind on reflection that it would be better for me not to participate in person in the canvass."[75]

This remoteness from the fray was what McClellan much preferred. He had been trained to generalship, and a general, particularly a general-in-chief, laid out the master strategy of the campaign, but left the fighting to subordinates. That was the duty of a commanding general. It also seemed to him the duty of a presidential candidate. Besides, he simply didn't like associating with politicians. "My own judgment," he wrote William C. Prime of the *Journal of Commerce*, "is that the fewer men I see the better. . . . I can't find any real use in seeing the politicians—rather the contrary."[76] Instead of going to Pennsylvania in October, McClellan and Nelly retreated for a week of quiet, far from the political clamor, at the country home of their friend Joseph W. Alsop in Middletown, Connecticut.

It was with soldiers that McClellan felt most comfortable. And he expected them to vote for him in overwhelming numbers. He was writing many of his fellow officers, old friends who had served under him in the Army of the Potomac, urging their help with the soldier vote. A Union-wide McClellan Legion was formed of veterans to rally the ex-soldiers and men home from the army on furlough and sick leave. Generally the first thing these legions did was to denounce the Chicago platform. J. Henry Liebenau, of the McClellan Legion in New York City, wrote the general that they had repudiated the platform "as an insult to the soldier" and instead embraced "your frank and honest Letter of Acceptance."

McClellan wrote Liebenau, assuring him that "you, and they, may rest satisfied that I remain the same man that I was when I had the honor to command the Army of the Potomac, and that I shall never willingly disappoint their confidence."[77]

McClellan was drawn out into public only three times as the campaign rolled along, the first time early in the canvass when his neighbors in Orange held a large demonstration of support. Crowds from as far away as New York City thronged into the town. Some 10,000 serenaded him, and he responded briefly. Later, in September, he showed himself at a rally in Newark.

He was not seen again publicly for nearly two months, until a giant McClellan meeting in the streets of New York City on November 5, when for two and a half hours he silently reviewed his political army from the balcony of the Fifth Avenue Hotel.

Unlike McClellan, Lincoln was wholly at home with politicians, but publicly he lay as low as his opponent in the campaign, minding the war and avoiding the issues, but pulling wires, throwing levers, and twisting arms quietly behind the scenes—as was his way.

He wrote one supporter who had asked him to make a speech or at least write a statement for a big pro-Union political meeting: "I beg you to pardon me for having concluded that it is not best for me now to write a general letter to a political meeting. First, I believe it is not customary for one holding the office, and being a candidate for re-election, to do so." Besides, where would it stop? Address one, and he would be obliged to address others.[78]

Lincoln was just as happy as McClellan to sit out the campaign publicly, since he believed it was "very difficult to say sensible things."[79] As in 1860, he believed he had already said all that needed saying. He had laid the groundwork and he believed the country understood the stakes and what the election meant. The people knew exactly where he stood and what he intended to do and not do if reelected.[80]

At a serenade in October, Lincoln did take aim at two rumors that had surfaced. One was that if defeated he would, between then and the end of his term, do what he could to ruin the government. The other was that McClellan, if elected, would at once seize control.

"I hope the good people will permit themselves to suffer no uneasiness on either point," Lincoln told the serenaders. "I am struggling to maintain government, not to overthrow it. I am struggling especially to prevent others from overthrowing it. I therefore say, that if I shall live, I shall remain President until the fourth of next March; and that whoever shall be constitutionally elected therefor in November, shall be duly installed as President . . . and that in the interval I shall do my utmost that whoever is to hold the helm for the next voyage, shall start with the best possible chance to save the ship."[81]

Blasting his opponent personally in public was the farthest thing from either candidate's mind. To hear his political friend Alexander McClure from Pennsylvania tell it, Lincoln wouldn't even do it in private. McClure wrote that never in the campaign did he hear Lincoln speak of McClellan in any other way than with the highest personal respect and kindness. He never questioned McClellan's loyalty to the government or the cause. He simply believed that if elected the general would be powerless, despite all his patriotism and loyalty to the Union, to prevent its dissolution.[82]

If Lincoln was lying low on the public stage, talking no issues and making no appeals for public support, he loomed huge behind the curtain. It was his way to row with muffled oars, but row he did—furiously.[83] He had not been a politician for thirty years—one of the shrewdest in the country—for nothing. Unlike McClellan, he had well-honed political instincts. He knew where the political levers were, and there were few he wasn't pulling.

Elihu Washburne said of him, "He is as good a politician as he is a President, and if there was no other way to get those votes he would go round with a carpet-bag and collect them himself."[84] That was not McClellan's way.

Lincoln thrust his hand into the affairs of the Republican speakers' bureau, asking supporters to speak, selecting the ones he thought best suited to this stump or that one. He often told state committees what to do if he felt they needed telling. He didn't hesitate to hire and fire government jobholders if necessary to advance the campaign.[85]

Even promotions in the army appeared to have been, in some cases, contingent on correct party alignment. Secretary of War Stanton was widely viewed as an implacable and merciless enforcer of deviators. Col. John H. Ferry wrote McClellan on October 3 that his commission was revoked after he was seen at the Chicago convention.[86]

Lincoln required a certain degree of support from his party's maverick-minded politicians. They could vote against administration bills, they could call him all the unflattering names they wished, but he expected them to support first his renomination and now his reelection. Those who refused were cut off from patronage and promotion. He had no mercy on open defectors.[87]

In May, after the Pomeroy Circular incident that killed Salmon Chase's presidential aspirations, Senator Pomeroy asked Lincoln for an audience to get some patronage to bestow. The senator complained of being starved out during the last few months in favor of his fellow Kansas senator, the hated Jim Lane. He wanted some of the pie. "He did not get any," John Hay reported in his diary.[88]

Dunning federal employees for political contributions—ten percent or more per paycheck—was a common practice with whatever party was in power, and a big source of Republican campaign funding. Lincoln didn't hesitate to tap it. Henry Raymond, in his capacity as head of the

Union Party campaign, systematically levied war contractors, as well as customs officers and other federal employees. The Union National Committee not only tweaked their paychecks, but put government employees to work distributing pro-Lincoln campaign literature.

"The National Republican Committee have taken full possession of all the Capitol buildings," a Democrat complained, "and the committee rooms of the Senate and House of Representatives are filled with clerks, busy in mailing Lincoln documents all over the loyal States."[89]

Even newspapers were strong-armed—given or denied government advertising according to the warmth of their political support. Lincoln hadn't objected to any paper expressing its preference for the nomination of any Union Party candidate. But the patronage of the government would be given to none that opposed the election of whoever was finally and fairly nominated by the regular Union National Convention—who after June 8 happened to be himself.[90]

Cabinet members all gave willingly to the campaign, as much as five hundred dollars each, except Gideon Welles, who frowned on such activity. "These large individual subscriptions are not in all respects right or proper," Welles huffed into his diary. Nor did he like where the money was likely to go—wasted or absorbed by electioneers, or worse.[91]

Indeed, Welles was a burr under Raymond's saddle. When Raymond came to him to collect a party assessment on paydays from the huge 6,000-man workforce at the Brooklyn Navy Yard, which had a $4-million annual payroll, Welles balked. The whole idea rankled him, and he refused to enforce it. To a great extent, he argued in his diary, money so raised is "misused, misapplied, and perverted and prostituted. A set of harpies and adventurers pocket a large portion of the money extorted." Such fund-raising "would and ought to destroy any party," Welles complained. "No administration could justify and sustain itself that would misuse power and the public means as they propose. Such action would sooner or later destroy the government. Their measures would not stand the test of investigation, and would be condemned by the public judgment. . . . They are not republican but imperial."[92]

Welles had no use for Raymond in the first place, trained as the editor was in the vicious New York school of politics. "Raymond," Welles told his diary, "has in party matters neither honesty nor principle himself, and believes that no one else has. He would compel men to vote, and would buy up leaders. Money and office, not argument and reason, are the means which he would use."[93] Raymond, for his part, was baffled that Welles should bridle at a such a well-established political practice as extorting money from government employees. He tried again and again to win the secretary's cooperation. Failing to do so himself, he sent one agent after another to try his hand. The secretary wouldn't budge.[94] Welles was strong for Lincoln, but the president was going to have to win without his help in this matter.

In early September, just as the campaign was beginning, James Gordon Bennett predicted in the *Herald* that the race would be "one of the toughest in our political history." He argued that Lincoln was already in the saddle, and had "the whip hand of patronage and the spur of power" to help him draw all the speed possible out of his Republican charger. However, Bennett wrote, "the McClellan nag has been only recently bitted, and is not yet, by any means, quite 'bridle wise.'" Bennett wrote, "Now, all this kind of talk as to Mr. Lincoln's alleged 'unpopularity' and the 'public approval' with which Gen. McClellan is regarded must amount, for the present at least, to just about the value of a peck measure of moonshine."[95]

In truth, at that point, there was not yet enough wind in the air to test, no clear signals yet of what was going to happen in this unique election. But some clear road signs loomed. There were to be several state elections between then and November, the first of which would be in Vermont and Maine. They would tell something. And in October three huge states—Pennsylvania, Ohio, and Indiana—with nearly enough electoral votes among them to pick a president, would hold elections for lesser offices. How they turned out would point the direction of the wind.

2 4

THE MONTH OF
SPLENDID AUGURIES

——————

A S THE STATE ELECTIONS IN PENNSYLVANIA, OHIO, AND INDIANA
went, wrote James Gordon Bennett at the *New York Herald,*
"so will the Presidential election go in November."[1] As one
politician explained it, state elections "decided the Presidential election
in 1856 and 1860 and will probably do so again in 1864."[2]

"If [Pennsylvania] goes right in October," a friend nervously wrote
Manton Marble, "all will be right!—but if not, the fence men will
fall over to the Republican side, and the heart of our people will be
gone."[3]

But first, even before Pennsylvania, Ohio, and Indiana, in the first two
weeks in September, Vermont and Maine would vote. John Nicolay and
John Hay, keeping with the wartime motif, put it this way: the Vermont
and Maine elections in September were "the picket firing"; the elections
in Pennsylvania, Ohio, and Indiana in October were the "grand guard
fighting"; and the national election in November was to be the "final
battle all along the line."[4]

The picket firing brought good news to Lincoln. In Vermont on September 6, the Union Party candidate for governor and all of its candidates for Congress were swept into office by a 20,000-vote majority.
The pro-Union margin in the legislature was five to one.

A week later Maine voters went to the polls in a severe northeast
rainstorm that blew all day. That night, James G. Blaine, managing the
Republican campaign in the state, sent two telegrams to Lincoln. The
first was received at 8:40 in the evening and said, "The State Election
today has resulted in a great victory for the Union cause." The Republican governor had been reelected by a large majority with the entire
congressional ticket. The second telegram, received at eleven o'clock,

read, "The Union majority in Maine will reach 20,000. We will give you thirty thousand (30,000) in November."

Lincoln, ever vigilant in the telegraph office, wired back: "On behalf of the Union, thanks to Maine."[5]

The Republican journals were jubilant. They called the outcome in Maine "the day star in the East."[6] Horace Greeley at the *Tribune* called it a "Waterloo defeat" for the Democrats: "Everywhere," he said, "they have been routed, 'Horse, foot and Dragoons.'"[7]

As heartwarming as these New England heralds of November were for the Union Party, they were by no means conclusive. Both Maine and Vermont were Republican strongholds. They had been expected to go that way. The real test was yet to come, in the October states.

Both parties were crying urgently for help in those three big election-day harbingers. Republicans in Indiana were conceived as underdogs, and they were desperate. Republican governor Oliver P. Morton, running for reelection, was full of angst. Not only was the campaign in his state important, he wrote a friend in August, but the contest was going to be severe. To help his cause, he was about to arrest a bevy of Sons of Liberty Democrats and put them on public trial. But that still might not be enough. "If we use all the means within our reach, it is within the power of the Union Party to save the state," he wrote, but the need for outside speakers was urgent. He "must have help on the stump from abroad."[8]

The race in Pennsylvania, considered too close for comfort by both parties, was keeping people awake nights. The choice of a president depended upon the result of the elections in Pennsylvania, a Democratic worker wrote August Belmont. "Unless we carry the state at the Congressional elections in October," he said, "we will meet with a most disastrous repulse in November." He begged for help. "Can you not address prominent Pennsylvanians & urge them to duty?" he implored Belmont. "Can you not send speakers & funds? Can you not send documents? Can you not do something? Sir, if you do not I tell you we are lost. We want organization & enthusiasm and there is none. Sir, you know this to be the most apathetic state in the Union. The invading Confederates could have burned half the towns in the state, before tardy Pennsylvanians would have risen from their lethargy for the defense of their firesides. Nothing short of an earthquake or general deluge would awaken our people to action. . . . The party carrying the state in October will carry it in November. . . . Do something Sir at once. All depends on October."[9]

James Gordon Bennett could tell them how to do it, and he did.

"The great question for the democrats now," he wrote, "is how to carry Pennsylvania. We will kindly answer this question for them. It is a curious philosophical fact that the politicians of Pennsylvania are found in strata, like the coal and the petroleum oil, and they can be got at by the same means, viz: a liberal expenditure of capital." Like coal and petroleum, Bennett explained, they are "for sale in large or small quantities. . . . The campaign literature in vogue there is greenbacks, and the only word the stump speakers need utter is cash."[10]

Bennett even had a word of advice for Belmont: get rid of that copperhead, George Pendleton, on the ticket immediately or all is lost. In early October he advised Belmont to exercise the right to reconvene the still-unadjourned Democratic convention and replace that "bad stick of timber" with an acceptable Union man as McClellan's running mate, or kiss the election good-bye.[11]

As the campaigns in the three states wound down, the common opinion was that Pennsylvania would give a respectable majority for the Union candidates; Ohio would go the same way by a huge margin; and Indiana would tip to the Democrats.[12]

Many Democrats were pessimistic. On October 7, Charles Mason, the Democratic point man in Washington who had tried in vain to persuade McClellan to go to Pennsylvania, began his diary entry as he always did, with the weather report—it was a beautiful day—and then wrote that "the political prospect looks all the while more discouraging." On election day, the eleventh, Mason reported another beautiful day and just as much angst. "I am preparing myself to hear nothing but ill news," he wrote.[13]

Sunset Cox, who was in an uphill fight to keep his congressional seat in Ohio, wrote McClellan on election day, "The battle is over. It is 6 P.M. & the polls are closed. . . . I have made an earnest & honest fight." He said he would now rest for a while and "if the State goes greatly against us, I will—after a respite—go to some state, where I can do some good."[14]

On the evening of the eleventh, Lincoln and John Hay started for the telegraph office at about eight o'clock. They found the building in a state of preparation for a siege. Stanton had locked the doors and taken the keys upstairs. A shivering messenger, pacing to and fro in the moonlight over the withered leaves, took the president and his secretary around by the Navy Department and conducted them into the War Office by a side door.[15]

Inside and down to raisins, Lincoln waited. The first returns came in from Ohio with the welcome news of the election of Rutherford B. Hayes and his Republican colleague from the hard-fought Cincinnati districts. Ohio was doing what it was expected to do. The news coming in from Indiana, however, was surprising—and gratifying: the Republicans were winning that state as well. Hay was more than thankful. He believed the result there would rescue Indiana from sedition and civil war, and probably save Illinois in November. A copperhead governor in Indiana would have been a central rallying point for the "lurking treason" existing there. Hay knew that the loss of the executive governments in those two states, Illinois and Indiana, would be disastrous and paralyzing.[16]

The anxious Lincoln stayed at the telegraph office until after midnight. Pennsylvania was still undecided. As he was leaving to return to the White House, he wired Simon Cameron: How does it stand now? Cameron's answer didn't come in until about nine the next morning. Then he reported that returns were trickling in slowly, but it looked as if the Republicans had picked up four new congressional seats and a comfortable majority in the legislature.[17] The home vote was close. The soldier vote was likely to decide the final outcome.

Lincoln had kept an eye out all evening for news of how the soldiers were voting. And it was coming in nearly unanimous for the Union candidates—about ten to one in the western armies, closer in the eastern. The heaviest soldier opposition had come from the immediate neighborhood, from Carver Army Hospital, which Lincoln and Stanton passed on a regular basis on the way out to the country. It had gone one vote in three against the Republicans. Lincoln turned to Stanton and said wryly, "That's hard on us, Stanton! They know us better than the others."[18]

By next morning it was clear that Ohio had piled up a whopping 50,000-vote majority for the Union Party. The voters there turned the congressional delegation completely around. It had been fourteen Democrats and five Republicans; in the next Congress it would be seventeen Republicans and only two Democrats. Sunset Cox had been voted out of office. The pro-Republican *Ohio State Journal,* who called Cox "this little dodger," offered a requiem: "The sun has verily set upon our friend of the pensive hour. So good night, Mr. Cox."[19]

Indiana continued to surprise everybody. Morton was reelected by 20,000 votes and the Republicans had gained four House seats. The ardent copperhead congressman, Daniel W. Vorhees, who was to Indiana what Vallandigham was to Ohio, had been defeated. The *Indianapolis Journal* was certain the conspiracy trial had added 10,000 votes to the Union Party majority.[20] Both Ohio and Indiana would have solid Republican legislatures.

Pennsylvania was still undecided. It would take nearly the rest of the month before the soldier vote would verify a 13,000-vote Republican majority. Until then both sides would claim victory. On October 19, the *New York Herald* reported that "the organs of both parties keep up their lying about the results." Pennsylvania was not turning out to be a reliable straw in the wind. The state could go either way in November.

The Republican reaction to these three critical state elections was tempered by that uncertainty. Otherwise their immediate reaction was a shout of optimism and joy. John Hay wrote to John Nicolay, who was in Missouri on a mission for Lincoln, that "Indiana is simply glorious. The surprise of this good thing is its chief delight." On the thirteenth, Lincoln wired Governor Morton, "Bravo, for Indiana, and for yourself personally."[21]

Henry Raymond at the *Times* called October 11 with its Union Party victories "an eventful day in the history of this continent. A battle was fought then whose results shall reach further than those of any engagement fought during this war. . . . Tuesday's silent battle of voters has decided the destiny of the Republic." A political analyst who wrote regularly for the *Times* under the name "A Veteran Observer," proclaimed that "the skies look bright. The nation, I think, is saved. Let it be made a certainty on the Ides of November."[22]

Speaking as the Union Party's national chairman, Raymond hailed the "splendid auguries," and said the signs were in the political alignments. "The Union victories of September in Vermont and Maine," he wrote in an official statement, "indicated unmistakably the feelings of New England. New York has never failed to sympathize in political sentiment, with Pennsylvania. Illinois always votes with Indiana, and the overwhelming majority in Ohio renders certain the verdict of the mighty West."[23]

Many Democrats were gloomy. Charles Mason reported another fine day in his diary on October 13 and said the results in Ohio and Indiana were "too much to be overcome in November." The next day he looked up at a full moon and said, "There is scarcely any hope, still we must conduct ourselves as though success was within our reach."[24]

There were many Democrats, however—and Republicans as well—who believed everything was still as up in the air as Mason's moon, that the election in November was yet to be won or lost. Even Mason, at the end of October, was feeling more sanguine. "No one can yet tell the final result," he told his diary.[25]

And some Republicans slipped into a postelection depression. On October 17, Elihu Washburne wrote Lincoln from Galena, Illinois: "It is no use to deceive ourselves about this State. . . . Everything is at sixes and sevens; and no head or tail to anything. There is imminent danger of losing the State." Lincoln, while cautious, wasn't buying into that depth of pessimism. "Stampeded," he wrote on the envelope. Ten days later Washburne was feeling better. "Logan is carrying all before him in Egypt," he wrote Lincoln.[26]

Manton Marble at the *New York World* was keeping the Democratic faith almost singlehandedly. He expected an entirely different outcome in November. For days he continued to call the close vote in Pennsylvania a Democratic victory. And he charged that an outrageous fraud vote had stolen Indiana for the Republicans. But he vowed it would all be made right in November.

"The knell of the Republican party is sounded," he shouted in the *World* on the day after the elections. On the last day of October he was still predicting that it was curtains for Lincoln: "In spite of the most gigantic system of official patronage and of organized corruption which the world has ever seen, the party devoted to the administration of Abraham Lincoln has found itself utterly unable to stem the tide of popular indignation, which is fast sweeping it from power."[27]

James Gordon Bennett was not convinced either party was a certain winner. On the surface it looked good for the Republicans. The Chicago platform was undermining the Democrats disastrously. The tide was evidently setting in the Republican direction. Yet, he believed, it still might be turned. Lincoln had showed softness in Pennsylvania, Ohio, and Indiana; his majorities in those states were down from 1860. As for the alleged frauds, Bennett didn't give them much credence. "Against the genuine votes of the people in a national election," he wrote, "the fraudulent votes put in are but as the bubbles on the surface of a mighty stream."[28]

In the midst of all the stirred-up political dust—the day after the election, on October 12—Chief Justice Roger Taney died. It was time; he was eighty-seven years old and had been twenty-eight years on the bench, appointed by Andrew Jackson. But still it was a perplexing turn of events and a weird piece of timing.

He "went home to his fathers," John Hay wrote in his diary. "The elections carried him off. . . ." Raymond said his dying was "almost like some strange visitation."[29]

The abolitionist radicals were glad to see him go, for he had been the leading justice in the Dred Scott decision in the 1850s, in which the majority of the court had ruled that Congress had no power to limit slavery in the territories. Ben Wade had said in 1863, "I prayed with earnestness for the life of Taney to be prolonged through Buchanan's Administration, and by G—— I'm a little afraid I've overdone the matter."[30] George Strong, the aristocratic New York Republican, wrote in his diary, "The Hon. old Roger B. Taney has earned the gratitude of his country by dying at last. Better late than never."[31]

Speculation began immediately over who Lincoln would appoint in his place. A good deal of the guesswork centered on Salmon P. Chase, a prospect that was likely to cause the ex-treasury secretary, now out on the stump, to campaign ever harder for the president.

Lincoln attended Taney's funeral with Seward, Bates, and Dennison shortly before six o'clock in the morning on October 15. By seven o'clock the body was leaving town—on its way to the railroad station, where a funeral train of two cars would carry it to Frederick, Maryland, for burial.

That done, the nation turned back to the election campaign.

Predictions were now flying everywhere. Many were looking closer at the three October states, noting that among them they accounted for sixty electoral votes, two more than half the number needed to win the presidency, and concluding that the Lincoln-Johnson ticket was certain of election.

Manton Marble was having none of this. He had counted the certain votes, the uncertain ones, the likely ones, and the unlikely ones, and concluded this: certain for McClellan, 126; probable for McClellan, 49; certain for Lincoln, 35; may go to Lincoln, 51. There was no way Lincoln could win. "In all human probability," Marble wrote, "General McClellan will be honestly elected President on the 8th of November next. . . ." He did admit, however, that there was still so large a margin of doubt that Democrats couldn't afford to consider the matter settled.[32]

Marble's pro-Democratic cohort at the *Journal of Commerce*, William C. Prime, was using an entirely different, less optimistic set of figures. He predicted it would be razor-close, but that McClellan would

win. "We are gaining daily in my opinion . . . ," he wrote McClellan
on October 20. "We can't tell what will happen within a fortnight or
three weeks, but the *set* of the tide is now with us." S. L. M. Barlow
agreed with that assessment. "I think the case may be fairly stated to
be this—" he wrote McClellan, "we have an even chance of success."
McClellan wrote him back on October 27, "All the news I hear is *very*
favorable. There is every reason to be most hopeful."[33]

Lincoln was being his own cautious self. On the evening of October
13, two days after the elections in Ohio, Indiana, and Pennsylvania, he
walked over as usual to the telegraph office. Major Eckert and the
cipher operators were all there. The president appeared to them unusually weary and depressed as he sat down to scan the political landscape
and consider the probabilities. After the results of October had been
fully discussed all around, the talk turned to the presidential canvass in
November. After pondering a short while, Lincoln reached for a telegraph blank and began toting up the likely electoral vote.

In the first column he entered the names of eight states he conceded
to McClellan: New York, Pennsylvania, New Jersey, Delaware, Maryland, Missouri, Kentucky, Illinois. They added up to 114. He then
listed the states he expected to carry: all of New England, Michigan,
Wisconsin, Minnesota, Iowa, Oregon, California, Kansas, Indiana,
Ohio, and West Virginia. They added up to 117. Major Eckert added
to the pro-Lincoln list Nevada's three electoral votes. The grand total
was 120. By this rough accounting Lincoln would win the presidency
by a mere six electoral votes. This was well below the comfort zone.[34]

On the same day, Jacob Thompson, the Confederate agent in
Canada, was doing his own arithmetic and throwing in the towel. That
day he wrote Jefferson Davis, "We now look upon the reelection of
Lincoln in November as almost certain."[35]

The largest voting bloc in the canvass, the one that could make the difference and that was being madly courted, was far from the polling
place, would vote absentee, and carried a gun.

In no presidential election in the nation's past had the soldier vote
mattered. It hadn't existed. Always before when a soldier went off to
war he lost his franchise, for the only place a man could legally vote
was at his home polling place. And the tented field was nobody's home
polling place.

When the war came there was no legislation in the country, in any
state, that allowed a soldier or a sailor to vote anywhere outside his

home district. Leave your state and you lost your vote. It wasn't fair, but that was the way it was. Wisconsin and Minnesota were the first states, early in the war, to pass laws to allow their soldiers to vote in the field. Ohio and Vermont followed. Now, as the election approached in 1864, thirteen states allowed voting in the field and would count the votes separately. Four others had laws to permit soldiers to vote from the seat of war by proxy, but their vote would not be counted separately. In five states—Indiana, Illinois, Delaware, New Jersey, and Oregon—the soldiers remained disenfranchised unless they could find a way to get home on election day. But how the soldiers voted could well dictate the outcome.

Legislation to permit soldiers to vote had not been easily won. Until this war nobody had ever thought such a thing as voting in the field would ever be necessary or that it could be legally done. There was also an objection to giving soldiers under control of the military power the right to vote in civil matters. It was feared that their officers would dictate how they voted.

The real problem was politics. It was a partisan thing. Soldier voting bills were uniformly supported by the Republicans and uniformly opposed by the Democrats. No voting bill or constitutional amendment permitting soldiers to vote in the field had yet been passed by a legislature under Democratic control. In part this was because Republicans were for it, and Democrats had to oppose whatever Republicans were for. But an even larger reason was the suspicion that the soldiers would vote Republican. This suspicion had been borne out in October in Ohio, Pennsylvania, and Indiana.[36]

The presidential contest was different, however. The Democratic candidate was George McClellan, one of the most popular generals with his soldiers who had ever put on a uniform. And McClellan, his mind lit by the memory of the overwhelming huzzahs that had greeted his every ride through his army, had no doubt that his men would stand by him in November. He expected to win the soldier vote. Manton Marble at the *New York World* wrote in October that "we are as certain of two-thirds of that vote for General McClellan as that the sun shines."[37]

Charles A. Dana, the assistant secretary of war, had an entirely different impression. He was spending most of his time this fall arranging for soldiers to go home and vote, or for taking ballots in the field. Why would he be doing that if they were just going to vote him and his bosses out of a job? Dana was dealing with a constant stream of telegrams requesting extensions of leave of absence for officers, furloughs for men—sometimes whole regiments—and requests for men on detached service and convalescence to be sent home to vote. "All the power and influence of the War Department . . . ," Dana said, "was employed to secure the re-election of Mr. Lincoln. The political struggle was most intense, and the interest taken in it, both in the White House and in the War Department, was almost painful."[38]

The Democratic concern was not that they couldn't carry the soldier vote, but that they would be cheated out of it. The plan of the Democratic campaign for October had as one of its aims to appoint a committee to confer with Lincoln, Grant, and Sherman and to take every other precaution to keep the soldier vote free from fraud. Charles Mason in Washington called on Stanton in late September to secure his pledge of fairness. Stanton and Lincoln promised that the Democrats would have the same rights as the Republicans. Lincoln's attitude was "that all loyal men may vote, and vote for whom they please."[39]

This didn't necessarily ease the minds of either Democrats or Republicans. Less than two weeks before the election, Marble protested in the *World:* "We charge, and it can be proved, that letters from Democrats here to soldiers in the army, containing McClellan electoral tickets, have been opened, the McClellan tickets taken out and Lincoln tickets put in." Senator Morgan of New York unearthed a Democratic effort to get the principal officers in the army committed to McClellan with the expectation of swaying the soldier vote—changing it if necessary. Even the retired general of the armies, Winfield Scott, was being heavily lobbied. But, although not considered unfriendly to McClellan, he was staying out of it.[40]

Lincoln had an entirely different slant on the political mood of the soldiers than McClellan did. He was good at sensing political tides and preferences, and he believed the soldiers would vote for the Union Party. He was doing all he could to get them in the approximate neighborhood of a ballot box on election day, first in the state elections in October and now in the general election. Since Indiana had no soldier voting law, the two Indianans, Schuyler Colfax and Oliver Morton, both urged the president to get their boys home to vote in the state elections in October. After the fall of Atlanta, Lincoln wrote General Sherman suggesting, but not ordering, him to permit Indiana's soldiers, "or any part of them, [to] go home and vote at the State election," if he could do it without endangering his army. "They need not remain for the Presidential election," Lincoln assured Sherman, "but may return to you at once." Sherman complied, and even the Nineteenth Vermont

Volunteers and the Sixtieth Massachusetts, to their surprise, found themselves voting in the Indiana election.[41]

The day McClellan was nominated in Chicago was the day he seemed to lose traction with his soldiers. Their letters home began showing it. It was not the general, whom they still esteemed, who was turning them off. It was the company he was keeping.

A political cartoon pictured a soldier saying, "I would vote for you General, if you were not tied to a Peace Copperhead." His companion added, "Good bye, 'little Mac'—if thats your company, Uncle Abe gets my vote." No theme in the letters home was more common than this disillusionment with McClellan. And not even his letter forswearing the war-failure plank blunted the feeling.[42]

A colonel in the Army of the Potomac, normally a strong McClellan man, in writing to his wife after the Chicago convention, said, "The nomination of McClellan is not well received in the army, from the fact that they put that abominable traitor, Pendleton, on as Vice President. The ticket has no chance here. McClellan's friends . . . have abandoned him." By early October he was writing her, "I have not come across an officer or a man that will vote for McClellan and Pendleton. Why, we don't touch the Chicago platform!" In mid-October, he reported a vote in his division that had run seven to one in favor of the administration, and in his corps, ten to one. "This has always been considered the Democratic Corps," the colonel wrote. "If this is the way it goes here, dear help the Democrats in the other parts of the Army that McClellan never had anything to do with. . . . He can't win at all."[43]

The main army that McClellan had "never had anything to do with" was in the West. From there one soldier wrote, "There were in the Western Army many McClellan men at the time of his nomination, but since the platform has been read and then to know that the nomination of McClellan was made unanimous on the motion of that Traitor Vallandigham is more than the admirers of little 'Mac' could stand and I can assure that 'Mac' has lost thousands of votes within three weeks." A surgeon in Sherman's army wrote: "I would hide my head with shame sooner than vote for any man nominated under the Chicago banner. Should McClellan be elected, I think that the question of 'Union' is at an end." Another wrote of McClellan that he was "like a verdant spooney [a person who is amorous in a silly, sentimental way] whom old gamesters have inveigled into their snares." He said he couldn't vote for him on either a peace or a war platform.[44]

Yet another of Sherman's soldiers wrote his wife that he was for Lincoln against McClellan, for "we must have the man who dares to say: the Nation must live. We can trust ourselves to no other pilot."[45]

One self-appointed pollster decided to take a survey of the 186th New York as it was marching up Broadway. "Old Abe or Little Mac?" he shouted at four different points along the line. He swore nine voices out of ten answered, "Old Abe"—with a will.[46]

Lincoln is reported to have confided to the reporter Henry Wing, in one of their talks in the dark days of August, "Henry, I would rather be defeated with the soldier vote behind me than to be elected without it." Wing is reported to have said, "You will have it, Mr. Lincoln. You will have it. They'll vote as they shoot."[47]

That probably gratified Lincoln. But perhaps something a German soldier said after the presidential nominations were known would have gratified him just as much. "I goes for Fader Abraham," the soldier said. "Fader Abraham, he likes the soldier-boy. Ven he serves tree years he gives him four hundred tollar, and reenlists him von veteran. Now Fader Abraham, he serve four years. We reenlist him four years more, and make *von veteran of him*."[48]

There was one segment of the fighting man's vote, however, that no Republican was seriously courting in the canvass: the sailors. Many, perhaps most, tars were Irish, and the Irish were overwhelmingly Democratic. Another reason not to stir them up politically had to do with the fact that the administration had stopped issuing the "spirit ration" to sailors in 1862. They had cut off their grog, a very unpolitic thing to do. You don't do that to sailors, particularly if they are Irish. Jack Tar, therefore, was a Democrat and a hopeless case for Republicans.[49]

One final splendid augury came to Lincoln two weeks before the election, and her name was Sojourner Truth.

Sojourner was known in the North as the slave preacher. The celebrated antislavery novelist, Harriet Beecher Stowe, described her as an African prophetess. Born a slave, she was a compelling advocate of equal rights for blacks and women, who saw her mission in life to help set the world "right side up." She was unable to read and write, and her real name was Isabella Van Wagener.[50]

When she was born was a matter of some mystery, for she seemed ageless. She was tall—nearly six feet—and spare and somewhere around seventy in 1864, but indignantly denied the widespread rumor in the army camps, which she visited often, that she had nursed George Washington. She was a beacon in the North. When she showed up at the camps of black regiments, the men would be mustered in a line and she would distribute her bounty—gifts for them that she had solicited by lecturing and singing—with motherly bits of advice. Among her songs, one from her own soul and sung to "John Brown's Body," went in part this way:

> *We are done with hoeing corn;*
> *We are colored Yankee soldiers,*
> *As sure as you are born.*
> *When Massa hears us shouting,*
> *He will think 'tis Gabriel's horn*
> *As we go marching on.*[51]

In the fall of 1864, Sojourner had it in mind to visit the president before the election. She left her home in Battle Creek, Michigan, where she said she had been busy "scouring copperheads" as once she had scoured brass doorknobs.[52]

She reached Washington in late October and found that she was unable on her own to get an appointment to see Lincoln. She enlisted Lucy Coleman, a white Massachusetts-born schoolteacher, who had become an antislavery lecturer, to arrange it for her. They went up together to the White House and were admitted, with a host of others, to one of Lincoln's "beggars' operas."

It was about eight in the morning, and as they waited, listening to the appeals of others to the president, Sojourner was struck that he was showing as much kindness to the colored petitioners as to whites, as if there were no difference. There was one colored woman who was sick and likely to be turned out of her house on account of her inability to pay her rent. Lincoln listened to her with much attention, and spoke to her with kindness. He said he had given so much he could give no more, but told her where to go for help.

When Sojourner's time came, Lucy Coleman said to Lincoln, "This is Sojourner Truth, who has come all the way from Michigan to see you."

Lincoln rose, gave Sojourner his hand, bowed, and said, "I am pleased to see you."

"Mr. President," she began, "when you first took your seat I feared you would be torn to pieces, for I likened you unto Daniel, who was thrown into the lions' den; and if the lions did not tear you into pieces,

I knew that it would be God that had saved you; and I said if He spared me I would see you before the four years expired, and He has done so, and now I am here to see you for myself."

Lincoln congratulated her on having been spared, and she continued, "I appreciate you, for you are the best President who has ever taken the seat."

Lincoln replied, "I expect you have reference to my having emancipated the slaves in my proclamation."

He then named several of his predecessors—among them Washington—and said, "They were all just as good, and would have done just as I have done if the time had come."

Lincoln pointed toward the Potomac and said, "If the people over the river had behaved themselves, I could not have done what I have; but they did not, and I was compelled to do these things."

Sojourner replied, "I thank God that you were the instrument selected by Him and the people to do it."

Lincoln showed her a Bible that had been presented to him on July 4 by the colored people of Baltimore. It was a book of pulpit size, bound in violet-tinted velvet with bands of solid gold. On a gold plate on the left-hand cover was a design representing the president in a cotton field striking the shackles from the wrists of a slave, who held one hand aloft as if invoking blessings on the head of his benefactor. At the benefactor's feet was a scroll on which was written, "Emancipation." On the Bible's other cover, on a similar plate, was the inscription, "To Abraham Lincoln, President of the United States, the friend of Universal Freedom. From the loyal colored people of Baltimore as a token of respect and gratitude."

"This is beautiful indeed," Sojourner told Lincoln; "the colored people have given this to the Head of the Government, and that Government once sanctioned laws that would not permit its people to learn enough to enable them to read this Book. And for what? Let them answer who can."

Sojourner had her own little book, and Lincoln took it and wrote, "For Aunty Sojourner Truth, October 29, 1864," and signed it "A. Lincoln."

As she rose to leave, Lincoln took her hand and said he would be pleased to have her call again. [53]

The time was now at hand. All that was left was to vote.

"The day has come—the day of fate," wrote Henry Raymond at *The*

New York Times. "Before the morning's sun sets, the destinies of this republic, so far as depends on human agency, are to be settled for weal or for woe. . . . We are making this decision not for ourselves simply. We are settling the lot of the generations that shall come after us. If the people err,

> *The child will rue, that is unborn,*
> *The* voting *of this day.*"[54]

Manton Marble at the *New York World* was no less leaden and somber and no less concerned for generations yet unborn. For the first time in the campaign, he and Raymond agreed on something. "Choose for yourselves this day!" Marble shouted editorially, "For with this day's setting sun your irrevocable verdict will have been passed; and with it the weal or woe of yourselves and of your children's children assured through years on years to come."[55]

The day before the election, Maj. Gen. William B. Franklin wrote his old commander and dear friend, George McClellan, saying, "This will not reach you until it has been determined whether Providence intends that our country shall soon begin to prosper again, or whether it must go to a depth which imagination has not yet sounded."[56]

Alexander McClure wrote to Lincoln from Pennsylvania, "The work is as well done as it can be done, & well enough I have no doubt. We shall carry the State by from 5,000 to 10,000 on the home vote, & it may be more, unless all signs are deceptive. We should have had much more, but it is too late for complaint, & we shall have enough. I go home to-morrow greatly encouraged by the conviction that your Election will be by a *decisive* vote, & give you all the moral power necessary for your high & holy trust. . . ."[57]

Noah Brooks wrote that all of Washington was in its "quadrennial hegira"—gone home to vote. Scarcely a government bureau was left in running order, the Army of the Potomac was once more in motion—toward the ballot box—and a drenching rain was falling.[58]

2 5

OYSTERS AT MIDNIGHT

T HE WEATHER WAS HEAVY — ANOTHER DULL, GLOOMY, RAINY DAY
across the North, one of the many the nation had endured in
this nearly four years of war.

"You would never dream," Elizabeth Blair Lee wrote her husband
from Philadelphia, "that anything important was going on here today—
things look as quiet as on any other rainy day."[1]

There was a hush around Washington. The White House was virtually
deserted. It was cabinet meeting day, but only two members attended,
the same two who nearly always came — Bates and Welles. Stanton was
sick with the chills and fever. Seward, Usher, and Dennison had all gone
home to their states to vote. Fessenden was shut up with the New York
financiers.[2]

Everybody else not home voting, it seemed to John Hay, was ashamed
of it and was staying away from the president. Lincoln was in a pensive mood and was thinking about the campaign just ended. "It is a
little singular," he said to his secretary, "that I, who am not a vindictive
man, should have always been before the people for election in canvasses marked for their bitterness."[3]

Lincoln was anxious. Just before the cabinet meeting he said to
Noah Brooks, "I am just enough of a politician to know that there was
not much doubt about the result of the Baltimore convention, but
about this thing I am far from certain; I wish I were certain."[4]

Tad burst into Lincoln's office and hustled his father to the window
to see the soldiers "voting for Lincoln and Johnson." The boy pointed
to the Pennsylvania soldiers quartered on the White House grounds,
who were on the south lawn, voting under the supervision of a com-

mission sent from their state. Lincoln saw Jack, Tad's pet turkey, long since pardoned as Christmas dinner, strutting among the voters.

"What business has the turkey stalking about the polls in that way?" Lincoln asked. "Does he vote?"

Tad said, "No, he's not of age."[5]

And Lincoln laughed.

Thousands of voters who were old enough were defying the weather and streaming to the polls across the North. In New York a heavy fog hung over the city and the harbor—a wet, muggy day. Rain was falling occasionally, and liquor was flowing not at all, banned throughout the city for election day—yet another reason for the Irish to vote Democratic.

In army camps around the North, there was the extraordinary spectacle of soldiers being citizens, the sword sustaining rather than suppressing the ballot box.[6] In the Shenandoah Valley it was like an Indian summer. Wilbur Fisk, a private in the Second Vermont, wrote from there, "Election day, to-day, and warm and foggy at that. . . . Thousands of bits of paper are falling into ballot-boxes today, all over our country. It is a little thing, and can be done very easily, but mighty consequences may hang on the result. It is almost a new thing in the history of the world, when such great results as whether this country shall be governed by one principle, or another in almost deadly hostility to it, can be decided by such simple means. God hasten the day when *all* questions may be decided in the same way, and then war, with its terrible list of horrors, will be remembered as one of the evils buried forever in the grim Past."[7]

Deacon John Phillips, who was 105 years old and had voted for George Washington, was perhaps thinking something of the same thing as his son, Col. Edward Phillips, age seventy-nine, took him to his polling place at the town hall in Sturbridge, Massachusetts. Phillips was the oldest man in Sturbridge, and perhaps the oldest voter in the country. He entered the polling place between two unfurled flags, and all inside rose in his honor. Phillips was a lifelong Democrat of the Jeffersonian school. But when offered two ballots, to take his choice, he said, "I vote for Abraham Lincoln."[8]

At about noon, a telegram arrived in Washington from Maj. Gen. Ben Butler in New York City. "The quietest city ever seen," it said.[9]

Butler was a man who got around. At Fort Monroe on November 1, a week before the election, he had received a telegram from Stanton. "Report at once in person to the Secretary of War," it said. Was he dismissed? Promoted? Reassigned? What? Butler had no idea what it meant. But he ordered his vessel coaled as soon as possible for two days' sailing, and then telegraphed the wire to Grant at City Point.

Grant wired back, ordering him to start immediately for Washington and be guided by orders from there. Still puzzled, Butler arrived in Washington the next morning. Stanton handed him a sheaf of papers and told him to read them. The papers were reports of planned interference in the election in New York, reportedly a far wider, far better organized uprising than the draft riots of the year before. It was feared that the entire vote of the city of New York was to be deposited for McClellan, that Republicans were to be driven from the polls, and that several thousand rebels were in New York to lead the movement.

Stanton's intention was to send Beast Butler to New York with troops to prevent all this happening.

This sort of damage prevention was right up Butler's alley, and everybody knew it. If there was anybody in the country who could thwart such an outrage with iron-handed effect, it was Butler. Just the idea of this scourge of New Orleans being in New York with several thousand troops might be enough to give would-be rioters serious second thoughts.

Ordered to report to Maj. Gen. John Dix, commanding in New York, and assured of five thousand troops and at least two batteries of Napoleon guns to follow, Butler left Washington that night. He saw the problem clearly. He believed the reports of uprising, while alarming, were much exaggerated. But he knew he had to carry this thing off with great delicacy. The challenge was to have his troops ready to put down a riot in the city, and yet not have them seen as an intimidating presence. Indeed they must not actually be in New York.

There was both a political and logistical problem. The political problem was that many of the soldiers being sent to him by Grant for this duty were New Yorkers, and the law said that if they were in New York on election day, their votes, already cast in the field, would be invalid. The logistical problem was where to put them in light of that fact. With his accustomed innovative approach to problems of this sort, Butler ordered up a fleet of ferryboats, anchored them in New Jersey waters, and began putting his arriving New Yorkers in them. On election day, steam was to be kept up in the boilers and cables ready to be slipped at a moment's notice.

On November 5, Butler issued his first general order to his little army. They were there, he told them, to preserve the peace, protect public property, prevent and punish unlawful interference in the election, and to ensure calm and quiet. They were not there to interfere, but "to see to it that there is no interference with the election of any body, unless the civil authorities are overcome with force by bad men."

On the day before the election, Butler wired Stanton that he was ready. All of his troops had arrived, and all dispositions had been made. "All will be quiet here," he promised the secretary.

On election day, Butler had telegraph lines snaking into his headquarters at the Hoffman Hotel from more than sixty points in the city. At each polling place he stationed an officer in plain clothes in command of scouts and detective officers. Any disturbance was to be telegraphed to him immediately. Each officer was also under orders to report hourly on the state of quiet at the polls. Gunboats were discreetly covering Wall Street and the worst sections of the city, and a brigade of infantry was ready to land on the Battery. A revenue cutter was guarding the cable over the North River, and another gunboat was watching the High Bridge on the Harlem River.

The upshot of all this unobtrusive military presence, as the Loyal League committee in New York put it, was an "extraordinary degree of tranquility . . . a tranquility, quietness, and good order unprecedented in our political history."

The only special irregularity that had been reported to Butler, waiting at the Hoffman Hotel, was that August Belmont had lost his vote. George Strong, the New York Republican, knew all about that. Strong had been standing in line for nearly two hours at his polling place, waiting his turn to vote. A little ahead of him in line was Belmont. Strong listened as the Democratic national chairman's vote was challenged on grounds that he had bet on the election. Disenfranchised, the Democratic national chairman stalked off in a rage.

Otherwise, New York was as quiet as the tomb. Butler had wired Washington at noon telling them so.[10]

By evening a raw, drizzling rain was still falling in New York City. After dark, when the polls had closed, the crowds began coming out. They jammed into Printing House Square to read the return bulletins posted by the *Times* and the *Tribune*. They collected before the *Herald* office, blocking the streets in every direction, standing, the paper reported, "in solid phalanx, as compactly and regularly arranged as a regiment in the field, swaying and moving as one immense body."

An enormous crowd of partisans thronged Republican headquarters at Cooper Union, where young Abram Dittenhoefer was giving his last speech of the campaign, often interrupted by the chairman to announce the latest returns. Henry Raymond had directed that the rooms of the Astor House be made ready to be thrown open in celebration when the signs were propitious. The Democrats, expecting the city to go heavily for McClellan, took returns at Tammany Hall. As the evening progressed, one gentleman of an inquiring mind wanted to know what should be done in case McClellan was swindled out of the presidency.[11]

In Philadelphia, Chestnut Street from Third to Broad was filled by nine o'clock in the evening with people flocking to the different political headquarters. National Hall and Concert Hall were filled. Ward parades of both political persuasions, playing music and carrying banners and torches, were on the move. One partisan Republican device carried through the streets read, "We are coming, Father Abraham, with an overwhelming majority." Another said, "Get out of the way for Abe and Andy."[12]

In Washington the night was rainy, steamy, and dark. Lincoln and Hay started to the telegraph office from the White House at about seven o'clock. They splashed through the grounds to the side door, where a soaked and smoking sentinel was standing in his own vapor, his huddled-up frame covered by a rubber cloak.

As Lincoln entered, the cipher operators handed him a dispatch from John W. Forney, the hotly partisan editor of two major Pennsylvania newspapers, claiming a 10,000-vote majority in Philadelphia.

"Forney is a little excitable," Lincoln said.

Another return from Baltimore reported a 15,000-vote majority in that city, 5,000 statewide. Charles Sumner wired from Boston, claiming a 5,000-vote lead. Major Eckert stomped in, muddy and shaking the rain from his cloak. He had taken a tumble crossing the street.

The president sent over the first returns to Mary at the White House, saying, "She is more anxious than I," and went into Stanton's room.

Gideon Welles and Assistant Secretary of the Navy Gustavus Fox soon appeared. Fox hailed the defeat of Henry Winter Davis in Maryland, and tied it to the departure of Senator John P. Hale of New Hampshire, who had been a particular nemesis of the Navy Department, and called both a blessing. "There are two fellows that have been especially malignant to us," Fox said, "and retribution has come upon them both."

"You have more of that feeling of personal resentment than I," Lincoln said. "Perhaps I may have too little of it, but I never thought it paid. A man has not time to spend half his life in quarrels. If any man ceases to attack me, I never remember the past against him. It has seemed to me recently that Winter Davis was growing more sensible to his own true interests and has ceased wasting his time by attacking me. I hope for his own good he has. He has been very malicious against me but has only injured himself by it."

Hay remembered how the president had often said, "I am in favor of short statutes of limitations in politics."[13]

Assistant Secretary of War Charles Dana arrived at about eight-thirty and found Lincoln and Stanton together in the secretary's office. Eckert was coming in constantly with telegrams bearing returns. Stanton read them and Lincoln looked at them and commented. In a lull, Lincoln called Dana over to a seat beside him.

"Dana," he said, "have you ever read any of the writings of Petroleum V. Nasby?"

"No, sir," admitted Dana, "I have only looked at some of them, and they seemed to be quite funny."

"Well, let me read you a specimen."

Lincoln pulled out a thin, yellow-covered booklet from his breast pocket and began reading aloud. As he read along, Stanton squirmed with impatience. But Lincoln paid him no mind. He read a page or a story, paused to consider a new election telegram, then opened the book again and went on with a new passage. Chase came in, then Whitelaw Reid, the radical correspondent from the *Cincinnati Gazette,* interrupting the reading.

Stanton pulled Dana aside and, sotte voce and indignant, said that when the safety of the republic was thus at issue—when the control of an empire was to be determined by a few figures brought in by the telegraph—the idea that the leader, the man most deeply concerned, not merely for himself but for his country, could turn aside to read such balderdash and to laugh at such frivolous jests was to his mind repugnant, even damnable.[14] It must be remembered that Stanton had more than once called Lincoln "a d——d fool," and that he was another of those who probably required a surgical operation to get a joke into his head.

There was nothing for a long while from New York, the chosen battleground of the Democrats. Then the first returns came in claiming a 10,000-vote margin for Lincoln.

"I don't believe that," Lincoln said. When Horace Greeley telegraphed near midnight that it looked to be 4,000, Lincoln thought that more reasonable. Pennsylvania continued to be a concern. Neither Lincoln nor Stanton was happy with the returns coming in from that key state.

Lincoln said, "As goes Pennsylvania, so goes the Union, they say."[15]

It was approaching midnight, and the dim contours of this election outcome were beginning to take shape. It would be a while before it could
all be sorted out, added up, and nailed precisely. But it looked to be a
victory for the president, an overwhelming triumph, comfortable in the
popular vote, a landslide in the electoral vote.

By midnight, Lincoln was certain of carrying all of New England,
Maryland, Ohio, Indiana, Michigan, Wisconsin, and probably Delaware. There was still no word from Illinois, Iowa, or any of the Trans-
Mississippi states. But at about one o'clock in the morning, word came
from Chicago claiming a 20,000-vote bulge statewide. The wires were
working badly because of the storm, which had worsened. Nothing
further would be heard from the West for two days, but the claim in
Illinois was close to correct. Pennsylvania was now looking safe. New
York was uncertain, but it would soon begin tipping to Lincoln.[16]

New England and the rich central West—Ohio, Illinois, Indiana,
Michigan, Wisconsin, Iowa, Minnesota, where the Northwest Con-
spiracy was supposed to center—were giving Lincoln strong majorities.
He was doing worst in the middle states, barely winning in New York,
Pennsylvania, and Connecticut, and losing in New Jersey and, finally,
Delaware. The far West, when its results came in, would be solid for
him—Kansas, California, Oregon, Nevada.

There were two kinds of immigrants to America, with two different
political profiles. In the Midwest they were immigrants who had drifted
from the eastern seaboard to settle on land far from New York, where
they had first landed in the New World. They were more "American-
ized" than the immigrants who had stayed in New York City—and
they were voting for Lincoln. The immigrants who had stayed, or
migrated only a short distance to the manufacturing villages in Connecticut, were heavily Irish, and they were voting for McClellan. In
some districts of New York and Pennsylvania the vote could almost be
divided by race. New England was heavily abolitionist. It had nowhere
to go but to Lincoln.[17]

Lincoln was faring well in most cities of the North, except in New
York State, where McClellan was winning every city but Rochester, and
in Detroit and Milwaukee, with their heavy ethnic populations. He was
faring poorly with Catholic immigrants everywhere. These newcomers
to America, working men mainly, had little sympathy with a war for
black freedom. Protestants were going largely for Lincoln.

Lincoln, as expected, was carrying the agricultural areas inhabited largely by the native-born. He was winning the vote of skilled urban workers and professionals. McClellan was drawing his heaviest vote from among the immigrant proletariat in the big cities and in some rural areas with strong foreign majorities.[18]

When it was all over and all the votes were counted, Lincoln would win by a 411,428 margin over McClellan—2,213,665 to 1,802,237. In the electoral vote he would win by a devastating 212 to 21. McClellan would carry only three states, New Jersey, Kentucky, and Delaware.[19]

The hurt for the Democrats didn't stop there. The election was to leave the North with but one Democratic governor, Joel Parker in New Jersey. Even Horatio Seymour had been defeated in New York— "cheated out of the vote," Manton Marble insisted.[20] The Republicans were also in control of most of the state legislatures, giving them the power to name U.S. senators and further tighten their grip on Congress.

But on the presidential level it was not the rout it would appear. The Democrats were a singed cat, the appearance of disaster far worse than it actually was. More than four million voted, and Lincoln was winning fifty-five percent of the popular vote. But it had not been a cakewalk. The president had won but 350,000 more votes than he had in 1860, when it had been a four-way race. A shift of 80,000 well-placed votes in certain key states would have thrown the election to McClellan. The country still seemed to lean Democratic, with thousands of their number defecting to vote for the Union.[21]

Where the Democratic debacle was all it appeared to be was where McClellan least expected it—in the vote of his beloved soldiers. They were going overwhelmingly against him. No other part of the electorate was rejecting him so emphatically. In the Army of the Potomac, his old command, he was winning but three votes in ten. Among Pennsylvania's soldiers in the Army of the Potomac, who had the largest number voting in the field, only six of fifty-one regiments were giving their old commander a majority. In Sherman's army in the West it was worse— only two votes in ten. Of the total of 150,635 soldier votes finally counted separately, McClellan would win but 33,748 to Lincoln's 116,887.[22]

The soldier vote wasn't deciding the election. Only in Maryland was it making a difference, and there it didn't affect the presidential outcome. That state's new constitution abolishing slavery would win by a slim 475-vote margin. The soldier vote would decide it.[23]

The massive soldier defection from McClellan was, as suspected, not so much a vote against him as against the company he had been forced to keep. One of Lincoln's friends put it this way: "The soldiers are quite as dangerous to Rebels in the rear as in front."[24]

By midnight, all in the telegraph office were congratulating Lincoln on his reelection. He took it calmly and said he was free to confess he felt relieved of suspense and was glad the verdict of the people was so likely to be clear, full, and unmistakable.[25] Major Eckert came in carrying supper, and Lincoln began awkwardly shoveling out fried oysters to all.

At about two o'clock a messenger came from the White House to tell the president that a crowd of Pennsylvanians was serenading his empty chamber. So he returned to the Executive Mansion to speak to them.

"I am thankful to God for this approval of the people," he told them. "But while deeply grateful for this mark of their confidence in me, if I know my heart, my gratitude is free from any taint of personal triumph. I do not impugn the motives of any one opposed to me. It is no pleasure to me to triumph over any one; but I give thanks to the Almighty for this evidence of the people's resolution to stand by free government and the rights of humanity."[26]

Then Lincoln went to bed. Ward Lamon, the marshal of the District of Columbia, Lincoln's old Illinois friend, now his bodyguard, came to John Hay's room to talk for a while. Then, taking a glass of whiskey and refusing Hay's offer of a bed for the night, he went out and rolled himself up in borrowed blankets and his cloak, and lay down outside Lincoln's door.

There he passed the rest of the night with his small arsenal of pistols and bowie knives. In the morning Hay found the blankets at his door and Lamon gone.[27]

Lincoln's life had been assured for another night. The election returns were telling him his political life had been assured for another four years.

Punch, the irreverent British humor magazine, which endlessly made fun of the president from over the ocean, conceded in verse, with just a touch of admiration: old Abe, of the "rueful phiz" and "shambling graces," had risen, phoenixlike, from the ashes.[28]

Epilogue

Worth More Than
a Battle Won

———

O N ELECTION DAY, GEORGE MCCLELLAN RESIGNED HIS COMMIS-
sion in the army. The day after, he was also resigned to the outcome of the canvass and ready to call it quits in politics.

"The smoke has cleared away," he said in a letter to his mother, "and
we are beaten!"

To his friend Barlow he wrote that "I was fully prepared for the
result and not in the slightest degree overcome by it. For my country's
sake I deplore the result—but the people have decided with their eyes
wide open and I feel that a great weight is removed from my mind . . .
and have abandoned Public life forever—I can imagine no combination
of circumstances that can ever induce me to enter it again. . . ."

To Manton Marble he wrote that they had conducted themselves
with dignity and had nothing to be ashamed of. It was "a struggle of
honor patriotism & truth against deceit selfishness & fanaticism, and I
think that we have well played our parts. The mistakes made were not
of our making. . . ."[1]

Henry Raymond, who had also been elected to Congress from New
York, had the avalanche he so much wanted. "We accept it without
surprise," he said in the *Times*.[2] James Gordon Bennett, however, was
impressed, indeed slightly over the top in his reaction. "One of the
most signal political triumphs in the records of human history . . . ," he
called it, "one of the most remarkable, imposing and sublime events in
the vicissitudes of any nation on the face of the globe since the mirac-
ulous crossing of the Red Sea by the children of Israel."[3]

More than one weary participant looked at it and called it a political passage without parallel. "One of the greatest national acts in all

history," the political theorist and head of the Loyal Publication Society, Francis Leiber, called it. The celebrated New England essayist Ralph Waldo Emerson wrote, "Seldom in history was so much staked on a popular vote. —I suppose never in history."[4]

John Hay spoke of the quiet and orderly character of the canvass, calling that quality "the pivotal centre of our history." "It proves," he said, "our worthiness of free institutions, and our capability of preserving them without running into anarchy or despotism."[5]

George Strong, the aristocratic New York diarist, said yes to that, and was surprised that it was so. *"Laus Deo!"* he told his diary. "The crisis has been past, and the most momentous popular election ever held since ballots were invented has decided against treason and disunion. My contempt for democracy and extended suffrage is mitigated. The American people can be trusted to take care of the national honor."[6]

Many were just glad it was over and were ready to get back to business. Charles Francis Adams Jr., the Union cavalryman, wrote his brother, Henry, "This election has relieved us of the fire in the rear and now we can devote an undivided attention to the remnants of the Confederacy."[7]

Democratic reaction ranged from outrage to the resignation McClellan felt. The *Springfield State Register* in Illinois, a Lincoln neighbor, but no friend, called the outcome "the heaviest calamity that ever befell this nation . . . the farewell to civil liberty, to a republican form of government, and to the unity of these states."[8]

Manton Marble wrote, "We will not affect to conceal the profound chagrin and sorrow with which we contemplate the result." But he was a loyal citizen and could only agree in the end with the *Boston Post,* which wrote, "The ballot-box has spoken, and we abide the result."[9] Marble wasn't likely to stop believing, however, that the ballot box had spoken with a forked and fraudulent tongue. He might even be inclined to agree with one reaction to the big Republican majority: "The Almighty himself must have stuffed the ballot-boxes."[10]

Charles Mason, the Democrat in Washington, looked up at the sky the day after the election and wrote, "A gloomy day without much rain. Our election news is all more gloomy than the weather."[11]

William C. Prime, the editor of the *Journal of Commerce,* wrote his friend McClellan, "While I mourn for the country, we have made a gallant fight. . . . Now for repose, if we can find it. I don't believe that you are as disappointed as your friends are."[12]

The Democrat whom Lincoln succeeded in the White House, James Buchanan, was thinking, Better him than me. Much as he deplored the defeat, Buchanan wrote a friend, the Republicans "have won the elephant; & they will find difficulty in deciding what to do with him."[13]

Who would want such a thankless job anyhow, so freighted with problems that no administration could successfully contend with them? That was the way such reasoning went. A friend of McClellan's wrote him, "Had you succeeded you would have had congratulations enough. You were not elected—let me be one to congratulate you on the result."[14]

The Confederacy was deeply disappointed, both with the result and with the fact that it was not accompanied by violence. It was a more complete Republican victory than most of the South expected. "There is no use disguising the fact," one Confederate said, "that our subjugation is popular at the North." The *Richmond Examiner* said, "The Yankee nation has committed itself to the game of all or nothing; and so must we." Many in the Confederate army, however, were not ready to be so committed. There followed an epidemic of desertions by discouraged rebel soldiers, aggravating further what was already a desperate problem.[15]

Two editors who had supported Lincoln through the darkest and brightest days could now sit back in satisfaction. George William Curtis at *Harper's Weekly* had said in August, the darkest of days, "Two years ago I was the only Lincoln man I knew hereabouts, and I have come round to the same position. Yet he will be elected, or we are dreary humbugs."[16]

Joseph Medill at the *Chicago Tribune* had written in that same dreary month, "Through all this fiery ordeal Mr. Lincoln has continued to have not only the confidence but the love of the masses of the people. Every body has his own little fault to find with him. . . . But never were the people of a great nation more unanimous in favor of sustaining any public officer than are the Union masses of the North in favor of Mr. Lincoln."[17]

They had been prophets speaking in the wilderness.

Now, on the night following the election, a clergyman in Middletown, Connecticut, during a torchlight display, hung a transparency over his door quoting Genesis 22:15: "The angel of the Lord called unto Abraham out of heaven the second time."[18]

Lincoln's Illinois friend, A. G. Henry, ventured to congratulate the president, calling him "our more than *political friend.*"[19]

Our more than political friend was feeling a mixed sense of satisfaction, accomplishment, and weariness. The day after the election, he told Noah Brooks, "Being only mortal, after all, I should have been a little mortified if I had been beaten in this canvass before the people; but that sting would have been more than compensated by the thought that the people had notified me that all my official responsibilities were soon to be lifted off my back."[20]

This politically astute man knew better than most why he still had these responsibilities on his back. "I am here," he told another friend, "by the blunders of the Democrats. If, instead of resolving that the war was a failure, they had resolved that I was a failure, and denounced me for not more vigorously prosecuting it, I should not have been reelected."[21]

On the night of November 10, two days after the election, a procession with banners, lanterns, and transparencies marched to the White House. A crowd surged around the entrance, blocking off the semicircular drive. A band brayed martial music. Cannon parked in the driveway barked, rattling the windows in the Executive Mansion. Tad flew from window to window, arranging a small illumination of his own. Lincoln stood at the window over the portico and spoke from a written text.[22]

The election, he told the serenaders, had been "a necessity. We can not have free government without elections; and if the rebellion could force us to forego, or postpone a national election, it might fairly claim to have already conquered and ruined us. . . . It has been demonstrated that a people's government can sustain a national election, in the midst of a great civil war. Until now it has not been known to the world that this was a possibility. It shows also how *sound,* and how *strong* we still are."

Then Lincoln reached out, appealing, as he often had before, for a union of hearts. "But the rebellion," he said, "continues; and now that the election is over, may not all, having a common interest, re-unite in a common effort, to save our common country? For my own part I have striven, and shall strive to avoid placing any obstacle in the way. So long as I have been here I have not willingly planted a thorn in any man's bosom. . . . May I ask those who have not differed with me, to join with me, in this same spirit towards those who have?"[23]

When he had finished, and the procession moved away toward Secretary of State Seward's house, Lincoln turned from the window and said, "Not very graceful, but I am growing old enough not to care much for the manner of doing things."[24]

The next day the cabinet met. Lincoln reached into the drawer of his desk and took out the queerly pasted note that, in the bleak days of August, he had asked them to sign, sight unseen.

"Gentlemen," he said, "do you remember last summer I asked you all to sign your names to the back of a paper of which I did not show you the inside? This is it. Now, Mr. Hay, see if you can get this open without tearing it?"

After some cutting, Hay got it open and Lincoln read it aloud.

It was dated August 23, and it said, "This morning, as for some days past, it seems exceedingly probable that this Administration will not be reelected. Then it will be my duty to so cooperate with the President elect, as to save the Union between the election and the inauguration; as he will have secured his election on such ground that he cannot possibly save it afterwards."

Then Lincoln said to his cabinet, "You will remember that this was written at a time . . . when as yet we had no adversary, and seemed to have no friends. I then solemnly resolved on the course of action indicated above. I resolved, in case of the election of General McClellan, being certain that he would be the candidate, that I would see him and talk matters over with him. I would say, 'General, the election has demonstrated that you are stronger, have more influence with the American people than I. Now let us together, you with your influence and I with all the executive power of the Government, try to save the country. You raise as many troops as you possibly can for this final trial, and I will devote all my energies to assisting and finishing the war."

Seward said, "And the General would answer you 'Yes, Yes'; and the next day when you saw him again and pressed these views upon him, he would say, 'Yes, Yes'; & so on forever, and would have done nothing at all."

"At least," Lincoln said, "I should have done my duty and have stood clear before my own conscience."[25]

On November 10, when the outcome of the election was clear, U. S. Grant sent a telegram from City Point to Washington. It read, "The election having passed off quietly, no bloodshed or riiot [sic] throughout the land, is a victory worth more to the country than a battle won."[26]

Out on the picket line, when the news reached there, the sentinels in his army fired their muskets, to share the good news with the Confederates across the Petersburg trenches.[27]

And Lincoln said, "We have talked of elections until there is nothing more to say about them."[28]

In Appreciation

—————

I N THE END, WHEN THE WRITING MUST BE DONE, A WRITER ENDS UP
a loner. Nobody else but he or she can then do it. But on the way
to getting to that point and beyond, many helping hands have given
a boost and must be thanked.

My thanks begin at home. My wife, Kathleen Lively, was not only
superhumanly patient and forgiving of my living in another century for
yet another three years, but made library runs to bring home books,
and then dogged my heels, checking every word, sentence, paragraph,
and page with open book and red pencil to make sure that what I was
writing about that century and my friends in it squared with the known
facts. The other things she did to help this project along, in addition to
pursuing her own separate career, are numberless.

Without librarians, any writer of history is dead in the water. I have
many to thank, beginning with Trudi Ensey, the interlibrary loan librar-
ian at the Arlington (Texas) Central Library, who chased down books
I couldn't get anywhere else. The four great university libraries in the
Dallas–Fort Worth metroplex—the University of Texas at Arlington,
Texas Christian, Southern Methodist, and the University of North
Texas—were ever cooperative. Even as far down the road south as Bay-
lor University, the librarians were more than ready and willing to help.

Jennifer Lee at Brown University's John Hay Library in Providence,
Rhode Island, was also most helpful. And the librarians at the Library
of Congress, particularly in its Manuscript Division, were ready guides.
The division's resident Civil War specialist, Dr. John R. Sellers, was
especially so, graciously giving of his enormous knowledge of the collection and sending me documents I couldn't get without another trip
east.

Bryce Suderow, a Civil War researcher in Washington, D.C., spent hours nearly going blind copying a three-foot-tall stack of newspaper clippings about the election of 1864 so I could nearly go blind reading them. His contribution to the finished product was enormous.

Peter St. J. Ginna, the editor at Crown Publishers who worked with me to trim and fine-tune the final manuscript, was professional, sensitive, incisive, and usually right throughout the process. Two other editors at Crown, Dakila Divina and Ayesha Pande, were also most helpful and have my thanks.

My literary agent, Mike Hamilburg, again proved himself impossible to live without, and must be thanked for every book that I manage to write.

Two book-length monographs on the election of 1864 have been published: William Frank Zornow's *Lincoln & the Party Divided,* in 1954, and David E. Long's recent *The Jewel of Liberty,* in 1994. I found both of these fine works excellent guides, indispensable in researching and writing my own story of this incredible campaign.

And finally, I can never thank enough my many friends in the nineteenth century, Republican and Democrat, great and not so great, famous and not so famous, men and women, young and old, political and apolitical, straitlaced and bizarre, who wrote what they saw and thought, and wrote it so well and so memorably. If they hadn't done that, this book could never have been written.

As Abraham Lincoln said in a far different context in a far different time, "thanks to all."

NOTES

In all the notes that follow, only the author, the short title of the work, and the page numbers are cited. In every case the full bibliographical information on every work can be found presented alphabetically in the Sources section beginning on page 415.

Prologue: A Walk to the Telegraph Office

1. Brooks, *Mr. Lincoln's Washington*, 235.
2. Leech, *Reveille in Washington*, 278.
3. Hay, *Lincoln and the Civil War*, 76, 90.
4. This fragment of description of Washington in the fall of 1863 is borrowed from Brooks, *Mr. Lincoln's Washington*, 240; and French, *Witness to the Young Republic*, 457.
5. Brooks, *Mr. Lincoln's Washington*, 240.
6. Mason, *Diary*, entry for 15 November 1863, Remey Family Papers.
7. My description of Lincoln on the walk from the White House to the War Department owes much to Bates, *Lincoln in the Telegraph Office*, 7.
8. Lincoln's inward-turning is noted in Nicolay, *Personal Traits of Abraham Lincoln*, 191–92.
9. Brooks, *Mr. Lincoln's Washington*, 139.
10. Hay, *Lincoln and the Civil War*, 77.
11. This brief rundown on the freedom front is borrowed from Arnold, *The Life of Abraham Lincoln*, 344–45.
12. Lincoln, *Collected Works* 7:254.
13. For a more detailed summary of legislation, statecraft, state-making, and weapon development in Lincoln's first three years, see Squires, "Some Enduring Achievements of the Lincoln Administration," 191–211.

14. Segal, *Conversations with Lincoln,* 46.

15. Long, *The Civil War Day by Day,* 420–21.

16. Nicolay, *Lincoln's Secretary,* 180–81.

17. Nicolay and Hay, *Abraham Lincoln* 7:384.

18. Hay, *Lincoln and the Civil War,* 91.

19. Nicolay and Hay, *Abraham Lincoln* 7:385.

20. Lincoln's letter to Conkling is in *Collected Works* 6:406–10.

21. Nicolay and Hay, *Abraham Lincoln* 9:246.

22. Gurowski, *Diary* 3:28, 35, 37.

23. Hay, *Lincoln and the Civil War,* 99.

24. Leech, *Reveille in Washington,* 280.

25. Hay, *Lincoln and the Civil War,* 123–24.

26. Brooks, *Mr. Lincoln's Washington,* 12, 234–35.

27. For a description of Brooks and his closeness to Lincoln, see Staudenraus's introduction, ibid., 16, 18.

Chapter 1. That Subject of the Presidency

1. The image of Pennsylvania Avenue on a dust-blown day is from French, *Witness to the Young Republic,* 431.

2. Lowell, "The President's Policy," 236.

3. These opening paragraphs describing Lincoln in the cipher room draw heavily on *Lincoln in the Telegraph Office,* by David Homer Bates, one of the wartime cipher operators. See particularly pages 3–11, 38–42, 131, 138–46, 204–5.

4. Pratt, "The Repudiation of Lincoln's War Policy in 1862," 140.

5. Cary, *George William Curtis,* 161.

6. *New York Herald,* 7 October 1863.

7. Lincoln, *Collected Works* 5:350.

8. Harbison, "The Elections of 1862 as a Vote of Want of Confidence in President Lincoln," 503.

9. Adams, *Richard Henry Dana* 2:264.

10. Nicolay and Hay, *Abraham Lincoln* 7:375.

11. Hertz, *Abraham Lincoln: A New Portrait* 2:914.

12. Ibid.

13. *New York Herald,* 7 October 1863.

14. Ibid., 15 October 1863.

15. *New York Daily Tribune,* 12 October 1863.

16. *Dictionary of American Biography,* s.v. "Curtin, Andrew Gregg."

17. Welles, *Diary* 1:469–70.

18. Hesseltine, *Lincoln and the War Governors,* 334–35.

19. *New York World,* 17 October 1863.

20. *Chicago Tribune,* 23 October 1863.

21. Lincoln, *Collected Works* 7:24n.

22. Ibid., 7:24.

23. Nevins, *The War for the Union* 3:451.

24. Lincoln, *Collected Works* 6:540, 540–41n.

25. Brooks, "Personal Recollections of Abraham Lincoln," 228.

26. Segal, *Conversations with Lincoln,* 70, 75.

27. George, "A Long-Neglected Lincoln Speech," 27.

28. Gurowski, *Diary* 3:80.

29. Hay's diaries are sprinkled with these nicknames for Lincoln. See, for instance, *Lincoln and the Civil War,* 2, 5, 8.

30. Nicolay, *Personal Traits of Abraham Lincoln,* 221.

31. Hay, *Lincoln and the Civil War,* 76.

32. Ibid., 91.

33. *New York Herald,* 24 November 1863.

34. Ibid., 1 November 1863.

35. Carr, *Missouri: A Bone of Contention,* 284. There is a good summary of Blair's Union Club organization in Carr, 267–84. Also see Smith, *The Francis Preston Blair Family in Politics,* 2:22–24.

36. Thorndike, *The Sherman Letters,* 167.

37. Smith and Judah, *Life in the North During the Civil War,* 110.

38. *New York Herald,* 5 November 1863.

39. Hay, *Lincoln and the Civil War,* 112.

Chapter 2. Little Mac

1. *Ohio Statesman,* 19 May 1853, in Lindsey, *"Sunset" Cox,* 10.

2. Brooks, *Mr. Lincoln's Washington,* 109, 303. For a description of Cox, also see *Dictionary of American Biography,* s.v. "Cox, Samuel Sullivan."

3. Cox's dinner conversation is recounted in Hay, *Lincoln and the Civil War,* 143–44.

4. Carpenter, *Six Months at the White House,* 227.

5. McClellan, *Civil War Papers,* 583.

6. Ibid., 548.

7. There is a summary of McClellan's association with leading New York Democrats during this time in Stephen Sears's excellent biography, *George B. McClellan,* 344–45. For details about the home bought for McClellan by these Democrats, see Myers, *General George Brinton McClellan,* 405.

8. Manton Marble to James W. Wall, 30 March 1864, Marble Papers.

9. Sears, *George B. McClellan,* 345–46.

10. Ibid., 346–47.
11. For McClellan's view of administration politicians, see his *Civil War Papers,* 85–86, 106–7, 113–14.
12. McClellan often wrote his wife, Nelly, of his vision of himself as the savior of the Union. For some examples, which also touch on his ambivalent attitude toward overtly reaching for power, see ibid., 82, 86, 112–13.
13. Ibid., 548, 549n.
14. The Harrison's Landing letter is reproduced in full in ibid., 344–45.
15. Nicolay and Hay, *Abraham Lincoln* 5:449–50.
16. McClellan, *Civil War Papers,* 558–59.
17. Sears, *George B. McClellan,* 358.
18. *New York Times,* 14 October 1863.
19. Hay, *Lincoln and the Civil War,* 143.
20. *New York Daily Tribune,* 25 December 1863.
21. McClellan's letter to Lincoln is in his *Civil War Papers,* 560–62.
22. McClellan's exchange with his mother, Elizabeth B. McClellan, is in ibid., 562–63.

Chapter 3. Busy Laying Pipe

1. The weather report is courtesy of Brooks, *Mr. Lincoln's Washington,* 259–60.
2. Long, *The Civil War Day by Day,* 428, 431–32.
3. George F. Brown to Lyman Trumbull, 12 November 1863, Trumbull Papers.
4. *New York Herald,* 9 November 1863.
5. Browne, *The Every-Day Life of Abraham Lincoln,* 363.
6. Gurowski, *Diary* 1:16.
7. *New York Herald,* 9 October 1863.
8. Ibid., 12 November 1863.
9. Brooks, *Mr. Lincoln's Washington,* 61.
10. Hart, *Salmon Portland Chase,* 435.
11. Brooks, *Mr. Lincoln's Washington,* 176–77, 351, 275.
12. Hart, *Salmon Portland Chase,* 421, 432.
13. Viele, "A Trip with Lincoln, Chase and Stanton," 814.
14. Belden and Belden, *So Fell the Angels,* 64.
15. Brooks, "Personal Recollections of Abraham Lincoln," 229.
16. Schuckers, *The Life and Public Services of Salmon Portland Chase,* 613–14, 641.
17. Ibid., 604. Also see Lloyd, "The Home-Life of Salmon Portland Chase," 534.
18. Lloyd, "The Home-Life of Salmon Portland Chase," 534.
19. Warden, *An Account of the Private Life and Public Services of Salmon Portland Chase,* 582.

20. Schuckers, *The Life and Public Services of Salmon Portland Chase*, 595, 630, 604; Peacock, *Famous American Belles of the Nineteenth Century*, 211–12.

21. Blue, *Salmon P. Chase*, 207.

22. Warden, *An Account of the Private Life and Public Services of Salmon Portland Chase*, 567–68.

23. Brooks, *Mr. Lincoln's Washington*, 177.

24. Warden, *An Account of the Private Life and Public Services of Salmon Portland Chase*, 562.

25. Schuckers, *The Life and Public Services of Salmon Portland Chase*, 386–87.

26. The description of Chase at home, at work, and en route is mainly from Schuckers, *The Life and Public Services of Salmon Portland Chase*, 599, 601–4, 619, 630. The description of his office is created from a drawing facing page 212.

27. Nicolay and Hay, *Abraham Lincoln* 6:254.

28. Ibid., 8:311, 313.

29. Ibid., 6:254.

30. Warden, *An Account of the Private Life and Public Services of Salmon Portland Chase*, 564, 562.

31. Schuckers, *The Life and Public Services of Salmon Portland Chase*, 379–80.

32. McClure, *Abraham Lincoln and Men of War Times*, 119.

33. Hay, *Lincoln and the Civil War*, 130.

34. Schuckers, *The Life and Public Services of Salmon Portland Chase*, 494.

35. John Nicolay to John Hay, 17 February 1864, Nicolay Papers; Brooks, *Mr. Lincoln's Washington*, 349.

36. Warden, *An Account of the Private Life and Public Services of Salmon Portland Chase*, 565.

37. Welles, *Diary* 1:498.

38. Thomas, *Abraham Lincoln*, 412.

39. Hay, *Lincoln and the Civil War*, 53.

40. Ibid., 107.

41. Adams, *Richard Henry Dana* 2:265.

42. Bates, *Diary*, 310.

43. Welles, *Diary* 1:529.

44. Hay, *Lincoln and the Civil War*, 110.

45. Rice, *Reminiscences of Abraham Lincoln*, 390.

46. Hay, *Lincoln and the Civil War*, 100–1.

47. Keckley, *Behind the Scenes*, 128–30.

48. McClure recounts this conversation and tells Lincoln's Little Egypt story in *Lincoln and Men of War Times*, 120–23.

49. Ibid., 123.

50. Thomas, *Abraham Lincoln*, 412–13.

51. Russell, *My Diary North and South*, 27.

52. Schurz, *The Reminiscences of Carl Schurz* 2:169. See also Ross, *Proud Kate*, 32.

53. Kate's portrait is drawn from a grab bag of sources: Russell and Schurz as cited; Hay, *Lincoln and the Civil War*, 105–6; Brooks, *Mr. Lincoln's Washington*, 61; Belden and Belden, *So Fell the Angels*, 5–6; Ross, *Proud Kate*, 63–64, 66, 104, 55; Leech, *Reveille in Washington*, 281; Peacock, *Famous American Belles of the Nineteenth Century*, 213, 215, 217, 206–7, 209–11; Smith, *The Life and Letters of James Abram Garfield* 1:242; Howard, *Civil War Echoes*, 130; Ellis, *Sights and Secrets of the National Capital*, 429; Bowers, *The Tragic Era*, 252, 254–55; Hart, *Salmon Portland Chase*, 420.

54. Keckley, *Behind the Scenes*, 124–26.

55. Belden and Belden, *So Fell the Angels*, 83; Sokoloff, *Kate Chase for the Defense*, 99.

56. Ross, *Proud Kate*, 128.

57. Sokoloff, *Kate Chase for the Defense*, 91–92.

58. What the bride and groom wore is described in *The New York Times*, 15 November 1863; Brooks, *Mr. Lincoln's Washington*, 260–61; Leech, *Reveille in Washington*, 281; *Washington Evening Star*, 13 November 1863.

59. *New York Times*, 15 November 1863; *Cincinnati Daily Gazette*, 20 November 1863. Also see Sokoloff, *Kate Chase for the Defense*, 90; Ross, *Proud Kate*, 121; and Leech, *Reveille in Washington*, 282.

60. *New York Times*, 15 November 1863; *Cincinnati Daily Gazette*, 20 November 1863.

61. Belden and Belden, *So Fell the Angels*, 97, 94. Also see Leech, *Reveille in Washington*, 281.

62. *Cincinnati Daily Gazette*, 20 November 1863.

Chapter 4. The Men Who Faced Zionwards

1. *Cincinnati Daily Commercial*, 23 November 1863.

2. Nicolay and Hay, *Abraham Lincoln* 8:190.

3. For a discussion of Lincoln's objective at Gettysburg, see Donald, *Lincoln*, 460–63.

4. These first few descriptive paragraphs owe much to the prologue in Garry Wills's excellent work, *Lincoln at Gettysburg*, 19–40. The description of Lincoln and his party arriving and the serenading that bewildered the night with music are from Young, *Men and Memories*, 59. The serenaders singing "We Are Coming, Father Abraham," I owe to Rathvon, "I Heard Lincoln at Gettysburg."

5. Quote from a writer in *Lincoln Lore* 293 (19 November 1934).

6. Ibid.; Young, *Men and Memories,* 63; *Cincinnati Daily Commercial,* 23 November 1863; *Washington Chronicle,* 20 November 1863.

7. The quote is from Hay, *Letters of John Hay and Extracts from Diary* 1:124–25.

8. *Cincinnati Daily Commercial,* 23 November 1863.

9. Ibid.

10. *Washington Chronicle,* 20 November 1863.

11. Wills, *Lincoln at Gettysburg,* 34–35; Young, *Men and Memories,* 65; *Cincinnati Daily Commercial,* 23 November 1863; Hay, *Letters of John Hay and Extracts from Diary* 1:125.

12. Young, *Men and Memories,* 62–63; *Cincinnati Daily Commercial,* 23 November 1863.

13. Carr, "Lincoln at Gettysburg," 145.

14. Nicolay and Hay, *Abraham Lincoln* 8:192.

15. This snapshot account of Lincoln delivering his Gettysburg Address is distilled from Young, *Men and Memories,* 68; Carr, "Lincoln at Gettysburg"; Wills, *Lincoln at Gettysburg,* 36; *Boston Daily Journal,* 23 November 1863.

16. Lamon, *Recollections of Abraham Lincoln,* 173.

17. Sandburg, *Abraham Lincoln: The War Years* 1:48.

18. Lincoln, *Collected Works* 7:25n, 24.

19. Bates, *Lincoln in the Telegraph Office,* 166; Smith, "President Lincoln," 427.

20. Gurowski, *Diary* 3:33.

21. Rice, *Reminiscences of Abraham Lincoln,* 337.

22. Nicolay and Hay, *Abraham Lincoln* 8:204–5.

23. Ibid., 8:219–20.

24. Ibid., 8:214.

25. *New York Herald,* 14 October 1863.

26. Laughlin, "Missouri Politics in the Civil War," 105.

27. This litany of Lincoln's offenses is distilled from Randall and Current, *Lincoln the President: Last Full Measure,* 117–18; and Welles, "Administration of Abraham Lincoln," 611.

28. Quoted in Williams, "Lincoln and the Radicals," 93.

29. Brooks, *Mr. Lincoln's Washington,* 96, 328.

30. Donald, *Lincoln Reconsidered,* 112; Donald, "Devils Facing Zionwards," 80–83.

31. Wilson, "The Original Chase Organization Meeting," 62.

32. Welles, "Administration of Abraham Lincoln," 622–23.

33. Hesseltine, *Lincoln's Plan of Reconstruction,* 121–22.

34. Quoted in Williams, *Lincoln and the Radicals,* 6.

35. *Congressional Globe,* 37 cong, 1 sess., 415.

36. Ibid., 37 cong., 3 sess., pt. 2, 1338.

37. Hesseltine, *Lincoln's Plan of Reconstruction,* 122. Also see Cole, "Abraham Lincoln and the South," 78.

38. Welles, "Administration of Abraham Lincoln," 617.

39. Ibid.

40. This view of radical aims is distilled from Williams, *Lincoln and the Radicals,* 6, 13–14, 294; and Viorst, *Fall from Grace,* 48–49, 55.

41. Thomas, *Abraham Lincoln,* 343.

42. Smith, *Chase and Civil War Politics,* 68–69.

43. Poore, *Perley's Reminiscences* 2:50–51.

44. *New York Daily Tribune,* 13 June 1862, reprinted in Williams, *Lincoln and the Radicals,* 3.

45. Lee, *Wartime Washington,* 375.

46. Hay, *Lincoln and the Civil War,* 31.

47. Ibid., 108.

Chapter 5. The Drumroll of Reconstruction

1. Schurz, *The Reminiscences of Carl Schurz* 2:35.

2. "Washington During the War," 25.

3. Pierce, *Memoir and Letters of Charles Sumner* 4:96.

4. *Diary of a Public Man,* 63.

5. Brooks, *Washington in Lincoln's Time,* 33.

6. Sumner, "Our Domestic Relations," 528.

7. Hay, *Lincoln and the Civil War,* 250.

8. Howard, *Civil War Echoes,* 39.

9. Sandburg, *Abraham Lincoln: The War Years* 1:100.

10. Welles, *Diary* 1:502–3.

11. Donald, *Charles Sumner and the Rights of Man,* 147.

12. Howard, *Civil War Echoes,* 11.

13. Pierce, *Memoir and Letters of Charles Sumner* 4:83.

14. Owen, "Political Results from the Varioloid," 665.

15. *New York Herald,* 17 October 1863.

16. The gambling hells of Washington are described in Ellis, *Sights and Secrets of the National Capital,* 400–9.

17. For this general description of Stevens I have drawn on Schurz, *The Reminiscences of Carl Schurz* 3:214; Brooks, *Mr. Lincoln's Washington,* 104, 301; Woodburn, *The Life of Thaddeus Stevens,* 609; Woodley, *The Great Leveler,* 16; Brodie, *Thaddeus Stevens,* 17, 31; Binckley, "The Leader of the House," 495.

18. Binckley, "The Leader of the House," 494.

19. *New York World*, 23 March 1864.

20. Poore, *Perley's Reminiscences*, 2:101; Brooks, *Washington in Lincoln's Time*, 100; Brooks, *Mr. Lincoln's Washington*, 104.

21. Binckley, "The Leader of the House," 496.

22. Ellis, *Sights and Secrets of the National Capital*, 155–56.

23. Woodley, *The Great Leveler*, 10.

24. Brodie, *Thaddeus Stevens*, 145.

25. Schurz, *The Reminiscences of Carl Schurz* 3:214.

26. Brooks, *Mr. Lincoln's Washington*, 104.

27. Schurz, *The Reminiscences of Carl Schurz* 3:215.

28. Woodburn, *The Life of Thaddeus Stevens*, 165.

29. Owen, "Political Results from the Varioloid," 662, 664.

30. McClure, *Lincoln and Men of War Times*, 265.

31. George M. Drake in the *Union Springs* (Alabama) *Times*, 24 July 1867, reprinted in Brodie, *Thaddeus Stevens*, 18–19.

32. For an excellent review of the development of the reconstruction issue, see Belz, *Reconstructing the Union*, 126–53.

33. Sumner, "Our Domestic Relations," 510.

34. The Wilson, Trumbull, and Stevens quotes are from *Congressional Globe*, 37 cong., 2 sess., 2734, 2972, 440.

35. Sumner, "Our Domestic Relations," 510, 520–25.

36. Young, *Men and Memories*, 59; Smith, *The Francis Preston Blair Family in Politics* 1:211–12.

37. Brooks, *Mr. Lincoln's Washington*, 178, 238.

38. Dana, *Recollections of the Civil War*, 170.

39. Hendrick, *Lincoln's War Cabinet*, 387.

40. Blair's Rockville speech was printed in full in *The New York Times*, 17 October 1863.

41. The description of the view over the magnificent distances and the integrated street horsecars is drawn from Eckloff, *Memoirs of a Senate Page*, 15; Brooks, *Washington in Lincoln's Time*, 192; and Brooks, *Mr. Lincoln's Washington*, 245.

42. This brief tour of Washington was distilled from Eckloff, *Memoirs of a Senate Page*, 16–18; and Ellis, *Sights and Secrets of the National Capital*, 447.

43. Brooks, *Mr. Lincoln's Washington*, 241–42; Milton, *The Age of Hate*, 4.

44. Ellis, *Sights and Secrets of the National Capital*, 113–14. Stevens is quoted in Milton, *The Age of Hate*, 1.

45. Brooks, *Mr. Lincoln's Washington*, 266–67; Eckloff, *Memoirs of a Senate Page*, 6.

46. This brief sketch of Colfax is stitched together from Ellis, *Sights and Secrets of the National Capital*, 157; Howard, *Civil War Echoes*, 134; Brooks, *Mr. Lincoln's Washington*, 108; Welles, *Diary* 1:481; Smith, *Chase and Civil War Politics*, 96.

47. Quoted in Burlingame, *The Inner World of Abraham Lincoln,* 291—from reminiscences by Franz Mueller in the Ida M. Tarbell Papers, Allegheny College.

48. Lincoln's message to Congress is in *Collected Works* 7:36–53. The proclamation follows on pages 53–56.

49. Hay, *Lincoln and the Civil War,* 131–32.

50. Lincoln, *Collected Works* 7:66; 102.

51. *New York Times,* 11 December 1863.

52. Donald, *Charles Sumner and the Rights of Man,* 178–79.

53. Dodd, "Lincoln's Last Struggle—Victory?", 52.

54. There is an excellent discussion of radical misgivings in Donald, *Charles Sumner and the Rights of Man,* 179–83.

55. Belz, *Reconstructing the Union,* 188.

56. Hay, "Life in the White House in the Time of Lincoln," 35.

57. Brooks, "A Boy in the White House," 59.

58. *Lincoln Lore* 141 (21 December 1931).

59. Lincoln, *Collected Works* 7:94, 95.

60. Gurowski, *Diary* 3:53, 57–58.

Chapter 6. The Common Man

1. Brooks, *Mr. Lincoln's Washington,* 273.

2. Weather and disaster report courtesy of Mason's diary entries, 1–4 January 1864, Remey Family Papers; Brooks, *Mr. Lincoln's Washington,* 273; Welles, *Diary* 1:503–4; Hay, *Lincoln and the Civil War,* 148; Gurowski, *Diary* 3:59; *New York Times,* 4 January 1864.

3. John Nicolay to his fiancée, Therena Bates, 15 January 1863, Nicolay Papers.

4. Hay, *Lincoln and the Civil War,* 169.

5. Brooks, *Mr. Lincoln's Washington,* 177; "Washington During the War," 26; Dana, *Recollections of the Civil War,* 170.

6. This mini-sketch of Seward owes much to Lindeman, *The Conflict of Convictions,* 174; Brooks, *Mr. Lincoln's Washington,* 61–62; Borrett, "An Englishman in Washington in 1864," 9; *New York Herald,* 1 December 1863; Rice, *Reminiscences of Abraham Lincoln,* 481; "Washington During the War," 25; Young, *Men and Memories,* 60.

7. Brooks, *Mr. Lincoln's Washington,* 274; Poore, *Perley's Reminiscences* 2:148–49.

8. Gurowski, *Diary* 3:58.

9. Hay, *Lincoln and the Civil War,* 9, 321, 20. The general description of the living tide borrows from Poore, *Perley's Reminiscences* 2:149; Milton, *The Age of Hate,* 16, 18; and Ellis, *Sights and Secrets of the National Capital,* 243.

10. Brooks, *Mr. Lincoln's Washington,* 274.

11. Ross, *Proud Kate,* 150.

12. Herndon and Weik, *Herndon's Life of Lincoln,* 385n.

13. Hay, *Lincoln and the Civil War,* 40. Getting at the real Mary Lincoln was no easy task. Gamaliel Bradford, in his entertaining essay on Mrs. Lincoln in *Wives,* carries this disclaimer: "I cannot ask my readers to give implicit belief to anything I say about Mrs. Lincoln, for I believe very little of it myself." (See page 19.) William Herndon, Lincoln's law partner, detested her, thinking her a shrew. So did Nicolay and Hay. Much of recent scholarship agrees with their assessment of her. For an example of this, see Burlingame, *The Inner World of Abraham Lincoln.*

14. Lindeman, *The Conflict of Convictions,* 154; Brooks, *Mr. Lincoln's Washington,* 60.

15. Hay, "Life in the White House in the Time of Lincoln," 34–35.

16. Arnold, *The Life of Abraham Lincoln,* 351–52. For descriptions of Lincoln's grip by two who had felt it, see "Washington During the War," 23; and Sala, "Lincoln's 'Cast Iron Grip,'" 438–40.

17. Brooks, *Mr. Lincoln's Washington,* 274.

18. Russell, *My Diary North and South,* 22.

19. Sandburg, "The Face of Lincoln," 3; Carpenter, *Six Months at the White House,* 217–18.

20. Bancroft, "An Audience with Abraham Lincoln," 447–48.

21. Present-day ophthalmologists studying Lincoln's photographs believe that this rightward tilt of the head indicates he may have suffered from what they call "left fourth cranial nerve palsy." A further sign of this is a noticeably larger show of white in the iris of his left eye than in his right, evident in some of his photographs—a condition called hypertropia. Left fourth cranial nerve palsy is sometimes associated with Marfan's syndrome, a malady affecting very tall people, which many doctors believe Lincoln had. But it is generally caused in adults by a trauma—a blow to the head sometime in life. Dr. Everett A. Moody, of Dallas, Texas, suggests that it may have been caused by blows to his head by pieces of firewood wielded by an angry Mary Lincoln. "There are signs of the palsy and the fact that he was a battered husband," says Dr. Moody, a leading specialist in muscle disorders of the human eye. "It all adds up." For an account of an attack on Lincoln by a wood-wielding Mary, see Hertz, *The Hidden Lincoln,* 141; Burlingame, *The Inner World of Abraham Lincoln,* 273.

22. "Washington During the War," 23.

23. Russell, *My Diary North and South,* 22–23.

24. Lindeman, *The Conflict of Convictions,* 155, 157.

25. "Washington During the War," 23.

26. Hertz, *The Hidden Lincoln,* 413–14.

27. Rice, *Reminiscences of Abraham Lincoln,* 442.

28. Carpenter, *Six Months at the White House,* 218, 230.

29. Rice, *Reminiscences of Abraham Lincoln,* 443.

30. Hertz, *The Hidden Lincoln,* 412–14.

31. Sandburg, "The Face of Lincoln," 2.

32. Rice, *Reminiscences of Abraham Lincoln,* 479; Henry Lee Jr. to his wife, 2 November 1861, Lee Family Papers.

33. Randall, *Lincoln the President: Midstream,* 405; Randall and Current, *Lincoln the President: Last Full Measure,* 319.

34. Lindemann, *The Conflict of Convictions,* 155; Rice, *Reminiscences of Abraham Lincoln,* 479.

35. Holzer, "'If I Had Another Face, Do You Think I'd Wear This One?'", 57.

36. Dittenhoefer, *How We Elected Lincoln,* 52.

37. Mitgang, *Lincoln as They Saw Him,* 354.

38. Lindeman, *The Conflict of Convictions,* 155.

39. Pratt, *Concerning Mr. Lincoln,* 88.

40. "Homely or Handsome," 22.

41. Carpenter, *Six Months at the White House,* 173–74.

42. Borrett, "An Englishman in Washington in 1864," 14.

43. Brooks, "Personal Recollections of Abraham Lincoln," 225.

44. Rice, *Reminiscences of Abraham Lincoln,* 451.

45. Carpenter, *Six Months at the White House,* 33.

46. Hertz, *The Hidden Lincoln,* 417–19.

47. Henry Ward Beecher to Salmon P. Chase, in Chase, *Diary and Correspondence of Salmon P. Chase,* 512.

48. Bradford, *Wives,* 26–27.

49. Douglass's account is in Rice, *Reminiscences of Abraham Lincoln,* 186, 193.

50. Schurz, *Speeches, Correspondence and Political Papers of Carl Schurz* 1:250–51.

51. Porter, *Campaigning with Grant,* 220.

52. Rice, *Reminiscences of Abraham Lincoln,* 218, 447–48.

53. Borrett, "An Englishman in Washington in 1864," 5.

54. The description of Lincoln's office is taken mainly from an account by a correspondent of the *New York World,* written after the president's assassination, 14 May 1865, reprinted in *Lincoln Lore* 531 (12 June 1939). It also draws on Rice, *Reminiscences of Abraham Lincoln,* 377; Carpenter, *Six Months at the White House,* 215–16; and Hay, "Life in the White House in the Time of Lincoln," 33.

55. John Nicolay to John Hay, 29 January 1864, Nicolay Papers.

56. Brooks, *Washington in Lincoln's Time,* 254.

57. Neill, "Reminiscences of the Last Year of President Lincoln's Life," 37.

58. These paragraphs on Lincoln's daily routine, except as otherwise specifically cited, are from Hay, "Life in the White House in the Time of Lincoln," 34–36.

59. Carpenter, *Six Months at the White House,* 223–24.

60. Young, *Men and Memories,* 79; Whitman, "Walt Whitman Describes Lincoln in 1864," 52. Whitman's account is also in Rice, *Reminiscences of Abraham Lincoln,* 467–70n.

61. McBride, *Personal Recollections of Abraham Lincoln,* 55.

62. Borrett, "An Englishman in Washington in 1864," 6–7; Whitman, "Walt Whitman Describes Lincoln in 1864," 52.

63. Borrett, "An Englishman in Washington in 1864," 7.

64. Hay, *Lincoln and the Civil War,* 143.

65. Greeley, *Recollections of a Busy Life,* 408.

66. Brooks, "Personal Recollections of Abraham Lincoln," 222.

67. Schurz, *Speeches, Correspondence and Political Papers* 1:251; Schurz, *Intimate Letters of Carl Schurz,* 340.

68. Rice, *Reminiscences of Abraham Lincoln,* 110.

69. Carpenter, *Six Months at the White House,* 36.

Chapter 7. Storks by the Frog Pond

1. This scene of New York in winter is suggested by a general description of the city under similar circumstances in Smith and Judah, *Life in the North During the Civil War,* 291–92.

2. The description of Belmont and his rise to prominence in America draws on Brooks, *Mr. Lincoln's Washington,* 375; Smith, *Sunshine and Shadow in New York,* 666; Kamaras, "George B. McClellan and the Election of 1864," 61; and Katz, *August Belmont,* 1–11, 18, 50–54, 60–67, 73–74, 91–115, 122–23.

3. See Katz, *August Belmont,* 125, for a convenient summary of what happened at the meeting.

4. *New York Daily Tribune,* 9 November 1860.

5. Fermer, *James Gordon Bennett and the New York Herald,* 266.

6. *Cincinnati Daily Commercial,* 4 September 1861 and 15 May 1862.

7. *New York Herald,* 24 June 1864; *New York Times,* 1 June 1864.

8. Roseboom, *A History of Presidential Elections,* 191–92.

9. Smith, *Sunshine and Shadow in New York,* 275.

10. Tarbell, *The Life of Abraham Lincoln* 1:396.

11. *Chicago Tribune,* 12 January 1864.

12. *New York Daily Tribune,* 20 January 1864.

13. Silbey, *A Respectable Minority,* 112.

14. Ibid., 10.

15. Quotes are from ibid., 81–82.

16. *New York Daily Tribune,* 14 January 1864.

17. *New York World,* 25 December 1863.

18. Isaac Welsh to Ben Wade, 31 January 1864, Wade Papers.

19. Hay, *Lincoln and the Civil War,* 79–80.

20. Ibid., 130.

21. Brooks, *Mr. Lincoln's Washington,* 13, 69.

22. D. M. Conoughy to Edward McPherson, 2 July 1864, McPherson Papers.

23. Silbey, *A Respectable Minority,* 124. Silbey's book is an excellent and perceptive study of the Democratic party during the Civil War.

24. McClellan, *Civil War Papers,* 564.

25. *New York Times,* 6 January and 27 February 1864.

26. Manton Marble to James W. Wall, 30 March 1864, Marble Papers.

Chapter 8. Crazy Jane and Beast Butler

1. Brooks, *Mr. Lincoln's Washington,* 277.

2. Mason, Diary, entry for 8 January 1864, Remey Family Papers.

3. "Washington During the War," 27.

4. Brooks, *Mr. Lincoln's Washington,* 101.

5. Lincoln, *Collected Works* 7:137. Also see Mason, Diary, entry for 20 January 1864, Remey Family Papers.

6. Barnes, *Memoir of Thurlow Weed,* 444.

7. Miers, *Lincoln Day by Day,* 3:233.

8. Herndon and Weik, *Herndon's Life of Lincoln,* 304.

9. Welles, *Diary* 1:501, 509.

10. Ibid., 528.

11. Lowell, "The President's Policy," 238–39, 240, 242–43, 249.

12. John Nicolay to Therena Bates, 11 January 1863 and 25 February 1864, Nicolay Papers.

13. Rice, *Reminiscences of Abraham Lincoln,* 56–57.

14. Ibid., 100.

15. Carpenter, *Six Months at the White House,* 47–48.

16. Garrison, *William Lloyd Garrison* 4:97.

17. *Harper's Weekly,* 2 January 1864.

18. *Chicago Tribune,* 5 January 1864.

19. Garrison, *William Lloyd Garrison* 4:104, 117.

20. Hay, *Lincoln and the Civil War,* 152–53.

21. A summary of endorsements is in the *Chicago Tribune,* 27 February 1864. On the feeling out in the country see Zornow, "The Attitude of the Western Reserve Press on the Re-election of Lincoln," 37.

22. *Wilkes' Spirit of the Times,* 30 January 1864, reprinted in Wilson, "The Original Chase Organization Meeting," 76, 78. For Wilkes's general attitude, also see Butler, *Private and Official Correspondence* 5:135.

23. *New York Herald,* 29 January 1864.

24. *Congressional Globe,* 38 cong., 2 sess., part 1, 400.

25. Pratt, *Concerning Mr. Lincoln,* 111.

26. Young, "Anna Elizabeth Dickinson and the Civil War," 59–60.

27. Venet, *Neither Ballots nor Bullets,* 54.

28. Young, "Anna Elizabeth Dickinson and the Civil War," 65.

29. Ibid., 66.

30. Ibid., 61.

31. Venet, *Neither Ballots nor Bullets,* 55.

32. Young, "Anna Elizabeth Dickinson and the Civil War," 62.

33. Venet, *Neither Ballots nor Bullets,* 42; Young, "Anna Elizabeth Dickinson and the Civil War," 62. My description of Anna owes much to Young's article, which is based on his doctoral dissertation of the same title from the University of Illinois in 1941.

34. Mason reported the weather for the week in his diary, Remey Family Papers.

35. Venet, *Neither Ballots nor Bullets,* 125.

36. Brooks, *Mr. Lincoln's Washington,* 280; Brooks, *Washington in Lincoln's Time,* 74.

37. The stage is described in the *Washington Chronicle,* 17 January 1864, the stage fright by Venet in *Neither Ballots nor Bullets,* 48.

38. Brooks, *Mr. Lincoln's Washington,* 281–82.

39. Young, "Anna Elizabeth Dickinson and the Civil War," 69; Venet, *Neither Ballots nor Bullets,* 125–27.

40. *Washington Chronicle,* 17 January 1864.

41. Young, "Anna Elizabeth Dickinson and the Civil War," 70.

42. I am indebted to Trefousse, *Ben Butler,* 166, for this convenient wrap-up of the two men's contrasting natures.

43. Holzman, *Stormy Ben Butler,* 76.

44. Hay, *Lincoln and the Civil War,* 115.

45. Holzman, *Stormy Ben Butler,* 5.

46. Butler, *Butler's Book,* 108.

47. Chase, *Diary and Correspondence of Salmon P. Chase,* 316, 346.

48. Butler, *Private and Official Correspondence* 4:454.

49. Ibid., 4:417.

50. Butler, *Butler's Book,* 82. For a charming profile of Sarah Butler, see Bradford, *Wives,* 199–234. Butler's monumental five-volume *Private and Official Corre-*

spondence of General Benjamin F. Butler is larded with many letters to and from her, illuminating a unique couple in a unique marriage.

51. Hay, *Lincoln and the Civil War,* 183.

52. Butler, *Butler's Book,* 417.

53. Ibid., 543.

54. Three of the best sources on Butler are the five volumes of his voluminous correspondence, *Private and Official Correspondence of General Benjamin F. Butler;* his autobiography, *Butler's Book;* and Holzman's *Stormy Ben Butler.*

Chapter 9. The Pudding Don't Rise

1. John Nicolay to Therena Bates, 17 February 1864, Nicolay Papers.

2. Weather report for February 10 is from Bates, *Diary,* 329; and Mason, Diary, Remey Family Papers.

3. The fire is described in McBride, *Personal Recollections of Abraham Lincoln,* 44–45; Lee, *Wartime Washington,* 346, 347n; John Nicolay to Therena Bates, 12 February 1864, Nicolay Papers.

4. This brief portrait of Bates owes much to Hendrick, *Lincoln's War Cabinet,* 46–47, 385.

5. Segal, *Conversations with Lincoln,* 228.

6. Bates, *Diary,* 390.

7. Ibid., 350.

8. Bates's half-hour talk with Lincoln is recounted from ibid., 333–34.

9. *New York Herald,* 17 October 1863.

10. Ibid., 20 October 1863.

11. Schuckers, *The Life and Public Services of Salmon Portland Chase,* 52.

12. Ibid., 395.

13. Belden and Belden, *So Fell the Angels,* 67–69.

14. Details of this first meeting, with the list of names, is in Wilson, "The Original Chase Organization Meeting," 61–70.

15. Brooks, *Washington in Lincoln's Time,* 128; Ellis, *Sights and Secrets of the National Capital,* 125.

16. Wilson, "The Original Chase Organization Meeting," 63.

17. Hay, *Lincoln and the Civil War,* 138.

18. Dittenhoefer, *How We Elected Lincoln,* 72.

19. Hay, *Lincoln and the Civil War,* 152.

20. Schuckers, *The Life and Public Services of Salmon Portland Chase,* 497.

21. Warden, *An Account of the Private Life and Public Services of Salmon Portland Chase,* 563–64.

22. Schuckers, *The Life and Public Services of Salmon Portland Chase,* 498.

23. Wilson, "The Original Chase Organization Meeting," 63–64. The document is reprinted in full in Wilson's monograph, pages 71–76.

24. The *Enquirer* is quoted in ibid., 64.

25. The text of the circular is reprinted in Nicolay and Hay, *Abraham Lincoln* 8:319–20.

26. Welles, *Diary* 1:529.

27. John Nicolay to John Hay, 17 February 1864, Nicolay Papers.

28. Nicolay and Hay, *Abraham Lincoln* 8:321.

29. Lincoln, *Collected Works* 7:213.

30. My profile of Blair draws largely from Smith, *The Francis Preston Blair Family in Politics* 2:112–17. Also see Brooks, *Mr. Lincoln's Washington,* 309–10.

31. Lee, *Wartime Washington,* 316.

32. Smith, *The Francis Preston Blair Family in Politics* 2:115.

33. Lee, *Wartime Washington,* 393n; 358, 392.

34. Hay, *Lincoln and the Civil War,* 133; Smith, *The Francis Preston Blair Family in Politics* 2:113.

35. Gurowski, *Diary* 3:59.

36. Lincoln, *Collected Works* 6:554–55.

37. Welles, *Diary* 2:20.

38. Blair's speech is in *Congressional Globe,* 38 cong., 1 sess., appendix, 46–51. For quotes, see page 50.

39. Smith, *The Life and Letters of James Abram Garfield* 1:375–76.

40. Smith, *Chase and Civil War Politics,* 135; Schuckers, *The Life and Public Services of Salmon Portland Chase,* 502–3.

41. Warden, *An Account of the Private Life and Public Services of Salmon Portland Chase,* 576.

42. Smith, *Chase and Civil War Politics,* 132–33.

43. Both quotes are from Barnes, *Memoir of Thurlow Weed,* 445.

44. *New York Herald,* 12 March 1864.

45. Quoted in *Lincoln Lore* 1102 (22 May 1950).

Chapter 10. Let Him Have the Presidency

1. Lincoln, *Collected Works* 7:134n.

2. Williams, *McClellan, Sherman and Grant,* 105.

3. McClure, *Abraham Lincoln and Men of War Times,* 180.

4. Williams, *McClellan, Sherman and Grant,* 97–98.

5. Commager, *The Blue and the Gray* 2:1083.

6. Strong, *Diary,* 409.

7. Nicolay, Memorandum of Grant's Visit to Washington, 8 March 1864, Nicolay Papers; Nicolay and Hay, *Abraham Lincoln* 9:58–59.

8. *New York Herald,* 18 December 1864.

9. *New York Daily Tribune,* 18 December 1864.

10. Hay, *Lincoln and the Civil War,* 143–44.

11. Tarbell, *The Life of Abraham Lincoln* 2:188.

12. Welles, *Diary* 1:481.

13. Tarbell, *The Life of Abraham Lincoln* 2:188–89.

14. Grant, *The Papers of Ulysses S. Grant* 9:542.

15. All this about Jones and Grant, and Jones making his way to the train station, is from Tarbell, *The Life of Abraham Lincoln* 2:187.

16. Grant, *The Papers of Ulysses S. Grant* 9:541.

17. Ibid., 543.

18. This account of Jones's summons to Washington and his conversation with Lincoln is his own, reproduced in Tarbell, *The Life of Abraham Lincoln* 2:187–88. Details about what was said in the meeting differ. See, for instance, Wilson, "Reminiscences of General Grant," 954; and Richardson, *A Personal History of Ulysses S. Grant,* 380–81. At least one modern Grant biographer is skeptical of Jones's version altogether, doubting, for one thing, whether Lincoln would ever say to anybody, "My son. . . ." (See McFeely, *Grant,* 163–64.) Since Jones was present, however, and none of these other gentlemen were, I have taken his account on faith.

19. Sherman's quotes and the sailor quote are all from Nicolay and Hay, *Abraham Lincoln* 8:338–39.

20. Macdonell, "America Then and Now," 51.

21. The scene at the registration desk and the signing of the register are from Garland, *Ulysses S. Grant,* 257; and Porter, *Campaigning with Grant,* 21–22.

22. Welles, *Diary* 1:539.

23. Adams, *Richard Henry Dana* 2:271.

24. Williams, *McClellan, Sherman and Grant,* 82.

25. This brief profile of Grant in motion and at rest is a tapestry stitched together from Adams, *Richard Henry Dana* 2:271; Poore, *Perley's Reminiscences,* 2:150; Williams, *McClellan, Sherman and Grant,* 81–82; Brooks, *Mr. Lincoln's Washington,* 290; Borrett, "An Englishman in Washington in 1864," 10; Lyman, *Meade's Headquarters,* 80, 83; Foote, *The Civil War* 3:9; and Porter, *Campaigning with Grant,* 14–15.

26. Lee, *Wartime Washington,* 358.

27. Welles, *Diary* 1:540.

28. Lyman, *Meade's Headquarters,* 156, 81.

29. Grant's dining-hall reception is built from differing accounts in Brooks, *Washington in Lincoln's Time,* 134–35; Richardson, *A Personal History of Ulysses S. Grant,* 383; and Grant, "Reminiscences of Gen. U. S. Grant," 73.

30. Nicolay, Memorandum of Grant's Visit to Washington, 8 March 1864, Nicolay Papers. As usual in firsthand accounts, details differ over what was actually said when these two great men of the war met for the first time. No two versions are the same. Horace Porter reports that Lincoln said, "Why, here is General Grant! Well, this is a great pleasure, I assure you." (*Campaigning with Grant,* 19.) Grant's son Frederick remembers Lincoln saying, "I am most delighted to see you, General." (Grant, "Reminiscences of Gen. U. S. Grant," 74.) I have used Nicolay's version because he, like young Grant, was present, but wrote what he remembered in a memorandum later that same evening when it was fresh in his memory. Whatever Lincoln said, he doubtless subjected Grant to his cast-iron handshake.

31. Brooks, *Mr. Lincoln's Washington,* 290. Nicolay, Memorandum of Grant's Visit to Washington, 8 March 1864, Nicolay Papers.

32. Carpenter, *Six Months at the White House,* 56.

33. This account, and the account of what followed the remainder of the evening, is from Nicolay's memorandum cited above.

34. The account of the presentation ceremony is from Nicolay and Hay, *Abraham Lincoln* 8:341–43.

35. Richardson, *A Personal History of Ulysses S. Grant,* 386.

36. Brooks, *Mr. Lincoln's Washington,* 311; *Love's Labor Lost,* act 1, sc. 1, lines 100–1.

37. Mason, Diary, entries of 22 and 23 March 1864, Remey Family Papers; French, *Witness to the Young Republic,* 447.

38. Grant, *Personal Memoirs* 2:407–8.

39. George McClellan to Elizabeth McClellan, 13 March 1864, McClellan Papers.

Chapter 11. The Editor Generals
1. Macdonell. "America Then and Now," 53.

2. Bates, *Diary,* 362.

3. Carpenter, *Six Months at the White House,* 17.

4. *New York Herald,* 29 March 1864.

5. Carpenter, *Six Months at the White House,* 160.

6. *New York Herald,* 30 March 1864.

7. Mitgang, *Lincoln as They Saw Him,* 389.

8. Hertz, *The Hidden Lincoln,* 95. Also see Donald, *Lincoln's Herndon,* 127.

9. Brooks, *Washington in Lincoln's Time*, 261.

10. Carpenter, *Six Months at the White House*, 153.

11. Ibid., 155.

12. The description of Greeley is a pastiche from Bungay, *Off-Hand Takings*, 237, 239–40; O'Laughlin, "Lincoln and the Press," 38; Bradford, *As God Made Them*, 134; Shortall, "Horace Greeley," 2–3; Seitz, *Horace Greeley*, 1–3, 24, 75; Stoddard, *Horace Greeley*, xi; Isely, *Horace Greeley and the Republican Party*, 10–11; Carpenter, *Six Months at the White House*, 152; Andrews, *The North Reports the Civil War*, 10.

13. Shortall, "Horace Greeley," 2; Seitz, *Horace Greeley*, 17.

14. This picture of Greeley at work is borrowed mainly from Seitz, *Horace Greeley*, 17–18, 10. Also see Bungay, *Off-Hand Takings*, 243.

15. The story is from Johnson, "Horace Greeley in Church," Greeley Papers.

16. Seitz, *Horace Greeley*, 8.

17. Bradford, *As God Made Them*, 144–45.

18. Welles, *Diary* 2:83.

19. McClure, *Abraham Lincoln and Men of War Times*, 291.

20. *Chicago Tribune*, 27 February 1864.

21. Greeley, *Recollections of a Busy Life*, 295.

22. Trietsch, *The Printer and the Prince*, 248.

23. Young, *Men and Memories*, 51.

24. Hale, *Horace Greeley*, 275.

25. Trietsch, *The Printer and the Prince*, 233–34.

26. Bungay, *Off-Hand Takings*, 390.

27. Andrews, *The North Reports the Civil War*, 13; Sandburg, *Abraham Lincoln: The War Years* 1:12.

28. Starr, "James Gordon Bennett—Beneficent Rascal," 35.

29. I have relied in this description of Bennett on Fermer, *James Gordon Bennett and the New York Herald*, 1, 328; Smith, *Sunshine and Shadow in New York*, 523; Croffutt, "Bennett and His Times," 199; Starr, "James Gordon Bennett—Beneficent Rascal," 33; and Seitz, *The James Gordon Bennetts*, 206–7.

30. Young, *Men and Memories*, 209.

31. Croffutt, "Bennett and His Times," 199.

32. Fermer, *James Gordon Bennett and the New York Herald*, 1.

33. Starr, "James Gordon Bennett—Beneficent Rascal," 35–36.

34. O'Laughlin, "Lincoln and the Press," 39; Fermer, *James Gordon Bennett and the New York Herald*, 37.

35. Smith, *Sunshine and Shadow in New York*, 512; Fermer, *James Gordon Bennett and the New York Herald*, 40n; Starr, "James Gordon Bennett—Beneficent Rascal," 33.

36. *New York Herald,* 6 May 1835, quoted in Starr, "James Gordon Bennett—Beneficent Rascal," 34.

37. Parton, "The New York Herald," 390.

38. Ibid., 389.

39. Starr, "James Gordon Bennett—Beneficent Rascal," 34; Fermer, *James Gordon Bennett and the New York Herald,* 1–2.

40. Quoted in Sandburg, *Abraham Lincoln: The War Years* 1:12.

41. An excellent rundown of Bennett's positions is in Crouthamel, *Bennett's New York Herald and the Rise of the Popular Press,* 142–47.

42. *New York Herald,* 19 February 1864.

43. Hay, *Lincoln and the Civil War,* 215; Lincoln, *Collected Works* 6:120.

44. Brown, *Raymond of the Times,* 161, 165.

45. Maverick, *Henry J. Raymond and the New York Press,* 17, 28.

46. Andrews, *The North Reports the Civil War,* 10–11.

47. Welles, *Diary* 2:87–88.

48. Andrews, *The North Reports the Civil War,* 11.

49. O'Laughlin, "Lincoln and the Press," 37–38.

50. Ellis, "The *Chicago Times* During the Civil War," 135, 167–71; Andrews, *The North Reports the Civil War,* 29–30.

51. *New York Herald,* 30 December 1863, and 11 June and 19 February 1864.

52. Welles, *Diary* 2:142.

53. Starr, "James Gordon Bennett—Beneficent Rascal," 36.

54. *New York Herald,* 17 April 1864.

55. *Chicago Tribune,* 29 February and 9 January 1864.

56. *New York World,* 19 March 1864; *New York Daily Tribune,* 1 March 1864.

57. Greeley to Mark Howard, 10 January 1864, in Dittenhoefer, *How We Elected Lincoln,* 74.

58. Greeley to Rebekah M. Whipple, 8 March 1864, Greeley Papers.

59. Dittenhoefer, *How We Elected Lincoln,* 77; *New York Daily Tribune,* 1 April 1864.

60. *New York Herald,* 27 April 1864.

61. Welles, "Administration of Abraham Lincoln," 621; Welles, *Diary* 2:4.

62. *New York Times,* 4 April 1864.

63. *New York Herald,* 3, 7, 9 and 11 April 1864.

64. The McClellan meeting was reported in detail in the *New York Herald,* 18 March 1864.

65. *New York World,* 10 and 11 March 1864.

66. *New York Herald,* 5 March 1864.

67. *New York World,* 19 March 1864.

Chapter 12. The Confederate Connection

1. Bill, *The Beleaguered City,* 193.

2. Ibid., 202.

3. Jones, *A Rebel War Clerk's Diary,* 348–51.

4. Ibid., 351.

5. The litany of inflated prices in Richmond in the spring of 1864 can be found in Jones, pages 348–61, and in Varina Davis, *Jefferson Davis, Ex-President of the Confederate States of America* 2:530–33. Also see Bill, *The Beleaguered City,* 202.

6. Jones, *A Rebel War Clerk's Diary,* 358, 361.

7. There is an excellent summary of the South's plight in the *American Annual Cyclopoedia* for 1863, p. 203.

8. Quoted in *The New York Times,* 12 March 1864.

9. *Augusta Constitutionalist,* 22 January 1864, in Nelson, *Bullets, Ballots, and Rhetoric,* 11.

10. *Chicago Tribune,* 26 February 1864.

11. Lee, *The Wartime Papers of R. E. Lee,* 508–9.

12. Davis, *The Rise and Fall of the Confederate Government* 2:611.

13. *Augusta Chronicle & Sentinel,* 6 March 1864, in Nelson, *Bullets, Ballots, and Rhetoric,* 38.

14. *Richmond Examiner,* 30 March 1864, in ibid., 42.

15. Davis, *Jefferson Davis, Ex-President of the Confederate States of America* 2:494, 496.

16. Hay, *Lincoln and the Civil War,* 171–72.

17. Pollard, *Southern History of the War* 2:181.

18. Nelson, *Bullets, Ballots, and Rhetoric,* 35–36.

19. Davis, *Jefferson Davis, Ex-President of the Confederate States of America* 2:496–97; Chesnut, *Mary Chesnut's Civil War,* 601.

20. Most of the detail of Joe's fall and death is from Varina's own account in *Jefferson Davis, Ex-President of the Confederate States of America* 2:496–97.

21. Chesnut, *Mary Chesnut's Civil War,* 601.

22. Davis, *Jefferson Davis, Ex-President of the Confederate States of America* 2:497.

23. Mary's eloquent descriptions of that night in the executive mansion and at the funeral are in *Mary Chesnut's Civil War,* 601–2; 609.

24. Davis, *Jefferson Davis, Constitutionalist* 6:220.

25. Clay is described in Kinchen, *Confederate Operations in Canada and the North,* 37–38.

26. Davis, *Jefferson Davis, Constitutionalist* 6:236–38.

27. U.S. War Department, *The War of the Rebellion,* ser. 1, vol. 43, pt. 2, 930. Henceforth this source will be cited as *O.R.*

28. Thompson's list of goals is distilled largely from Hines, "The Northwest Conspiracy," 500, 508. Thomas H. Hines and his cohort, John B. Castleman, who actually wrote this account of operations in Canada for Hines, were both intimately involved from first to last.

29. Ibid., 505. Also see Kinchen, *Confederate Operations in Canada and the North*, 31.

30. Holcombe and Hines are described in Horan, *Confederate Agent*, 4–5, 85–86. Also see Castleman's book, written after the war: *Active Service*, 9–10; and Gray, *The Hidden Civil War*, 167.

31. Many of these plans are described in Thompson's report of 3 December 1864 to Confederate Secretary of State Judah Benjamin, in *O.R.*, ser. 1, vol. 43, pt. 2, 930–36.

32. Cleary's account of the chase of the *Thistle* is in Hines, "The Northwest Conspiracy," 444–45.

33. For accounts of Thompson's early maneuvering, his meeting with Vallandigham, and his eagerness for the ball to begin, see Hines, "The Northwest Conspiracy," 508–9; Castleman, *Active Service*, 144–47; and Kinchen, *Confederate Operations in Canada and the North*, 42–44, 57.

Chapter 13. An Unquiet Spring

1. E. Howard to Manton Marble, 3 May 1864, Marble Papers.

2. Gurowski, *Diary* 3:159, 191.

3. John Nicolay to Therena Bates, 24 April and 21 March 1864, Nicolay Papers.

4. Brooks, *Mr. Lincoln's Washington*, 324.

5. *New York Times*, 28 May 1864.

6. *New York Daily Tribune*, 17 May 1864.

7. Gurowski, *Diary* 3:159.

8. McClure, *Abraham Lincoln and Men of War Times*, 124.

9. Lincoln, *Collected Works* 7:111.

10. Nicolay, *Personal Traits of Abraham Lincoln*, 280. His name for such cases are from the same source, page 281.

11. Neill, "Reminiscences of the Last Year of President Lincoln's Life," 35.

12. Lincoln, *Collected Works* 7:208.

13. Butler, *Private and Official Correspondence* 3:396–97, 400.

14. Merrill, "General Benjamin F. Butler in the Presidential Campaign of 1864," 546–47.

15. Butler, *Private and Official Correspondence*, 4:510, 546.

16. Hendrick, *Lincoln's War Cabinet*, 51. Cameron is reputed to have said that, but there is no evidence he ever did. Whether he believed it or not is an open question.

He did once say, "There is no rest for the wicked and who is not wicked?" (Bradley, *Simon Cameron*, 423.)

17. According to Butler's later account, when Cameron offered him the vice presidency he replied, "Please say to Mr. Lincoln that while I appreciate with the fullest sensibility this act of friendship and the compliment he pays me, yet I must decline." He then laughed and said, "With the prospect of the [upcoming military] campaign, I would not quit the field to be Vice-President, even with him as President, unless he will give me bond with sureties, in the full sum of his four years' salary that he will die or resign within three months after his inauguration." It is a wonderful story that begs to be believed, but there is no hard evidence that Lincoln made such an offer to Butler, either directly or indirectly. For testimony that he did, see McClure, *Abraham Lincoln and Men of War Times*, 442–43; Rice, *Reminiscences of Abraham Lincoln*, 157–60; Butler, *Butler's Book*, 631–35; and Butler, "Vice Presidential Politics in '64," 331–34. For a scholarly interpretation that accepts the McClure-Butler version, see Merrill, "General Benjamin F. Butler in the Presidential Campaign of 1864," 537–70. For an equally scholarly interpretation that emphatically does not accept it, see Horowitz, "Benjamin Butler: Seventeenth President?", 191–203. Lacking sufficient hard evidence, I have downplayed the affair in the narrative.

18. Butler, *Private and Official Correspondence* 4:29, 59.

19. Adams, *Richard Henry Dana* 2:271–72.

20. *New York Times*, 9 May 1864.

21. Grant, *Memoirs* 2:416.

22. Lincoln, *Collected Works* 7:324.

23. Jones, *A Rebel War Clerk's Diary*, 365.

24. Ibid., 366.

25. Goss, *Recollections of a Private*, 266.

26. Brooks, *Mr. Lincoln's Washington*, 179.

27. Wheeler, *Voices of the Civil War*, 381–82. Private Warren Lee Goss also describes the skull-strewn battlefield in *Recollections of a Private*, 267.

28. Swinton, *Campaigns of the Army of the Potomac*, 418, 429, 437.

29. Goss, *Recollections of a Private*, 264.

30. Swinton, *Campaigns of the Army of the Potomac*, 427, 429, 439.

31. *New York Daily Tribune*, 9 May 1864.

32. Goss, *Recollections of a Private*, 272.

33. Hay, *Lincoln and the Civil War*, 180.

34. Stiles, *Four Years under Marse Robert*, 248, 266.

35. Ford, *A Cycle of Adams Letters* 2:130.

36. Long, *The Civil War Day by Day*, 495.

37. Grant, "Preparing for the Campaigns of '64," 116n.

38. Welles, *Diary* 2:33.
39. Brooks, *Mr. Lincoln's Washington,* 316–17.
40. This story of Lincoln and Wing is told by Tarbell, in *A Reporter for Lincoln,* 1–13. Also see Crozier, *Yankee Reporters,* 382–91; and Bullard, *Famous War Correspondents,* 406–8.
41. Hay, *Lincoln and the Civil War,* 180–81.
42. Brooks, *Mr. Lincoln's Washington,* 318–19.
43. Swinton, *Campaigns of the Army of the Potomac,* 404.
44. The monumental storm is described in Chittenden, *Recollections of President Lincoln and His Administration,* 252.
45. Thomas, *Abraham Lincoln,* 423.
46. Brooks, *Mr. Lincoln's Washington,* 320–21; Welles, *Diary* 2:44–45.
47. Chittenden, *Recollections of President Lincoln and His Administration,* 251.
48. Brooks, *Mr. Lincoln's Washington,* 322–23.
49. Welles, "The Opposition to Lincoln in 1864," 372.
50. Tarbell, *A Reporter for Lincoln,* 53–54.

Chapter 14. The Cleveland 400

1. For the description of Frémont and his character, background, and upbringing in these and subsequent paragraphs, I am indebted to Bartlett, *John C. Frémont and the Republican Party,* 1–2; Bungay, *Off-Hand Takings,* 37, 41; Nevins, *Frémont: The West's Greatest Adventurer,* 703–4, 707; and particularly to Nevins's later revised biography, *Frémont: Pathmarker of the West,* 1–16.
2. Nevins, *Frémont: Pathmarker of the West,* 69–71.
3. Welles, *Diary* 2:41–42.
4. Nelson, *Bullets, Ballots, and Rhetoric,* 48–49.
5. Hay, *Lincoln and the Civil War,* 133.
6. Nicolay and Hay, *Abraham Lincoln* 9:29–30.
7. McPherson, *The Political History of the United States of America During the Great Rebellion,* 410.
8. *New York World,* 6 May 1864.
9. *New York Herald,* 8 and 18 May 1864.
10. *New York Times,* 6 May 1864; Bates, *Lincoln in the Telegraph Office,* 193–94; Barnes, *Memoir of Thurlow Weed,* 446.
11. McPherson, *The Political History of the United States of America During the Great Rebellion,* 411.
12. *New York Herald,* 24 December 1863; *New York World,* 5 December 1863; *New York Times,* 2 July 1864.
13. Phillips, *Speeches, Lectures, and Letters,* 294.

14. Nicolay and Hay, *Abraham Lincoln* 9:32–33.

15. *New York World,* 31 May 1864; Hendrick, *Lincoln's War Cabinet,* 436–37.

16. *New York World,* 31 May 1864.

17. Both quoted in Bartlett, *John C. Frémont and the Republican Party,* 104.

18. Hendrick, *Lincoln's War Cabinet,* 437; Welles, *Diary* 2:43.

19. *Cleveland Plain Dealer,* 2 June 1864.

20. *Chicago Tribune,* 3 June 1864.

21. Bates, *Lincoln in the Telegraph Office,* 195.

22. *Cleveland Plain Dealer,* 2 June 1864; Alexander, *A Political History of the State of New York* 3:6.

23. McPherson, *The Political History of the United States of America During the Great Rebellion,* 412.

24. Ibid., 413, 413n.

25. *Chicago Tribune,* 3 June 1864.

26. Welles, *Diary* 2:43.

27. Hay, *Lincoln and the Civil War,* 184.

28. *New York Herald,* 1 June 1864; *Chicago Tribune,* 3 June 1864.

29. Zornow, "The Cleveland Convention, 1864," 49; Alexander, *A Political History of the State of New York* 3:92.

30. McPherson, *The Political History of the United States of America During the Great Rebellion,* 414.

31. *New York Herald* 2 June 1864.

32. *New York Times,* 2 and 3 June and 2 July 1864.

Chapter 15. What! Am I Renominated?

1. Law, "From the Wilderness to Cold Harbor," 139; Swinton, *Campaigns of the Army of the Potomac,* 485.

2. Tarbell, *A Reporter for Lincoln,* 51.

3. Law, "From the Wilderness to Cold Harbor," 141.

4. Goss, *Recollections of a Private,* 315.

5. Gurowski, *Diary* 3:246; Lee, *Wartime Washington,* 389.

6. Hay, *Lincoln and the Civil War,* 185.

7. Ibid.

8. Bates, *Diary,* 373–74.

9. Gurowski, *Diary* 3:249.

10. Hendrick, *Lincoln's War Cabinet,* 437–38; Nicolay and Hay, *Abraham Lincoln* 9:29.

11. John Nicolay to John Hay, 5 June 1864, Nicolay Papers.

12. *New York Daily Tribune,* 6 June 1864.

13. Brooks, *Mr. Lincoln's Washington,* 246, 325–26.

14. Smith, *Sunshine and Shadow in New York,* 317; Milton, *The Age of Hate,* 23; Brown, *Raymond of the Times,* 251–52.

15. Stoddard, "The Story of a Nomination," 267–68.

16. Speer, *Life of General James H. Lane,* 280; Stoddard, *Inside the White House in War Times,* 238–39.

17. Stoddard was present, and this account of the Grand Council meeting and Lane's rising to speak is recounted in his memoir, *Inside the White House in War Times,* 239–40.

18. Hay, *Lincoln and the Civil War,* 9, 289.

19. *New York Herald,* 14 October 1863.

20. *Dictionary of American Biography,* s.v. "Lane, James Henry."

21. Lewis, "The Man the Historians Forgot," 85–87.

22. Brooks, *Mr. Lincoln's Washington,* 316.

23. Hay, *Lincoln and the Civil War,* 177.

24. The account of Lane's speech and the reaction to it are in Stoddard, *Inside the White House in War Times,* 240–42.

25. The Front Street Theatre and its arrangement are described from a mix of sources: Welles, *Diary* 2:30; Brooks, *Mr. Lincoln's Washington,* 328–29; White, *Autobiography* 1:117; *Baltimore Gazette,* 8 June 1864; *New York Herald,* 8 June 1864.

26. Seilhamer, *History of the Republican Party,* 138.

27. *Baltimore American,* 8 June 1864; *Baltimore Sun,* 8 June 1864; *Proceedings of the First Three Republican National Conventions,* 176 (hereafter cited as *Proceedings*).

28. For a description of Morgan, see Rawley, *Edwin D. Morgan,* 137–38, 267–68.

29. McPherson, *The Political History of the United States of America During the Great Rebellion,* 403.

30. *Proceedings,* 180.

31. Brooks, *Mr. Lincoln's Washington,* 330.

32. *Proceedings,* 185–86; Brown, *Raymond of the Times,* 253.

33. Milton, *The Age of Hate,* 46, 51.

34. *Proceedings,* 189; Milton, *The Age of Hate,* 51–52.

35. Brooks, *Mr. Lincoln's Washington,* 331.

36. Laughlin, "Missouri Politics During the Civil War," 267.

37. Carr, "Why Lincoln Was Not Renominated by Acclamation," 505.

38. *Proceedings,* 215–16.

39. Hendrick, *Lincoln's War Cabinet,* 439–40.

40. Brown, *Raymond of the Times,* 251, 254; Milton, *The Age of Hate,* 23.

41. *Proceedings,* 225–26.

42. Brooks, *Mr. Lincoln's Washington,* 335.

43. Hendrick, *Lincoln's War Cabinet,* 440–41.

44. The following description of how the president was renominated is taken from *Proceedings,* 227–34, unless otherwise cited.

45. Brooks, *Washington in Lincoln's Time,* 144.

46. Speer, *James H. Lane,* 283–84.

47. Brooks, "Two War-Time Conventions," 724.

48. Campbell's frustrated attempt to second Lincoln's nomination is described in Brooks, *Mr. Lincoln's Washington,* 337; and Brooks, *Washington in Lincoln's Time,* 144–45. With an assist from Hay, *Lincoln and the Civil War,* 186.

49. The outburst on the floor against Missouri, Widdicombe's account of it, and the intercession by Lane and Stone are from Stevens, "Lincoln and Missouri," 111.

50. Brooks, *Mr. Lincoln's Washington,* 337–38; Brooks, *Washington in Lincoln's Time,* 146; Brooks, "Two War-Time Conventions," 725.

51. Brooks, "Two War-Time Conventions," 726. There are several conflicting versions of how Lincoln heard of his nomination. The painter Francis Carpenter says the president heard first of Johnson's nomination, when a wire came in announcing it. "What!" Carpenter has the president exclaiming, "do they nominate a Vice-President before they do a President?" "Why," said the astonished telegraph operator, "have you not heard of your own nomination? It was sent to the White House two hours ago." To that Lincoln said, "It is all right. I shall probably find it on my return." (Carpenter, *Six Months at the White House,* 163.) Yet another version puts Lincoln at Grover's Theatre on the day of his nomination, where Lincoln said to Grover, "There is a convention, as I suppose you know, Mr. Grover, and I thought I would get away for a little while, lest they make me promise too much." At about nine o'clock a messenger from the White House came with a telegram carrying news of his nomination. "Well," the president is reputed to have said to Grover, "they have nominated me again." Grover congratulated him and predicted his reelection. "I think it looks that way," Lincoln said, "but I am a little curious to know what man they are going to harness up with me." (Grover, "Lincoln's Interest in the Theater," 947.)

52. McClure, *Abraham Lincoln and Men of War Times,* 105.

53. Howard, *Civil War Echoes,* 23–24.

54. Speer, *James H. Lane,* 284.

55. McClure, *Abraham Lincoln and Men of War Times,* 115–17, 446.

56. Ibid., 446.

57. Dittenhoefer, *How We Elected Lincoln,* 80, 83.

58. McClure, *Abraham Lincoln and Men of War Times*, 443.

59. Sumner, "Our Domestic Relations," 521. For description and background on Johnson I have drawn on Milton, *The Age of Hate*, 86–87, 90, 92, 96, 120–21; Winston, *Andrew Johnson*, 243, 246–47; Stryker, *Andrew Johnson*, 95, 132; Trefousse, *Andrew Johnson*, 17–18, 20–22, 152, 155–56.

60. Foote, *The Civil War* 1:51.

61. Stryker, *Andrew Johnson*, 98.

62. Brownlow's remarks at the convention are in *Proceedings*, 198–99.

63. Brooks, "Two War-Time Conventions," 723.

64. Lincoln, *Collected Works* 7:377–78n.

65. McClure, *Abraham Lincoln and Men of War Times*, 431.

66. Ibid., 260.

67. The controversy over whether Lincoln favored Johnson, and, even more pointedly, sent selected emissaries to the convention to make certain he was nominated, churns on even to this day. My political instincts are conditioned by presidential politics in the twentieth century, where it is unthinkable that a presidential candidate would not dictate his choice of a running mate, and that everybody would not know it. It seems inconceivable in light of political reality today that a candidate, particularly one so astute as Lincoln, would leave such an important matter in such a critical and close election to chance. But in the nineteenth century such direct interference was not necessarily the modus operandi. The argument that Lincoln interfered directly is a persuasive one, believed by many leading historians, but it is waged essentially on the testimony and documentation of but one man, Alexander McClure, who claimed emphatically that Lincoln conspired to see Johnson nominated and kept it hidden from many people, Hamlin included, despite his disclaimer to Nicolay. McClure's veracity has been questioned on other matters, and it must be questioned here. The only "hard" evidence we have is Lincoln's reply to Nicolay, which was a strictly hands-off position. In light of that, I have reluctantly shied from telling the story from McClure's point of view. I have concluded about that what Lincoln concluded about James Gordon Bennett—too pitchy to touch. For the argument that Lincoln interceded from beginning to end and how he did it, see McClure, *Abraham Lincoln and Men of War Times*, 425–49. For strong dissents and a spirited defense of Lincoln's neutrality in the matter, see Fehrenbacher, "The Making of a Myth: Lincoln and the Vice Presidential Nomination in 1864," 273–90; Glonek, "Lincoln, Johnson, and the Baltimore Ticket," 255–71; and Hamlin, *The Life and Times of Hannibal Hamlin*, 461–89, 591–615.

68. Quoted in the *New York Daily Tribune*, 24 June 1864.

69. Winston, *Andrew Johnson*, 257.

70. *New York World,* 9 June 1864.

71. Mason, Diary, entry for 12 June 1864, Remey Family Papers.

72. *New York Herald,* 10 and 11 June 1864.

73. Lincoln, *Collected Works* 7:381n.

74. Ibid., 380, 384.

75. Quote is by Charles Francis Adams Jr., in Long, *The Civil War Day by Day,* 515. The casualty figures are from Swinton, *Campaigns of the Army of the Potomac,* 491–92.

Chapter 16. War Weariness

1. Welles, "The Opposition to Lincoln in 1864," 368.

2. Gurowski, *Diary* 3:236.

3. Brooks, *Mr. Lincoln's Washington,* 342–43.

4. Quoted in Mellon, *The Face of Lincoln,* 6.

5. Nicolay, *Lincoln's Secretary,* 186.

6. Lincoln, *Collected Works* 7:394–95.

7. From "Hope and Peace," printed in the *West Moreland* (Pennsylvania) *Republican,* and sent 30 May 1864 from Johnstown, Pennsylvania, McClellan Papers.

8. McClellan, *Oration of Maj.-Gen. McClellan,* 14–16, 19, 23, 33–34.

9. Nelson, *Bullets, Ballots, and Rhetoric,* 95.

10. Manton Marble to George McClellan, 16 June 1864, McClellan Papers.

11. *New York Herald,* 25 June 1864.

12. *Chicago Tribune,* 23 June 1864.

13. B. F. Meyers to George McClellan, 22 June 1864; Samuel S. Cox to McClellan, 4 August 1864, McClellan Papers.

14. The Democratic meeting and some of the tug-of-war is described in Katz, *August Belmont,* 126–27.

15. Samuel S. Cox to George McClellan, 9 June 1864, McClellan Papers.

16. McClellan, *Civil War Papers,* 579.

17. Manton Marble to George McClellan, 13 June 1864, McClellan Papers.

18. McClellan, *Civil War Papers,* 580.

19. Samuel S. Cox to Manton Marble, 20 June 1864, Marble Papers.

20. Earl Goodrich to Manton Marble, 27 June 1864, Marble Papers.

21. James C. Conkling to Lyman Trumbull, 29 June 1864, Trumbull Papers.

22. Chateau 64 to Manton Marble, 5 July 1864, Marble Papers.

23. Starr, "Was There a Northwest Conspiracy?", 327.

24. Hines, "The Northwest Conspiracy," 502.

25. Ibid., 507.

26. For descriptions and statistical background on this Northwestern tie to the South, see Hubbart, "'Pro-Southern' Influences in the Free West," 45–54; and Starr, "Was There a Northwest Conspiracy?", 324.

27. Nicolay and Hay, *Abraham Lincoln* 8:3, 8.

28. This litany of insurgent activity is from a report by Joseph Holt, the Union judge advocate general, issued 8 October 1864, and reprinted in *O.R.,* ser. 2, vol. 7, 943–49.

29. Milton, *Abraham Lincoln and the Fifth Column,* 280.

30. Holt report, in *O.R.,* ser. 2, vol. 7, 949, 953.

31. Klement, *Dark Lanterns,* 138.

32. Nicolay and Hay, *Abraham Lincoln* 8:13.

33. Lincoln's visit to the army is described in Porter, *Campaigning with Grant,* 216–24.

34. Ibid., 223.

Chapter 17. Showdown at the Capitol

1. Brooks, *Mr. Lincoln's Washington,* 344–45.

2. Ibid., 345–46.

3. This image of the Capitol dome is from Macdonell, "America Then and Now," 52.

4. Brooks, *Mr. Lincoln's Washington,* 345.

5. Fessenden, *Life and Public Services of William Pitt Fessenden,* 1:325; Jellison, *Fessenden of Maine,* 180.

6. Carman and Luthin, *Lincoln and the Patronage,* 245.

7. Brooks, *Mr. Lincoln's Washington,* 352.

8. Welles, *Diary* 2:62.

9. Field, *Memories of Many Men,* 300.

10. Chase, *Inside Lincoln's Cabinet,* 217.

11. Lincoln, *Collected Works* 7:412–13.

12. Nicolay and Hay, *Abraham Lincoln* 9:93.

13. Lincoln, *Collected Works* 7:413–14.

14. Ibid., 414n.

15. Lincoln later recounted these four occasions to Maunsell Field himself, which Field in turn recounted in his *Memories of Many Men,* 302–4.

16. Chittenden, *Recollections of President Lincoln and His Administration,* 379.

17. Hay, *Lincoln and the Civil War,* 198.

18. Lincoln, *Collected Works* 7:420.

19. Chase, *Inside Lincoln's Cabinet,* 223.

20. Lincoln, *Collected Works* 7:419.

21. Chase, *Inside Lincoln's Cabinet,* 225; Warden, *An Account of the Private Life and Public Services of Salmon Portland Chase,* 628.

22. Quoted in Hendrick, *Lincoln's War Cabinet,* 451.

23. *New York World,* 1 July 1864.

24. *New York Herald,* 1 and 3 July 1864.

25. Hay, *Lincoln and the Civil War,* 199.

26. *New York World,* 1 July 1864.

27. Hay, *Lincoln and the Civil War,* 201.

28. The account of Fessenden's nomination, its swift confirmation, and his and Lincoln's reactions are in ibid., 201–3.

29. Brooks, *Mr. Lincoln's Washington,* 349.

30. Howard, *Civil War Echoes,* 24.

31. Field, *Memories of Many Men,* 307.

32. Ibid., 307. Also see the rankings of various senators by the Washington correspondent of the *Cincinnati Daily Commercial,* reprinted in the *Chicago Tribune,* 4 March 1864; and Howard, *Civil War Echoes,* 26.

33. Williams, "Lincoln and the Radicals," 93.

34. Chase, *Inside Lincoln's Cabinet,* 226; Schuckers, *The Life and Public Services of Salmon Portland Chase,* 385.

35. Chase, *Inside Lincoln's Cabinet,* 227.

36. Ibid., 228.

37. Fessenden, *Life and Public Services of William Pitt Fessenden* 1:319.

38. Ibid., 320.

39. Jellison, *Fessenden of Maine,* 182.

40. Fessenden, *Life and Public Services of William Pitt Fessenden* 1:320–21.

41. Jellison, *Fessenden of Maine,* 182.

42. Comment of both papers quoted in ibid., 182–83.

43. Field, *Memories of Many Men,* 298.

44. Brooks, *Washington in Lincoln's Time,* 152.

45. Howard, *Civil War Echoes,* 133.

46. Brooks, *Washington in Lincoln's Time,* 28.

47. Brooks, *Mr. Lincoln's Washington,* 350.

48. Nicolay and Hay, *Abraham Lincoln* 9:113.

49. Quoted by Wendell Phillips in a speech reprinted in the *New York Herald,* 27 October 1864.

50. These views of Davis and his allies are in Hesseltine, *Lincoln's Plan of Reconstruction,* 115–16.

51. *Richmond Examiner,* 12 March and 15 April 1864, quoted in Nelson, *Bullets, Ballots, and Rhetoric,* 12.

52. William B. Hill to John Cresswell, 19 February 1864, Cresswell Papers.

53. The ultimate intentions of the radicals are well described in Williams, *Lincoln and the Radicals,* 319.

54. Nicolay and Hay, *Abraham Lincoln* 9:115; Welles, *Diary* 2:95.

55. Belz, *Reconstructing the Union,* 214–16.

56. Brooks, *Washington in Lincoln's Time,* 34.

57. Howard, *Civil War Echoes,* 22–23.

58. Welles, *Diary* 2:95.

59. This little composite of Wade's traits is drawn from Ellis, *Sights and Secrets of the National Capital,* 123–24; Brooks, *Washington in Lincoln's Time,* 34; Riddle, *The Life of Benjamin F. Wade,* 86, 88; and Trefousse, *Benjamin Franklin Wade,* 219–20.

60. Chase, *Inside Lincoln's Cabinet,* 229.

61. Brooks, "Two War-Time Conventions," 727.

62. The description of the president's room is courtesy of Ellis, *Sights and Secrets of the National Capital,* 89.

63. Hay, *Lincoln and the Civil War,* 204.

64. Buell, "Zachariah Chandler," 272; Howard, *Civil War Echoes,* 53.

65. Harris, *Public Life of Zachariah Chandler,* 54.

66. The description of Chandler's walk and dress are from Howard, *Civil War Echoes,* 53.

67. The events and what was said in the president's room are reported by Hay, in *Lincoln and the Civil War,* 204–5.

68. Bates, *Diary,* 382.

69. Hay, *Lincoln and the Civil War,* 205–6.

70. Brooks, *Washington in Lincoln's Time,* 154.

71. Lincoln, *Collected Works* 7:433.

72. Quoted in Belz, *Reconstructing the Union,* 227–28.

Chapter 18. Get Down, You Fool!

1. *O.R.,* ser 1, vol. 37, pt. 1, 174.

2. Both quotes are from Nicolay and Hay, *Abraham Lincoln* 9:158, 159.

3. Welles, *Diary* 2:68.

4. The description of Early owes much to Wise, *The End of an Era,* 228. Also see Sorrel, *Recollections of a Confederate Staff Officer,* 49, 56; and Douglas, *I Rode with Stonewall,* 33.

5. Stiles, *Four Years under Marse Robert,* 189.

6. Ibid., 190.

7. Douglas, *I Rode with Stonewall,* 292. Also see Bradwell, "First of Valley Campaign by General Early," 231, and "Early's March to Washington in 1864," 176.

8. Wallace, *An Autobiography* 2:702.

9. Ibid., 2:713.

10. Roe, "Recollections of Monocacy," 433.

11. Wallace, *An Autobiography* 2:742, 751.

12. Worsham, *One of Jackson's Foot Cavalry,* 151.

13. This brief account as the battle continued and time passed is from Wallace, *An Autobiography* 2:265–96.

14. Worsham, *One of Jackson's Foot Cavalry,* 155.

15. Welles, *Diary* 2:69–70.

16. *Chicago Evening Journal,* 20 July 1864, quoted in Andrews, *The North Reports the Civil War,* 591.

17. Lincoln, *Collected Works* 7:437.

18. Ibid., 437–38.

19. Brooks, "Two War-Time Conventions," 730.

20. Lincoln, *Collected Works* 7:438n.

21. Andrews, *The North Reports the Civil War,* 593.

22. Lincoln, *Collected Works* 7:438.

23. Welles, *Diary* 2:71.

24. Brooks, "Two War-Time Conventions," 730.

25. Worsham, *One of Jackson's Foot Cavalry,* 155–56.

26. Andrews, *The North Reports the Civil War,* 592; Brooks, "Two War-Time Conventions," 730.

27. Early, *A Memoir of the Last Year of the War for Independence,* 48.

28. This sequence of events at the Blair house was later told to Elizabeth Blair Lee by Jim Byrne, and is recounted in *Wartime Washington,* 413.

29. Welles, *Diary* 2:70.

30. Lee, *Wartime Washington,* 413.

31. Seward, *Reminiscences of a War-Time Statesman,* 246.

32. Hay, *Lincoln and the Civil War,* 208.

33. These developments and Early's train of reasoning are recorded in his *A Memoir of the Last Year of the War for Independence,* 50–52.

34. Stevens, *Three Years in the Sixth Corps,* 374.

35. The account of Lincoln's conversation with Wright on the parapets is from *Lincoln Lore* 699 (31 August 1942). This event, Lincoln under fire at Fort Stevens on 12 July, has been the subject of endless telling, retelling, and romanticizing, particularly the part where Holmes told the fool to get down. Evidently years after the event, Holmes, who was by then the great Supreme Court Justice, told the story to a few close friends. Perhaps the most dramatic retelling is by Alexander Woollcott in his "Get Down, You Fool," 169–73. For evenhanded analyses of these various stories, see Cramer, *Lincoln under Enemy Fire,* and Hicks, "Lincoln, Wright and

Holmes," 323–32. I have read the various versions and reconstructed the scenario as I think it might logically have happened.

36. Lee, *Wartime Washington,* 411.

37. Douglas, *I Rode with Stonewall,* 295–96.

38. Dana, *Recollections of the Civil War,* 230–31.

39. Lee, *Wartime Washington,* 402.

40. Ibid., 404–5.

41. Quoted in Hendrick, *Lincoln's War Cabinet,* 389.

42. Lincoln, *Collected Works* 7:439–40.

43. Welles, *Diary* 2:76–77.

44. The noodles quote is in the *New York Herald,* 27 July 1864. Bennett's oft-repeated, unsolicited advice is, for instance, repeated in the issues of 13, 14, 15, 17, 20, and 28 July, and 4 and 5 August.

45. *New York Times,* 13 July 1864.

46. Ibid., 16 July 1864; *Chicago Tribune,* 20 July 1864.

47. Quoted in the *Chicago Tribune,* 11 August 1864.

48. Kean, *Inside the Confederate Government,* 164.

49. Hay, *Lincoln and the Civil War,* 210.

50. *New York Herald,* 29 July 1864.

Chapter 19. The Peaceseekers

1. This picture of Greeley, his mood, and his beliefs is stitched together from various sources: Kirkland, *The Peacemakers of 1864,* 66–67; Van Deusen, *Horace Greeley,* 296, 302, 308–9; Horner, *Lincoln and Greeley,* 299; Dunlap, "President Lincoln and Editor Greeley," 100.

2. Welles, "Lincoln's Triumph in 1864," 454.

3. Kinchen, *Confederate Operations in Canada and the North,* 75–76.

4. *New York World,* 22 July and 2 August 1864.

5. Bates, *Diary,* 388.

6. My own interpretation after staring at Jewett's photograph in Meredith, *Mr. Lincoln's Contemporaries,* 203.

7. *New York Times,* 1 August 1864.

8. *O.R.,* ser. 4, vol. 3, 584.

9. Kinchen, *Confederate Operations in Canada and the North,* 76.

10. Sanders is described in Curtis, "George N. Sanders—American Patriot of the Fifties," 80–81. Also see Kinchen, *Confederate Operations in Canada and the North,* 41; and Castleman, *Active Service,* 134–36.

11. Lincoln, *Collected Works* 7:435n.

12. Cullom, *Fifty Years of Public Service*, 101.
13. Nicolay and Hay, *Abraham Lincoln* 9:217.
14. Lincoln, *Collected Works* 7:435.
15. Hay, *Letters of John Hay and Extracts from Diary* 1:213.
16. Lincoln, *Collected Works* 7:441n.
17. Ibid.
18. Ibid., 440.
19. Ibid., 441–42.
20. Hay's account is in *Letters of John Hay and Extracts from Diary* 1:212–13.
21. Lincoln, *Collected Works* 7:443n.
22. Castleman, *Active Service*, 136; Kirkland, *The Peacemakers of 1864*, 80–81.
23. Lincoln, *Collected Works* 7:451n.
24. Hay, *Letters of John Hay and Extracts from Diary* 1:214–15.
25. Lincoln, *Collected Works* 7:451.
26. The train of events at Niagara is from Hay's account in *Letters of John Hay and Extracts from Diary* 1:215–17.
27. Kinchen, *Confederate Operations in Canada and the North*, 83–84.
28. Welles, *Diary* 2:83.
29. Bennett's editorial comments are in the *New York Herald*, 21, 22, 27, and 29 July 1864.
30. *New York World*, 22 July 1864.
31. *New York Times*, 1 August 1864.
32. Tarbell, *The Life of Abraham Lincoln* 2:198.
33. Gilmore, *Down in Tennessee*, 236.
34. This story of Jaquess in 1863 is stitched together from accounts in Nicolay and Hay, *Abraham Lincoln* 9:201–3; Gilmore, *Down in Tennessee*, 235; Kirkland, *The Peacemakers of 1864*, 86–89; Horner, *Lincoln and Greeley*, 324.
35. Lincoln's thinking about the prospects for peace and his attitude and actions in approving the Jaquess-Gilmore mission are explained in Nicolay and Hay, *Abraham Lincoln* 9:206–7.
36. Lincoln, *Collected Works* 7:429.
37. From a lecture by Gilmore in Pawtucket on August 10, 1864, as reported in the *Providence Press* and reprinted in *The New York Times* of 14 August.
38. Nicolay and Hay, *Abraham Lincoln* 9:208.
39. Gilmore, *Personal Recollections of Abraham Lincoln and the Civil War*, 259.
40. U.S. Navy Department, *Official Records of Union and Confederate Navies in the War of the Rebellion*, ser. 2, vol. 3, 1192. Henceforth this source will be cited as *O.R., Navy*.
41. Nicolay and Hay, *Abraham Lincoln* 9:209–11.

42. Gilmore, *Personal Recollections of Abraham Lincoln and the Civil War,* 272.

43. Welles, *Diary* 2:83–84.

44. Lincoln, *Collected Works* 7:459–60.

45. Ibid., 461, 461n.

Chapter 20. The Wild Howl of Summer

1. John Nicolay to Therena Bates, 20 July 1864, Nicolay Papers.

2. Ben Wade to Horace Greeley, 1 August 1864, Greeley Papers.

3. *New York Daily Tribune,* 5 August 1864.

4. Nicolay and Hay, *Abraham Lincoln* 9:125.

5. Butler, *Private and Official Correspondence* 5:8.

6. Brooks, *Washington in Lincoln's Time,* 156–57.

7. Holland, *The Life of Abraham Lincoln,* 477–78.

8. Butler, *Private and Official Correspondence* 5:8.

9. Bennett's comments and suggestions are in the *New York Herald,* 6 and 11 August 1864.

10. *New York Times,* 9 and 20 August 1864.

11. Ibid., 28 May 1864.

12. *Richmond Examiner,* 12 August 1864, reprinted in the *New York World,* 16 August 1864.

13. Butler, *Private and Official Correspondence* 5:9.

14. *New York Times,* 16 August 1864.

15. Zornow, "The Attitude of the Western Reserve Press on the Reelection of Lincoln," 36.

16. *New York Times,* 30 August 1864.

17. Brooks, *Washington in Lincoln's Time,* 157–58; McClure, *Abraham Lincoln and Men of War Times,* 105.

18. Welles, "Lincoln's Triumph in 1864," 455; McClure, *Abraham Lincoln and Men of War Times,* 105.

19. These four letters to Butler are in his *Private and Official Correspondence* 5:43, 47–48, 55, 67.

20. John Nicolay to Therena Bates, 28 August 1864, Nicolay Papers.

21. *New York Times,* 10 August 1864.

22. Gurowski, *Diary* 3:90.

23. Lincoln, *Collected Works* 7:514n.

24. Raymond's letter is in ibid., 7:517–18n.

25. Swett's observations are in two letters to his wife, reprinted in Tarbell, *The Life of Abraham Lincoln* 2:201–3.

26. John Nicolay to Therena Bates, 21 August 1864, Nicolay Papers.

27. Hay, *Lincoln and the Civil War*, 212–13.

28. This face-off with Stevens at the White House is from a handwritten paper titled "The Interview Between Thad Stevens & Mr. Lincoln as Related by Col. R. M. Hoe," in the Nicolay Papers.

29. Nicolay and Hay, *Abraham Lincoln* 9:250; Cullom, *Fifty Years of Public Service*, 99.

30. Brooks, *Mr. Lincoln's Washington*, 362–63.

31. McClure, *Abraham Lincoln and Men of War Times*, 113–15.

32. Mills's diary account of the conversation is in Lincoln, *Collected Works* 7:506–8.

33. Butler, *Private and Official Correspondence* 5:35.

34. Eaton's mission to Grant is described in Eaton, *Grant, Lincoln and the Freedmen*, 186–91. Also see Tarbell, *The Life of Abraham Lincoln* 2:199–200.

35. Lincoln, *Collected Works* 7:512.

36. John Nicolay to John Hay, 25 August 1864, Nicolay Papers.

37. Nicolay and Hay, *Abraham Lincoln* 9:221.

38. Hay, *Lincoln and the Civil War*, 237.

39. Butler, *Private and Official Correspondence* 5:67–68.

40. The *New York Sun* on 30 June 1889, twenty-five years later, printed a long article about this call for a new convention to pick a new nominee replacing Lincoln, and reprinted a host of letters from participants and would-be participants. Greeley's letter and the letters touching on the call and its signing, which are quoted below, are all from that article—unless otherwise cited.

41. Butler, *Private and Official Correspondence* 5:81.

42. Ibid., 68.

43. Ibid., 8–9, 117.

44. Ibid., 68, 119.

45. These sentiments are from various letters from Butler to his wife, in ibid., 39, 94, 112.

46. Cyrus H. McCormick to Manton Marble, 17 August 1864, Marble Papers.

47. Hines, "The Northwest Conspiracy," 509.

48. *New York Times*, 11 August 1864.

49. *New York Daily Tribune*, 12 August 1864.

50. *New York World*, 11 August 1864.

51. Both of these warnings not to send him politicians are from McClellan, *Civil War Papers*, 586.

52. Sidney Brooks to George McClellan, 15 July 1864, McClellan Papers.

53. Stephen L. Mersh to George McClellan, 12 August 1864, ibid.

54. Blair's visit with McClellan is from the account in Nicolay and Hay, *Abraham Lincoln* 9:247–49.

55. McClellan, *Civil War Papers*, 583–84.

Chapter 21. The Band Played "Dixie"

1. Brooks, *Washington in Lincoln's Time*, 164.
2. Brooks, "Two War-Time Conventions," 732.
3. Lincoln, *Collected Works* 7:524n.
4. Hay, *Lincoln and the Civil War*, 211.
5. *Philadelphia Inquirer*, 14 November 1864.
6. Samuel S. Cox to Manton Marble, 21 August 1864, Marble Papers.
7. S. L. M. Barlow to Manton Marble, 21 August 1864, ibid.
8. Ibid., (undated) August 1864.
9. Brooks, *Mr. Lincoln's Washington*, 365.
10. Ibid.
11. Brooks's account of the train trip to Chicago is in his "Two War-Time Conventions," 732.
12. Katz, *August Belmont*, 128.
13. *New York World*, 30 August 1864; *New York Herald*, 28 August 1864; *New York Times*, 28 August 1864.
14. *Chicago Times*, 25 August 1864.
15. *Chicago Tribune*, 27 August 1864.
16. Ibid., 28 August 1864.
17. *New York World*, 26 August 1864.
18. Brooks, *Mr. Lincoln's Washington*, 369; *New York Herald*, 28 August 1864.
19. Brooks, *Mr. Lincoln's Washington*, 366.
20. *New York World*, 26 August 1864.
21. *New York Times*, 30 August 1864.
22. *New York Herald*, 28 August 1864; *Chicago Tribune*, 29 August 1864.
23. Katz, *August Belmont*, 131–32.
24. *New York Herald*, 24 August 1864.
25. Katz, *August Belmont*, 128–29.
26. S. L. M. Barlow to George McClellan, 16 June 1864, McClellan Papers.
27. Macdonell, "America Then and Now," 52; Detroit Post and Tribune, *Zachariah Chandler*, 272; Brooks, *Mr. Lincoln's Washington*, 25–26, 44, 69, 105.
28. Brooks, *Mr. Lincoln's Washington*, 105–6.
29. *Chicago Tribune*, 8 September 1864.
30. Klement, *Dark Lanterns*, 170.
31. I owe this account of the Confederates in Chicago to Nelson, *Bullets, Ballots, and Rhetoric*, 110–11.
32. *New York Daily Tribune*, 1 September 1864.
33. *New York World*, 26 August 1864; *New York Herald*, 30 August 1864.
34. Brooks, "Two War-Time Conventions," 732; Brooks, *Mr. Lincoln's Washington*, 370.

35. *New York Daily Tribune,* 1 September 1864.

36. *Official Proceedings of the Democratic National Convention,* 3–4. Henceforth this will be cited as *Official Proceedings.*

37. Ibid., 11.

38. Most of the detail describing the activity on the convention floor is taken from the *Official Proceedings.* Where called for, specific pages will be cited. The description of the long devotional exercises is from pages 11–12.

39. Ibid., 23.

40. Brooks, "Two War-Time Conventions," 733; Brooks, *Mr. Lincoln's Washington,* 371.

41. Klement, *The Limits of Dissent,* 284–85.

42. The resolutions are reprinted in full in the *Official Proceedings,* 27.

43. Brooks, "Two War-Time Conventions," 733. Also see *Official Proceedings,* 27–28.

44. Silbey, *A Respectable Minority,* 126.

45. Nicolay and Hay, *Abraham Lincoln* 9:258; *Official Proceedings,* 28.

46. *Official Proceedings,* 29.

47. Brooks, "Two War-Time Conventions," 732; Klement, *The Limits of Dissent,* 279, 281.

48. *Official Proceedings,* 29.

49. Harris's harangue and the furor on the floor is in ibid., 30–33.

50. *New York Daily Tribune,* 5 September 1864. For a slightly different account, see Brooks, "Two War-Time Conventions," 733; and Brooks, *Mr. Lincoln's Washington,* 373.

51. *Official Proceedings,* 33.

52. Morgan's statement is in ibid., 34–35, the Maryland disclaimers on 36–37.

53. Ibid., 38.

54. Nicolay and Hay, *Abraham Lincoln* 9:255; *Official Proceedings,* 28.

55. *Official Proceedings,* 38–40.

56. The exchange in the darkness and adjournment is in ibid., 41–42.

57. For descriptions of Chicago that night, see Brooks, "Two War-Time Conventions," 733–34; Brooks, *Mr. Lincoln's Washington,* 375; *New York Daily Tribune,* 20 August 1864.

58. For this chain of events, see Brooks, "Two War-Time Conventions," 734; *New York Herald,* 1 September 1864; *Official Proceedings,* 46–47.

59. These speeches are in the *Official Proceedings,* 47–53.

60. Katz, *August Belmont,* 132–33; *New York Times,* 23 September 1864; Brooks, *Mr. Lincoln's Washington,* 304.

61. Brooks, *Mr. Lincoln's Washington,* 110–11; Brooks, *Washington in Lincoln's Time,* 170.

62. John Douglass to George McClellan, 5 September 1864, McClellan Papers.
63. Brooks, *Mr. Lincoln's Washington,* 378–79.
64. *New York Herald,* 1 September 1864.
65. Welles, "Lincoln's Triumph in 1864," 463.
66. Welles, *Diary* 2:132, 135–36.
67. Ibid., 136.
68. French, *Witness to the Young Republic,* 455.
69. Gurowski, *Diary* 3:328.
70. Quoted in Nelson, *Bullets, Ballots, and Rhetoric,* 110.
71. *Augusta Constitutionalist,* 9 September 1864, and *Richmond Dispatch,* 5 September 1864, both quoted in ibid., 114.

Chapter 22. Clearing the Track

1. Farragut, *The Life of David Glasgow Farragut,* 405.
2. Ibid., 417. Also see Johnson and Buel, *Battles and Leaders of the Civil War* 4:391, 406–8.
3. Lindeman, *The Conflict of Convictions,* 255.
4. Sherman, *Memoirs* 2:583.
5. Williams, *This War So Horrible,* 110.
6. Rawson, Personal Papers for 1864, Atlanta Historical Society.
7. Reed, *History of Atlanta, Georgia,* 194. Both Rawson and Reed's descriptions are more readily accessible in Carter, *The Siege of Atlanta,* 315–16.
8. Williams, *This War So Horrible,* 110.
9. Sherman, *Memoirs* 2:581–82. Also see Cox, *Atlanta,* 208; and Lewis, *Sherman: Fighting Prophet,* 407.
10. *O.R.,* vol. 38, pt. 5, 777.
11. *Chicago Tribune,* 5 September 1864.
12. Nicolay and Hay, *Abraham Lincoln* 9:305.
13. *O.R.,* ser. 1, vol. 43, pt. 2, 117–18.
14. Both quotes are from Nelson, *Bullets, Ballots, and Rhetoric,* 119–21.
15. Chesnut, *Mary Chesnut's Civil War,* 642.
16. Katz, *August Belmont,* 133; Sears, *George B. McClellan,* 375.
17. James Laurence to George McClellan, 31 August 1864, McClellan Papers.
18. George Ticknor Curtis to George McClellan, 1 September 1864; Charles Davies to George McClellan, 3 September 1864; Truman Seymour to George McClellan, 6 September 1864, all in the McClellan Papers.
19. *New York Evening Post,* 2 September 1864.
20. Clement Vallandigham to George McClellan, 4 September 1864, McClellan Papers.

21. *New York World,* 5 September 1864.

22. From clippings on reel 81, McClellan Papers.

23. Unidentified letter from Philadelphia, 19 September 1864, Marble Papers.

24. Nicolay, *Personal Traits of Abraham Lincoln,* 308–9.

25. Both letters are in McClellan, *Civil War Papers,* 593–94.

26. The text of McClellan's acceptance letter is in *Official Proceedings,* 60–61.

27. The quotes in order: N. C. Goodwin to George McClellan, 12 September 1864, Marble Papers; Washington Hunt to Manton Marble, 20 September 1864, Marble Papers. Amos Kendall to George McClellan, 10 September 1864, McClellan Papers. R. W. Clelland to Manton Marble, 10 September 1864, Marble Papers.

28. Lindsey, *"Sunset" Cox,* 867; Vallandigham, *A Life of Clement L. Vallandigham,* 367.

29. Nelson, *Bullets, Ballots, and Rhetoric,* 123; Kinchen, *Confederate Operations in Canada and the North,* 97.

30. *New York Times,* 10 September 1864.

31. Katz, *August Belmont,* 135; *New York Herald,* 11 September 1864.

32. McClellan, *Civil War Papers,* 597, 598.

33. Patrick O'Reilly to George McClellan, 19 September 1864, Marble Papers.

34. This chronology of Chandler's party-patching activity is from Detroit Post and Tribune, *Zachariah Chandler,* 273–75, which is a brief "insider biography" of the senator.

35. Chandler's letters to his wife during this period are in Harbison, "Zachariah Chandler's Part in the Reelection of Abraham Lincoln," 271–73.

36. The Lincoln-Wakeman-Bennett communication is in Lincoln, *Collected Works* 7:461n.

37. The offer to Greeley is described in Seitz, *Horace Greeley,* 267–69. Lincoln's invitation for Greeley to come see him is in Lincoln, *Collected Works* 7:482.

38. McClure, *Abraham Lincoln and Men of War Times,* 83; Logan, *Reminiscences of a Soldier's Wife,* 172–79.

39. Whittier, *The Letters of John Greenleaf Whittier* 3:1.

40. McPherson, *The Political History of the United States During the Great Rebellion,* 426.

41. *Proceedings,* 226.

42. Hay, *Lincoln and the Civil War,* 219–20.

43. Nicolay and Hay, *Abraham Lincoln* 9:339–40.

44. Lincoln, *Collected Works* 8:18.

45. Ibid., 18n.

46. Ibid., 20.

47. Harbison, "Zachariah Chandler's Part in the Reelection of Abraham Lincoln," 274.

48. Bennett's remarkable view of the coming political skedaddle is in the *New York Herald,* 23 August 1864.

49. *New York Sun,* 30 June 1889.

50. Smith and Judah, *Life in the North During the Civil War,* 122; Gurowski, *Diary* 3:366.

51. John Nicolay to Abraham Lincoln, 30 August 1864, Nicolay Papers.

52. *New York Daily Tribune,* 6 September 1864.

53. Ibid., 27 September 1864.

54. John Frazier Jr. to John Cresswell, 5 October 1864, Cresswell Papers.

55. Butler, *Private and Official Correspondence* 5:167.

56. Harbison, "Zachariah Chandler's Part in the Reelection of Abraham Lincoln," 275–76.

57. Welles, "Lincoln's Triumph in 1864," 464; *New York Sun,* 30 June 1889.

58. Quoted in McPherson, *The Struggle for Equality,* 283.

59. Young, "Anna Elizabeth Dickinson and the Civil War," 76.

60. Butler, *Private and Official Correspondence* 5:167.

61. Merrill, "General Benjamin F. Butler in the Presidential Campaign of 1864," 566.

62. Brown, *Raymond of the Times,* 255.

63. Brooks, "Two War-Time Conventions," 735.

Chapter 23. Striking Up a Hallelujah

1. *Philadelphia Inquirer,* 4 October 1864.

2. Gurowski, *Diary* 3:21.

3. *New York Times,* 29 September 1864.

4. Ibid., 3 September 1864.

5. *New York World,* 10 October 1864.

6. *Lincoln Lore,* 1100 (8 May 1950).

7. *New York World,* 10 October 1864.

8. Dittenhoefer, *How We Elected Lincoln,* 87–88.

9. Hay, *Lincoln and the Civil War,* 13, 15, 23.

10. E. W. Dennis to Joseph Holt, 24 October 1864, Holt Papers.

11. Ibid.

12. *New York Herald,* 18 September 1864.

13. Ibid.

14. Ibid., 23 September 1864.

15. Lincoln, *Collected Works* 8:3.

16. Mitchell, *Civil War Soldiers,* 189.

17. *New York World,* 8 October 1864.

18. *New York Herald,* 2 October 1864.

19. *New York Times,* 8 November 1864.

20. *New York World,* 17 October 1863.

21. Hay, *Lincoln and the Civil War,* 184.

22. Strong, *Diary,* 405.

23. *New York World,* 1 September and 1 and 26 October 1864.

24. Ibid., 1 October 1864.

25. Blaine, *Twenty Years of Congress* 2:43.

26. Zornow, "Campaign Issues and Popular Mandates in 1864," 207.

27. Dittenhoefer, *How We Elected Lincoln,* 87.

28. A summary of the criminations and recriminations is in the *New York Herald,* 4 November 1864.

29. Ibid.

30. Dittenhoefer, *How We Elected Lincoln,* 88.

31. Silbey, *A Respectable Minority,* 167.

32. Hay, *Lincoln and the Civil War,* 220; Zornow, "Campaign Issues and Popular Mandates in 1864," 198.

33. Lowell, "The Next General Election," 560.

34. McMaster, *A History of the People of the United States,* 527.

35. Laboulaye, "The Election of the President of the United States," 1–4.

36. The text of Holt's report is reprinted in *O.R.,* ser. 2, vol. 7, 930–53.

37. Nelson, *Bullets, Ballots, and Rhetoric,* 148–51.

38. Hay, *Lincoln and the Civil War,* 220.

39. The background on Croly and Wakeman is from Kaplan, "The Miscegenation Issue in the Election of 1864," 285–86, 342.

40. This brief summary with quotes and paraphrased passages is from a reprint version of the pamphlet: Croly, *Miscegenation,* 1–2, 8–9, 11, 16, 18–19, 29, 61.

41. Kaplan, "The Miscegenation Issue in the Election of 1864," 285n.

42. Ibid., 307.

43. *New York Daily Tribune,* 16 March 1864.

44. *New York World,* 17 March 1864.

45. Cox, *Eight Years in Congress,* 358–59, 365, 367–68.

46. The "Lincoln Catechism" is reprinted as an appendix in Hyman, "Election of 1864," 1214–44.

47. Kaplan, "The Miscegenation Issue in the Election of 1864," 322–23.

48. Ibid., 324–25.

49. *New York Daily News,* 4 April 1864.

50. *New York Herald,* 26 April 1864.

51. *New York World,* 23 and 26 September 1864.

52. *Chicago Tribune,* 18 March 1864. Also see Wood, *Black Scare,* 62, 73–75.

53. *Cincinnati Daily Gazette,* 25 October 1864, in Hyman, "Election of 1864," 1203.

54. *Philadelphia Inquirer,* 28 October 1864.

55. *New York Herald,* 27 October 1864.

56. *Chicago Tribune,* 5 and 22 October 1864. For a description of Logan's oratorical style, see *Dictionary of American Biography,* s.v., "Logan, John Alexander."

57. *New York Herald,* 5 November 1864.

58. *New York Times,* 31 October 1864.

59. McClellan, *Civil War Papers,* 615.

60. *New York World,* 20 October 1864.

61. Winthrop's speech is reprinted in Freidel, *Union Pamphlets of the Civil War,* vol. 2. See pages 1082–83, 1087, 1096, 1098, 1101.

62. McClellan, *Civil War Papers,* 616.

63. Gurowski, *Diary* 3:123.

64. *New York Times,* 1, 5, and 7 October 1864.

65. *New York World,* 8 October 1864.

66. Bennett's summaries and conclusion are in the *New York Herald,* 7 November 1864.

67. Ibid., 29 October 1864.

68. Grant, *The Papers of Ulysses S. Grant,* 12:16–17.

69. Gurowski, *Diary* 3:352.

70. Henry J. Raymond to Edward McPherson, 3 July 1864, McPherson Papers.

71. *New York Herald,* 5 November 1864.

72. Strong, *Diary,* 508–9.

73. Manton Marble explains this prevailing custom in the *New York World,* 29 September 1864. Lincoln, holding to the custom, had also shut his mouth in 1860. However, Stephen A. Douglas, his major opponent, shattered all norms in that campaign, traveling and speaking extensively and urgently of the danger facing the country. His effort neither headed off the crisis nor got him elected. The no-campaign tradition reinstated itself after the Douglas apostasy, and it was not until this century that presidential candidates began campaigning with the frenzy we see today. Now no candidate dares not campaign personally, until he has utterly exhausted himself and the electorate.

74. McClellan, *Civil War Papers,* 609n.

75. Ibid., 608.

76. Ibid., 611.

77. The Liebenau-McClellan exchange is in ibid., 612n; 612.

78. Lincoln, *Collected Works* 8:2.

79. Ibid., 7:198.

80. Tarbell, *The Life of Abraham Lincoln* 2:204.

81. Lincoln, *Collected Works* 8:52.

82. McClure, *Abraham Lincoln and Men of War Times,* 207.

83. The muffled-oars analogy is stolen directly from Donald, *Lincoln Reconsidered*, 67.

84. Rice, *Reminiscences of Abraham Lincoln*, 430.

85. Current, *The Lincoln Nobody Knows*, 209.

86. Dennett, "Lincoln and the Campaign of 1864," 53; McClellan, *Civil War Papers*, 613n.

87. One of the better descriptions of how Lincoln operated as a politician is in Donald, *Lincoln Reconsidered*, 57–81.

88. Hay, *Lincoln and the Civil War*, 181.

89. Carman and Luthin, *Lincoln and the Patronage*, 287.

90. Lincoln, *Collected Works* 7:197.

91. Welles, *Diary* 1:534.

92. Ibid., 2:97–98, 113, 123–24. For the size of the workforce and payroll at the Brooklyn Navy Yard, see Livingston, *President Lincoln's Third Largest City*, 101–2.

93. Welles, *Diary* 2:142.

94. Brown, *Raymond of the Times*, 262–63.

95. *New York Herald*, 2 September 1864.

Chapter 24. The Month of Splendid Auguries

1. *New York Herald*, 8 September 1864.

 2. John M. Harlan to R. F. Stevens, 7 September 1864, Marble Papers.

 3. Samuel North to Manton Marble, 28 September 1864, ibid.

 4. Nicolay and Hay, *Abraham Lincoln* 9:369.

 5. Blaine's telegrams and Lincoln's response are in Lincoln, *Collected Works* 8:3n, 2.

 6. *New York Herald*, 15 September 1864.

 7. *New York Daily Tribune*, 14 September 1864.

 8. Oliver P. Morton to W. M. Dunn, 22 August 1864, Holt Papers.

 9. M. H. J. to August Belmont, 10 September 1864, Marble Papers.

10. *New York Herald*, 18 September 1864.

11. Ibid., 5 October 1864.

12. Hazewell, "The Twentieth Presidential Election," 641.

13. Mason, Diary, Remey Family Papers.

14. Samuel S. Cox to George B. McClellan, 11 October 1864, McClellan Papers.

15. Hay, *Lincoln and the Civil War*, 227.

16. Nicolay and Hay, *Abraham Lincoln* 9:370; Hay, *Lincoln and the Civil War*, 229.

17. Lincoln, *Collected Works* 8:43, 43n, 44n.

18. Nicolay and Hay, *Abraham Lincoln* 9:370–71.

19. *Ohio State Journal*, 11 and 13 October 1864, in Lindsey, *"Sunset" Cox*, 86–87.

20. The opinion of the *Indianapolis Journal* is reported in Stampp, "The Milligan Case and the Election of 1864," 55.

21. Hay, *Lincoln and the Civil War,* 230; Lincoln, *Collected Works* 8:46.

22. *New York Times,* 15 and 25 October 1864.

23. Raymond's statement was printed in the *Chicago Tribune,* 19 October 1864.

24. Mason, Diary, Remey Family Papers.

25. Ibid., entry for 30 October 1846.

26. Nicolay and Hay, *Abraham Lincoln* 9:372.

27. *New York World,* 12, 28, and 31 October 1864.

28. *New York Herald,* 22 and 26 October and 1 November 1864.

29. Hay, *Lincoln and the Civil War,* 231; *New York Times,* 14 October 1864.

30. Hay, *Lincoln and the Civil War,* 53.

31. Strong, *Diary,* 500.

32. *New York World,* 13 October 1864.

33. McClellan, *Civil War Papers,* 615n, 617n, 617.

34. Bates, *Lincoln in the Telegraph Office,* 277–79; Lincoln, *Collected Works* 8:46.

35. Bates, *Lincoln in the Telegraph Office,* 295.

36. The standard work on this subject is Benton, *Voting in the Field,* privately published in 1915. See pages 5, 306–9, 312–13. Also see Long, *The Jewel of Liberty,* 217–18.

37. *New York World,* 14 October 1864.

38. Dana, *Recollections of the Civil War,* 260–61.

39. Memorandum on the Plan of Democratic Campaign for October 1864, Marble Papers; Mason, Diary, entry for 24 September 1864, Remey Family Papers; Lincoln, *Collected Works* 6:557.

40. *New York World,* 29 October 1864; Rawley, *Edwin D. Morgan,* 200.

41. Commager, *The Blue and the Gray* 1:297–98; Winther, "The Soldier Vote in the Election of 1864," 452–53.

42. Sears, *George B. McClellan,* 379.

43. McAllister, *The Civil War Letters of General Robert McAllister,* 495, 518, 520.

44. These comments are quoted in Long, *The Jewel of Liberty,* 224–25, 232.

45. Connolly, *Three Years in the Army of the Cumberland,* 262–63.

46. *New York Times,* 2 October 1864.

47. Tarbell, *A Reporter for Lincoln,* 70–71.

48. Carpenter, *Six Months at the White House,* 231.

49. *Lincoln Lore* 1698 (August 1979).

50. Carpenter, *Six Months at the White House,* 201; Mabee, "Sojourner Truth and President Lincoln," 519, 528–29; *Lincoln Lore* 809 (9 October 1944).

51. Quarles, *The Negro in the Civil War,* 228–29.

52. Ibid., 252.

53. Sojourner Truth's own account, from which this is taken, is in Carpenter, *Six Months at the White House*, 201–3. The Bible is described on page 197.

54. *New York Times*, 8 November 1864.

55. *New York World*, 8 November 1864.

56. W. B. Franklin to George B. McClellan, 7 November 1864, McClellan Papers.

57. Lincoln, *Collected Works* 8:81n.

58. Brooks, *Mr. Lincoln's Washington*, 383–84.

Chapter 25. Oysters at Midnight

1. Lee, *Wartime Washington*, 440n.

2. Brooks, *Mr. Lincoln's Washington*, 385.

3. Hay, *Lincoln and the Civil War*, 232–33.

4. Brooks, *Mr. Lincoln's Washington*, 385.

5. Brooks, *Washington in Lincoln's Time*, 196; Brooks, "Personal Reminiscences of Lincoln," 677.

6. Hyman, "Election of 1864," 1173.

7. Fisk, *Hard Marching Every Day*, 273.

8. Lincoln, *Collected Works* 8:118n.

9. Hay, *Lincoln and the Civil War*, 233.

10. These paragraphs about Butler in New York on election day are shaped from accounts in Butler, *Butler's Book*, 752–55, 759–61, 770, 1092; and Butler, *Private and Official Correspondence* 5:306–7, 310, 315, 326–27, 346. Belmont's rejection at the polls for betting is from Strong, *Diary*, 510.

11. The election-night color in New York City is distilled from Brown, *Raymond of the Times*, 267; and *New York Herald*, 9 November 1864.

12. *Philadelphia Inquirer*, 9 November 1864.

13. The opening scenes in the telegraph office and Stanton's room are from Hay, *Lincoln and the Civil War*, 233–35, 239.

14. Dana, *Recollections of the Civil War*, 261–62.

15. Brooks, *Mr. Lincoln's Washington*, 386.

16. Ibid.; Hay, *Lincoln and the Civil War*, 235.

17. *New York Times*, 23 November 1864.

18. This brief analysis owes much to Zornow, *Lincoln & the Party Divided*, 214–15; and Long, *The Jewel of Liberty*, 256–58.

19. McPherson, *The Political History of the United States of America During the Great Rebellion*, 623.

20. *New York World*, 11 November 1864.

21. Current, *The Lincoln Nobody Knows*, 212; Zornow, *Lincoln & the Party Divided*, 216, 219.

22. McPherson, *The Political History of the United States of America During the Great Rebellion,* 623; Sears, *George B. McClellan,* 385–86.

23. Benton, *Voting in the Field,* 313.

24. Lincoln, *Collected Works* 8:100n.

25. Brooks, *Mr. Lincoln's Washington,* 386–87.

26. Lincoln, *Collected Works* 8:96.

27. Hay, *Lincoln and the Civil War,* 236.

28. Mitgang, *Lincoln as They Saw Him,* 423.

Epilogue: Worth More Than a Battle Won

1. All three McClellan quotes are from his *Civil War Papers,* 619, 618, 624. The combination of circumstances to induce him to enter public life did come again. From 1878 to 1881 he was governor of New Jersey.

2. *New York Times,* 10 November 1864.

3. *New York Herald,* 14 November 1864.

4. Friedel, "The Loyal Publication Society," 376; Lindeman, *The Conflict of Convictions,* 259.

5. Hay, *Lincoln and the Civil War,* 242.

6. Strong, *Diary,* 511.

7. Ford, *A Cycle of Adams Letters* 2:223.

8. Quoted in Cole, "Lincoln and the Presidential Election of 1864," 137.

9. *New York World,* 10 November 1864. The *Boston Post* is quoted in the *World* on 11 November.

10. Nicolay, *Personal Traits of Abraham Lincoln,* 309.

11. Mason, *Diary,* Remey Family Papers.

12. William C. Prime to George McClellan, 11 November 1864, McClellan Papers.

13. Buchanan, *Works* 11:377.

14. F. Jefferson Coolidge to George McClellan, 25 November 1864, McClellan Papers.

15. Kean, *Inside the Confederate Government,* 177; Nelson, *Bullets, Ballots, and Rhetoric,* 157–58; *Richmond Examiner,* 11 November 1864.

16. Cary, *George William Curtis,* 182.

17. *Chicago Tribune,* 13 August 1864.

18. Carpenter, *Six Months at the White House,* 231.

19. A. G. Henry to Lyman Trumbull, 22 November 1864, Trumbull Papers.

20. Brooks, "Personal Recollections of Abraham Lincoln," 226.

21. Nicolay, *Personal Traits of Abraham Lincoln,* 289.

22. Brooks, *Mr. Lincoln's Washington,* 387–88; Brooks, *Washington in Lincoln's Time,* 200.

23. Lincoln, *Collected Works* 8:101.

24. Hay, *Lincoln and the Civil War,* 239.
25. Hay recounts this in ibid., 237–38. The text of the memorandum is also in Lincoln, *Collected Works* 7:514.
26. Grant, *The Papers of Ulysses S. Grant* 12:398.
27. Rogers, "McClellan's Candidacy with the Army," 959.
28. Lincoln, *Collected Works* 8:154.

SOURCES

―――

Abrahams, Samuel. "Lincoln's Political Opposition in 1864." *Negro History Bulletin* 12 (1948–49): 7–9, 18.

Adams, Charles Francis. *Richard Henry Dana: A Biography.* 2 vols. Boston: Houghton Mifflin, 1890.

Alexander, DeAlva Stanwood. *A Political History of the State of New York.* 4 vols. 1909, 1923. Reprint, New York: Ira J. Friedman, 1969.

Alvord, Henry E. "Early's Attack Upon Washington, July, 1864." In *War Papers* read before the commandery of the District of Columbia of the Military Order of the Loyal Legion of the United States. Vol. 1, no. 26, 1897. Reprint, Wilmington, N.C.: Broadfoot Publishing Co., 1993.

American Annual Cyclopoedia and Register of Important Events, 1862–64. Vols. 2–4. New York: D. Appleton & Co., 1863–65.

Andrews, J. Cutler. *The North Reports the Civil War.* Pittsburgh: University of Pittsburgh Press, 1955.

Arnold, Isaac Newton. *The Life of Abraham Lincoln.* 1884. Reprint, Lincoln: University of Nebraska Press, 1994.

Augusta Chronicle & Sentinel.

Augusta Constitutionalist.

Baltimore American.

Baltimore Gazette.

Baltimore Sun.

Bancroft, T. B. "An Audience with Abraham Lincoln." *McClure's Magazine* 32 (February 1909): 447–50.

Barnes, Thurlow Weed. *Memoir of Thurlow Weed.* Boston: Houghton Mifflin, 1884.

Bartlett, Ruhl J. *John C. Frémont and the Republican Party.* 1930. Reprint, New York: Da Capo Press, 1970.

Bates, David Homer. *Lincoln in the Telegraph Office: Recollections of the United States Military Telegraph Corps During the Civil War*. New York: Century Co., 1907.

———. *Lincoln Stories Told by Him in the Military Office in the War Department During the Civil War*. New York: William Edwin Rudge, 1926.

Bates, Edward. *The Diary of Edward Bates, 1859–1866*. Edited by Howard K. Beale. Annual Report of the American Historical Association for 1930. Vol. 4. Washington, D.C.: U.S. Government Printing Office, 1933.

Belden, Thomas Graham, and Marva Robins Belden. *So Fell the Angels*. Boston: Little, Brown, 1956.

Belz, Herman. *Reconstructing the Union: Theory and Policy During the Civil War*. Ithaca, N.Y.: Cornell University Press, 1969.

Benton, Josiah Henry. *Voting in the Field: A Forgotten Chapter of the Civil War*. Boston: Privately printed, 1915.

Bill, Alfred Hoyt. *The Beleaguered City: Richmond, 1861–1865*. 1946. Reprint, Westport, Conn.: Greenwood Press, 1980.

Binckley, J. W. "The Leader of the House." *Galaxy* 1 (July 1866): 493–500.

Binkley, Wilfred E. *President and Congress*. New York: Alfred A. Knopf, 1947.

Blaine, James G. *Twenty Years of Congress: From Lincoln to Garfield*. 2 vols. Norwich, Conn.: Henry Bull Publishing Co., 1884–86.

Blue, Frederick J. *Salmon P. Chase: A Life in Politics*. Kent, Ohio: Kent State University Press, 1987.

Boatner, Mark Mayo III. *The Civil War Dictionary*. New York: David McKay, 1959.

Bogue, Allan G. *The Earnest Men: Republicans of the Civil War Senate*. Ithaca, N.Y.: Cornell University Press, 1981.

Borrett, George. "An Englishman in Washington in 1864." *The Magazine of History with Notes and Queries* 38 (1929): 5–15.

Boston Daily Journal.

Boston Globe.

Boston Post.

Bowen, Catherine Drinker. *Yankee from Olympus: Justice Holmes and His Family*. Boston: Little, Brown, 1944.

Bowers, Claude G. *The Tragic Era: The Revolution after Lincoln*. New York: Blue Ribbon Books, 1929.

Bradford, Gamaliel. *As God Made Them: Portraits of Some Nineteenth-Century Americans*. Boston: Houghton Mifflin, 1929.

———. *Wives*. New York: Harper & Brothers, 1925.

Bradley, Erwin Stanley. *Simon Cameron: Lincoln's Secretary of War—A Political Biography*. Philadelphia: University of Pennsylvania Press, 1966.

Bradwell, Isaac G. "Early's March to Washington in 1864." *Confederate Veteran* 28 (May 1920): 176–77.

———. "First of Valley Campaign by General Early." *Confederate Veteran* 19 (May 1911): 230–31.

Brodie, Fawn M. *Thaddeus Stevens: Scourge of the South*. New York: W. W. Norton, 1959.

Brooks, Noah. "A Boy in the White House." *St. Nicholas* 10 (November 1882): 57–65.

———. *Mr. Lincoln's Washington: Selections from the Writings of Noah Brooks, Civil War Correspondent*. Edited by P. J. Staudenraus. South Brunswick, N.J.: Thomas Yoseloff, 1967.

———. "Personal Recollections of Abraham Lincoln." *Harper's New Monthly Magazine* 31 (July 1865): 222–230.

———. "Personal Reminiscences of Lincoln." *Scribner's Monthly* 15 (1878): 673–81.

———. "Two War-Time Conventions." *Century Magazine* 49 (March 1895): 723–36.

———. *Washington in Lincoln's Time*. Edited by Herbert Mitgang. New York: Rinehart & Co., 1958.

Brown, Francis. *Raymond of the Times*. New York: W. W. Norton, 1951.

Browne, Francis Fisher. *The Every-Day Life of Abraham Lincoln: A Narrative and Descriptive Biography with Pen-Pictures and Personal Recollections by Those Who Knew Him*. Chicago: Browne & Howell, 1913.

Buchanan, James. *The Works of James Buchanan*, vol. 11. Edited by John Bassett Moore. 1910. Reprint, New York: Antiquarian Press, 1960.

Buell, Walter. "Zachariah Chandler." *Magazine of Western History* 4 (1886): 271–78, 338–52, 432–44.

Bullard, F. Lauriston. *Famous War Correspondents*. Boston: Little, Brown, 1914.

Bungay, George W. *Off-Hand Takings, or, Crayon Sketches of the Noticeable Men of Our Age*. New York: De Witt & Davenport, 1854.

Burlingame, Michael. *The Inner World of Abraham Lincoln*. Urbana: University of Illinois Press, 1994.

Burnham, W. Dean. *Presidential Ballots, 1836–1892*. Baltimore: Johns Hopkins Press, 1955.

Butler, Benjamin F. *Butler's Book: Autobiography and Personal Reminiscences of Major-General Benj. F. Butler*. Boston: A. M. Thayer & Co., 1892.

———. *Private and Official Correspondence of General Benjamin F. Butler During the Period of the Civil War*. Edited by Jessie A. Marshall. 5 vols. Norwood, Mass.: Plimpton Press, 1917.

———. "Vice-Presidential Politics in '64." *North American Review* 141 (October 1885): 331–34.

Carman, Harry J., and Reinhard H. Luthin. *Lincoln and the Patronage*. New York: Columbia University Press, 1943.

Carpenter, Francis B. *Six Months at the White House with Abraham Lincoln*. New York: Hurd and Houghton, 1867.

Carr, Clark E. "Lincoln at Gettysburg." *Transactions of the Illinois State Historical Society* Publication No. 11 (1906): 138–52.

———. "Why Lincoln Was Not Renominated by Acclamation." *Century Magazine* 73 (February 1907): 503–6.

Carr, Lucien. *Missouri: A Bone of Contention*. Boston: Houghton Mifflin, 1896.

Carter, Samuel III. *The Siege of Atlanta, 1864*. New York: St. Martin's Press, 1973.

Cary, Edward. *George William Curtis*. Boston: Houghton Mifflin, 1894.

Castleman, John B. *Active Service*. Louisville, Ky.: Courier-Journal Job Printing Co., 1917.

Catton, Bruce. *Grant Takes Command*. Boston: Little, Brown, 1968.

Chase, Salmon P. *Diary and Correspondence of Salmon P. Chase*. Vol. 2 of the *Annual Report of the American Historical Association, 1902*. Washington, D.C.: U.S. Government Printing Office, 1903.

———. *Inside Lincoln's Cabinet: The Civil War Diaries of Salmon P. Chase*. Edited by David Donald. New York: Longmans, Green and Co., 1954.

Chesnut, Mary. *Mary Chesnut's Civil War*. Edited by C. Vann Woodward. New Haven, Conn.: Yale University Press, 1981.

Chester, Giraud. *Embattled Maiden: The Life of Anna Dickinson*. New York: G. P. Putnam's Sons, 1951.

Chicago Evening Journal.

Chicago Times.

Chicago Tribune.

Chittenden, L. E. *Recollections of President Lincoln and His Administration*. New York: Harper & Brothers, 1891.

Cincinnati Daily Commercial.

Cincinnati Daily Enquirer.

Cincinnati Daily Gazette.

Cleveland Plain Dealer.

Cole, Arthur C. "Abraham Lincoln and the South." *Lincoln Centennial Association Papers*. Springfield, Ill.: Lincoln Centennial Association, 1928.

———. "Lincoln and the Presidential Election of 1864." *Transactions of the Illinois State Historical Society* 23 (1917): 130–38.

Coleman, Charles H. "The Use of the Term 'Copperhead' During the Civil War." *Mississippi Valley Historical Review* 25 (September 1938): 263–64.

Commager, Henry Steele, ed. *The Blue and the Gray: The Story of the Civil War as Told by Participants*. 1950. Reprint, New York: The Fairfax Press, 1982.

Congressional Globe.

Congressional Record.

Connolly, James A. *Three Years in the Army of the Cumberland: The Letters and Diary of Major James A. Connolly.* Edited by Paul M. Angle. Bloomington: Indiana University Press, 1959.

Cooling, Benjamin Franklin. *Jubal Early's Raid on Washington, 1864.* Baltimore: Nautical & Aviation Publishing Company of America, 1989.

Coulter, E. Merton. *The Confederate States of America, 1861–1865.* Baton Rouge: Louisiana State University Press and the Littlefield Fund for Southern History of the University of Texas, 1950.

Cox, Jacob D. *Atlanta.* 1882. Reprint, Wilmington, N.C.: Broadfoot Publishing Co., 1989.

Cox, Samuel S. *Eight Years in Congress, from 1857–1865: Memoir and Speeches.* New York: D. Appleton and Co., 1865.

Cramer, John Henry. *Lincoln under Enemy Fire: A Complete Account of His Experiences During Early's Attack on Washington.* Baton Rouge: Louisiana State University Press, 1948.

Cresswell, John A. J. Papers. Manuscript Division, Library of Congress.

Croffut, William A. "Bennett and His Times." *Atlantic Monthly* 147 (February 1931): 196–206.

Croly, David Goodman [and George Wakeman]. *Miscegenation: The Theory of the Blending of the Races, Applied to the White Man and Negro.* 1864. Reprint, Upper Saddle River, N.J.: Literature House/Gregg Press, 1970.

Crouthamel, James L. *Bennett's New York Herald and the Rise of the Popular Press.* Syracuse, N.Y.: Syracuse University Press, 1989.

Crozier, Emmet. *Yankee Reporters, 1861–65.* New York: Oxford University Press, 1956.

Cullom, Shelby M. *Fifty Years of Public Service: Personal Recollections of Shelby M. Cullom.* Chicago: A. C. McClurg & Co., 1911.

Current, Richard N. *The Lincoln Nobody Knows.* New York: McGraw-Hill, 1958.

———. *Old Thad Stevens: A Story of Ambition.* Madison: University of Wisconsin Press, 1942.

Curtis, George Ticknor. *McClellan's Last Service to the Republic, Together with a Tribute to His Memory.* New York: D. Appleton and Co., 1886.

Curtis, Merle E. "George N. Sanders—American Patriot of the Fifties." *South Atlantic Quarterly* 27 (January 1928): 79–87.

Dana, Charles A. *Recollections of the Civil War: With the Leaders at Washington and in the Field in the Sixties.* New York: D. Appleton and Co., 1898.

Davis, Jefferson. *Jefferson Davis, Constitutionalist: His Letters, Papers and Speeches.* Edited by Rowland Dunbar. 10 vols. New York: Press of J. J. Little & Ives Company for the Mississippi Department of Archives and History, 1923.

————. *The Rise and Fall of the Confederate Government.* 2 vols. New York: D. Appleton and Co., 1881.

Davis, Stanton Ling. *Pennsylvania Politics. 1860–1863.* Cleveland: The Bookstore, Western Reserve University, 1935.

Davis, Varina. *Jefferson Davis, Ex-President of the Confederate States of America: A Memoir by His Wife.* 2 vols. New York: Belford Co., 1890.

Davis, William C. *Jefferson Davis: The Man and His Hour.* New York: HarperCollins, 1991.

Dennett, Tyler. *John Hay: From Poetry to Politics.* New York: Dodd, Mead, 1934.

————. "Lincoln and the Campaign of 1864." *Abraham Lincoln Association Papers* (1936): 31–58.

Detroit Post and Tribune. *Zachariah Chandler: An Outline Sketch of His Life and Public Services.* Detroit: Post and Tribune Co., 1880.

Diary of a Public Man and a Page of Political Correspondence, Stanton to Buchanan. New Brunswick, N.J.: Rutgers University Press, 1946.

Dictionary of American Biography. 22 vols. New York: Charles Scribner's Sons, 1928–36.

Dittenhoefer, Abram J. *How We Elected Lincoln: Personal Recollections of Lincoln and Men of His Time.* New York: Harper & Brothers, 1916.

Dodd, William E. *Lincoln or Lee.* New York: Century Co., 1928.

————. "Lincoln's Last Struggle—Victory?" *Lincoln Centennial Association Papers* (1927): 49–98.

Donald, David Herbert. *Charles Sumner and the Rights of Man.* New York: Alfred A. Knopf, 1970.

————. "Devils Facing Zionwards." In *Grant, Lee, Lincoln and the Radicals: Essays on Civil War Leadership.* Edited by Grady McWhiney. Evansville, Ill.: Northwestern University Press, 1964.

————. *Lincoln.* New York: Simon & Schuster, 1995.

————. *Lincoln Reconsidered: Essays on the Civil War Era.* New York: Alfred A. Knopf, 1956.

————. *Lincoln's Herndon.* New York: Alfred A. Knopf, 1948.

Douglas, Henry Kyd. *I Rode with Stonewall.* 1940. Reprint, Chapel Hill: University of North Carolina Press, 1968.

Dudley, Harold M. "The Election of 1864." *The Mississippi Valley Historical Review* 18 (March 1932): 500–18.

Dunlap, Lloyd A. "President Lincoln and Editor Greeley." *Abraham Lincoln Quarterly* 5 (June 1948): 94–110.

Early, Jubal A. "The Advance on Washington in 1864." *Southern Historical Society Papers* 9 (1881): 297–312.

————. *A Memoir of the Last Year of the War for Independence in the Confederate States of America.* New Orleans: Blelock & Co., 1867.

Eaton, John. *Grant, Lincoln and the Freedmen: Reminiscences of the Civil War.* 1907. Reprint, New York: Negro Universities Press, 1969.

Eckloff, Christian F. *Memoirs of a Senate Page, 1855–1859.* Edited by Percival G. Melbourne. New York: Broadway Publishing Co., 1909.

Ellis, John B. *Sights and Secrets of the National Capital.* Chicago: Jones, Junkin & Co., 1869.

Ellis, L. E., Mrs. "The Chicago Times During the Civil War." In *Illinois State Historical Society Transactions for the Year 1932.* Publication no. 39, Illinois State Historical Library.

Fahrney, Ralph R. *Horace Greeley and the Tribune in the Civil War.* Cedar Rapids, Iowa: Torch Press, 1936.

Farragut, Loyall. *The Life of David Glasgow Farragut, First Admiral of the United States Navy, Embodying His Journal and Letters.* New York: D. Appleton and Co., 1879.

Fehrenbacher, Don E. "The Making of a Myth: Lincoln and the Vice-Presidential Nomination in 1864." *Civil War History* 41 (December 1995): 273–90.

Fermer, Douglas. *James Gordon Bennett and the New York Herald: A Study of Editorial Opinion in the Civil War Era, 1854–1867.* New York: St. Martin's Press, 1986.

Fesler, Mayo. "Secret Political Societies in the North During the Civil War." *Indiana Magazine of History* 14 (September 1918): 183–286.

Fessenden, Francis. *Life and Public Services of William Pitt Fessenden.* 2 vols. Boston: Houghton Mifflin, 1907.

Field, Maunsell B. *Memories of Many Men and of Some Women.* New York: Harper & Brothers, 1875.

Fischer, LeRoy H. *Lincoln's Gadfly, Adam Gurowski.* Norman: University of Oklahoma Press, 1964.

Fisk, Wilbur. *Hard Marching Every Day: The Civil War Letters of Private Wilbur Fisk, 1861–1865.* Edited by Emil and Ruth Rosenblatt. Lawrence: University Press of Kansas, 1992.

Foote, Shelby. *The Civil War: A Narrative.* 3 vols. New York: Random House, 1958–1974.

Ford, Worthington Chauncey, ed. *A Cycle of Adams Letters, 1861–1865.* 2 vols. Boston: Houghton Mifflin, 1920.

Freidel, Frank. "The Loyal Publication Society: A Pro-Union Propaganda Agency." *Mississippi Valley Historical Review* 26 (December 1939): 359–76.

————, ed. *Union Pamphlets of the Civil War, 1861–1865.* 2 Vols. Cambridge: The Belknap Press of Harvard University, 1967.

French, Benjamin Brown. *Witness to the Young Republic: A Yankee's Journal, 1828–1870.* Edited by Donald B. Cole and John J. McDonough. Hanover: University Press of New England, 1989.

Garland, Hamlin. *Ulysses S. Grant: His Life and Character.* New York: Macmillan Co., 1920.

Garrison, Wendell P., and Francis J. Garrison. *William Lloyd Garrison, 1805–1879: The Story of His Life Told by His Children.* 4 vols. New York: Century Co., 1885–1889.

George, Joseph, Jr. "A Long-Neglected Lincoln Speech: An 1864 Election Preliminary." *Journal of the Abraham Lincoln Association* 16 (Summer 1995): 23–28.

Gilmore, James R. [Edmund Kirke, pseud.] *Down in Tennessee, and Back by Way of Richmond.* New York: Carlton, 1864.

———. *Personal Recollections of Abraham Lincoln and the Civil War.* Boston: L. C. Page and Co., 1898.

Gladden, Washington. *Recollections.* Boston: Houghton Mifflin Co., 1909.

Glonek, James F. "Lincoln, Johnson, and the Baltimore Ticket." *Abraham Lincoln Quarterly* 6 (March 1951): 255–71.

Goss, Warren Lee. *Recollections of a Private: A Story of the Army of the Potomac.* New York: Thomas Y. Crowell & Co., 1890.

Grant, Frederick D. "Reminiscences of Gen. U. S. Grant." A paper read before the Illinois Commandery of the Loyal Legion of the United States, 27 January 1910. Reprinted in *Journal of the Illinois State Historical Society* 7 (April 1914): 72–76.

Grant, Ulysses S. *The Papers of Ulysses S. Grant.* Edited by John Y. Simon. 20 vols. Carbondale, Ill.: Southern Illinois University Press, 1967–1995.

———. *Personal Memoirs of U.S. Grant.* 1894. Reprint, New York: AMS Press, 1972.

———. "Preparing for the Campaigns of '64." In *Battles and Leaders of the Civil War,* vol. 4. Edited by Robert Underwood Johnson and Clarence Clough Buel. 1887. Reprint, Secaucus, N.J.: Castle, n.d.

Gray, Wood. *The Hidden Civil War: The Story of the Copperheads.* New York: Viking Press, 1942.

Greeley, Horace. Papers. Manuscript Division, Library of Congress.

———. *Recollections of a Busy Life.* New York: J. B. Ford & Co., 1868.

Green, Anna Maclay. "Civil War Public Opinion of General Grant." *Journal of the Illinois State Historical Society* 22 (April 1929): 1–64.

Grover, Leonard. "Lincoln's Interest in the Theater." *Century Magazine* 77 (1908–09): 943–50.

Gurowski, Adam. *Diary.* 3 vols. 1862–1866. Reprint, New York: Burt Franklin, 1968.

Hale, William Harlan. *Horace Greeley: Voice of the People.* New York: Harper & Brothers, 1950.

Hamlin, Charles Eugene. *The Life and Times of Hannibal Hamlin.* Cambridge: River-side Press, 1899.

Harbison, Winfred A. "The Election of 1862 as a Vote of Want of Confidence in President Lincoln." *Papers of the Michigan Academy of Science Arts and Letters* 14 (1930): 499–513.

———. "Zachariah Chandler's Part in the Reelection of Abraham Lincoln." *Mississippi Valley Historical Review* 22 (September 1935): 267–76.

Harper, Robert S. *Lincoln and the Press.* New York: McGraw-Hill, 1951.

Harper's Weekly.

Harris, Wilmer C. *Public Life of Zachariah Chandler, 1851–1875.* Lansing: Michigan Historical Commission, 1917.

Hart, Albert Bushnell. *Salmon Portland Chase.* Boston: Houghton Mifflin, 1899.

Hay, John. *Letters of John Hay and Extracts from Diary.* 3 vols. Washington, D.C.: n.p., 1908.

———. "Life in the White House in the Time of Lincoln." *Century Magazine* 41 (November 1890): 33–37.

———. *Lincoln and the Civil War in the Diaries and Letters of John Hay.* Edited by Tyler Dennett. New York: Dodd, Mead, 1939.

Hazewell, C. C. "The Twentieth Presidential Election." *Atlantic Monthly* 14 (November 1864): 633–41.

Headley, John W. *Confederate Operations in Canada and New York.* New York: Neale Publishing Co., 1906.

Hendrick, Burton J. *Lincoln's War Cabinet.* Boston: Little, Brown, 1946.

Henry, Robert Selph. *The Story of the Confederacy.* 1936. Reprint, Gloucester, Mass.: Peter Smith, 1970.

Herndon, William H. "Analysis of the Character of Abraham Lincoln." *Abraham Lincoln Quarterly* 1 (September 1941): 343–83; (December 1941): 403–41.

——— and Jessie W. Weik. *Herndon's Life of Lincoln.* Edited by Paul M. Angle. Cleveland: World Publishing Co., 1930.

Hertz, Emanuel. *Abraham Lincoln: A New Portrait.* 2 vols. New York: Horace Liveright, 1931.

———. *The Hidden Lincoln: From the Letters and Papers of William H. Herndon.* New York: Viking Press, 1938.

Hesseltine, William B. *Lincoln and the War Governors.* New York: Alfred A. Knopf, 1948.

———. *Lincoln's Plan of Reconstruction.* Tuscaloosa, Ala.: Confederate Publishing Co., 1960.

Hicks, Frederick C. "Lincoln, Wright and Holmes at Fort Stevens." *Journal of the Illinois State Historical Society* 39 (September 1946): 323–32.

Hines, Thomas H. "The Northwest Conspiracy." *Southern Bivouac* New Series 2 (December 1886): 437–45; (January 1887): 500–510; (February 1887): 567–74; (April 1887): 699–704.

Hofstadter, Richard. *The American Political Tradition and the Men Who Made It.* New York: Vintage Books, 1974.

Holland, Josiah G. *The Life of Abraham Lincoln.* Springfield, Mass.: Gurdon Bill, 1866.

Holt, Joseph. Papers. Manuscript Division, Library of Congress.

Holzer, Harold. "'If I Had Another Face, Do You Think I'd Wear This One?'" *American Heritage* 34 (February/March 1983): 56–63.

Holzman, Robert S. *Stormy Ben Butler.* New York: Macmillan, 1954.

"Homely or Handsome." *Chicago Tribune* in *The Magazine of History with Notes and Queries* 34 (1927): 21–29.

Horan, James D. *Confederate Agent: A Discovery in History.* New York: Crown Publishers, 1954.

Horner, Harlan Hoyt. *Lincoln and Greeley.* 1953. Reprint, Westport, Conn.: Greenwood Press, 1971.

Horowitz, Murray M. "Benjamin Butler: Seventeenth President?" *Lincoln Herald* 77 (Winter 1975): 191–203.

Howard, Hamilton Gay. *Civil War Echoes: Character Sketches and States Secrets.* Washington, D.C.: Howard Publishing Co., 1907.

Howe, Mark DeWolfe. *Justice Oliver Wendell Holmes: The Shaping Years, 1841–1870.* Cambridge: Belknap Press of Harvard University Press, 1957.

Hubbart, Henry Clyde. "'Pro-Southern' Influences in the Free West, 1840–1865." *Mississippi Valley Historical Review* 20 (June 1933): 45–62.

Humphreys, Andrew A. *The Virginia Campaign of '64 and '65: The Army of the Potomac and the Army of the James.* 1883. Reprint, Wilmington, N.C.: Broadfoot Publishing Co., 1989.

Hyman, Harold M. "Election of 1864." In *History of American Presidential Elections, 1789–1968*, vol. 2. Edited by Arthur M. Schlesinger Jr., Fred L. Israel, and William P. Hansen. New York: Chelsea House Publishers/McGraw-Hill, 1971.

Indianapolis Journal.

Isely, Jeter Allen. *Horace Greeley and the Republican Party, 1853–1861: A Study of the New York Tribune.* Princeton, N.J.: Princeton University Press, 1947.

Jackson, Donald Dale. *Twenty Million Yankees: The Northern Home Front.* Civil War Series. Alexandria, Va.: Time-Life Books, 1985.

Jellison, Charles A. *Fessenden of Maine: Civil War Senator.* Syracuse, N.Y.: Syracuse University Press, 1962.

Johnson, Oliver. "Horace Greeley in Church." Typescript copy of article from *Christian Register.* Greeley Papers, Manuscript Division, Library of Congress.

Johnson, Robert Underwood, and Clarence Clough Buel, eds. *Battles and Leaders of the Civil War.* 4 vols. 1887. Reprint, Secaucus, N.J.: Castle, n.d.

Jones, George R. *Joseph Russell Jones.* Chicago: Privately printed, 1964.

Jones, John B. *A Rebel War Clerk's Diary.* Edited by Earl Schenck Miers. New York: Sagamore Press, 1958.

Kamaras, Nicholas P. "George B. McClellan and the Election of 1854." Ph.D. diss., University of Delaware, 1976.

Kane, Joseph Nathan. *Facts about the Presidents: A Compilation of Biographical and Historical Data.* New York: H. W. Wilson, 1959.

Kaplan, Sidney. "The Miscegenation Issue in the Election of 1864." *Journal of Negro History* 34 (July 1949): 274–343.

Katz, Irving. *August Belmont: A Political Biography.* New York: Columbia University Press, 1968.

Kean, Robert Garlick Hill. *Inside the Confederate Government: The Diary of Robert Garlick Hill Kean.* Edited by Edward Younger. New York: Oxford University Press, 1957.

Keckley, Elizabeth. *Behind the Scenes; or, Thirty Years a Slave, and Four Years in the White House.* 1868. Reprint, Salem, N.H.: Ayer Company Publishers, 1985.

Kinchen, Oscar A. *Confederate Operations in Canada and the North: A Little-Known Phase of the American Civil War.* North Quincy, Mass.: Christopher Publishing House, 1970.

Kirkland, Edward Chase. *The Peacemakers of 1864.* New York: Macmillan, 1927.

Klement, Frank L. *Dark Lanterns: Secret Political Societies, Conspiracies, and Treason Trials in the Civil War.* Baton Rouge: Louisiana State University Press, 1984.

———. *The Limits of Dissent: Clement L. Vallandigham & the Civil War.* Lexington: University Press of Kentucky, 1970.

Kushner, Howard I., and Anne Hummel Sherrill. *John Milton Hay: The Union of Poetry and Politics.* Boston: Twayne Publishers, 1977.

Laboulaye, Edouard. "The Election of the President of the United States." *Lincoln Lore* 1520 (October 1964).

Lamon, Ward Hill. *Recollections of Abraham Lincoln, 1847–1865.* Edited by Dorothy Lamon Teillard. 1895. Reprint, Lincoln: University of Nebraska Press, 1994.

Laughlin, Sceva Bright. "Missouri Politics during the Civil War." *Missouri Historical Review* 23 (April 1929): 400–26; (July 1929): 583–618; 24 (October 1929): 87–113; (January 1930): 261–84.

Law, E. M. "From the Wilderness to Cold Harbor." In *Battles and Leaders of the Civil War,* vol. 4. Edited by Robert Underwood Johnson and Clarence Clough Buel. 1887. Reprint, Secaucus, N.J.: Castle, n.d.

Lee, Elizabeth Blair. *Wartime Washington: The Civil War Letters of Elizabeth Blair Lee.* Edited by Virginia Jeans Laas. Urbana: University of Illinois Press, 1991.

Lee Family. Papers. Documents Division, Library of Congress.

Lee, Robert E. *The Wartime Papers of R. E. Lee*. Edited by Clifford Dowdey and Louis A. Manarin. Boston: Little, Brown for the Virginia Civil War Commission, 1961.

Leech, Margaret. *Reveille in Washington, 1860–1865*. New York: Harper & Brothers, 1941.

Leonard, Ann. "'Smiler' Colfax and President Lincoln." *Lincoln Herald* 97 (Spring 1995): 4–29.

Lewis, Lloyd. "The Man the Historians Forgot." *Kansas Historical Quarterly* 8 (February 1939): 85–103.

———. *Sherman: Fighting Prophet*. New York: Harcourt, Brace & World, 1958.

Lincoln, Abraham. *The Collected Works of Abraham Lincoln*. Edited by Roy P. Basler. 8 vols. New Brunswick, N.J.: Rutgers University Press, 1953.

Lincoln Lore.

Lindeman, Jack, ed. *The Conflict of Convictions: American Writers Report the Civil War—A Selection and Arrangement from the Journals, Correspondence and Articles of the Major Men and Women of Letters Who Lived Through the War*. Philadelphia: Chilton Book Co., 1968.

Lindsey, David. *"Sunset" Cox: Irrepressible Democrat*. Detroit: Wayne State University Press, 1959.

Livermore, Mary A. *My Story of the War: A Woman's Narrative*. Hartford, Conn.: A. D. Worthington and Co. 1889.

Livingston, E. A. *President Lincoln's Third Largest City: Brooklyn and the Civil War*. Glendale, N.Y.: Budd Press, 1994.

Lloyd, Demarest. "The Home-Life of Salmon Portland Chase." *Atlantic Monthly* 32 (November 1873): 526–38.

Logan, Mary S. *Reminiscences of a Soldier's Wife: An Autobiography*. New York: Charles Scribner's Sons, 1913.

Long, A. L. "General Early's Valley Campaign." *Southern Historical Society Papers* 3 (1877): 112–22.

Long, David E. *The Jewel of Liberty: Abraham Lincoln's Re-Election and the End of Slavery*. Mechanicsburg, Pa.: Stackpole Books, 1994.

Long, E. B., with Barbara Long. *The Civil War Day by Day: An Almanac, 1861–1865*. Garden City, N.Y.: Doubleday, 1971.

Lowell, James Russell. "The Next General Election." *North American Review* 99 (October 1864): 557–72.

———. "The President's Policy." *North American Review* 98 (January 1864): 234–60.

Lyman, Theodore. *Meade's Headquarters, 1863–65: Letters of Colonel Theodore Lyman from the Wilderness to Appomattox*. Edited by George R. Agassiz. 1922. Reprint, Freeport, N.Y.: Books for Libraries Press, 1970.

McAllister, Robert. *The Civil War Letters of General Robert McAllister.* Edited by James I. Robertson Jr. New Brunswick, N.J.: Rutgers University Press, 1965.

McBride, Robert W. *Personal Recollections of Abraham Lincoln.* Indianapolis: Bobbs-Merrill, 1926.

McClellan, George B. *The Civil War Papers of George B. McClellan: Selected Correspondence, 1860–1865.* Edited by Stephen W. Sears. New York: Ticknor & Fields, 1989.

———. *Oration of Maj.-Gen. McClellan.* New York: Sheldon & Co., 1864.

———. Papers. Manuscript Division, Library of Congress.

McClure, Alexander K. *Abraham Lincoln and Men of War Times: Some Personal Recollections of War and Politics During the Lincoln Administration.* Philadelphia: Times Publishing Co., 1892.

McFeely, William S. *Grant: A Biography.* New York: W. W. Norton, 1981.

McMaster, John Bach. *A History of the People of the United States During Lincoln's Administration.* New York: D. Appleton and Co., 1927.

McPherson, Edward. Papers. Manuscript Division, Library of Congress.

———. *The Political History of the United States of America During the Great Rebellion, 1860–1885.* 1865. Reprint, New York: Da Capo Press, 1972.

McPherson, James M. *The Struggle for Equality: Abolitionists and the Negro in the Civil War and Reconstruction.* Princeton, N.J.: Princeton University Press, 1964.

McWhiney, Grady. *Battle in the Wilderness: Grant Meets Lee.* Fort Worth, Texas: Ryan Place Publishers, 1995.

———, ed. *Grant, Lee, Lincoln and the Radicals: Essays on Civil War Leadership.* Evansville, Ill.: Northwestern University Press, 1964.

Mabee, Carleton. "Sojourner Truth and President Lincoln." *New England Quarterly* 61 (December 1988): 519–29.

Macdonell, Lady Agnes. "America Then and Now: Recollections of Lincoln." *Magazine of History with Notes and Queries* Extra no. 65 (1919): 46–54.

Marble, Manton M. Papers. Manuscript Division, Library of Congress.

Martin, Edward Winslow [James Dabney McCabe]. *The Life and Public Services of Schuyler Colfax.* New York: United States Publishing Co., 1868.

Mason, Charles. Diary. Typescript. Remey Family Papers, Manuscript Division, Library of Congress.

Matthews, Albert. "Origin of 'Butternut' and 'Copperhead.'" In *Publications of the Colonial Society of Massachusetts* 20 (April 1918): 205–37.

Maverick, Augustus. *Henry J. Raymond and the New York Press.* Hartford, Conn.: A. S. Hale and Co., 1870.

Mellon, James, ed. *The Face of Lincoln.* New York: Viking Press, 1979.

Meredith, Roy. *Mr. Lincoln's Contemporaries: An Album of Portraits by Mathew B. Brady.* New York: Charles Scribner's Sons, 1951.

Merrill, Louis Taylor. "General Benjamin F. Butler in the Presidential Campaign of 1864." *Mississippi Valley Historical Review* 33 (March 1947): 537–70.

Michie, Peter S. *General McClellan.* New York: D. Appleton and Co., 1901.

Miers, Earl Schenck. *Lincoln Day by Day: A Chronology, 1809–1865.* 3 vols. 1861–1865. Washington: Lincoln Sesquicentennial Commission, 1960.

Milton, George Fort. *Abraham Lincoln and the Fifth Column.* New York: Vanguard Press, 1942.

———. *The Age of Hate: Andrew Johnson and the Radicals.* New York: Coward-McCann, 1930.

Mitchell, Reid. *Civil War Soldiers.* New York: Viking, 1988.

Mitchell, Stewart. *Horatio Seymour of New York.* Cambridge: Harvard University Press, 1938.

Mitgang, Herbert, ed. *Abraham Lincoln: A Press Portrait.* Athens: University of Georgia Press, 1989.

———, ed. *Lincoln as They Saw Him.* New York: Rinehart & Co., 1956.

Moore, Charles. "Zachariah Chandler in Lincoln's Second Campaign." *Century Magazine* 50 (July 1895): 476–77.

Moos, Malcolm Charles. *The Republicans: A History of Their Party.* New York: Random House, 1956.

Mott, Frank Luther. *American Journalism: A History, 1690–1960.* Third edition. New York: Macmillan, 1962.

Myers, William Starr. *General George Brinton McClellan: A Study in Personality.* New York: D. Appleton-Century Co., 1934.

Neill, Edward D. "Reminiscences of the Last Year of President Lincoln's Life." In *Glimpses of the Nation's Struggle,* vol. 1. A series of papers read before the Minnesota Commandery of the Military Order of the Loyal Legion of the United States. 1887. Reprint, Wilmington, N.C.: Broadfoot Publishing Co., 1992.

Nelson, Larry E. *Bullets, Ballots, and Rhetoric: Confederate Policy for the United States Presidential Contest of 1864.* University, Ala.: University of Alabama Press, 1980.

Nevins, Allan. *Frémont: Pathmarker of the West.* New York: Longmans, Green and Co., 1955.

———. *Frémont: The West's Greatest Adventurer.* 2 vols. New York: Harper & Brothers, 1928.

———. *The War for the Union.* 4 vols. New York: Charles Scribner's Sons, 1959–1971.

Newman, Ralph G., ed. *Lincoln for the Ages.* Garden City, N.Y.: Doubleday, 1960.

New York Daily News.

New York Evening Post.

New York Herald.

New York Sun.

New York Times.

New York Tribune.

New York World.

Nicolay, Helen. *Lincoln's Secretary: A Biography of John G. Nicolay.* New York: Longmans, Green and Co., 1949.

———. *Personal Traits of Abraham Lincoln.* New York: Century Co., 1912.

Nicolay, John G. "Lincoln's Gettysburg Address." *Century Magazine* 47 (February 1894): 596–608.

———. Papers. Manuscript Division, Library of Congress.

———, and John Hay. *Abraham Lincoln: A History.* 10 vols. New York: Century Co., 1890.

Oates, Stephen B. *With Malice Toward None: The Life of Abraham Lincoln.* New York: Harper & Row, 1977.

Oberholtzer, Ellis Paxson. *Jay Cooke: Financier of the Civil War.* Philadelphia: George W. Jacobs & Co., 1907.

Official Proceedings of the Democratic National Convention Held in 1864 at Chicago. Chicago: Times Steam Book and Job Printing House, 1864.

Ohio State Journal.

Ohio Statesman.

O'Laughlin, John Callan. "Lincoln and the Press." *Abraham Lincoln Association Papers.* Springfield, Ill.: Abraham Lincoln Association, 1931.

Owen, Robert Dale. "Political Results from the Varioloid: A Leaf of History." *Atlantic Monthly* 35 (June 1875): 660–70.

Painter, Nell Irvin. *Sojourner Truth: A Life, a Symbol.* New York: W. W. Norton, 1996.

Parrish, William E. *Turbulent Partnership: Missouri and the Union, 1861–1865.* Columbia: University of Missouri Press, 1963.

Parton, James. *General Butler in New Orleans: History of the Administration of the Department of the Gulf in the Year 1862.* New York: Mason Brothers, 1864.

———. *The Life of Horace Greeley, Editor of the New York Tribune.* New York: Mason Brothers, 1855.

———. "The New York Herald." *North American Review* 102 (April 1866): 373–419.

Paul, George E. "A Boy Who Heard Lincoln's Gettysburg Address." *The Magazine of History with Notes and Queries* 25 (1923): 119–21.

Peacock, Virginia Tatnall. *Famous American Belles of the Nineteenth Century.* Philadelphia: J. B. Lippincott, 1900.

Philadelphia Inquirer.

Phillips, Wendell. *Speeches, Lectures, and Letters.* Boston: Walker, Wise, and Co., 1864.

"Picture of a Candidate, 1860: A Pen Portrait of Lincoln." *Abraham Lincoln Quarterly* 1 (December 1940): 207–9.

Pierce, Edward L. *Memoir and Letters of Charles Sumner.* 4 vols. Boston: Roberts Brothers, 1894.

Pleasants, Samuel Augustus. *Fernando Wood of New York.* New York: Columbia University Press, 1948.

Pollard, Edward A. *The Lost Cause: A New Southern History of the War of the Confederates.* 1867. Reprint, New York: Bonanza Books, n.d.

——. *Southern History of the War.* 1866. Reprint, New York: Fairfax Press, 1977.

Pond, George E. *The Shenandoah Valley in 1864.* 1883. Reprint, Wilmington, N.C.: Broadfoot Publishing Co., 1989.

Poore, Benjamin Perley. *Perley's Reminiscences of Sixty Years in the National Metropolis.* 2 vols. Philadelphia: Hubbard Brothers, 1886.

Porter, Horace. *Campaigning with Grant.* Edited by Wayne C. Temple. Bloomington: Indiana University Press, 1961.

——. "Lincoln and Grant." *Century Magazine* 30 (October 1885): 939–47.

Potter, David M. "Horace Greeley and Peaceable Secession." *Journal of Southern History* 7 (May 1941): 145–59.

Pratt, Harry E., ed. *Concerning Mr. Lincoln: In Which Abraham Lincoln is Pictured as He Appeared to Letter Writers of His Time.* Springfield, Ill.: Abraham Lincoln Association, 1944.

——. "The Repudiation of Lincoln's War Policy in 1862—Stuart-Swett Congressional Campaign." *Journal of the Illinois State Historical Society* 24 (1931): 129–40.

Proceedings of the First Three Republican National Conventions of 1856, 1860 and 1864. . . . Minneapolis: Charles W. Johnson, 1893.

Providence Press.

Quarles, Benjamin. *The Negro in the Civil War.* Boston: Little, Brown, 1953.

Randall, James G. *Lincoln the President: Midstream.* Vol. 3 of *Lincoln the President.* New York: Dodd, Mead, 1952.

——. *Lincoln the President: Springfield to Gettysburg.* Vol. 2 of *Lincoln the President.* New York: Dodd, Mead, 1945.

——, and Richard N. Current. *Lincoln the President: Last Full Measure.* Vol. 4 of *Lincoln the President.* New York: Dodd, Mead, 1955.

——, and David Donald. *The Civil War and Reconstruction.* 2nd edition, revised. Boston: Little, Brown, 1969.

Randall, Ruth Painter. *Lincoln's Sons.* Boston: Little, Brown, 1955.

Rathvon, William R. "I Heard Lincoln at Gettysburg." *Christian Science Monitor,* 18 November 1963.

Rawley, James A. *Edwin D. Morgan, 1811–1883: Merchant in Politics.* New York: Columbia University Press, 1955.

———. "Lincoln and Governor Morgan." *Abraham Lincoln Quarterly* 6 (March 1951): 272–300.

Rawson, Mary. Personal Papers for 1864. Atlanta Historical Society, Atlanta, Ga.

Reed, Wallace P., ed. *History of Atlanta, Georgia.* Syracuse, N.Y.: D. Mason & Co., 1889.

Remensnyder, Junius B. "With Lincoln at Gettysburg." *Magazine of History with Notes and Queries* 32 (1926): 7–15.

Rhodes, James. *History of the United States from the Compromise of 1850 to the McKinley-Bryan Campaign of 1896.* 8 vols. 1892–1919. Reprint, Port Washington, N.Y.: Kennikat Press, 1967.

Rice, Allen Thorndike, ed. *Reminiscences of Abraham Lincoln by Distinguished Men of His Time.* New York: North American Review, 1885.

Richardson, Albert D. *A Personal History of Ulysses S. Grant.* Hartford, Conn.: American Publishing Co., 1868.

Richmond Dispatch.

Richmond Examiner.

Riddle, Albert G. *The Life of Benjamin F. Wade.* Cleveland: William W. Williams, 1887.

———. *Recollections of War Times: Reminiscences of Men and Events in Washington, 1860–1865.* New York: G. P. Putnam's Sons, 1895.

Roe, Alfred S. "Recollections of Monocacy." In *Personal Narratives of Events in the War of the Rebellion.* Papers read before the Rhode Island Soldiers and Sailors Historical Society. Vol. 4. 1883–1885. Reprint, Wilmington, N.C.: Broadfoot Publishing Co., 1993.

Rogers, Earl M. "McClellan's Candidacy with the Army." *Century Magazine* 40 (October 1890): 959.

Roseboom, Eugene H. *A History of Presidential Elections: From George Washington to Richard M. Nixon.* 3rd edition. New York: Macmillan, 1970.

Ross, Ishbel. *Proud Kate: Portrait of an Ambitious Woman.* New York: Harper & Brothers, 1953.

Russell, William Henry. "A Biography of Alexander K. McClure." Ph.D. diss., University of Wisconsin, 1953.

Russell, William Howard. *My Diary North and South.* Edited by Fletcher Pratt. New York: Harper & Brothers, 1954.

Sala, George Augustus. "Lincoln's 'Cast-Iron Grip.'" *Journal of the Illinois State Historical Society* 41 (December 1948): 438–40.

———. *My Diary in America in the Midst of War.* 2 vols. London: Tinsley Brothers, 1865.

Sandburg, Carl. *Abraham Lincoln: The War Years.* 4 vols. Sangamon Edition. New York: Charles Scribner's Sons, 1943.

————. "The Face of Lincoln." In Frederick Hill Meserve and Carl Sandburg, *The Photographs of Abraham Lincoln*. New York: Harcourt, Brace, 1944.

Schafer, Joseph. "Who Elected Lincoln?" *American Historical Review* 47 (October 1941): 51–63.

Schlesinger, Arthur M. Jr. *History of U.S. Political Parties*. Vol. 2: *1860–1910: The Gilded Age of Politics*. New York: Chelsea House Publishers/R. R. Bowker Co., 1973.

Schuckers, Jacob W. *The Life and Public Services of Salmon Portland Chase*. New York: D. Appleton and Co., 1874.

Schurz, Carl. *Intimate Letters of Carl Schurz, 1841–1869*. Edited by Joseph Schafer. 1928. Reprint, New York: Da Capo Press, 1970.

————. *The Reminiscences of Carl Schurz*. Edited by Frederic Bancroft and William A. Dunning. 3 vols. New York: McClure Co., 1907–1908.

————. *Speeches, Correspondence and Political Papers of Carl Schurz*. Edited by Frederic Bancroft. 6 vols. 1913. Reprint, New York: Negro Universities Press, 1969.

Sears, Stephen W. *George B. McClellan: The Young Napoleon*. New York: Ticknor & Fields, 1988.

Segal, Charles M., ed. *Conversations with Lincoln*. New York: G. P. Putnam's Sons, 1961.

Seilhamer, George O. *History of the Republican Party*. Vol. 1: *Narrative and Critical History, 1856–1898*. New York: Judge Publishing Co., n.d.

Seitz, Don C. *Horace Greeley: Founder of the New York Tribune*. 1926. Reprint, New York: AMS Press, 1970.

————. *The James Gordon Bennetts Father and Son: Proprietors of the New York Herald*. Indianapolis: Bobbs-Merrill, 1928.

Seward, Frederick W. *Reminiscences of a War-Time Statesman and Diplomat, 1830–1915*. New York: G. P. Putnam's Sons, 1916.

Shakespeare, William. *Love's Labor's Lost*. In *The Complete Works of William Shakespeare*. Vol. 1. New York: Bantam Books, 1988.

Sherman, William Tecumseh. *Memoirs of General W. T. Sherman*. 2 vols. in 1. New York: Library of America, 1990.

Shortall, John G. "Horace Greeley." Typescript. Horace Greeley Papers. Manuscript Division, Library of Congress.

Sifakis, Stewart. *Who Was Who in the Civil War*. New York: Facts on File Publications, 1988.

Silbey, Joel H. *A Respectable Minority: The Democratic Party in the Civil War Era, 1860–1868*. New York: W. W. Norton & Co., 1977.

Smith, Donnal V. *Chase and Civil War Politics*. Columbus: F. J. Heer Printing Co., 1931.

Smith, George Winston, and Charles Judah. *Life in the North During the Civil War: A Source History*. Albuquerque: University of New Mexico Press, 1966.

Smith, Goldwin. "President Lincoln." *Macmillan's Magazine*. Reprinted in *The Living Age* 84 (1865): 426–30.

Smith, Matthew Hale. *Sunshine and Shadow in New York*. Hartford, Conn.: J. B. Burr and Company, 1868.

Smith, Paul S. "First Use of the Term 'Copperhead.' " *American Historical Review* 32 (July 1927): 799–800.

Smith, Theodore C. *The Life and Letters of James Abram Garfield*. 2 vols. 1925. Reprint, Hamden, Conn.: Archon Books, 1968.

Smith, William Ernest. *The Francis Preston Blair Family in Politics*. 2 vols. New York: Macmillan, 1933.

Sokoloff, Alice Hunt. *Kate Chase for the Defense*. New York: Dodd, Mead, 1971.

Sorrel, G. Moxley. *Recollections of a Confederate Staff Officer*. 1905. Reprint, Dayton, Ohio: Press of Morningside Bookshop, 1978.

Speer, John. *Life of General James H. Lane*. Garden City, Kans.: John Speer, 1896.

Squires, J. Duane. "Some Enduring Achievements of the Lincoln Administration, 1861–1865." *Abraham Lincoln Quarterly* 5 (December 1948): 191–211.

Stampp, Kenneth M. "The Milligan Case and the Election of 1864 in Indiana." *Mississippi Valley Historical Review* 31 (June 1944): 41–58.

Starr, Louis M. "James Gordon Bennett—Beneficent Rascal." *American Heritage* 6 (February 1955): 32–37.

Starr, Stephen Z. "Was There a Northwest Conspiracy?" *Filson Club Historical Quarterly* 38 (October 1964): 323–41.

Stevens, George T. *Three Years in the Sixth Corps*. 1866. Reprint, New York: Time-Life Books, 1984.

Stevens, Thaddeus. Papers. Manuscript Division, Library of Congress.

Stevens, Walter B. "Lincoln and Missouri." *Missouri Historical Review* 10 (January 1916): 63–119.

Stiles, Robert. *Four Years under Marse Robert*. 1903. Reprint, Dayton, Ohio: Morningside, 1988.

Stoddard, Henry Luther. *Horace Greeley: Printer, Editor, Crusader*. New York: G. P. Putnam's Sons, 1946.

Stoddard, William O. *Inside the White House in War Times*. New York: Charles L. Webster & Co., 1890.

———. "The Story of a Nomination." *North American Review* 138 (March 1884): 263–73.

Storey, Moorfield. *Charles Sumner*. Boston: Houghton Mifflin, 1900.

Strong, George Templeton. *The Diary of George Templeton Strong: The Civil War, 1860–1865*. Edited by Allan Nevins and Milton Halsey Thomas. New York: Macmillan, 1952.

Stryker, Lloyd Paul. *Andrew Johnson: A Study in Courage*. New York: Macmillan, 1929.

Sumner, Charles. "Our Domestic Relations; or, How to Treat the Rebel States." *Atlantic Monthly* 12 (October 1863): 507–29.

Swinton, William. *Campaigns of the Army of the Potomac.* 1866. Reprint, Secaucus, N.J.: Blue & Grey Press, 1988.

Tarbell, Ida M. *The Life of Abraham Lincoln.* 2 vols. New York: Lincoln Memorial Association, 1900.

———. *A Reporter for Lincoln: Story of Henry E. Wing, Soldier and Newspaperman.* New York: Book League of America, 1929.

Thayer, William Roscoe. *The Life and Letters of John Hay.* 2 vols. Boston: Houghton Mifflin, 1915.

Thomas, Benjamin P. *Abraham Lincoln: A Biography.* New York: Alfred A. Knopf, 1952.

Thorndike, Rachel Sherman, ed. *The Sherman Letters: Correspondence between General Sherman and Senator Sherman from 1837 to 1891.* 1894. Reprint, New York: Da Capo Press, 1969.

Tidwell, William A. *April '65: Confederate Covert Action in the American Civil War.* Kent, Ohio: Kent State University Press, 1995.

Tredway, G. R. *Democratic Opposition to the Lincoln Administration in Indiana.* Indianapolis: Indiana Historical Bureau, 1973.

Trefousse, Hans L. *Andrew Johnson: A Biography.* New York: W. W. Norton, 1989.

———. *Ben Butler: The South Called Him BEAST!* New York: Twayne Publishers, 1957.

———. *Benjamin Franklin Wade: Radical Republican from Ohio.* New York: Twayne Publishers, 1963.

———. *The Radical Republicans: Lincoln's Vanguard for Racial Justice.* New York: Alfred A. Knopf, 1969.

———. "Zachariah Chandler and the Withdrawal of Frémont in 1864: New Answers to an Old Riddle." *Lincoln Herald* 70 (Winter 1968): 181–88.

Tribune Almanac and Political Register for 1864. New York: Tribune Association, 1864.

Trietsch, James H. *The Printer and the Prince: A Study of the Influence of Horace Greeley upon Abraham Lincoln as Candidate and President.* New York: Exposition Press, 1955.

Trumbull, Lyman. Papers. Manuscript Division, Library of Congress.

Union Springs (Alabama) *Times.*

U.S. Navy Department. *Official Records of the Union and Confederate Navies in the War of the Rebellion.* 30 vols. Washington, D.C.: Government Printing Office, 1894–1922.

U.S. War Department. *The War of the Rebellion: A Compilation of the Official Records of the Union and Confederate Armies.* 70 vols. in 128 parts. 1880–1901. Reprint, Harrisburg, Pa.: Historical Times, 1985.

Vallandigham, James L. *A Life of Clement L. Vallandigham.* Baltimore: Turnbull Brothers, 1872.

Van Deusen, Glyndon G. *Horace Greeley: Nineteenth-Century Crusader.* Philadelphia: University of Pennsylvania Press, 1953.

Vandiver, Frank E. *Jubal's Raid: General Early's Famous Attack on Washington in 1864.* New York: McGraw-Hill, 1960.

Venet, Wendy Hamand. *Neither Ballots nor Bullets: Women Abolitionists and the Civil War.* Charlottesville: University Press of Virginia, 1991.

Viele, Egbert L. "A Trip with Lincoln, Chase and Stanton." *Scribner's Monthly* 16 (October 1878): 813–22.

Viorst, Milton. *Fall from Grace: The Republican Party and the Puritan Ethic.* New York: Simon and Schuster, 1968.

Voigt, David Quentin. "'Too Pitchy to Touch'—President Lincoln and Editor Bennett." *Abraham Lincoln Quarterly* 6 (September 1950): 139–61.

Wade, Benjamin Franklin. Papers. Manuscript Division, Library of Congress.

Wallace, Lew. *An Autobiography.* 2 vols. New York: Harper & Brothers, 1906.

Warden, Robert B. *An Account of the Private Life and Public Services of Salmon Portland Chase.* Cincinnati: Wilstach, Baldwin & Co., 1874.

Washington Chronicle.

"Washington During the War." *Macmillan's Magazine* 6 (May 1862): 16–29.

Washington Evening Star.

Webb, Alexander S. "Through the Wilderness." In *Battles and Leaders of the Civil War,* vol. 4. Edited by Robert Underwood Johnson and Clarence Clough Buel. 1887. Reprint, Secaucus, N.J.: Castle, n.d.

Weed, Thurlow. *Autobiography of Thurlow Weed.* Edited by Harriet A. Weed. Boston: Houghton Mifflin, 1883.

Welles, Gideon. "Administration of Abraham Lincoln." *Galaxy* 24 (November and December 1877): 608–24, 733–45.

———. *Diary of Gideon Welles.* 3 vols. Boston: Houghton Mifflin, 1911.

———. "Lincoln's Triumph in 1864." *Atlantic Monthly* 41 (April 1878): 454–68.

———. "The Opposition to Lincoln in 1864." *Atlantic Monthly* 41 (March 1878): 366–76.

West Moreland (Pennsylvania) *Republican.*

Wheeler, Richard. *Voices of the Civil War.* New York: Thomas Y. Crowell, 1976.

White, Andrew Dickson. *Autobiography.* 2 vols. New York: Century Co., 1905.

White, Horace. *The Life of Lyman Trumbull.* Boston: Houghton Mifflin, 1913.

Whitman, Walt. Thomas Biggs Harned Collection of the Papers of Walt Whitman, Manuscript Division, Library of Congress.

———. "Walt Whitman Describes Lincoln in 1864." *Magazine of History with Notes and Queries* 33 (1927): 52–53.

Whittier, John Greenleaf. *The Letters of John Greenleaf Whittier.* Edited by John B. Pickard. Vol. 3, 1861–1892. Cambridge: Belknap Press of Harvard University Press, 1975.

Wiley, Bell Irvin. "Billy Yank and Abraham Lincoln." *Abraham Lincoln Quarterly* 6 (June 1950): 103–20.

Wilkes' Spirit of the Times.

Williams, Hiram Smith. *This War So Horrible: The Civil War Diaries of Hiram Smith Williams.* Edited by Lewis N. Wynne and Robert A. Taylor. Tuscaloosa: University of Alabama Press, 1993.

Williams, T. Harry. *Lincoln and His Generals.* New York: Alfred A. Knopf, 1952.

———. *Lincoln and the Radicals.* Madison: University of Wisconsin Press, 1941.

———. "Lincoln and the Radicals: An Essay in Civil War History and Historiography." In *Grant, Lee, Lincoln and the Radicals: Essays on Civil War Leadership.* Edited by Grady McWhiney. Evansville, Ill.: Northwestern University Press, 1964.

———. *McClellan, Sherman and Grant.* New Brunswick, N.J.: Rutgers University Press, 1962.

Wills, Garry. *Lincoln at Gettysburg: The Words that Remade America.* New York: Simon and Schuster, 1992.

Wilson, Charles R. "McClellan's Changing Views on the Peace Plank of 1864." *American Historical Review* 38 (April 1933): 498–505.

———. "New Light on the Lincoln-Blair-Frémont 'Bargain' of 1864." *American Historical Review* 42 (October 1936): 71–78.

———. "The Original Chase Organization Meeting and the Next Presidential Election." *Mississippi Valley Historical Review* 23 (June 1936): 61–79.

Wilson, James Harrison. "Reminiscences of General Grant." *Century Magazine* 30 (October 1885): 947–54.

Winston, Robert W. *Andrew Johnson: Plebeian and Patriot.* New York: Henry Holt and Co., 1928.

Winther, Oscar O. "The Soldier Vote in the Election of 1864." *New York History* 25 (October 1944): 440–58.

Wise, John S. *The End of an Era.* Boston: Houghton Mifflin, 1899.

Wood, Forrest G. *Black Scare: The Racist Response to Emancipation and Reconstruction.* Berkeley: University of California Press, 1968.

Woodburn, James Albert. *The Life of Thaddeus Stevens.* Indianapolis: Bobbs-Merrill Co., 1913.

Woodley, Thomas Frederick. *The Great Leveler: The Life of Thaddeus Stevens.* New York: Stackpole Sons, 1937.

Woodward, W. E. *Meet General Grant.* New York: Liveright, 1965.

Woollcott, Alexander. "'Get Down, You Fool!'" *Atlantic Monthly* 161 (February 1938): 169–73.

Worsham, John H. *One of Jackson's Foot Cavalry.* Edited by James I. Robertson Jr. 1964. Reprint, Wilmington, N.C.: Broadfoot Publishing Co., 1987.

Young, James Harvey. "Anna Elizabeth Dickinson and the Civil War: For and Against Lincoln." *Mississippi Valley Historical Review* 31 (June 1944): 59–80.

Young, John Russell. *Around the World with General Grant.* 2 vols. New York: American News Co., 1879.

———. "Lincoln at Gettysburg." Newspaper clipping in the Thomas Biggs Harned Collection of the Papers of Walt Whitman, Manuscript Division, Library of Congress.

———. *Men and Memories: Personal Reminiscences.* Edited by May D. Russell Young. Second edition. New York: F. Tennyson Neely, 1901.

Zornow, William Frank. "The Attitude of the Western Reserve Press on the Re-election of Lincoln." *Lincoln Herald* 50 (June 1948): 35–39.

———. "Campaign Issues and Popular Mandates in 1864." *Mid-America* 35 (October 1953): 195–216.

———. "The Cleveland Convention, 1864, and Radical Democrats." *Mid-America* 36 (January 1954): 39–53.

———. "Indiana and the Election of 1864." *Indiana Magazine of History* 45 (March 1949): 13–38.

———. *Lincoln & the Party Divided.* Norman: University of Oklahoma Press, 1954.

———. "McClellan and Seymour in the Chicago Convention of 1864." *Journal of the Illinois State Historical Society* 43 (Winter 1950): 282–95.

———. "Treason as a Campaign Issue in the Re-Election of Lincoln." *The Abraham Lincoln Quarterly* 5 (June 1949): 348–63.

———. "The Union Party Convention at Baltimore in 1864." *Maryland Historical Magazine* 45 (September 1950): 176–200.

INDEX

———※———